WORLDS ON THE MOVE

Toda Institute Book Series on Global Peace and Policy

Series Editor: Majid Tehranian

Published and forthcoming:

WORLDS ON THE MOVE

Globalization, Migration, and Cultural Security

Edited by

Jonathan Friedman
& Shalini Randeria

I.B. TAURIS
LONDON · NEW YORK

in association with
The Toda Institute for Global Peace and Policy Research

Published in 2004 by I.B.Tauris & Co Ltd
6 Salem Road, London W2 4BU
175 Fifth Avenue, New York NY 10010
www.ibtauris.com
in association with the Toda Institute for Global Peace and Policy Research

In the United States and Canada distributed by Palgrave Macmillan, a division of
St. Martin's Press
175 Fifth Avenue, New York NY 10010

ISBN 1 86064 951 3
EAN: 978 1 86064 951 6

A full CIP record for this book is available from the British Library

Typeset in Baskerville 11/12 pt by Q3 Bookwork
Printed and bound in Great Britain by MPG Books Ltd, Bodmin

Contents

Contributors

Asu Aksoy is a researcher working on Turkish migrant identity in Europe. She is based in London and Istanbul.

Helmuth Berking teaches sociology and cultural anthropology at the Free University of Berlin. Publications include *Sociology of Giving* (1999); and *Staedte im Globalisierungsdiskurs* (2002).

Michael Bommes is professor of sociology at the institute for social sciences at the University for Education, Freiburg, Germany. He was Jean Monnet Fellow at the European University Institute in Florence in 1997/1998 and is a Permanent Fellow at the Institute for Migration Research and Intercultural Studies at the University of Osnabrueck. Main research areas are sociological theory, migration sociology, and sociology of the welfare state. Recent book publications are *Migration und Nationaler Wohlfahrtsstaat: Ein differenzierungstheoretischer Entwurf* (1999); co-author with Albert Scherr of *Soziologie der Sozialen Arbeit*; and co-editor with Andrew Geddes of *Immigration and Welfare: Challenging the Borders of the Welfare State* (2000).

Ayse Caglar is an assistant professor at the Institute of Ethnology, Free University of Berlin. Since completing her MA. and Ph.D in anthropology from the McGill University she has been based in Berlin. She has recently completed an (joint) ESRC project, "Negotiating spaces: Media and Cultural Practices in the Turkish Diaspora in Britain, France, and Germany" for the Transnational Communities Programme. Her work concentrates on migration, consumption, and popular culture. She is currently working on the transnationalizing process of Turkish immigrants in Europe. She has published in several journals including *New Community*, *Journal of Material Culture, and Cultural Dynamics*. Her most recent publication is "Constraining Metaphors and the Transnationalisation of Spaces in Berlin" in *Journal of Ethnic and Migration Studies* (October 2001). She is a Jean Monnet Fellow at the Robert Schuman Centre for Advanced Studies at the European University in Florence for 2001–2002.

Arif Dirlik is Knight Professor of social sciences at the University of Oregon. His most recent publications include *Postmodernity's*

Histories, Places and Politics in an Age of Globalization (edited with Roxann Prazniak); *Chinese on the American Frontier* (edited); and *History After the Three Worlds* (edited with Vinay Bahl and Peter Gran).

Katherine P. Ewing, Ph.D. University of Chicago 1980, is associate professor of cultural anthropology at Duke University. She is currently investigating Turkish community and identity in Germany, with a focus on diasporic Islamic practice. Her areas of specialization include South Asia and the Middle East, with field research in Pakistan, Turkey, and among Muslims in Europe. In her most recent book, *Arguing Sainthood* (1997), she examined how the Sufi mystical tradition has been a focus of religious and political controversy in Pakistan and how this controversy plays out in the lives of individuals. She has also published numerous other articles and the edited volume *Shariat and Ambiguity in South Asian Islam* (1988).

Richard Falk is Albert G. Milbank Professor of International Law and Practice Emeritus at Princeton University. He is the author of *Human Rights Horizons* (2000); and *Religion and Humane Global Governance* (2001).

Jonathan Friedman is Directeur d'études at the Ecole des Hautes Etudes en Sciences Sociales in Paris and professor of social anthropology at the University of Lund, Sweden. He has written extensively on issues related to global system history, the anthropology and ethnography of global/local articulations, ethnicity, and indigenous movements. He has done fieldwork in Hawai'i since the late 70s. His publications include *Cultural Identity and Global Process* (editor) (1994); *Consumption and Identity* (1994); *System Structure and Contradiction in the 'Evolution' of Asiatic Social Formations* (1998); and *PC Worlds: An Anthropology of Political Correctness* (forthcoming).

Tschanguiz Pahlavan is a leading Iranian political scientist whose articles and books in Persian, German, and English have earned him an international reputation. His studies have primarily focused on the Iranian civilization and its spread throughout the West Asian region.

James N. Rosenau is University Professor of International Affairs at The George Washington University. His books include *Turbulence in World Politics* (1990); *Along the Domestic-Foreign Frontier* (1997); and *Distant Proximities: Dynamics Beyond Globalization* (forthcoming).

Kevin Robins is Professor of Communications, Goldsmiths College, University of London. He is the author of *Into the Image: Culture and Politics in the Field of Vision* (1996); and co-editor (with David Morley) of *British Cultural Studies* (2001).

Werner Schiffauer is professor for social and cultural anthropology in Frankfurt (Oder), Germany. He has worked on the transformation of rural and urban Turkey, Turkish migration to Germany, Islam in Europe, and on the comparative analysis of European multicultural societies. Recently he published *Die Gottesmänner: Islamisten in Deutschland. Eine Studie zur Herstellung religiöser Evidenz* (2000).

Boaventura de Sousa Santos is full professor at the School of Economics, University of Coimbra, Department of Sociology and Director of the Centro de Estudos Sociais (Center of Social Studies), School of Economics, University of Coimbra. He has also taught at the University of Wisconsin, Madison, London School of Economics, University of São Paulo, Catholic University of Rio de Janeiro, University of Los Andes (Bogotá), and is currently Distinguished Legal Scholar, Institute for Legal Studies, Law School, University of Wisconsin, Madison. His recent publications include *Toward a New Common Sense: Law, Science and Politics in the Paradigmatic Transition* (1995); *La globalización del derecho: los nuevos caminos de la regulación y la emancipación* (1998); *Reinventar a Democracia* (998); *Globalizing Institutions: Case Studies in Regulation and Innovation* (co-editor) (2000); and *A Cor do Tempo Quando Foge* (2001).

Saskia Sassen is the Ralph Lewis Professor of Sociology at the University of Chicago, and Centennial Visiting Professor at the London School of Economics. She is currently completing her forthcoming book *Denationalization: Economy and Polity in a Global Digital Age* (Princeton University Press, 2003) based on her five-year project on governance and accountability in a global economy. Her most recent books are *Guests and Aliens* (1999); and her edited book *Global Networks/ Linked Cities* (2002). *The Global City* is out in a new fully updated edition in 2001. Her books have been translated into twelve languages. She is co-director of the Economy Section of the Global Chicago Project, a member of the National Academy of Sciences Panel on Urban Data Sets, a member of the Council of Foreign Relations, and chair of the newly formed Information Technology, International Cooperation and Global Security Committee of the SSRC.

Majid Tehranian is professor of international communication at the University of Hawai'i, and director of the Toda Institute for Global Peace and Policy Research. His publications include 20 books and over 100 articles. His work has been translated into a dozen languages. He also edits *Peace & Policy* as well as the Toda Institute Book Series.

Peter van der Veer is Professor of Comparative Religion and Director of the Research, Centre for Religion and Society at the University of Amsterdam. He is also co-director of the International Institute for the Study of Islam in the Modern World (ISIM) in Leiden. Among his many publications are *Religious Nationalism* (1994); and *Imperial Encounters* (2001).

Preface

Diasporas have become a visible phenomenon of our world. Wherever we go in the major metropolitan world centers, we run into not only China and India Towns, but we also witness the happy or forlorn individual faces of old and recent immigrants from a variety of other nations flooding the airports, shopping centers, and city parks. Although, as Jonathan Friedman points out, the total numbers may not exceed two percent of the world population, diasporas have significantly impacted world politics and economics. The anti-immigrant reactions have led to the rise of right-wing movements in Austria, Australia, France, Germany, Italy, and the United States for tightening immigration policies.

In the meantime, the accelerating free flow of capital and cultural products, facilitated by the expanding global telecommunication system, has created an anomaly. The desire to migrate from low to high income and security regions in the world is exploding. That explosion manifests itself in legal immigration to places such as the Silicon Valley, where the Chinese, Indian, and Iranian engineers dominate the scene, as well as illegal immigration. The latter is managed by an underworld specializing in drugs, prostitution, and sweatshops.

The impact of the "worlds on the move" on globalization, migration, and identity negotiations is the subject matter of this remarkable book written and edited by a distinguished group of scholars. The book significantly complements the Toda Institute Book Series on Human Security and Global Governance. It appears at a time that post-colonial migration has been largely replaced by migration of professionals, political refugees, and traffickers. This has added to the complexity of the problem. There are no panaceas. But the volume demonstrates how capital and labor movements are inextricably tied to the development of an increasingly lop-sided world system. The uneven development of the world has created growing gaps within and among countries while at the same time localizing the global and globalizing the local conflicts. Witness the global environmental and local Palestinian-Israeli conflicts. In such a world, global problems such as migration cannot be left to local and national remedies alone. They need a global approach and global institutions to deal with them. Unilateral approaches, to global terrorism, for instance, will probably prove at the end counter-productive.

This volume drives that lesson home with respect to population movements. For that reason, it is a book worthy of attention by scholars and policy makers alike.

Majid Tehranian
May 3, 2002

Introduction

Throughout Europe there has been an explosive increase in debates concerning the "immigrant problem", "fortress Europe", cultural racism, skinheads, transnational crime and the like. This is not merely a media issue but has filled the pages of academic journals as well. The problems involved are quite real. Since the mid-80s there has been a very rapid increase in migration to Western Europe. This is a period of global upheaval as well as globalization. And, of course, the issues are not simply European. Migration and its consequences have also become major topics of discussion in immigrant-based countries such as the United States, Canada, and Australia during the past 15 years. It is even a serious issue in Japan and in many of the countries of Southeast Asia. While the kinds of questions may differ, there are also similar problems of violence, increasing criminality, and marginality. While in Southeast Asia and even Japan, as in the Persian Gulf oil states, there are policies of non-integration and even marginalization, in Europe it is precisely non-integration that has proven to be the most serious problem. And while the causes of emigration are quite varied, there are clearly global systemic connections involved that link these flows of population. The proliferation of intra-state conflicts and forced migrations has increased markedly as well as, often related, ecological and economic crises and social disintegration. At the same time there is real economic globalization and imaginary visions of a "brave new world" produced in many quarters, from CNN to UNESCO to academic journals such as *Public Culture*. Even here, however, there is a growing awareness of the conflictual and contradictory nature of contemporary mass migration. It might, and shall, be suggested here that while discourses of globalization proliferate throughout the media, the boardrooms, and the classrooms, the global transformations that we confront are of a more complex and profound nature.

The primary focus of this collection is the issue of global migration and its impact on a world that is already undergoing a great many other transformations. Migration should not be understood as an extraneous factor to these changes but as one of their major components. It cannot be separated from the political debates concerning integration, multiculturalism, and the future of democratic institutions. Migration is not simply a demographic phenomenon. It is a socially constituted process in which cultural identity, economic, and political strategies play a definitive role. This is an old anthropological matter. There are forms of social life that are structured by nomadism of various kinds and sedentarism is itself a phenomenon that needs to be understood within a larger framework of intersocietal connections of great historical depth. Within the civilizations of the past three millennia there has been a continuous and systematic articulation between regional movements of traders, craftsmen, and specialists in transport and larger sedentary populations. There have also been periods of mass migration and population displacement in periods of civilizational decline or rupture. If populations such as the Gypsies represent remnants of such itinerant populations in Europe, they also indicate the extensive transformations of social space that have occurred in the past century and which have destroyed their conditions of existence by eliminating their former functions within a larger division of labor. And if large-scale migration has always posed problems for sedentary populations, these have also varied greatly depending on the nature of the state systems within which they moved. Thus the socio-cultural context or frame within which people and peoples have moved in the history of our species needs to serve as a baseline for a comprehension of the present. Helots, slaves, traders, and mass migrations are part and parcel of the history of commercial civilizations, and we have undoubtedly much to learn from the kind of comparison that is not the subject of this book but which could certainly help us in future attempts at greater understanding.

The contemporary world is increasingly depicted in terms such as transnationalism, accentuating the long-distance, cross-border identifications and practices that seem to characterize many contemporary migrating populations. The degree to which this occurs is rarely stated by proponents of transnationalization and some of the contributors to this volume challenge the general validity of this position. We note here that the transnational requires a national and that the actual percentage of people on the international move is extremely small, within two percent of the world's population, so that our current focus must be understood in proper perspective. The themes that we have posited here require that we address a number of crucial problems.

First we need to understand the causes not only of contemporary migration but also of the ways in which migration becomes the formation of transnational groups, local minorities, and everything in between. There is an older discussion of migration and ethnicity, primarily from the United States, which delineates the transition from migratory to ethnic status and to eventual integration into the host society, a description that was elevated to the status of general process that should be expected to occur everywhere. The image of the disappearing ethnic was dominant in the decades following World War II until in the 70s it was discovered that ethnicity was reappearing with a vengeance. This was not merely an issue of migration but of regional, indigenous, and other identities as well (Esman 1994). More recently it has become commonplace to conflate migration and identity so that immigrants are often simply equated with moving cultures. While this may seem to some to be appropriate for the contemporary world, it is just as faulty conceptually as the former assimilationist assumptions. In order to grasp the relation between demography and cultural formations it is necessary to understand the way in which movement itself takes on a particular meaning for those who move and not merely for those who observe. While it is true that technological change has made migration cheaper and transnational communication easier and both more rapid due to "time-space compression" (Harvey 1989), this is not sufficient to understand why transnational communities seem to have proliferated in recent years. First the phenomenon, as we indicated above, is as old as commercial civilizations, so speed is not enough to account for its existence. Secondly, such organization is based on human intentionality, and the latter can never be reduced to the technology of movement. We need to grasp the social conditions within which such transnational worlds are created, worlds that involve economic, kinship, religious, and other cultural relations over long distances. This is an endeavor that requires investigation of political structures and their transformation, global economic processes, cultural strategies, and broad issues of identity formation that is greatly aided by a multidisciplinary approach afforded here.

We need to understand the nature of the relations that develop within host politics in the presence of large-scale migration. This is historically as well as geographically variable. While most of the examples discussed here come from the contemporary West, there are interesting contrasts that need to be considered such as those provided by Pahlavan for Iran. The particular configuration of state institutions, mechanisms of accommodation, and incorporation, but also strategies adopted by migrant populations are all crucial in working out the complexities of the articulation between global migration and host states. This allows for a more comprehensive analysis of the particular problems faced by nation-states, especially welfare states by relativizing them both historically and geographically.

The issue of localization of migrant populations needs to be seen in contrast to and articulation with the formation of diasporic or transnational identities. These are issues that are especially relevant to discussions of integration and minority formation. Reterritorialization is sometimes a term applied to such processes, taken up by several of the chapters in this collection. It is in an ethnographic understanding of the negotiation of identities at the neighborhood level, in relations between immigrants and state agencies, and in everyday forms of social interaction, that we can grasp the way in which global forces inform, and sometimes form, local structures. The constitution of local fields is an inescapable aspect of immigration. The fact of long distance communication of satellite dish transnationalism is also a fact of creation of a local sphere, perhaps of enclavization, of ethnic public spaces which themselves undergo changes in the larger local context of the host society. The study of generations and intergenerational relations has been and is still an important key to understanding the way in which localities are created and destroyed.

All of these processes occur within a world system that is undergoing major transformation, altering the political, economic, and cultural contexts within which migration occurs. The transformation includes the transformation of the nation-state itself and emergence, not only of international working class migration and refugees, but of transnational elites and corresponding global institutional frameworks, from the World Trade Organization (WTO) and related organizations to millions of non-governmental organizations (NGOs), mafias specializing in weapons, women and "refugees", and international high-tech mercenary firms. It should be stressed that while this might appear to be a chaos of different phenomena, they seem to be related systemically to one another and it is of utmost importance that these relations are subjected to investigation.

There have been innumerable books and collections dealing with migration, ethnic conflict and multiculturalism. There have been fewer works that have tried to combine the issues of cultural identity, globalization, and migration in an interdisciplinary framework as is done here; one that seeks to offer a variety of theoretical approaches to the issues as well.

In a conference held at the House of World Cultures in Berlin in October 1999, a number of researchers from various fields were invited to address issues related to "globalization and cultural security: migration and negotiations of identity". The presentations ranged from theoretical models to concrete analyses and the resultant chapters cover issues ranging from the relation between economic globalization and migration to the study of the construction of immigrant and cosmopolitan identities and their concomitant discourses. No matter how one interprets the current period of globalization, whether a global novelty or a repetition of a process that has occurred in the past, there are a number of invariant parameters that seem to be generally accepted as relevant to its description. There is a rapid increase in the globalization of capital and in the geographical decentralization of accumulation. This is part of a process whereby Western nation-states have, according to some, been weakened, both financially and also culturally. New areas of the world have risen from underdeveloped status 30 years ago to major players in the world economy, not least East and Southeast Asia. While immigration may have increased significantly in the past decades, there has been a general shift from labor migration to refugees. This is itself an aspect of a larger transformation in the nature of migration as well as the nature of the state itself. The earlier migration was predicated on relatively rapid integration into an expanding labor force. The situation in Northern Europe from the late 70s, followed more recently by other regions, is one in which demand for labor suddenly collapsed and in which the increase in conflicts and immiseration has led to a different kind of migratory process, one predicated on refugee status where nation-states are increasingly incapable of absorbing immigrants into national labor markets. A great many things changed in this period and whether these changes amount to the emergence of something fundamentally new has been debated (Hirst & Thompson 1996; Castells 1997). However, the newness of contemporary globalization is less interesting than the fact that it is part of a global process whose effects are both powerful and historically significant. The conference concentrated on a particular aspect of contemporary globalization, which has occupied many national governments and international agencies.

The themes of the book fall roughly into three broad categories. The first of these is the nature of the global processes that have generated the contemporary situation. This includes issues that link economic globalization to processes of sociocultural fragmentation as well as the formation of transnational networks and identities, not merely in reference to ethnic groups but to transnational classes and class fractions. The issue of whether the nation-state is being challenged by globalization is also discussed here many viewing this as a complex process in which the nation may indeed be becoming weaker while the state is growing stronger. The issue of cultural security is also taken up in this section in relation to a world in which proliferating conflicts are increasingly defined in terms of cultural identities and their supposed incompatibilities.

The second section deals with more specific issues involving the negotiation of identity. These chapters deal with the ways in which immigrant identities are constituted, the way in which rights are constructed and negotiated within the public sphere, with the way in which locality and place are constructed in arenas pervaded by migratory experiences, the historical and contemporary nature of cosmopolitan identities, and the interaction of media and identity formation. The final section deals with political and legal regimes that very much affect the outcomes of migration. The transformation of the national territorially based state, the emergence of new structures in the European Union, the issues of exclusion and inclusion inscribed in the logic of the state are among the issues explored here. The question of the welfare state is also broached in this section since its capacity of absorption is one of the crucial problems that links migration to the issue of integration. The institutional forms of attachment of persons to territories is a currently debated issue; the nature of citizenship and its possible variations, the rights of refugees and other immigrants present current challenges to the structure of the nation-state and may be leading to fundamental reorganization. This is especially pertinent in the European Union where the facilitation of internal labor migration is a stated goal at the same time as there is significant structural unemployment. International immigration, which is officially controlled more strictly and under attack as well, still has clear links to "flexible" sweatshop and plantation exploitation. These and other problems are all discussed in the light of the larger global systemic processes that have altered the very conditions of existence of the state, not least of the nation-state. Thus the mechanisms for the regulation and deregulation of capital flows, commodity flows and flows of people are closely connected to shifting state functions and interests rather than exposing a weakening of a nation-state confronted with "the forces of demography".

This very brief summary is a mere indication of what can be found within these rich and varied chapters. We have chosen not to provide extensive discussions of each chapter some of which are quite long. Rather we hope that the reader will find food for thought and discussion here. Our purpose has been to explore a certain field of relations, which cannot be covered by any one discipline or perspective. There are quite different approaches to the issues involved in understanding such large-scale phenomena, but there is a broader consensus on the importance of scale and of situating the processes of migration, identification, conflict, and security within the larger dynamic arena. This is a book that hopes to be able to combine the study of specific processes; be they institutional or legal processes within nation-states, or the way teenagers identify against their immigrant parents and *with* a specific territorial arena, and the global processes that configure their conditions of existence.

Jonathan Friedman

Part One: GLOBAL SYSTEM, MIGRATION, AND CULTURAL SECURITY

CHAPTER 1

Cultural Security and Global Governance: International Migration and Negotiations of Identity

Majid Tehranian

"There is no greater sorrow in life than the loss of one's native land."
— *Euripides, 431 B.C.*

Cultural security is a dimension of human security that has received little attention. It consists of the security of personal and collective identity negotiations that are so characteristic of our mobile postmodern world. It includes but is not limited to freedom of thought, conscience, language, speech, life style, ethnicity, gender, association, assembly, as well as cultural and political participation. Most modern democratic constitutions pay lip service to such freedoms, but premodern and modernist prejudices impose severe constraints on identity negotiations and cultural security. The dual process of globalization and localization, aptly called by Robertson (1994) *glocalization*, has imposed another constraint. Globalized local conflicts, such as those in Palestine-Israel, the Persian Gulf, Somalia, Rwanda-Burundi, Bosnia, and Kosovo have created increasing forced and voluntary migrations accompanied by cultural insecurities for the immigrants, refugees, and displaced persons.

This essay focuses on such insecurities and the problem of dealing with them in the present international migration regime. It argues that the present world system both facilitates and represses pluralization of identities. On the one hand, the nation-states are fundamentally biased against pluralization of identities and

3

protection of the human rights of migrants and minorities. On the other hand, an emerging Pancapitalist regime facilitates increasing international mobility and cosmopolitan identities. Pancapitalism is also generating three distinctly different types of international labor migration: manual, intellectual, and political. While the first two result from market demand for labor and voluntary migration, the third is a consequence of revolutions, civil wars, ethnic cleansing, and forced migration.

The latter is partly due to the facts of enormous diversity within the territorial states. There are some 6,000 living languages in the world today and only about 200 territorial states. As increasing numbers of ethnic minorities struggle for cultural and political survival and sovereignty, the world will face mounting conflicts between the nation-state system and ethno-nationalist movements. Any reform of global governance must take account of increasing international mobility and multiple identities. Cultural security requires new forms of global governance that recognize the multiple layers of possible identity from local to national, regional, and global. The essay proposes the creation of a new UN sponsored legal regime of multiple identities and citizenships to remedy some aspects of the situation.

What Is Cultural Insecurity?

Cultural security can be best understood by its opposite. Some examples of cultural insecurity are well known; others may be obscure. Here are some of the most flagrant cases of cultural insecurity:

- A Bahaii in Iran is a non-entity. Under the Shah's regime, a Bahaii could not declare his or her faith in an application for civil service employment. Under the Islamic Republican regime, he or she is subject to arrest and execution as an apostate.
- A Kurd in Turkey is called a Mountain Turk. S/he is denied to have his or her own cultural identity, the right to speak her language and to recreate her culture. Although Kurds constitute some 22 percent of the population of Turkey, they are denied regional autonomy in eastern Turkey where 13 million of them live. In fact, Kurds are perhaps the most stateless nation in the world. Their population of 26 million is mostly divided between Turkey, Iran, Iraq, and Syria, in all of which they suffer various degrees of discrimination (Table 1.1).

4

Table 1.1. Who are the Kurds?

The Kurds are the descendants of Indo-European tribes who settled among the inhabitants of the Zagros Mountains in various epochs, but probably mainly during the second millennium BC. The first mention of Kurds, as 'Cyrtii', occurred in the 2nd century BC. At the time of the Arab conquest in the 7th century AD, the term 'Kurd' was used to denote nomadic people. The Kurds today, numbering at least 26 million, struggle to obtain political recognition and rights as national communities within the state boundaries in which they find themselves. They form the largest ethnic community in the Middle East without a state of its own.

Population estimates (1993) (in rounded figures.)

Country	Total population	Kurds	% Kurdish
Iran	61,000,000	6,100,000	10%
Iraq	19,300,000	4,400,000	23%
Syria	13,400,000	1,100,000	8%
Turkey	60,000,000	13,200,000	22%
Former Soviet Union	500,000		
Elsewhere	700,000		
Total	26,000,000		

Source: *Minority Rights Group* report, "The Kurds", by David McDowall, 1997

- A girl in Afghanistan under the Taliban regime had no right to schooling let alone any other human rights.
- A woman in Saudi Arabia cannot elect or be elected to public office. She is also not allowed to drive a car or ride a bicycle.
- Females in many parts of Africa are subjected to genital circumcision and mutilation.
- A Turkish "guest worker" in Germany is frequently someone who has lived, worked, and been married with children for several decades. His children for the most part are more German in culture than Turkish, yet until recently they could not be German citizens.
- Many third or fourth generation Koreans in Japan continue to live there without rights of citizenship.
- Since the establishment of Israel in 1948, 3.3 million Palestinians have been driven out of their homeland and are living as refugees around the world, some of them in tents.
- The rise of anti-immigrant sentiments in Europe is creating great cultural insecurity for some 15 million foreign born immigrants. The success of right wing political parties such as that of Freedom

Party in Austria, in October 1999, may increase the hostilities. Despite official warnings to the contrary, following the terrorist attack of September 11, 2001 on the United States, counter-terrorist measures have sometimes assumed ethnic profiling.

- There are about 3.7 million people who have been displaced by the civil war in the former Yugoslavia. Ethnic cleansing in Bosnia and Kosovo drove them away from their homes.

- The genocide of half a million Tutsi civilians in Rwanda and the displacement of about 2 million, in 1994, has created cultural insecurity for both Tutsi and Hutu tribal enemies.

There are an estimated 27.4 million displaced persons around the world under the protection of the United Nations High Commissioner for Refugees (UNHCR), of whom 14.5 milion are considered refugees. Some of these refugees have been given temporary asylum, but as UNHCR (1995, 16) reports, "states are increasingly taking steps to obstruct the arrival of asylum seekers, to contain displaced people within their homeland, and to return refugees to their country of origin."

On a more positive note, UNHCR (1995, 14) reports that:

> States and other members of the international community have found themselves responding to the causes and consequences of human displacement with innovative forms of action: the creation of a 'safety zone' in northern Iraq; the deployment of human rights monitors within Rwanda; the intervention of a regional peacekeeping force in Liberia; the use of UN troops to protect the delivery of humanitarian assistance in Bosnia and Herzegovina; the introduction of 'regional safe havens' for Haitian asylum seekers; and the establishment of a war crimes tribunal for former Yugoslavia and Rwanda.

We may add the establishment of the International Criminal Court (1998) and the UN intervention in East Timor (1999) to this list. However, the international human rights regime is characterized by a paradox. One the one hand, in the post-Cold War years, the discourse of human rights has been intensified by great and small powers. On the other hand, in places such as Rwanda, Bosnia, Kosovo, and East Timor, we have witnessed genocide without a timely and adequate response from the international community.

What Is Cultural Security?

What is the root of the problem? While national security, both internal and external, is on the top of every state's agenda, followed perhaps by economic security, human security in general and cultural security in particular are frequently relegated to the back burner. In fact, given the nation-state system, cultural security is often considered in terms that are at odds with human security. Ever since the rise of nationalism in Europe and its spread to the rest of the world, states have tried as best as they can to mould and homogenize their population around preconceived notions of nationhood. This often consists of unity of language, ethnicity, ideology, and sometimes religion. The democratic states, and nowadays even the not-so-democratic states, have often established constitutions that guarantee such cultural rights as freedom of speech and assembly. However, as we all covertly know, there are three kinds of lies: lies, damned lies, and constitutions!

The concept of cultural security as employed in this essay basically means the freedom to negotiate one's identity. But are identities negotiable? In response to that question, five schools of thought seem to have developed: primordialist, constructivist, instrumentalist, situationalist, and communitarian (see Table 2.2).

The primordialist position takes its inspiration from Clifford Geertz (1973). Geertz (1963) saw ethnic identity resulting "from being born into a particular religious community, speaking a particular language, or even a dialect of a language and following particular social practices. These congruities of blood, speech, custom and so on, are seen to have an ineffable, and at times, overpowering coerciveness in and of themselves."

Geertz thus deviated from the dominant modernization paradigm that emphasized modernity's homogenizing effects. He pointed to the visceral force of primordial identities of common historical memories, language, and religion that reassert themselves in the processes of modernization. Other cultural determinists, such as Johan Galtung, have developed cosmological theories that hypothesize preordained behavior by such nations as the Americans, the Russians, the Japanese, and the Iranians. This follows in the tradition of the "national character" studies of the 19th and 20th centuries. As always ready to produce a new ideological framework for the latest American foreign policy twists and turns, Samuel Huntington (1996) has turned from praise of military regimes to cultural explanations to account for the post-Cold War conflicts. He has thus predicted a "clash of civilizations" in which the West will be pitted against a Confucian-Islamic alliance. Although they belong to opposite political poles, Galtung and Huntington have thus elevated primordial identities to the level of major forces in history.

Table 1.2. Theories of Identity Formation

Identity formation	Primordialist	Constructivist	Instrumentalist	Situationalist	Communitarian
Political: Civic Identity	Deep attachment to traditional authorities	Imagined communities of ethnicity, nationhood, etc.	Hegemonic project of domination and resistance	Power relation to the political 'other'	Core solidarity with an epistemic community plus alliances with other epistemic communities
Economic: Status Identity	Common economic life	Construction of new economic lives	Class domination and resistance	Status situation relative to the 'other'	Status negotiations of identity
Cultural: Primordial Identity	Common myths, religion, language	Common project, e.g. nationalism	Symbolic domination and resistance	Malleable cultural posturing *vis-à-vis* the other	Cultural negotiation of identity

By contrast, Benedict Anderson (1983) has proposed that identity is a psychic order that is socially constructed. By studying the rise of nationalism in Southeast Asia, Anderson has shown how the introduction of print has historically created "imagined communities" of peoples that commonly share language and historical memories. We can further argue that the introduction of electronic media has extended the boundaries of nationhood beyond the literate population to encompass the illiterate masses speaking a common language. Today, the Internet is creating new imagined global communities of common interests, ideologies, and epistemologies.

The instrumentalists mostly come from an economistic perspective on migration and identity formation. While Marxists focus on class conflict, liberal economists emphasize market forces. Classical Marxists saw migration as a way of providing cheap labor for capital. This stands in sharp contrast to the classical and neo-liberal instrumentalist views of migration that consider population movements under capitalism resulting mainly from the worldwide supply and demand for labor. Borjas (1990, 225–8) for instance, suggests that the United States government should deregulate the immigration market by selling visas to the highest bidders. That proposal provides grist for the mill of world system theories that argue migration accentuates the domination of periphery by core countries. In addition to the flight of financial capital that takes place through transfer of corporate profits, brain drain of the highly skilled professionals is a flight of human capital from periphery to core countries. These factors as well as exploitation of cheap labor by transnational capital perpetuate uneven development, employing the resources of poor countries to make the rich even richer (Castles & Kosack 1985; Cohen 1987; Sassen 1988).

By contrast, situationalists come from anthropological and psychological perspectives converging into cultural studies (Friedman 1994; Wallman 1986). We define ourselves always in relation to others, they argue. As situations change our definitions of ourselves also change. Identity formations are thus relational and dynamic rather than fixed and static. Globalization processes have created great population movements at the top and bottom of the social structure. Identity formations are thus differentiating along new class, ethnic, and life style configurations in a complex variety of situations and hybrid identities.

Without negating some validity in each of the above theoretical positions, the communitarian position (Tehranian 1992; K. K. Tehranian 1998, 2000) focuses on community formation as the critical factor. To have a nation, it is not enough to have a common language. The British, Americans, Canadians, Australians, South Africans, and New Zealanders are six different nations divided by a common language. The Swiss are a nation with four different official languages; the Indians have sixteen official languages. What is important is to establish a national community of common historical memories, interests, and symbolic practices. Community formations, however, are inextricably tied to power struggles. Different hegemonic projects within a potential or actual national, regional, or global community emphasize different sets of historical memories, interests, and symbolic practices. Accelerating international migration, both physically and virtually through cyberspace has thus led to increasing multiple epistemic communities and identities.

Cultural security becomes a problem in the context of such power struggles. As the case of Iran dramatically demonstrates, the same national community can be reconfigured with radically different cultural and political consequences. The monarchist and secularist versus republican and Islamic visions and regimes fundamentally have differed in their views of Iranian history, cultural identity, position of women, and relations with the outside world. While the monarchist regime was based on the military and emphasized pre-Islamic historical memories and identities, the Islamic regime is based on clerical hegemony and draws its inspiration from the Islamic period and cultural practices. The cultural security of different segments of population has been thus compromised under the two regimes. The two nations have now been physically separated by the migration of some 3 million Iranians to many parts of the world where they can negotiate hybrid identities in relation to their host countries. For instance, there are an estimated 250,000 diaspric Iranians in Southern California that have developed their own epistemic community of Yellow Pages and media systems with its own distinct Irangeles imprint (Naficy 1993; Kelly *et al.* 1993).

Pancapitalism, Labor, and Migration

As an emerging mode of production and regulation, global capitalism or Pancapitalism (Tehranian 1999a, 1999b) is creating three distinctly different types of international migration, each leading to a variety of cultural insecurities. International labor migrations may be termed *manual, intellectual,* and *political.* While the first two result from market demand for labor and voluntary migration, the third is a consequence of revolutions, civil wars, ethnic cleansing, and forced migration.

The Pancapitalist regime needs two distinctly different kinds of cheap manual labor. Export processing zones in the newly industrializing countries (NICs) heavily depend on especially trained labor for routine and repetitive tasks. Pancapitalism has also created a class of newly rich countries and individuals in need of domestic services. Because they are cheap and malleable, young women frequently supply both types of manual labor. Hence, there is a feminization of migration. As Castles and Miller (1998, 25, 150) report,

> In many cases, migration decisions are made by the elders (especially the men), and people and women are expected to obey patriarchal authority. The family may decide to send young women to the city or overseas, because the labor of the young men is less dispensable on the farm. Young women are also often seen as more reliable in sending remittances. Such motivations correspond with increasing international demand for female labor as factory workers for precision assembly or as domestic servants, contributing to growing feminization of migration ... about 1.5 million Asian women were working abroad by the mid-1990s, and in many migratory movements they outnumbered men. For instance, two-thirds of Indonesian migrants from 1984 to 1994 were women. About half of Philippine overseas contract workers (OCWs) in 1994 were female. Most migrant women are concentrated in jobs regarded as 'typically female': domestic workers, entertainers (often a euphemism for prostitution), restaurant and hotel staff, assembly-line workers in clothing and electronics.

With the transfer of billions of petrodollars to the Persian Gulf oil exporting countries in the 1970s and 1980s, demand for manual labor resulted in a flood of migration from Asia to that region (Castles & Miller 1998, 147). By 1985, there were 3.2 million Asian workers in the Persian Gulf States, of whom 2 million were in Saudi Arabia. Recruitment declined as oil prices fell sharply in the late 1980s and 1990s. In the aftermath of the Persian Gulf War of 1990–91, about 450,000 Asians were forced to leave Kuwait. In particular, the politically undesirable Palestinians and Yemenis were compelled to leave Kuwait and Saudi Arabia. The Gulf states generally, and Saudi Arabia particularly, have developed a quasi-caste system in which European migrants are placed on top while Arab and Asian migrants are positioned in the middle and bottom of the social structure. In some of the Arab countries of the Persian Gulf, a new business has come about providing visas for foreign workers only to pass them on for whatever services (including prostitution) they can render.

The second type of demand for labor generated by Pancapitalism takes place at the opposite pole of the labor market, i.e. to satisfy the need for highly skilled, intellectual labor. In contrast to national capitalism that focused on manufacturing, global Pancapitalism is critically dependent on knowledge and financial service industries entailing overseas assignments. As Castles and Miller (1998, 167–168) have noted,

> The internationalization of production, trade, and finance is leading to increasing mobility of highly qualified personnel … The head of ILO's migrant workers section termed Western Europe's growing number of professionals, technicians, and kindred foreign workers the 'highly invisible' migrants. He estimated that they comprised one-quarter of legally resident aliens living in the EC and included 2 million citizens of European Free Trade Association (EFTA) countries, which have since joined with the EC to create the world's most populous free trade zone, the European Economic Area. The remainder of the EC's highly invisible migrants consists of Americans, Canadians, and Japanese. However resident alien populations, such as Turks in Germany, who are stereotypically seen as blue-collar workers, also include surprising numbers of professionals and entrepreneurs.

The third category of international migration under the Pancapitalist regime consists of victims of revolutions, civil wars, and ethnic cleansing who are forced to migrate. Such migrants may or may not appear in the UNHCR's statistics of refugees (Table 1.3). The political migrants may be considered an unintended consequence of a postwar bipolar regime in which dictatorial regimes were propped up in the Third World countries by the Western or Soviet bloc. In Eastern Europe, Asia, Africa, and Latin America, such regimes have sooner or later succumbed to social and political upheavals such as those in Cuba, Vietnam, Cambodia, Iran, Afghanistan, the Philippines,

Table 1.3. Estimated Number of Refugees Under UNHCR Mandate, 2001
Source: http://www.unher.ch/cgi-bin/texis/vtx/home?page=basics

Region	1 Jan. 2001
Asia	8,450,000
Africa	6,072,900
Europe	5,571,700
North America	1,047,100
Latin America & Caribbean	575,600
Oceania	76,000
Total	21,793,300

Indonesia, and communist countries in Eastern Europe. This in turn has resulted in waves of political migrations from those countries into Western Europe and North America. Civil wars such as those in Somalia and Ethiopia are also in part legacies of the Cold War era in which different sides were supported and armed by the Soviet and Western camps. Colonial policies of divide and rule in Congo and Rwanda also have contributed to the postcolonial civil wars. Despite its human rights rhetoric, Pancapitalism continues to support dictatorships wherever they guarantee safe havens for foreign investment, as in the Persian Gulf States. To that extent, we may expect continuing waves of migrants when and if revolutions occur in any of the client states.

The Kurdish migrants in Germany and the Iranian students abroad present two interesting cases of unintended consequences. About two thirds of Turkish guest workers in Germany are of Kurdish origin. Germany thus became a base of operation for Kurdish nationalism. Kurdish migrants in Germany and Lebanon have significantly assisted the Kurdish insurgency in Turkey (Castles & Miller 1998, 122–23). Iranian students in Western Europe and North America present another case of unintended political consequences of migration. While opposition to the Shah was severely repressed in Iran, starting in 1959, students who were sent abroad formed a Confederation of Iranian Students (CIS) that led to the struggle against the monarchical dictatorship until it finally succeeded in the revolution of 1979 (Shokat 1999; Matin 1999). During the 1960s and 1970s, the CIS also played a significant role in the European student movement, particularly in Germany.

Trends in International Migration

Accelerating international migration in the last few centuries has both enhanced and undermined cultural security. The diffusion of the human rights discourse and its incorporation into state constitutions and international declarations have, no doubt, legitimated cultural security as an issue in global and national governance. Castles and Miller (1998, 8–9) have identified five contemporary trends in international migration that have created unique problems and opportunities for cultural security. Their list consists of globalization, acceleration, differentiation, feminization, and politicization of migration. However, we should add commodification of migration to the list as another significant trend.

Globalization of Migration

Although population movements across spatial boundaries have been recurrent in history, international migration took on new proportions in 1492 when Columbus sailed for the New World. We may identify at least three distinct waves in international migration that have been driven by different motivations and consequences. In the first colonial wave of modern migration, the Europeans moved into "empty" territories and nearly wiped out the indigenous population of North and South America and the Pacific islands (Stannard 1989, 1992). They also brought millions of Africans as slaves to work the newly established plantations in the New World. In the second postcolonial wave, starting in 1945, international migration reversed itself. Millions of Asians, Africans, and Latin Americans sought better standards of living or refuge in North America and Europe. In the current third wave of globalized migration, beginning with the oil shock of 1973, international migration has proliferated in many different directions. Most notably, immigrants have come from Asia, Africa, and Eastern Europe moving toward the rich oil producing countries of South West Asia, Western Europe, Australia, New Zealand, and North America. In addition, millions of global nomads are roaming around the world as transnational corporate or government employees, guest workers, refugees, or tourists.

Acceleration of Migration

Although there has been acceleration in the rate of international migration in the 1973–1993 period, this is not an inexorable trend. During this period, the rise in migration was mainly due to the rising fortune of the oil exporting countries that attracted guest workers from all over the world, the fall of the communist regimes in Eastern Europe, and civil wars in Afghanistan, Yugoslavia, Iraq, Rwanda, and Tajikistan. Government policies that restrict migration can and have had a depressing effect on the rate of population movements.

Differentiation of Migration

Whereas in the first wave of migration, the main objective was colonization, in the second phase the purpose was chiefly to seek higher standards of living in the mother country. In the third wave, however, types of migrants and their motivations have proliferated. Revolutions in Cuba and Iran, for instance, drove millions of Cubans and Iranians out of their countries into Western Europe and

North America. These immigrants are mostly high status professionals. By contrast, the civil wars in Vietnam, Cambodia, Afghanistan, Tajikistan, and Yugoslavia have driven out masses of people who cannot all easily pursue a new professional life in their host countries. The unification of Germany is another unique case in which low income East Germans flooded the high income West Germany. The migrations in Africa (Rwanda, Burundi, Congo, Sudan, etc.) are mostly motivated by civil and tribal warfare. The complexity of this picture makes global policy formation more difficult if not impossible.

Feminization of Migration

Another notable trend in migration is the increase of women in the ranks of migrants. There are pull as well as push factors in this phenomenon. On the one hand, this trend may be considered a reflection of the increasing entry of women into the labor force. On the other hand, in many instances such as those in the rich oil exporting countries or post-communist Europe, women are preferred by the host countries as house workers, concubines, or prostitutes.

Politicization of Migration

While certain countries such as the United States, France, and Britain have a long history of immigration, others such as Nordic countries, Australia, Canada, and New Zealand have embarked on multiculturalism rather recently. The latter countries are thus facing more severe tests than the former. When newly arrived immigrants make up 25 percent of the population of a relatively homogenous country such as Sweden, the cultural shock to the old inhabitants can be severe. Even in the old immigration countries, temporary labor migrants can pose a sensitive political issue. The rise of anti-immigrant feelings in the face of rising unemployment in Europe and North America has thus politicized international migration. The presence of huge numbers of cheaply available migrant labor, some without legal papers, has often been supported by business and opposed by the labor unions. Language is another politicized issue. A number of individual states in the United States have already passed legislation to impose English as the sole language in schools and places of work.

Commodification of Migration

The latter two trends suggest a sixth trend reminiscent of the colonial period when large numbers of slaves or immigrants were brought by the colonists to provide labor for their plantations. Australia started as a penal colony; the British and the Dutch brought Indians and Chinese to their colonies (Indonesia, Malay, and Fiji) to provide cheap and reliable labor. American landlords brought Asian and Portuguese labor to Hawaii to work their sugar plantations. In some of the Persian Gulf states today citizens can bring immigrants to work for them. While this provides for immigrants' remittances to their mother countries (the Philippines, Pakistan, India, and Bangladesh), it also has opened up the door to abuse. There are agencies that specialize in bringing women and children from abroad to serve their new masters as servants and concubines. There are also sweatshops in New York and Los Angeles that employ illegal immigrants with few human rights except those granted by their new bosses.

International Migration Policies and Governance

International migration policies are caught in a complex web of national, regional, and global policies.

National Policies

The variety of national policies on international migration has made the development of an international migration regime difficult if not impossible. We may identify at least three basic national policies: Exclusionary, Assimilationist, and Multiculturalist. States can also follow a mix of policies with respect to different segments of their migrant population.

Exclusionary policies, typified by those in Germany and Israel with respect to Turkish and Palestinian guest workers, consider the arrangements of a temporary duration and mostly deny the migrants the rights of citizenship.

Assimilationist policies have been widely practiced in the older immigrant societies such as Britain, France, the United States, and Israel (in the case of its Palestinian citizens). Assimilationist policies expect the immigrants to leave their past identities behind and dissolve into the French, American, or Israeli national melting pots. Theodore Roosevelt's famous dictum that "we do not need hyphen-ated Americans" reflects the underlying spirit of such policies. Assimilationist policies, however, have run into serious difficulties with the North Africans in France, Mexicans in the United States, and Eastern European and Oriental Jews in Israel. In each case, ties with past religious or national identities have proved too strong to break.

Since the 1960s when cultural roots assumed a new importance in the lives of African-Americans in the United States, ethnic consciousness among old and new immigrants has inspired a new Multiculturalist policy alternative. Such policies have already been followed consciously in Britain, Canada, Australia, and New Zealand, but they are matters of controversy in France and the United States (Schlesinger 1992; Berman 1992; Taylor & Gutman 1994; D'Souza 1996). Multiculturalist demands and practices on the part of new migrants have, in turn, led to new anti-immigrant sentiments in Germany, France, Scandinavia, and the United States. Such sentiments have combined with the rise of Islamic militancy to create a poisoned international atmosphere for Muslim immigrants.

The UN Refugee Convention and Protocol forbid governments from forcibly returning refugees to where they can be persecuted. This violation of the international agreements is known as *refoulement*. Since its exercise often brings disrepute in the international community, governments often forcibly return those refugees whose legal status as "refugees" has not yet been determined. World Refugee Survey 1999 (US Committee for Refugees 2000, p. 13) reports significant numbers that have been returned in this fashion.

Regional Policies

We may recognize at least two distinct migration policies at the regional level: open and closed labor migration. The European Union has pioneered a policy of open labor migration within its own boundaries that accompanies its drive towards monetary and political union. Other regional organizations, however, lag behind and mostly continue to practice closed national borders. Although there is some receptivity to intra-regional migration, as evidenced in the Arab, Iranian, and East Asian regions, migrants continue to be treated as "foreign" to be employed and discharged in mostly menial jobs as necessary.

Global Policies

Conflicting national policies toward migrants do not add up to an international migration policy. However, global attitudes and policies toward one category of migrants, namely refugees, have evolved in response to major historical disasters. As the Minority Rights Group points out (www.minorityrights.org), the international

Table 1.4. Origin of Major Refugee Populations in 1999 (Ten Largest Groups)[1]
Source: http://www.unhcr.ch/cgi-bin/texis/vtx/home?page=basics

Country of origin[2]	Main countries of asylum	Refugees
Afghanistan	Pakistan/Iran	3,580,400
Burundi	Tanzania	568,000
Iraq	Iran	512,800
Sudan	Uganda/D.R. Congo/Ethiopia/ Kenya/C.A.R./Chad	490,400
Bosnia-Herzegovina	Yugoslavia/Croatia/USA/Sweden/ Netherlands/Denmark	478,300
Somalia	Kenya/Ethiopia/Yemen/Djibouti	447,800
Angola	Zambia/D.R. Congo/Namibia	432,700
Sierra Leone	Guinea/Liberia	400,800
Eritrea	Sudan	376,400
Vietnam	China/USA	370,300

1. An estimated 3.8 million Palestinians who are covered by a separate mandate of the U.N. Relief and Works Agency for Palestine Refugees in the Near East (UNRWA) are not included in this report. However, Palestinians outside the UNWRA area of operations such as those in Iraq or Libya, are considered to be of concern to UNHCR.
2. This table includes UNHCR estimates for nationalities in industrialized countries on the basis of recent refugee arrivals and asylum seeker recognition.

system to assist refugees has emerged out of World Wars I and II. The right to claim asylum was thus formally established in Article 14 of the Universal Declaration of Human Rights. At the end of the World War II, 6 million people were displaced in Europe. Their numbers soon swelled by refugees fleeing the political turmoils that led to the division of most of Europe into Western and Soviet blocs. In the office of the UN High Commissioner for Refugees (UNHCR), the United Nations established a new international mechanism in December 1950. In 1951, the Geneva Convention on the Status of Refugees came into force. It provided a mechanism in international law for individual protection. Under the Convention a refugee is defined as any person who has "a well-founded fear of being persecuted for reasons of race, religion, nationality, membership of a particular social group or political opinion."

From the 1970s attention shifted from Europe to the newly decolonized states in the South. Just as the formation of nation-states and the dissolution of empires had resulted in conflict and mass movements in Europe, so did the collapse of colonial empires and the formation of new states lead to internal and international conflicts and new waves of refugees. For two decades these movements had little direct impact on Europe. Refugees moved to the neighboring states to be housed in camps or among the local population. European and North American governments and voluntary organizations provided assistance and UNHCR tried, with varying degrees of success, to coordinate relief and offer protection. Many of the host countries were among the world's poorest countries. During this period small numbers of people continued to seek asylum upon arrival in Europe and governments initiated some programs for accepting quotas of refugees from a specific crisis on a case-by-case basis.

Refugees from Vietnam arriving by boat in Hong Kong marked a change in the manner of caring for refugees in Europe. An international conference in 1979 allocated responsibility for resettling the refugees primarily in Western Europe and North America. This plan met with some reluctance in these regions, brought on by deepening economic recession and implementation of strict immigration policies. Yet the response was still considerably more generous than that given to new refugees in the 1980s and 1990s. In 1972, 13,000 people applied for asylum in Western Europe. By 1979 this number had increased to 77,000. The number of applications for asylum in Europe rose every year from 1983, when there were 73,700 applications, and reached a peak in 1992 when there were 692,685 applicants, many from the war in former Yugoslavia. The number of applicants has subsequently decreased every year. In 1995 there were 283,416 applicants and preliminary figures from 1996 show a further decrease. These numbers are much lower than the many millions of refugees assisted in Africa, the Middle East, and Asia.

In the mid-1980s, Western European governments concluded that they needed to harmonize their asylum policy. Two major events precipitated this process: the Single European Act (aimed at abolishing internal borders in the EU) and the dramatic increase of asylum-seekers arriving in Europe at a time when economic recession made newcomers 'unwelcome'. Restrictive changes in Europe have frequently originated in agreements reached at intergovernmental meetings between ministers. The resulting proposals have created largely uniform measures reducing the number of asylum-seekers and refugees in Europe.

In Western Europe and North America, new measures to deter asylum seekers have taken a number of forms. These include: new visa requirements; heavy fines on airlines and other transporters for carrying undocumented passengers; more difficult application procedures; long periods of detention for applicants, often in conditions worse than those experienced by prisoners; and, increasingly, restricted freedom of movement; prohibition on employment and political participation; lack of social welfare benefits and settlement provisions; and decreased opportunities for family reunification. The new measures extend to sending asylum-seekers back to the first country to which they fled ('country of first asylum') or to a 'third host country' outside of Europe. The asylum-seeker then risks forcible return to the country of persecution or an unending cycle of chain deportations.

Conclusion

This essay has argued that Pancapitalism has ushered a new third historical wave of international migration. In the first wave, lasting from beginning of history to the 16th century, global migration was primarily motivated by the search for new resources and habitats as well as military conquest. The second wave, dominated by the European migration into "the empty territories" of the New World and colonization of Africa, Asia, and America, lasted until the mid-20th century. The rise of Pancapitalism in the postwar period has inaugurated a third wave that is far more complex and multidimensional.

The essay also argues that three types of labor migration have characterized the third wave, including intellectual, manual, and displaced labor. The head of the International Organization of Migration (IMO) estimated the number of international migrants at 120 million in 1994 (Castles & Miller 1998, 4). Of these about 16 million are displaced labor (refugees and displaced persons). Another 30 million or so are considered foreign workers (manual labor) who transmit about $75 billion to their countries of origin as immigrants' remittances (World Bank 2000, 39). About 74 million migrants may be thus considered as intellectual labor.

Discounting the number of illegal immigrants and internal migration, these figures suggest that Pancapitalism is thriving in part because of the brain drain that migration of intellectual labor from less to more developed countries entails. Chinese, Indian, and Iranian engineers and scientists, for instance, heavily populate

Silicon Valley. According to the World Bank (2000, 39), "some countries in Sub-Saharan Africa, the Caribbean, Central America, and South Asia have lost one-third of their skilled workers." The loss should be weighed against immigrant remittances that constitute 50 percent more funds than total official development assistance provides.

The flow of international migration under Pancapitalism is generally from poorer to richer countries, reversing the process of European colonization of Africa, Asia, and Latin America. This has, in turn, created important diasporic communities and identities in Europe and North America. The Chinese, Indian, Pakistani, Turkish, Algerian, Hispanic, and Iranian Diaspora can be witnessed in the major metropolitan centers of Europe and North America (World Bank 2000, 40). One unfortunate consequence of the increasing visibility of immigrants is the rise of anti-immigrant sentiments and the politics of intolerance. Having had little experience with immigration, the more homogenous European countries such as Austria have thus stooped to the increasing popularity of right-wing and racist parties.

The problems of international migration are so complex and many-faceted that it is nearly impossible to offer solutions that cover all circumstances and predicaments. However, the postwar international refugee regime, consisting of the four Geneva conventions of 1949 and two additional protocols of 1977, is undergoing considerable stress. Because of the mounting refugee problems and domestic backlash against them, the gap between international law and practice has been widening (Newland 2000).

Globalization is clearly accelerating the flow of funds, ideas, services, goods, and people in that order. What Richard Falk (2000) has aptly called "predatory globalization" is creating increasing barriers to the flow of people while facilitating the flows of capital. But the dislocations that result from predatory globalization, and its concomitant militarization, are creating a desperate need for a new international migration and refugee regime. The old regime contains too many loopholes and escape clauses that states often employ to shirk their responsibilities.

The governance of the new regime should come perhaps under the umbrella of a new United Nations specialized agency that can coordinate the efforts of the UNHCR, the international organizations, national agencies, and non-governmental organizations dealing with refugee and migration problems. Recent experiences in Bosnia, Kosovo, Rwanda-Burundi, Kurdistan, Afghanistan, and

Tajikistan have shown that the existence of too many organizations in the management of migration and refugee problems leads to confusion and dissolution of responsibility. A United Nations Migration Organization (UNMO) may have, therefore, the following functions:

- To coordinate the work of national, intergovernmental, and non-governmental organizations in international migration.
- To facilitate the work of all organizations toward timely and effective humanitarian assistance to refugees, displaced persons, and international migrants.
- To provide early warning on refugee and migratory problems while developing appropriate policies for dealing with the outcomes.

To provide funds for UNMO, it is only fair that the beneficiaries of globalization should be prepared to pay for the human costs of globalization-*cum*-militarization. Ethnic cleansing, displacement, and refugees are part of those heart-wrenching costs. In the Iran-Iraq War of 1980–88, the Persian Gulf War of 1991, the civil wars in Somalia, former Yugoslavia, East Timor, Central America, Afghanistan, Rwanda-Burundi, and Tajikistan, great and regional power rivalries exacerbated the conditions and produced colossal human tragedies. Apart from internal conditions that gave rise to these conflicts, global economic and political forces also must assume their share of responsibility. A tax levied on international travel can provide a global fund for refugees to support the work of UNHCR and UNMO. The fund can be also supplemented by voluntary contributions from individuals and states.

We are increasingly living in a multicultural world of high population mobility. In spite of some government policies against it, many mobile professionals carry more than one passport. The nation-state system runs against the fact of an increasing global economy in which capital, trade, and investment are mobile but people are held back within the confines of the territorial states. It would be proactive to reach a new international agreement that allows mobile citizens to carry more than one passport and to permit stateless persons to carry a United Nations passport that entitles them to basic human rights in their temporary or permanent host countries.

CHAPTER 2

Emergent Spaces, New Places, and Old Faces: Proliferating Identities in a Globalizing World

James N. Rosenau

I was born in Argentina, my entire family is Argentinean, and culturally I have been raised Argentinean. Yet, at age four I moved out of Argentina and only returned on vacations. I grew up in Panama until I was thirteen and then moved to California. So where does that leave me? I speak perfect English and Spanish. Physically, I can pass as Californian, Panamanian, or Argentinean. I know many people that are in my same situation. In a sense, we identify with each other. We have created our own territory, imagined, but a territory nonetheless.

Virginia Barreiro, graduate student[1]

I see myself as a citizen of the world, and someone who is unmistakably American and Chinese. My parents are Chinese but I grew up in a small town in the Midwest. I have no attachment to a place, but I wish I had one. I am a scientist but I like philosophy. I am a social psychologist but I read a lot of anthropology, sociology, mythology, and political science. I am a shifting person of multicolored hues. I can disguise myself very well, and make it very difficult for others to know exactly where I come from. There are probably more people like me now than at any other time in human history.

James H. Liu, Senior Lecturer[2]

[Woods said it bothers him when people label him as African-American since he is one-quarter black, one-quarter Thai, one-quarter Chinese, one-eighth white, and one-eighth American Indian.] Growing up, I came up with this name. I'm a Cablinasian.

Tiger Woods, golfer[3]

These epigraphs suggest the major theme of this paper as well as personally and eloquently capturing three of its subthemes. The major theme is that an understanding of the links between contemporary culture, identity, and world affairs requires a commitment to the tracing of nuance. One of the subthemes is that the macro-complexities of modern life are fully experienced at the micro-levels of most (but not all) individuals. The second is that the identities of many (but not all) individuals are proliferating because, third, many (but not all) people are on the move.

The repeated "but not all" qualifier is intended to highlight the presence of pervasive and significant contradictions in world affairs that render the tracing of nuance challenging, mandatory, and difficult. It is challenging because to focus on the relevance of identities and cultures is to be concerned about the interactions between micro- and macro-phenomena, interactions that pose enormous conceptual, theoretical, and empirical problems in assessing the degree to which the micro-identities of individuals underlie the macro-cultures of collectivities, and vice versa. Tracing nuance is mandatory because the key contradictions are so sharp that they can tempt one into black-or-white forms of analysis, and it is difficult because of the numerous shades of gray on which the contradictions rest.

Today the contradictions of world affairs are widely considered to signify the advent of an age of globalization. But that is too simple. It underplays the complexities, contradictions, and the nuances of our time. These are best grasped by viewing the dynamics presently at work on a global scale as generating the emergence of a new epoch in human history, an epoch marked by profound transformations that, in turn, have fostered contradictions between the globalizing and the localizing, between the centralizing and the decentralizing, between the integrating and the fragmenting—to mention only the more conspicuous of the polarities presently unfolding at both the micro- and macro-levels. I have long summarized these contradictions by using the label "fragmegration". The term is a combination of fragmentation and integration, and it is designed to highlight the dynamics of contraction, which sustain localizing, decentralizing, and fragmenting forces on the one hand, and the dynamics of expansion through which globalizing, centralizing, and integrating forces unfold on the other hand.[4] The fragmegrative label may seem awkward at first, but it has the virtue of fusing in a single phrase the interactive polarities that underlie the emergent epoch (Rosenau 1983, 1994a).

To meet the analytic challenges posed by identity and culture in a fragmegrative context the ensuing analysis first sets forth the underlying macro-dynamics and contradictions of world affairs. In so doing, it highlights the transformative sources that have opened up new spaces and places in which large numbers of people (but not all) are encountering new cultures and identities through immigration and other forms of travel as well as by staying at home and having the world come to them electronically, through word of mouth, education, and new products and store fronts. The inquiry then turns to the micro-level and attempts to sort out how individuals cope with the dynamics of change and their encounters with new cultures and identities. The sorting-out effort follows two lines of inquiry. One focuses on immigrants and transnational elites as illustrative of people who are consistently confronted by questions of identity. The other is concerned more generally with how people link themselves to the several local and global worlds highlighted by fragmegration that are available for affiliation or rejection. Twelve worlds and their corresponding identities are specified and some suggestions are made as to the capacity of people to manage more than one of the identities and to estimate what might lead to shifts from any one of the identities to any of the others.[5] Together the two foci suggest what can well be called a "simultaneity of consciousness" and constitute an extension of an earlier effort to outline a psychology of fragmegration (Liu & Rosenau 1999). Hopefully it is a psychology that has the potential of clarifying the macro implications of the growing number of people whose experiences parallel those of Virginia Barriero, James Liu, and Tiger Woods.

An Emergent Epoch

As indicated by its powerful polarities, the new epoch is marked by an extensive multiplicity of opposites. The international system is less commanding, but it is still powerful. State sovereignty has eroded, but it is still vigorously asserted. Governments are weaker, but they can still throw their weight around. Scenes of unspeakable horror and genocide flicker on TV screens even as humanitarian organizations undertake remedial actions. The United Nations is asked to take on more assignments and not supplied with the funds to carry them out. Many people cling desperately to long-standing identities, but many others are expanding their repertoire of identities. At times publics are more demanding, but at other times they are more pliable. Citizens are both more active and more cynical. Borders still keep out intruders, but they are also more porous. Cultures are fraying even as they become more meaningful. Many identities are undergoing transformation even as some are becoming more rigid.

In sum, we have come to know that we live in a world that is deteriorating in some areas, remaining fixed in others, and thriving still in others which is another way of concluding that both order and disorder simultaneously sustain global structures. It is hardly surprising that each day brings word of a world inching slowly toward sanity even as it moves toward breakdown. From a fragmegrative perspective, the world is short on clear-cut boundaries that differentiate domestic and foreign affairs, with the result that local problems can become transnational in scope even as global challenges can have repercussions for small communities.[6] Viewed in this way, the global system has undergone such a vast disaggregation that the post-Cold War era has come to an end and been replaced, not by an age of globalization, but by the age of fragmegration—by processes that are neither unwavering nor unidirectional, that create their own negation even as they foster change, that result in fragile outcomes ever vulnerable to reversal, and that have collapsed the age-old struggle between tradition and innovation into a singular dynamic.

The diverse multiplicity of opposites underlies an endless series of tensions between core and periphery, between national and transnational systems, between communitarianism and cosmopolitanism, between cultures and subcultures, between states and markets, between territory and cyberspace, between patriots and urbanites, between decentralization and centralization, between universalism and particularism, between flow and closure (Meyer & Geschiere 1997), between pace and space (Luke & Tuathail 1998),[7] between self and Other, between the distant and the proximate—to note only the more conspicuous links between opposites that underlie the course of events. And each of these tensions is marked by numerous variants; they take different forms in different parts of the world, in different countries, in different markets, in different communities, in different professions, and in different cyberspaces, with the result that there is enormous diversity in the way people experience the tensions that beset their lives.[8]

In our heavily wired world, moreover, the integrating and fragmenting events usually occur simultaneously. And often they are causally related, with the causal links tending to cumulate and to generate a momentum such that integrative increments tend to give rise to disintegrative increments, and vice versa. It is important to stress the pervasiveness of the interactive foundations of the diverse tensions. To disaggregate them for analytic purposes, to confine inquiry only to globalizing dynamics or only to localizing dynamics, is to risk overlooking what makes events unfold as they do. The simultaneity of the good and bad, integrative and disintegrative, and coherent and incoherent lies at the heart of the emergent epoch. As one analyst puts it, "the distinction between the global and the local is becoming very complex and problematic" (Robertson 1990, 19).

Nor have the contradictions of the emergent epoch escaped the attention of publics. With the fragmenting forces of localization and the integrating dynamics of globalization so interwoven as to be products of each other, people have become increasingly aware of how fragmegration has intensified old identities and fostered new ones. However they may articulate their understanding, individuals everywhere have come to expect, to take for granted, that the advance of globalization poses threats to long-standing local and national ties, that some groups will contest, even violently fight, the intrusion of global norms even as others will seek to obtain goods, larger market shares, or generalized support beyond their communities. The forces of fragmentation are rooted in the psychic comfort people derive from the familiar, close-at-hand values and practices of their neighborhoods, just as the forces of integration stem from their aspirations to benefit from the distant products of the global economy, to realize the efficiencies of regional unity, to counter environmental degradation, to achieve coherent communities through policies of inclusion that expand their democratic institutions, and to acknowledge the meaning of the pictures taken in outer space that depict the earth as a solitary entity in a huge universe. Stated more generally, and in the succinct words of one astute observer, "There is a constant struggle between the collectivist and individualist elements within each human" (Triandis 1995, xiv).

The Sources of Change and Contradiction

To understand how fragmegrative dynamics are impacting on individuals at the micro-levels by collapsing time and space and thus rendering problematic the meaning of "home" and territory, it is useful to take note of the sources underlying the transformations unfolding at the macro-level of cultures, societies, states, and international systems. Anticipating the diversity of these sources, new technologies have facilitated the rapid flow of ideas, information, pictures, and money across continents; the transportation revolution has hastened the boundary-spanning flow of elites, tourists, immigrants (legal and illegal), migrants, and whole populations; the organizational revolution has shifted the flow of authority, influence, and power beyond traditional boundaries; and the economic revolution has redirected the flow of goods, services, capital, and ownership among countries. Taken together, these flows have

fostered a cumulative process that is both the source and consequence of eroding boundaries, integrating regions, proliferating
networks, diminishing territorial attachments, coalescing social
movements, weakening states, contracting sovereignty, dispersing
authority, demanding publics, and expanding citizen skills—all of
which also serve to generate counter-reactions intended to contest,
contain, or reverse the multiple flows and thereby preserve communities and reduce inequities. While each of these sources is powerful,
none of them can be listed as primary. They are all interactive and
each reinforces the others. None are sufficient but all are necessary
to sustain the age of fragmegration.

Technological Innovations

Stunning are the data depicting the ways in which a variety of
communications technologies—from the fax machine to the fiber
optic cable, from the VCR to the orbiting satellite, from television to
the Internet—continue to shrink the world and reduce the relevance
of geographic boundaries. Today there are more than one billion
telephones in active use throughout the world. In 1964 there was one
TV set for every 20 persons, whereas now there is one for every four.
Currently more than 200 functioning satellites orbit the Earth, each
capable of carrying tens of thousands of calls and several TV signals
at once. The number of Internet hosts, or networked computers,
grew more than six-fold between 1995 and 1999 (National
Geographic Society 1999). More than 1.4 billion e-mail messages are
estimated to cross national boundaries every day (Clinton 1999, 2).
Quite possibly, moreover, these dynamics are poised for another
step-level leap forward with the advent of the Internet, which is
growing by one million web pages a day (*ibid.*, 1), and new computer
technologies, which include the prospect of a chip 100 billion (repeat
100 billion) times faster than those available today (Markoff 1999,
A1). Future generations might look back to the latter part of the
1990s and the widening scope of the Internet as the historical starting
point for a new phase of modern globalization. It is not difficult to
extrapolate from these data the conclusion that increasingly people
have close encounters with foreign cultures through global networks
that offer the potential for a proliferation of identities.

The Skill Revolution

All too many observers of world affairs are inclined to treat
individuals at the micro-level as constants on the (often implicit)

grounds that collectivities at the macro-level, especially states, either ignore their publics or are able to mobilize their support when needed. Recently, however, it seems clear that people everywhere need to be regarded as variables in the sense that their analytic, emotional, and imaginative talents have undergone sufficient expansion to make a difference in the conduct of states and other macro-actors. Such variations are great enough to warrant referring to them as "the skill revolution" (Rosenau 1990). Taken together, the several dimensions of the skill revolution are pivotal to all the other sources of fragmegrative dynamics noted below. The data descriptive of enlarged skills are hardly voluminous and many are anecdotal, but those that have been systematically collected all point in the same direction (Rosenau & Fagen 1997; Neisser 1998). The skill revolution enables people to trace more readily the course of distant events back into their own homes, to know more precisely what they favor and oppose as situations unfold, to imagine more fully other cultures, to appreciate more explicitly the possibility that the identity and bases of their citizenship may be changing, and to engage more effectively in collective action. Given the contradictions that underlie the emergent epoch, the enhanced analytic skills of some people serve to expand their horizons to include transnational foci, while for others the skill revolution has facilitated a retreat to local concerns.

The Mobility Upheaval

The data reflecting new transportation technologies—mainly the jet aircraft—clearly indicate the huge extent to which time and space have been substantially reduced. The vastness of the encounters with distant cultures through foreign travel—what I call the "mobility upheaval"—can be readily depicted. The movement of people—everyone from the tourist to the terrorist and the immigrant to the jet-setter—has been so extensive that around five percent of the people alive today are estimated to be living in a country other than the one where they were born (Tharoor 1999, 7)[9] and in the United States nearly one in 10 residents is foreign born (Associated Press 1999). Indeed, every day one-half million airline passengers cross national boundaries (Clinton 1999, 2). And especially relevant to the concern here with the links between migration and culture is the pattern whereby "personal international calls have burgeoned, fed by immigrants talking to relatives or friends. The number of calls from the US to other countries in 1997 was 21 times that in 1980"

(National Geographic Society 1999). In 1965, on a worldwide basis 75 million people were migrants from another country, whereas the figure for 1999 was 125 million (*New York Times*, September 19, 1999, Sec. 4, p.4).

The Organizational Explosion

Hardly less so than the population explosion, recent years have witnessed a veritable explosion in the number of voluntary associations that have crowded onto the global stage. Fostered partly by environment and human rights issues, people have been reaching out to like-minded others to form associations or otherwise band together on behalf of common purposes. A sense of remoteness from the centers of decision has also energized people to come together. Still another source of the organizational explosion is the Internet and the ease with which associations can keep in touch with and mobilize their memberships. Indeed, not only have the new communications technologies facilitated the growth and coherence of associations, but they have also contributed to the mushrooming of networks and the decline of hierarchy as the basis for organizational structures.

Exact data on the extent and scope of the organizational proliferation are virtually impossible to compile (since self-reporting about membership size and issue concerns is not a characteristic trait of organizations), but some relevant materials have been developed.[10] It has been calculated, for example, that Indonesia had only one independent environmental organization twenty years ago, whereas now there are more than 2,000 linked to an environmental network based in Jakarta. Likewise, registered nonprofit organizations in the Philippines grew from 18,000 to 58,000 between 1989 and 1996; in Slovakia the figure went from a handful in the 1980s to more than 10,000 today; and in the US 70 percent of the nonprofit organizations—not counting religious groups and private foundations—filing tax returns with the Treasury Department are less than 30 years old and a third are less than 15 years old (Bornstein 1999). All the indicators, in short, point to an extensive proliferation of collectivities, to a global stage dense with actors. As noted below, the mushrooming of organizations at every level of community has important implications for the structures of the global system, the weakening of states, and the advent of authority crises. More importantly for present purposes, it is a development that has offered people a wide range of new opportunities to evolve new identities.

The Decline of the State and Territoriality

Although some analysts insist states are as viable and competent as ever (Ikenberry 1996), many (myself included) contend that they are in decline. To be sure, state institutions still have a modicum of authority and they are not about to disappear from the global stage. But their capacity to exercise their authority has lessened considerably. States cannot prevent ideas from moving across their borders. They cannot control the flow of money, jobs, and production facilities in and out of their country. They have only minimal control over the flow of people and virtually no control over the flow of drugs or the drift of polluted air and water. Their capacity to promote and maintain cohesion among the groups that comprise their society is at an all-time low as crime, corruption, and ethnic sensitivities undermine any larger sense of national community they may have had. Cynicism toward politicians and major institutions is widespread and people increasingly perceive no connection between their own welfare and that of their communities. Selfishness and greed have replaced more encompassing loyalties as attachments to territory have diminished. Thus many states are unable to enforce laws, prevent widespread corruption, collect taxes, or mobilize their armed forces for battle. They cannot collectively bring order to war-torn societies. In short, landscapes, those visions of territoriality, have become blurred and are being supplemented by ethnoscapes, financescapes, ideoscapes, mediascapes, technoscapes, and identiscapes (Appadurai 1996).[11]

As the capacities of states have eroded, so has territoriality lost much of its organizing focus. The history of states is a history of territorial division, of clear-cut links to geographically bound spaces, but in the emergent fragmegrative epoch these links have become frayed and some degree of de-territorialization has resulted from all the boundary-spanning flows noted above. The advent of the Internet and other electronic mechanisms for transgressing—better, ignoring—territorial units is illustrative in this respect, but it is only one of many ways in which the dynamics of globalization have rendered long-standing national boundaries porous and, in some cases, obsolete. An extreme projection of this trend has been recorded by one observer who argues, "The very epoch of the nation-state is near its end ... It may well be that the emergent post-national order proves not to be a system of homogeneous units (as with the current system of nation-states) but a system based on relations between heterogeneous units (some social movements, some

31

interest groups, some professional bodies, some nongovernmental organizations, some armed constabularies, some judicial bodies)" (Appadurai 1996, 19, 23).

Authority Crises

With people increasingly skillful, with states weakened, and with other types of organizations proliferating, governments everywhere are undergoing authority crises in which traditional conceptions of legitimacy are being replaced by performance criteria of legitimacy, thus fostering bureaucratic disarray, executive-legislative stalemate, and decisional paralysis that, in turn, enhances the readiness of individuals to employ their newly acquired skills on behalf of their perceived self-interests. Indeed, there is hardly a national government today that is not caught up in one or another form of crisis that severely restricts their capacity to frame innovative policies and move toward their goals. Nor are these crises confined just to governments and states. The fragmenting tendencies are also operative within other institutions and organizations, from the Catholic Church to the Mafia, from the multinational corporation to the political party. Given fragmegrative dynamics, it follows that some authority crises have enlarged the jurisdiction of intergovernmental organizations (IGOs) and nongovernmental organizations (NGOs), while others have contracted the range of national jurisdictions and extended that of local institutions. Equally important, the onset of authority crises has the potential of inducing people to redirect their loyalties and legitimacy sentiments that, in turn, may alter the allegiances collectivities and cultures can command.

Subgroupism

Since there is a widespread inclination to refer loosely to "nationalism" as a source of the fragmenting forces at work in the world, it is perhaps useful to be more precise about the collective nature of those decentralizing tendencies wherein individuals and groups feel readier to challenge authority and reorient their loyalties. The authority crises that result from such challenges can be either of an "upward" or a "downward" kind, depending on whether the aspiration is to relocate authority in more or less encompassing jurisdictions than those that operate at the national level. In a number of instances of both kinds of relocation, the motivation that sustains the change is not so deeply emotional to qualify as an "ism". The creation of subnational administrative divisions, for example, can stem from detached efforts to rationalize the work of a governmental agency or private organization, and the process of implementing the decentralized arrangements can occur in the context of reasoned dialogue and calm decision making. Often, however, intense concerns and powerful attachments—feelings and commitments strong enough to justify using terms like "transnationalism", "supra-nationalism", or "internationalism"—can accompany the press for new arrangements. Accordingly, it seems preferable to label the decentralizing tendencies of fragmegration as those of "subgroupism" and to reserve the concept of nationalism for those subgroup expressions that revolve around nations and feelings of ethnicity.

Subgroupism arises out of those deep affinities that people develop toward the close-at-hand associations, organizations, and subcultures with which they have been historically, professionally, economically, socially, or politically linked and to which they attach their highest priorities. Subgroupism values the in-group over the out-group, sometimes treating the two as adversaries and sometimes positing them as susceptible to extensive cooperation. Subgroupism can derive from and be sustained by a variety of sources, not the least being disappointment with—and alienation from—the perform-ances of the whole system in which the subgroup is located. Most of all, perhaps, its intensities are the product of long-standing historical roots that span generations and get reinforced by an accumulated lore surrounding past events in which the subgroup survived trying circumstances. For all of these reasons, moreover, subgroupism tends to beget subgroupism as new splits occur in subgroups after they achieve their autonomy. Just as some people in Quebec want out of Canada, for example, so do the Mohawks want out of Quebec. Indeed, it can be said that the proliferation of many identities is mirrored in the processes of subgroupism.

That subgroupism can be deeply implanted in the consciousness of peoples was manifestly apparent in the resurfacing of strong ethnic identities throughout Eastern Europe and the former Soviet Union when, after decades, the authoritarian domination of communist parties came to an end. In those cases, the subgroups were historic nations either repressed or co-opted by the USSR and their resur-gence in the 1990s can thus be readily regarded as expressions of nationalism. Not all, or even a preponderance, of decentralizing tendencies attach to nations, however. Governmental subdivisions, political parties, labor unions, professional societies, corporate head-quarters, and a host of other types of subgroups can also evoke

intense attachments, and it would grossly understate the relevance of
the decentralizing tendencies at work in world politics to ignore these
other forms of close-at-hand ties.

Especially relevant to our concerns here are the processes
whereby the relocation of authority in diverse directions has been
accompanied by—and contributed further to—a surge in the politics
of identity, in people redefining who they believe themselves to be in
such a way that their commitments to the state, their national loyalties, are lessening. In the United States, for example, serious
proposals have recently been voiced questioning the virtues of patriotism (Cohen 1996). A thoughtful proposal to rewrite the national
anthem has even found its way into the public domain (Hertzberg
1997). Stated differently, as the values of multiculturalism become
increasingly ascendant throughout the world, states are bound to be
weakened, with their capacity to sustain broad consensuses around
shared goals diminished and their ability to concert the energies of
citizens in support of policies reduced.

In short, subgroupism is inherent in the dynamics of fragmegration. It has resulted in rule-setting authority being dispersed widely
throughout the world's neighborhoods, communities, provinces, and
transnational cyberspaces.[12] As one observer aptly notes, the current
scene is marked by "a pluralism of authority" (Bauman 1992, 160).

The Bifurcation of Global Structures

As the density of the global stage increases with the proliferation of
organizations and as authority gets relocated to fill the vacuums left
by weakened states, global structures have undergone a significant
transformation, a bifurcation such that there are now two worlds of
world politics: the traditional state-centric world of sovereign states
and an emergent multi-centric world composed of diverse collectivities such as multinational corporations, ethnic minorities,
nongovernmental organizations (NGOs), professional associations,
social movements, and incipient communities. These two worlds are
still working out their respective domains as the emergent epoch
unfolds. While in some instances the actors in the two worlds go their
separate ways, most of the time they cooperate, conflict, or otherwise
interact even as they maintain the boundaries that separate them. In
effect, the traditional state-centric world now has a formidable rival
in the multi-centric world even as it is beset by authority crises and
under siege from skillful publics (Rosenau 1990, ch. 10). Indeed, the
bifurcation of global structures underlies the weakening of states by

creating spaces for the formation or consolidation of collectivities in the multi-centric world.

The Globalization of National Economies

If the communications revolution has been a prime stimulus of the tendencies toward decentralization through empowering citizens and subnational groups, the dynamics at work in the realm of economics are equally powerful as sources of centralizing tendencies. The globalization of capital, production, labor, and markets in the last few decades has resulted in financiers, entrepreneurs, workers, and consumers now being deeply enmeshed in transnational networks that have superseded the traditional political jurisdictions of national scope. Such a transformation has served to loosen the ties of producers to their states and workers to their firms, to expand the horizons within which citizens pondered their self-interests, and to contribute to the proliferation of organizations that can operate on a global scale to protect and advance the economic interests of their members. The rapid growth and maturation of the multi-centric world can in good part be traced to the extraordinary dynamism and expansion of the global economy. Most importantly for present purposes, the advent of the global economy has also accentuated the identity of most people as consumers and, in so doing, possibly weakened the ways in which they identify with other spaces that have commanded their sense of affiliation.

The Advent of Interdependence Issues

The evolution of the world economy is not the only source of centralizing tendencies at work in global life. In addition to the growing relevance of supranational actors such as the European Union, the institutions of which have increased their authority relative to its member states,[13] there are also a number of new, transnational problems that are crowding high on the world's agenda and undergoing globalization. Whereas the political agenda used to consist of issues that governments could cope with on their own or through interstate bargaining, conventional issues are now being joined by challenges that by their very nature do not fall exclusively within the jurisdiction of states and their diplomatic institutions. Six current challenges are illustrative: environmental pollution, currency crises, the drug trade, terrorism, AIDS, and the flow of refugees. Each of these issues embraces processes that involve participation by large numbers of citizens, that inherently and inescapably transgress

35

national boundaries, and that offer causes with which to identify. Several of the six issues are the focus of transnational social movements forged to ameliorate, if not to resolve, the challenges they present. To be an environmentalist today, for example, is to have an identity that for the most part did not exist in earlier epochs. Conceivably, in other words, such issues give some citizens pause about their states as the ultimate problem solvers and, in the case of those who join social movements, the issues may reorient people to ponder a restructuring of their loyalties.

The Multiple Flows of Culture

While the focus here is mainly on cultural phenomena as they are experienced at the micro-level by individuals, it is useful to stress that cultures are macro-phenomena in the sense that any culture is a socially constructed concept, a widely shared sct of norms and practices to which people subscribe as sources of their conduct both within and outside the culture. One of the consequences of fragmegrative dynamics, however, is that the coherence and boundaries of cultures, like those of states, have become porous and often frayed as other norms and practices intrude through the circulation of ideas and pictures from abroad, the mobility upheaval, the organizational explosion, the diverse products of a global economy, and the other dynamics enumerated above. Many observers view the ongoing diffusion of culture as a one-way process that begins in the United States and the West and then radiates around the rest of the world. For such analysts, globalization is the equivalent of Americanization. But once again this appears to be an oversimplified conception. McDonald's may be thriving in Asia and thousands of other locations around the world (Ritzer 1996), but its restaurants can have different meanings in different cultures even though a uniformity marks their exterior and interior designs. It is noteworthy, for example, that McDonald's alters its menu to suit the tastes and precepts of different cultures. No less relevant, Chinese, Japanese, Vietnamese, and Korean restaurants are frequented widely in the United States and Europe, and much the same can be said about the direction of intercultural flows in the fields of medicine, education, and religion. Indeed, history records other (and earlier) cultural flows no less noteworthy in their impact than those originating in the West. Hinduization and Islamization in Southeast Asia, for example, have long been cultural processes sustained by regional trading systems.

Furthermore, there are good reasons to presume that worldwide tastes in clothing, food, and music are not overwhelming and emasculating local customs. On the contrary, fragmegrative dynamics heighten the sensitivities of people to their cultures and identities. As they recognize and experience a greater awareness of the homogenizing processes inherent in globalizing processes, so does their involvement in these processes "trigger a search for fixed orientation points and action frames, as well as determined efforts to affirm old and construct new boundaries" (Meyer & Geschiere 1999, 2). The aforementioned fact that McDonald's has adapted its menu to the core preferences of host countries (Watson 1997) is suggestive of how local cultures are rooted in deep-seated habits and a resilience that tend to absorb rather than emulate the lures of the global economy. Thus the adoption of a foreign norm or practice does not necessarily reflect an inroad into a native culture. Consider, for example, how people whose rights are violated seek refuge in the human rights regime so as to preserve some of the basic premises of their own cultures:

> [T]he emergence of the global market has assisted the diffusion of human rights, since markets break down traditional social structures and encourage the emergence of assertive temperaments. But while markets do create individuals, as buyers and sellers of goods and labor, these individuals often want human rights precisely to protect them from the indignities and indecencies of the market. Moreover, the dignity such a person is seeking to protect is not necessarily derived from Western models. The women in Kabul who come to Western human rights agencies seeking their protection from the Taliban militias do not want to cease being Muslim wives and mothers; they want to combine respect for their traditions with certain "universal" prerogatives, like the right to an education or professional health care provided by a woman ... Human rights has gone global, but it has also gone local. (Ignatieff 1999, 59, 60)

That cultural flows are as infused with complexities and nuances as any other dimension of fragmegration is further—and nicely—summarized in this account of their multiple sources and directions:

> There is growing evidence that the consumption of the mass media throughout the world often provokes resistance, irony, selectivity, and, in general, agency. Terrorists modeling themselves on Rambo-like figures (who have themselves generated a host of non-Western counterparts); housewives reading romances and watching soap operas as part of their efforts to construct their own lives; Muslim family gatherings listening to speeches by Islamic leaders on cassette tapes; domestic servants in South India taking packaged tours to Kashmir; these

are all examples of the active way in which media are appropriated by people throughout the world. T-shirts, billboards, and graffiti as well as rap music, street dancing, and slum housing all show that the images of the media are quickly moved into local repertoires of irony, anger, humor, and resistance ... It is the imagination, in its collective forms, that creates ideas of neighborhood and nationhood, of moral economies and unjust rule, of higher wages and foreign labor prospects. *The imagination is today a staging ground for action, and not only for escape.* (Appadurai 1996, 7) (Italics added)

This last, italicized sentence is worth pondering. For all its defects, fragmegration has fostered circumstances whereby collective actions at the grass roots can be stimuli to change, given the will of publics to converge around and act upon their collective aspirations. In view of the skill revolution and the newly developed uses of the imagination, it is hardly surprising that people everywhere are forming organizations and rethinking their identities as they assert their interests and demand remedies for their grievances. Indeed, sensitivity to one's identities can be seen as a powerful fragmegrative dynamic in itself: often local cultures challenged by global discourses will translate and use them for their own purposes. In so doing, an impression is conveyed that a worldwide diffusion of values is occurring free of human agency. Of course, such is not the case. While people have become disposed to ask who they are and where they fit, thus giving rise to "[t]he intercontinental spread of identity discourse and identity politics during the last third of the twentieth century,"(Hannerz 1999, 328) it is important to stress that such a spread is due not simply to a diffusion of culture. The spread of human rights values, for example, stems not from the compelling nature of rights, but rather from the skill revolution that has facilitated greater appreciation of human rights. Since it is people who are asking who they are and where they fit, the worldwide spread of concern about identity occurs through the agency of individuals at the micro-level.

Micro-Dynamics of Fragmegration

Although extended and elaborate, the foregoing discussion is essentially background material for what follows. The ensuing pages take note of a number of points at which macro dimensions of fragmegration may shape (and be shaped by) the experience of individuals at the micro-level. In order to demonstrate the complexities inherent in the psychology of fragmegration as it sustains the links between culture and identity, the analysis of the micro-dimensions proceeds along two related but separate lines. One involves persons who physically move around the world and those who are more stationary and have the world come to them through various means of communications. More specifically, as previously indicated, the ensuing pages are divided between a focus on the simultaneity of consciousness as it is experienced by immigrants and transnational elites on the one hand and by all people—citizens as well as immigrants—on the other.

The Concepts of Culture and Identity

What follows assumes that, whatever the degree to which they shape each other, micro identities are constituent elements of macro-cultures. A culture is conceived to consist of established habits, values, attitudes, and practices that are widely shared, that have historical roots, and that are differentiated in diverse ways from the characteristics of other cultures. When people are born into or otherwise acquire a set of such habits, values, attitudes, and practices, they have an identity that links them to the culture. Identities, in other words, are embedded in cultures, but they are nonetheless micro-phenomena in the sense that it is individuals who internalize, maintain, or abandon a culture's characteristics.

A careful reading of the previous paragraph will reveal that I also presume that the concept of culture applies to a diverse array of collectivities. It refers not only to society-wide or ethnic-wide entities, but also to the habits, values, attitudes, and practices of whatever larger aggregate a person internalizes. It allows one to speak, say, of the culture of a corporation, a transnational movement, a city, or a NGO as well as the more traditional ethnic, religious, or national kinds of culture. More than that, it enables us to treat Virginia Barreiro and James Liu as having identities that attach to mobile, hybrid, and non-territorial cultures that neither can quite specify but that both feel they share with others.

Some might argue that this broad approach is needlessly stretching the concept of culture, rendering it devoid of any mean-ingful content and undermining the more fundamental and accepted conceptions of culture. Such reasoning would also lead to the contention that the foregoing formulation treats identities too loosely, that any activity can be viewed as deriving from some kind of identity, and that therefore this loose conception needlessly equates identities with roles. My response to this line of thought focuses on the contradictions, ambiguities, and complexities of the emergent epoch. These are so numerous, and their evolution in the future so obscure, that it seems unnecessarily constraining to employ narrow concepts of culture and identity. Faced with a plurality of authorities and an explosion of organizations, surely at least some people will evolve new identities that, in turn, are located in emergent cultures. And if this is so, it is important that culture and identity concepts be framed in sufficiently wide-ranging contexts to enable us to enlarge upon "the idea that the world is a collection of nameable groups" (Kelly 1999, 241).

Furthermore, while there is some overlap between identities and roles in the sense that both ascribe behavior and orientations to people, the two are not the same. Roles are largely defined by the expectations of others, whereas identities, being internalized, are defined by the self, by how a person feels and thinks about whatever array of habits, values, attitudes, and practices he or she perceives to be encompassed by each of his or her identities. But the line between external expectations and internalized self-definitions may not be clear-cut. The former can develop into the latter with a fair amount of ease, especially at a time of rapid and pervasive transformations in which the dynamic forces of fragmegration are tearing at cultures and proliferating identities as time and distance collapse, with the result that individuals are compelled or enabled to encounter new ideas, alternative cultures, and redefined identities. That is, present-day circumstances are conducive to people occupying new roles defined by new rule-setting authorities and, as they do, internalizing the habits, values, attitudes, and practices prescribed by the roles and thereby contributing to the formation of new identities and cultures.

Immigrants in a Fragmegrative World

As indicated by the foregoing epigraphs, persons whose lives are marked by prolonged residence in two or more countries are especially subject to the opportunities and vulnerabilities inherent in the contradictory pressures of fragmegration. This would include expatriots and mobile jet setters as well as immigrants, but it is the latter who may seek or acquire a passport from the host country, who thus most fully confront the challenges of acculturation, and who can therefore be regarded as quintessential cases for a probing of the possible ways in which a simultaneity of consciousness might operate.

Social identity theory is a major focus of the field of social psychology, and in the last two decades it is a focus that has witnessed a major theoretical advance in the form of what is called self-categorization theory (SCT) (Turner, Hogg, Oakes, Reicher, & Wetherell 1987). However, despite having provided a framework for integrating a number of social processes such as the dynamics of conformity, attitude polarization, stereotyping, and prejudice, SCT makes one assumption woefully lacking in nuance: it posits a mutual incompatibility between self-categorization as an individual and as a group. People are seen as unable to manage both categorizations at the same time, as either valuing themselves or their collective identities but not both. This incompatibility runs counter to the dynamics of fragmegration, which fosters multiple identities and induces people to shift back and forth between different identities as immediate circumstances shift back and forth from moment to moment. That is, reinforced by the skill revolution, the organizational explosion, and all the other macro characteristics enumerated above, a psychological theory of fragmegration presumes that some people have acquired the capacity for juggling more than one, even many, identities at the same time.

To be sure, this capacity may not be the case for everyone. There are no definitive data on the distribution of the enlarged capacity for multiple identities among people in developed and developing parts of the world, but it is reasonable to expect that such a talent will be more prevalent among mobile, well-educated, affluent business elites and intellectuals than among the poor and less educated. The former are the people most likely to have a consciousness about people and events that transcends simple categorizations into black and white. A simultaneity of consciousness, in other words, is about being able to maintain complex world views without collapsing them into simple dichotomies. It is about being able to see several sides of a story even when one is involved as a protagonist in the narrative. And perhaps most important, it is about being able to manage the ever-increasing multiplicity of identities that people are evolving in response to the ever-increasing opportunities and obligations fostered by the age of fragmegration. Consider, for example, Mexicans who move north: they "learn only in America that they have to have a specific 'identity'. In their home areas, patterns of self-identification are diffuse, permeable and multiple, but in America they are pressurized in all sorts of ways to cultivate and mark their own identity" (Meyer & Geschiere 1999, 8).[14]

A step toward rectifying the polarizing assumption of SCT was subsequently taken with developments in acculturation theory that focused on the tensions between the desire or motivation of immigrants to value their heritage culture and the desire or motivation to value their host culture. Viewing acculturation processes in the context of these tensions, four separate processes can be specified through a 2X2 matrix that differentiates four types of immigrants (Table 2.1): those who value both the host and heritage culture are located in the "integration" quadrant; those who value the host but not the heritage culture are classified in the "assimilation" category; those who value the heritage but not the host culture adhere to a "separation" strategy, and those who value neither are designated as "marginalized" (Berry, Kim, & Young 1989). Whatever may be the proportion of people who fall in the integration quadrant, they are immigrants comfortable identifying with their newly adopted culture as well as the one they left behind, and there is considerable evidence that this is the most beneficial acculturation strategy for a variety of immigrants (Berry, Kim, & Boski 1987; Dona & Berry 1994). Contrariwise, the separationists are likely to be the immigrants most intensely concerned about threats to the security of their culture emanating either from members of the host culture or from fellow immigrants who have assimilationist or integrationist attitudes.

Table 2.1. A Model of Immigrant Acculturation

	Devalue Host/ Majority Culture	Value Host/ Majority Culture
Devalue Heritage/Minority Culture	Marginalized	Assimilationist
Value Heritage/Minority Culture	Separationist	Integrationist

Yet, even this more nuanced conception of acculturation appears to fall short of what at least some modern immigrants experience. It leaves no space for immigrants whose self-categorization either does not fall in any of the quadrants or who are able to move freely among the quadrants as circumstances may warrant. Where, for example, might people like the three quoted in the epigraphs locate themselves? Each is a product of too many cultures to fit readily into any of the quadrants and, indeed, James Liu says that he is not only "a shifting person of multicolored hues," but also that he knows how to disguise his complex background. Equally important, the fourfold scheme presented in Table 2.1 does not make room for the proliferation of identities that has accompanied the organizational explosion. Immigrants with a higher education who move to new host cultures in order to pursue professional interests with which they closely identify may well exemplify a capacity to shoulder several identities at the same time.

In short, spaces need to be opened up in the formulation set forth in Table 2.1 to accommodate the growing number of immigrants whose educational and professional attainments are hypothesized to be the basis of a widening simultaneity of consciousness. Table 2.2 suggests the existence of these spaces, with the newly created space in the middle representing the greatest fusion of habits, values, attitudes, and practices from disparate cultures that lead, so to speak, to a hybridity composed of several identities and cultures. Not only can the authors of the three epigraphs be viewed as hybrids in this regard, but the first two also explicate a conviction that many others are in a similar situation and, in effect, crowding into the newly created space. And they may well be right. The world's ever greater sensitivity to the challenges faced by multicultural societies suggests, given the dynamics of the emergent epoch, that all the spaces created by opening up the 2X2 matrix are increasingly draining immigrants away from the fixed positions represented by the four quadrants in Table 2.1.[15] The creation of these spaces is not, however, analytically arbitrary. On the contrary, "[g]lobalization is not about the absence of or dissolution of boundaries, but about the dramatically reduced fee that time and space impose, and thus the opening up of new spaces and new times within new boundaries that were hitherto inconceivable" (van Binsbergen 1999, 275).

Table 2.2. Immigrant Acculturation Model with Spaces for Movement

	Devalue Host/ Majority Culture		**Value Host/ Majority Culture**
Devalue Heritage/ Minority Culture	Marginalized		Assimilationist
		Hybrids	
Value Heritage/ Minority Culture	Separationist		Integrationist

In sum, a nuanced conception of the links between immigrants, their identities, and their cultures requires us to avoid treating them as an undifferentiated group. Depending on the circumstances of the communities into which they move and the orientations they bring with them, immigrants can vary considerably.

Transnational Elites in a Fragmegrative World

Although many fewer in number than immigrants, another cluster of people who move widely around the world are those on the cutting edge of globalization—corporate executives with far-flung interests, intellectuals with colleagues in universities everywhere, artists and entertainers with worldwide audiences, to mention only some of those known variously as transnational elites, jet setters, or cosmopolitans who are likely to be highly educated and thus especially alert to the challenges of fragmegration. Presumably it is this group that is most capable of expanding their simultaneity of consciousness by adding new identities and cultural affiliations, possibly even shedding old identities and cultural affiliations from their repertoire of sensitivities. Put differently, it is this group whose old faces are fashioning emergent spaces in new places. That is, because of their leadership responsibilities, transnational elites are probably less territorially bound and more prone to juggle multiple identities derived from non-territorial ties they share with others in their field of endeavor than is the case for immigrants and other people whose range of activities are more confined.

But to what extent have transnational elites formed a common culture? Have their local and national identities been supplemented by a more varied and complex set of ties? Do their face-to-face interactions in conferences and via video communications foster loyalties to non-territorial elite communities that supersede their feelings for their countries of birth? Do they exhibit shared habits, values, attitudes, and practices irrespective of where they come from?

Clear-cut answers to such questions would serve as cogent evidence for the premise here that fragmegrative dynamics are fostering new identities and swelling the numbers of people capable of shouldering and juggling them. Unfortunately, however, little systematic data descriptive of the transnational elites have been generated. There is no lack of literature that posits a global elite culture, but as far as I know not even preliminary attempts to survey the affiliations, loyalties, and life styles of such people have been undertaken.[16] It would be helpful, for example, if systematic studies of transnational elites—say, of the 25,986 persons from 37 countries who held 1K status as frequent fliers on United Airlines (i.e. people who fly more than 100,000 miles a year) in 1995[17]—were conducted, but efforts to raise funds for extensive studies of them have been unsuccessful. Hence, it is necessary to conduct small, pilot studies or fall back on undocumented, varied, and contradictory (but often not implausible) impressions such as these:

> Since they embrace a wide variety of occupations—brokers, bankers, real estate promoters and developers, engineers, consultants of all kinds, systems analysts, scientists, doctors, publicists, publishers, editors, advertising executives, art directors, moviemakers, entertainers, journalists, television producers and directors, artists, writers, university professors—and since they lack a common political outlook, it is also inappropriate to characterize managerial and professional elites as a new ruling class. (Lasch 1995, 34)

> The transnational capitalist class (TCC) is transnational in at least three senses. Its members tend to have global rather than local perspectives on a variety of issues; they tend to be people from many countries, more and more of whom begin to consider themselves 'citizens of the world' as well as of their places of birth; and they tend to share similar lifestyles, particularly patterns of luxury consumption of goods and services ... This class sees its mission as organizing the conditions under which its interests and the interests of the system . . . can be furthered within the national and local context. (Sklair 1995, 71–72)

> Participants in this [Davos] culture know how to deal with computers, cellular phones, airline schedules, currency exchange, and the like. But they also dress alike, exhibit the same amicable informality, relieve tensions by similar attempts at humor, and of course most of them interact in English. Since most of these cultural traits are of Western (and mostly American) provenance, individuals coming from different backgrounds must go through a process of socialization that will allow them to engage in this behavior with seemingly effortless spontaneity ... But it would be a mistake to think that the "Davos culture" operates only in the offices, boardrooms, and hotel suites in which international business is transacted. It carries over into the lifestyles and presumably also the values of those who participate in it. Thus, for example, the frenetic pace of contemporary business is carried over into the leisure activities and the family life of business people. There is a yuppie style in the corporation, but also in the body building studio and in the bedroom. And notions of costs, benefits, and maximization spill over from work into private life. The "Davos culture" is a culture of the elite and ... of those aspiring to join the elite. Its principal social location is in the business world, but since elites intermingle, it also affects at least the political elites. There is, as it were, a yuppie internationale. (Berger 1997, 24)

> We may describe as transnational those intellectuals who are at home in the cultures of other peoples as well as their own. They keep track of what is happening in various places. They have special ties to those countries where they have lived, they have friends all over the world, they hop across the sea to discuss something with their colleagues; they fly to visit one another as easily as their counterparts two hundred years ago rode over to the next town to exchange ideas. (Konrad 1984)

Assuming that the occupational responsibilities of transnational elites encourage them to be concerned about the world, or major segments of it, what do they do about such concerns? On the grounds that a person's work tends to shape how one thinks about one's relations with others, with one's culture, and with one's country, most theorizing about the loyalties of transnational elites precedes from the assumption that these undergo change the greater their contacts abroad. Thus investigations are needed into whether the common experience of working across national boundaries conduces to traditional loyalties being supplanted, or at least supplemented, by transnational ties, as these commentaries suggest:

> Patriotism, certainly, does not rank very high in their hierarchy of virtues ... Their loyalties ... are international rather than regional, national, or local. They have more in common with their counterparts in Brussels or Hong Kong than with the masses of Americans not yet plugged into the network of global communications. (Lasch 1995, 6, 35)

> [A] new breed of men and women for whom religion, culture, and ethnic nationality are marginal elements in a working identity ... the word foreign has no meaning to the ambitious global businessperson ... How can the physical distinction between domestic and foreign have any resonance in a virtual world defined by electronic communications and intrinsically unbounded markets? (Barber 1996, 17, 29)

> Cosmopolitan is, in identity terms, betwixt and between without being liminal. It is shifting, participating in many worlds, without becoming part of them. It is the position and identity of an intellectual self situated outside of the local arenas among which s/he moves. The practice of cosmopolitanism ... is predicated on maintaining distance, often a superiority to the local. By this very self-definition, the cosmopolitan is unauthentic and quintessentially 'modern,' ... (Friedman 1994, 204)

If it is the case that the horizons of transnational elites have been enlarged, presumably their local- or national-community orientations and commitments toward home, church, professional organization, local community, ethnic group, and national system will be affected. But how? Will they incline toward alienation or an expanded form of civic responsibility? Opinions differ, but most analysts argue that alienation is more likely to prevail than civic responsibility:

> The question is whether the habits of citizenship are sufficiently strong to withstand the centrifugal forces of the new global economy. Is there enough of simple loyalty to place—of civic obligation, even when unadorned by enlightened self-interest—to elicit sacrifice nonetheless? We are, after all, citizens as well as

economic actors; we may work in markets, but we live in societies. How tight is the social and political bond when the economic bond unravels? (Reich 1991, 304)

Without national attachments ... people have little inclination to make sacrifices or to accept responsibility for their actions ... The new elites are at home only in transit, en route to a high-level conference, to the grand opening of a new franchise, to an international film festival, or to an undiscovered resort. Theirs is essentially a tourist's view of the world—not a perspective likely to encourage a passionate devotion to democracy ... To an alarming extent the privileged classes ... have made themselves independent not only of crumbling industrial cities but of public services in general ... In effect, they have removed themselves from the common life. (Lasch 1995, 6, 45, 47)

But will the cosmopolitan with a global perspective choose to act fairly and compassionately? Will our current and future symbolic analysts—lacking any special sense of responsibility toward a particular nation and its citizens—share their wealth with the less fortunate of the world and devote their resources and energies to improving the chances that others may contribute to the world's wealth? Here we find the darker side of cosmopolitanism. For without strong attachments and loyalties extending beyond family and friends, symbolic analysts may never develop the habits and attitudes of social responsibility. They will be world citizens, but without accepting or even acknowledging any of the obligations that citizenship in a polity normally implies. (Reich 1991, 309)

[O]n the one hand, the dominant global elites inhabiting the space of flows tend to consist of identity-less individuals ("citizens of the world"); while on the other hand, people resisting economic, cultural, and political disenfranchisement tend to be attracted to communal identity. (Castells 1997, 356)

As these diverse comments indicate, transnational elites may well be prone to evolving a variety of cultures that have not heretofore been part of the global scene. More important for present purposes, they highlight the substantial extent to which a psychology of fragmegration, with its simultaneity of consciousness and its creation of new spaces suggested by Table 2.2, has become part of the human condition. To be sure, the circumstances of elites are conducive to the development of such a psychology, but they are not so far removed from other educated groups as to be exceptional. Or at least they encourage one to undertake an effort to outline how all people may be subjected to the tensions that sustain the psychology of fragmegration.

Twelve Worlds in an Age of Fragmegration

So let us turn now to a brief, overall analysis of how a simultaneity of consciousness derived from the dynamics of fragmegration may impact on all individuals, irrespective of whether or not they are immigrants or transnational elites. To do so, twelve analytic categories—what I shall call "worlds"—seem sufficiently exhaustive and revealing to capture the diverse ways in which fragmegrative processes have generated a proliferation of identities and movement among them. The identities ascribed to those who live in each of these worlds are neither referred to nor consciously recognized by the persons they encompass—nor, indeed, by the literature on identity and culture. Yet, from an analytic perspective I find them helpful as a means of clarifying the diversity, nuances, and contradictions inherent in the tensions between the globalizing and localizing forces at work in a very complex epoch. Moreover, the scheme is useful in stressing the proliferation of identities and movement among them. As will be seen, it facilitates assessing the probability of people shifting from any one of the worlds to any of the others (a total of 132 possible shifts) either by replacing identities or shouldering multiple identities. In effect, the twelve worlds consist of emergent spaces and places in which old faces either become ensconced or move about.

The Proliferation of Identities

Before outlining the contours of the twelve worlds, it is useful to indicate why the present epoch is marked by a pervasive preoccupation with questions of identity, with a restless need for affiliation, thus intensifying and proliferating the identities available as a means of locating where one fits in the course of events. The explanation has several dimensions, all of them relatively simple. First, as some organizations fragment and others cohere, as some countries, economies, and societies break down while others move toward integration, as the pulls of de-territorialization compete ever more with the ties that bind people to territory, and as some social movements expand transnationally even as some ethnic and religious groups become increasingly exclusive, so do identities proliferate as these diverse processes pose powerful questions of who one is, of whether one's main affiliations are spatially near-at-hand or remote, and of whether one has a single or a multiplicity of identities. Second, the distinction between Self and Other—one important aspect of any identity—has become especially salient as people acquire more and more Selves and relate to more and more Others. Similarly, as patterns of migration intensify and more and more people occupy the amorphous space between Friend and

Enemy—that of the Stranger (Bauman 1990)—so do the ambiguities that can attach to identity deepen and broaden, thereby encouraging further self-reflection on where one fits in the interplay of contradictory forces that sustain the age of fragmegration.

It might even be argued that increasingly people have little choice but to think of themselves in terms of a multiplicity of identities. Gone are the days for most people when they could define themselves in terms of a singular geographic space. Instead there has been a "dissolution of self," (Gergen 1991, x) a fragmenting of interests, values, and affiliations such that individuals have different identities which can vary as widely as the different interests, values, and affiliations they may have. As one analyst puts it, "Small and enduring communities, with a limited cast of significant others, are being replaced by a vast and ever-expanding array of relationships" (ibid., xi). And as the emergent epoch proliferates identities, it may become increasingly difficult to maintain clarity with respect to them. In earlier epochs,

> If you say who you are, you could say where you came from; broadly speaking, what race you belong to, a nation state of which you are a citizen or subject; you have a class position, an established and relatively secure gender position. You knew where you fitted in the world ... whereas most of us now live with a sense of a much greater plurality, a sense of unfinished character of each of those. It is not that they have disappeared but they do not stitch us in place, locate us, in the way they did in the past. (Hall 1997, 62–3)

For many people, of course, a singular territorial space—"home"—still matters even as it seems more and more obscure and less and less capable of stitching us in place. A minuscule number may see themselves as citizens of the world, but most identify with a neighborhood, city, region, or country (and even the "world" is a territorial conception). Rooted in to a particular territorial space as they may be, however, people seem increasingly sensitive to the other identities they have evolved through the new relationships they have formed in response to the dynamics of fragmegration. Not only are they capable of differentiating among territorial spaces and maintaining an identity with more than one of the them—as a leader of the Northern League in Italy put it, "We care about being Lombards first and Europeans second. Italy means nothing to us" (Friggerio quoted in Viviano 1993, 1)—but they also appear able to sustain simultaneously the identities that attach to work, professions, social movements, global issues, and the many other aspects of their lives that are undergoing both fragmenting and integrative processes.

This capacity for maintaining multiple identities is a major feature of the fragmegrative era. With its advent, people can use their enlarged skills to construct priorities among their affiliations, emotionally attach themselves to more than one collective enterprise, and imagine themselves as tied to distant others who share their aspirations or fears. Put differently, in an era of fragmegration it is becoming increasingly difficult to think of oneself in constant, fixed ways, and increasingly easy to move from one identity to another—to appreciate that as the distant becomes ever closer, one's identity becomes ever more tied up with diverse local and global worlds.

What Happened to National Worlds?

As noted, twelve such worlds seem especially relevant. Four are local worlds, four are global worlds, and four are private worlds. Elsewhere I have elaborated on these at length (Rosenau forthcoming, chs. 4–7), but for present purposes it is sufficient to note them briefly as a means of indicating the diverse spaces that the age of fragmegration has opened up.

First, however, it is useful to acknowledge that the ensuing scheme does not include persons who identify with any national worlds. There are two reasons for this omission. First, in a era of globalizing dynamics that are reconfiguring conceptions of territory, time, and space, clarity is served by remaining focused on the way people experience the two central and opposing tendencies that underlie the epoch of fragmegration and to do so by viewing those persons who may manage to sustain either tendency in a national context as unable to focus just on national issues without favoring and occupying at least one local, global, or private world.

Second, and related, the inability to focus exclusively on national concerns derives from the processes whereby the unfamiliar aspects of the emergent epoch have begun to supersede the relevance of national worlds. Indeed, it can even be said that "the idea of the culturally cohesive national society has blinded us to the various ways in which the world as a whole has been increasingly 'organized' around sets of shifting definitions of the global circumstance" (Robertson 1997, 89). The implications of the shifts away from national conceptions are considerable. In the cogent words of one observer:

> These are dramatic times. We have entered the era of global politics but have grown up in an age of national politics. Globalization generates anxiety because

it places people within the reach of forces which are or seem to be outside the range of conventional forms of political control. Along with the sense of power-lessness comes the cognitive and emotional anxiety of conventional frames of reference losing their relevance, without new, hospitable and welcoming images being available. Political conventions, analytical frameworks, mental habits, all are under pressure. (Pieterse 1997, 79)

In short, the global is best seen in contrast to the local. Just as there can be no "we" without a "them" or no "self" without an "other", so can there be no global without a local.

Four Local Worlds

Before differentiating among the various local worlds, however, note needs to be taken of several characteristics they have in common. First, all the local worlds are populated by persons whose orientations and actions are, in contrast to counterparts in global worlds, small in scale and scope. Second, the notion of the local, of locality, has undergone more than a few changes of meaning as globalizing worlds have steadily encroached on local spaces throughout history. From rural crossroads to small villages, from small communities to urban sprawls, from national societies to sites in cyberspace, locality has both shrunk and grown in contrast to the global. Third, it follows that local worlds are not constants. They do undergo transformations. Variations occur in the way globalizing dynamics impinge upon their processes and structures. Such changes may not be as rapid or sweeping as those that occur in global worlds, but it is a mistake "to take for granted that the local is to the global more or less as continuity is to change" (*ibid.*, 19). Finally, whatever their bases for being linked to a particular local world, people are deeply attached to its premises and practices. Unlike their global counterparts, their local ties are deep-seated and not easily undone. Life's circumstances may moderate their connections or move some into one or another global world, but most will retain their original affiliations even as distant phenomena become more proximate.

The fragmenting dimensions of fragmegration involve movement toward or commitments to the local—to those proximate spaces that are, or seek to be, disengaged from a global context—either through indifference to, aversion to, or retreat from globalizing dynamics. There are huge and significant differences among these three paths to localism, the first being traversed by those I call the Traditional Locals, the second by the Resistant Locals, and the third by the Exclusionary Locals. The Traditional Locals are distinguished by an exclusive concern with the spatially close, with the geographically near-at-hand, with circumstances that can be directly encountered. On the other hand, the Resistant Locals and Exclusionary Locals contextualize proximity and allow for the spatially remote to be near-at-hand, but the Resistant Locals perceive the spatially remote as so threateningly close as to necessitate opposition while the Exclusionary Locals are inclined to retreat from distant developments they view as becoming too close.

Put differently, Traditional Locals work and think in terms of their immediate geographic space and, as such, are essentially isolated from the rest of the world. They do not experience the distant interconnectedness that can attach to proximity. Resistant Locals work and think in response to globalizing dynamics they regard as threatening and thus worthy of opposing. Their interconnectivities with the financescapes, technoscapes, ideoscapes, and mediascapes that pervade the global horizon are considered so noxious as to generate a need to ward off and overcome them. Exclusionary Locals are also aware of the interconnectivities, but they work and think more in terms of retreating from rather than resisting any links to globalized space. For them only ethnoscapes delineate the horizon. Their inclination is to assure their retreat by drawing boundaries between themselves and distant trends viewed as ominous.

But there is a fourth local world. It is populated by persons who, faced with global dynamics, are neither isolated from, nor aversive to, nor inclined to retreat from them. They are, rather, capable of absorbing external encroachments on their own terms without fearing their local world will lose its integrity. Indeed, by adapting the external inputs to local practices and norms without diminishing the distinctive features of their world, the Affirmative Locals—as I call them—can contribute to the integrative dimensions of fragmegration as much as they do to its divisive dimensions. In other words, Affirmative Locals cannot in any way be regarded as Traditional, Resistant, or Exclusionary Locals because they are not disruptive with respect to globalizing patterns. They work and think in a world that has imported foreign practices without substantially altering their small-scale orientations.

In sum, the differences among the four types of Locals involve historic ties to land (the Traditional Locals), long-standing patterns of life and power balances other than ethnicity that are felt to be threatened (the Resistant Locals), historic ties to an ethnicity that are felt to be under siege (the Exclusionary Locals), and changing ties that are regarded as acceptable (the Affirmative Locals). In effect, the Traditional Locals have always been secluded from globalizing dynamics, the Resistant Locals have long put up with the nonlinear "scapes" of the modern world but see them as fomenting changes that need to be contested, the Exclusionary Locals have lived in a more encompassing world but feel it has become so encroaching as to seek isolation from it, and the Affirmative Locals have learned to live with global encroachments. Stated in still another way, the Traditional Locals tend to live in closed communities, the Resistant Locals tend to live in political arenas, the Exclusionary Locals tend to live in enclaves, and the Affirmative Locals tend to live in open communities.

Four Global Worlds

Just as there are several local worlds, so are there at least four global worlds that are sufficiently different from each other to be foci of separate identities. All of them are populated by individuals who share tendencies to think and act on a scale that exceeds a local context. All of them are global in the sense that their daily routines are linked into distant developments; but at the same time each of the global worlds is differentiated by the ways in which large scale is conceived and non-territorial dynamics contextualized.

Three of the four global worlds consist of persons whose thoughts and actions are worldwide in scale and not confined to any spatially-bounded territory. One of these encompasses the Affirmative Globals, who share positive inclinations toward the processes of globalization—especially toward those fostering and sustaining a global marketplace—seeing them as moving humankind toward a greater integration and prosperity. In contrast, the Resistant Globals are no less worldwide in the scale of their orientations but they regard globalizing dynamics as detrimental to the well being of peoples. The third of these worlds is that of the Specialized Globals, which consists of persons whose territorial orientations are not locally-bounded but who are involved in only limited dimensions of global affairs such as environmental or human rights issues. Finally, there is the world of the Traditional Globals, whose scale of thought and action is large but territorially bounded. Foreign policy officials are quintessential (though not the only) examples of Traditional Globals inasmuch as they are concerned about problems that arise anywhere abroad even as their concerns are framed in terms of their country's interests and are thus territorially specific.

It follows that, taken as a whole, persons in the several global worlds contribute to both the fragmenting and integrative dynamics of fragmegration. They share a relative indifference to the dynamics of localization, but they can conflict intensely over whether the world is better off as a result of a globalizing economy, technologies that shrink distance, and a vast movement of people that renders long-standing boundaries ever more porous. Clashes between Affirmative and Resistant Globals are thus very much the substance of politics and power in the emergent epoch, with leaders in each group often seeking to garner support from like-minded counterparts in local worlds.

It seems likely that the dynamics of fragmegration are swelling the ranks of the several global worlds continuously and will continue to do so for the foreseeable future, with the terrorist attacks on the United States having further accelerated the movement toward global orientations. This growth pattern is perhaps especially discernible for non-elites who, with their skills enhanced by greater education and the new communications technologies, are exposed to diverse stimuli conducive to orienting them toward one or another global world. The growth pattern for elites in these worlds is likely to be slower, but even their ranks are expanding as the complexities of urban life and the global economy proliferate organizations and the number of leaders required to manage them. The number of such elites is probably more in the hundreds of thousands than in the millions, but it is reasonable to presume that the trend line traces an upward slope.

Four Private Worlds

While it is virtually impossible today for people not to have a simul-taneity of consciousness—since local clusters of beliefs bound by the dictates of distance and social space are nonetheless complemented by the consciousness created by distance-transcending forms of contact such as global television, electronic mail, chat lines, the world wide web, and international conferences—or otherwise be oblivious to what happens in distant places, being sensitive to the course of events is for many persons a source of discontent, a fear that the world is out of control and that it cannot readily get back on track. And the more people feel they have lost control over their lives, the more do they distrust the leaders and institutions that appear to be taking their communities in the wrong direction. Consequently, "the 90s is a world where people are searching for connections. But

54

there's a feeling of disconnection from all the old things people were born feeling they were supposed to feel connected to, like the church, God, institutions, school, and parental figures" (Spindler 1998, A25).

In many parts of the world, therefore, increasing numbers of people appear to have either tuned out or become deeply alienated from any world other than their own private one. Some of these are oblivious to what happens in any local or global world and others are purposeful in their remoteness, but all of them live exclusively in their own private worlds. For them there is no nearness and no farness; but only daily routine, precedent, avoidance, or disdain. Events on neither the local or global level are of interest to them, either because prior developments have alienated them or because for any number of reasons they have never evolved community concerns of any sort. Since we are interested in movement in and out of the various local and global worlds, these two groups can usefully be labeled the Alienated and the Passives,[18] both of whom engage in behavior and adhere to perspectives that help explain what attracts people to and deters them from involvement in one or another local or global world.

While the Passives consist mainly of people who have never been part of any local or global world, a preponderance of the Alienated are likely to have been in one or more worlds at some prior time and then subsequently rejected them. For any number of reasons—such as cynicism about politics, disdain for the affairs of any community, or pessimism over humankind's ability to control either distant or close-at-hand developments—they have been led to opt out of the public arena. Indeed, most of the Alienated explicitly and self-consciously want no part of any world. They are intensely passive rather than being routinely passive. They know there is an alternative to their passivity and have reasons to deny its viability. Being alienated, in other words, they are sufficiently engaged to return to the political arena if changes occur in any of the stimuli that fostered their alienation and continue to prevent their involvement in one or another community. It is an open question whether they are likely to return in large numbers. On the contrary, given a worldwide decline in the respect for politicians, governments, the media, and other public institutions, it may well be that increasing numbers of people will enter the ranks of the Alienated.

Quite different attributes can be ascribed to the Passives. Never having had occasion to experience any local or global world, they are unlikely to abandon their oblivion to the course of events. In effect, the dynamics of fragmegration have passed them by—or at least this is the case until such time as either the external world intrudes so rudely as to jolt them out of their passivity or their surroundings are wired and the words and pictures of communities invade their perceptual space and allow for a broadening of their concerns. Conceivably, one of the long-term impacts of the microelectronic revolution and the travel upheaval may be a steady diminution in the ranks of the Passives.

But qualifications are in order. Two distinct groupings among both the Alienated and Passives can be identified. In the former case it is helpful to differentiate between the Cynics, whose alienation is such that they refrain from engagement with any political world, and the Illegals, who are so self-conscious about their own alienation that they resort to illegal, even violent, behavior to express their contempt for all the local and global worlds. Similarly, in the case of the Passives it is plausible to distinguish between the Tuned-Out Passives who may be fully aware of their apathy but who do not avail themselves of ample opportunities afforded by time, energy, and resources to respond to the course of events, and the Circumstantial Passives whose daily conditions are such as to leave them no time, energy, or resources to care about anything beyond their daily efforts to maintain their subsistence. The circumstances of their life situations are marked by a lack of education and a hand-to-mouth existence that compels them to focus so intensely on the daily needs of food, clothing, and shelter that salience does not attach to any larger community.

Movement among the Twelve Worlds

Having framed a picture of people in fixed positions in response to fragmegrative dynamics, now we need to relax the presumption of constancy and focus on video images, on how people may shift—or decide not to shift—their position among the twelve worlds. The abandonment of the presumption of constancy allows for the specification of 132 changes from one of the worlds to any of the others.

Such movements among the twelve worlds can result from attitude changes induced by the intensification of issues without corresponding alterations in a person's roles or identities, or it can stem from the occupancy of new roles, the evolution of new identities, or from all these sources. None of these changes is easily made. Most people are deeply ensconced in long-standing ways of thinking and acting, ways that tend to be habitual and continuously reinforcing. People are normally comfortable in the roles and identities that support their attachment to a particular world. It is a comfort marked by inertia, by an inclination to sustain continuity in their lives.

For all the difficulties, habits, and inertia that inhibit change, however, the emergent epoch is one in which large numbers of people are vulnerable to fragmegrative dynamics that encourage movement from one world to another. Unlikely, implausible, and logically impossible as many of the 132 shifts may be, the skill revolution, organizational explosion, and mobility upheaval are often sufficiently powerful to overcome the statics of continuity. Like developments in macro-systems, and in good part responsive to societal and global changes, people at all levels of community tend to be more restless than content, more eager to stay ahead of the curve than fall behind it. Consequently, the twelve worlds are sites of continual fluctuation.

Movement among the worlds can be either fast- or slow-paced, either spasmodic or continuous, depending on the degree to which the course of events increasingly intrude. As the scope of relevant issues expands or contracts, corresponding incremental attitude shifts may occur, but in some instances an issue can be so intrusive as to be sudden and jolting for individuals, so much so that movement into another of the twelve worlds is virtually instantaneous as the intensity of fragmegration accelerates dramatically or rapidly enough to breakdown the pervasive resistance to change. A sudden and severe economic crisis, or an internal war that leads to refugee flight, is illustrative of conditions under which the plausible and the unlikely become the probable. Under such extreme circumstances it seems likely that the dynamics of change will, on balance, predominate over those of continuity as the dynamics of fragmegration quicken and people become increasingly aware of their vulnerability to distant events and trends that once seemed too remote to be of consequence. Most of the movement will then be away from private worlds and toward a bunching up around the outlooks of the several local or global worlds as people are induced for diverse reasons to value, or at least to accept, the pervasiveness of fragmegration.

A cogent example of a jolting event that induced movement to another world—from Tuned-Out Passive to Affirmative Global—is evident in the public position taken by Arundhati Roy, a novelist of renown in India, in response to her country's announced possession of a nuclear bomb:

If protesting against having a nuclear bomb implanted in my brain is anti-Hindu and anti-national, then I secede. I hereby declare myself an independent, mobile republic. I am a citizen of the earth. I own no territory. I have no flag. (Quoted in Bearak 1998, A4)

Such sharp changes, however, are likely to be relatively rare, if only because distant events usually do not clash so abruptly with one's values. Instead, most changes are incremental and evolutionary as people adjust slowly to transforming events and trends. A telling instance along these lines can be seen in this assessment of peasants in two Central American countries:

[I]n the real world, peasants normally do not move swiftly from quiescence to rebellion. They move incrementally, first trying that, now trying this, depending on whom they are addressing with such action ... [W]e come to realize how uncommon peasant revolution really is and to grasp the reasons for its infrequency. We begin to understand that from the peasant perspective, nonviolent behavior is always preferable if it is effective, and it often is ... Peasant politics is increasingly moving beyond the village to address wider issues and distant authorities. (Anderson 1994, xiii–xiv)

Immigrants, Elites, and Culture in the Twelve Worlds

But do any of these twelve worlds constitute a culture? Are attachments to any of them equivalent to new identities? Are any of them meaningful to immigrants or transnational elites? The last question is the easiest to answer. Yes, of course, they are meaningful to both groups. The earlier discussion of elites indicates most of them are likely to share the orientations of Affirmative Globals even if they may be isolated from others in that world who do not occupy top leadership positions. Likewise, any of the four local or global worlds are likely to be meaningful to immigrants. By virtue of their movement through space—indeed, by definition—all immigrants seem unlikely to live and think in any of the private worlds. At the very least they have left one local world for another and, in so doing, often they will probably find themselves in one or another of the global worlds. In many cases, their new worlds will treat them as strangers and be hostile to their presence. Those with special skills, on the other hand, may be welcomed in and adjust easily to their new worlds. But whatever the reasons why they emigrated, surely all immigrants will have had first-hand experience with fragmegrative dynamics and thereby heightened their simultaneity of consciousness.

58

As for the question of whether any of the twelve worlds constitute a culture that subsumes new identities, perforce the answer involves nuance. In an empirical sense it is difficult to argue that any of the worlds sustain a culture or set of identities. People do not identify themselves by any of the twelve labels or describe themselves as moving in one or another of the worlds. Indeed, those in each of the worlds are spread across all the continents and cannot be mobilized as a transnational social movement. In an analytic sense, however, the twelve worlds serve to further clarify a psychology of fragmegration. Those oblivious or opposed to the changes at work in the world continue to be committed to long-standing local or global spaces, whereas those open to change have evolved—or have the potential for evolving—a simultaneity of consciousness that allows for non-territorial commitments located in new spaces opened up by the dynamics of fragmegration. Both the long-standing and opened up spaces are portrayed in Table 2.3, which presumes that the spaces are populated by the immigrants, elites, and others in each of the twelve worlds who, at a high level of generalization, have common habits, values, attitudes, and practices. The table emphasizes that movement into the open spaces in the center is most likely to occur on the part of those in the two affirmative worlds and the specialized global world.

Table 2.3. Fragmegration Model with Spaces for Movement in Response to Change

	Oblivious to Change	**Open to Change**	**Opposed to Change**
Local Orientations	Traditional Locals Tuned-Out Passives Circumstantial Passives		Resistant Locals Exclusionary Locals Alienated Illegals
		Affirmative Locals Affirmative Globals Specialized Globals	
Global Orientations	Traditional Globals		Resistant Globals Alienated Cynics

Just as those located in three of the worlds appear to be open to change and the assumption of new identities, so can it be seen in Table 2.3 that movement out of the other nine worlds into new identities is inhibited by those who experience the fragmentation impulses embedded in fragmegration. This is especially the case of the local and global resistance identities, both of which are founded on opposition to the transformations that mark the emergent epoch. On the other hand, to be inhibited about moving into new identities is not to be prevented from doing so. The dynamics of fragmegration may intrude so fully into the lives of people as to unsettle their long-standing identities and encourage either movement toward new ones or confusion about them. An extreme case of such an intrusion is presently being felt today in the former Yugoslavia, where a series of wars has left everyone "stuck with having to reinvent himself, with having to construct new 'imagined communities' from the debris of the old Communist federation" (Finnegan 1999, 61).

Conclusions

Clearly, a psychology of fragmegration is rooted in complexities that defy easy summarization. While the foregoing analysis is doubtless longer and less clear-cut than necessary, the challenge of unraveling the many sources of proliferating identities—and the dynamics that heighten awareness of identity—is not easily met. The transformations that are fostering an emergent epoch are also generating uncertainty among individuals who have to contend with a lack of clarity over the directions in which their preferred cultures are moving, as well as clashes between global and local forces that leave them even more fully exposed to conflicting tensions over who they are and where they want to be in the future. No less complicating, a psychology of fragmegration operates differently for different people, depending on the degree to which their lives are caught up in the vortex of the clash of fragmenting and integrating dynamics.

It follows that considerable research and further theorizing is needed for our understanding of the psychology of fragmegration to advance. Different groups of people, from immigrants to transnational elites, need to be surveyed and interviewed if the interplay of localizing and globalizing forces is to be grasped as a source of new or reinforced identities and of cultural transformations.

Notes

1. In the Elliott School of The George Washington University. The quote is from a paper she wrote for a course on The Dynamics of Globalization (March 1999).
2. In social psychology at the Victoria University of Wellington, New Zealand. The quote is a composite of comments from notes for a paper entitled, "The Psychology of Fragmegration."

3. http//204.202.128.130/archive/news/Todays_Stories/970423/ 4_23_97_woods.htm/

4. Other terms suggestive of the contradictory tensions that pull systems toward both coherence and collapse are "chaord," a label that juxtaposes the dynamics of chaos and order, "glocalization", which points to the simultaneity of globalizing and localizing dynamics, and "regcal", a term designed to focus attention on the links between regional and local phenomena. The chaord designation is proposed in Hock (1994:1–2); the glocalization concept is elaborately developed in Robertson (1995); and the regcal formulation can be found in Tai and Wong (1998). Here the term "fragmegration" is preferred because it does not imply a territorial scale and broadens the focus to include tensions at work in organizations as well as those that pervade communities (Rosenau 1983, 1994).

5. It will be noted that I have chosen not to focus on the serious methodological and conceptual problems of analyzing fragmegrative dynamics. These consist of nonlinear processes in which feedback loops predominate over simple cause-and-effect sequences and are difficult to grasp not only because they are new and emergent. They are also elusive because those of us who study world affairs lack powerful methodological tools with which to analyze how the feedback loops link the macro to the micro, a culture to its identities, a state to its publics.

6. For an extended inquiry into the dynamics that have obscured the boundaries between national and international affairs, see Rosenau (1997).

7. The reference here is to "an increasingly pervasive and contentious political struggle between a 'discourse of pace' linked, on the one hand, to accelerating transitions, speeding flows, overcoming resistances, eliminating frictions, and engineering the kinematics of globalization, and, on the other hand, a 'discourse of place' centered upon solidifying porous borders, bolstering breached containments, arresting eroded identities, and revitalizing faded essences." Luke and Tuathail (1998: 73).

8. These tensions are explored more fully in Rosenau (forthcoming).

9. Some colleagues feel that the five percent figure is unduly high, and one recalls reading somewhere that a figure of two percent is closer to the truth.

10. For several decades the Union of International Associations has published an annual compilation, the *Yearbook of International Organizations*, of established governmental and nongovernmental organizations active in the global arena.

11. All but the last of these "scapes" are discussed in Appadurai (1996, 33–37). I am indebted to David Earnest for the addition of "identiscapes" as a concept designed to capture that dimension of the emergent epoch which embraces the normative content of transborder affiliations.

12. Elsewhere I have suggested some conceptual innovations that may help clarify the macro dimensions of the emergent epoch, especially the ways in which authority is undergoing disaggregation and relocation as that of the state lessens. See Rosenau (1999).

13. For a recent example of this trend, see McNeil, Jr. (2000).

14. However, the notion implicit in this observation that identities are imposed on immigrants or otherwise derived from the exigencies of globalization is

somewhat simplistic. The processes whereby people evolve new identities involve responding to a multiplicity of demands and pressures, some of which originate in close-at-hand, local circumstances as well as in the dynamics of a globalizing world.

15. Of course, there are limits to movement in and out of the spaces represented in Tables 2.1 and 2.2. Most notably, adhering to a simultaneity of consciousness is presumably extremely difficult under strong polarizing conditions such as war or other forms of intense intergroup conflict.

16. PricewaterhouseCoopers has surveyed those attending the World Economic Forum in Davos, Switzerland, but the resulting data pertain more to e-business than to the culture and identity questions of concern here. See *Inside the Mind of the CEO: The 2000 Global Survey Report* (January 2000), at www.pwcglobal.com. Based on extremely limited resources (less than $5,000), my office recently sent a mail questionnaire that focuses on the cultural and identity concerns raised here to a sample of some 3,000 persons in *Who's Who in America*, hardly an adequate solution to the problem, but at least it is a beginning. As of this writing, approximately an eighth of the 880 returned questionnaires have been coded and they appear to reflect patterns consistent with several of the observations quoted here.

17. Personal communication from Stephanie Burnham, United Airlines Headquarters, dated May 23, 1996.

18. While there are other terms that capture the notion of alienation and passivity—such as apathy, indifference, nonparticipation, disconnected, and apolitical—these terms seem most descriptive as labels for those who do not live in any of the local or global worlds.

CHAPTER 3

Globalization, Transnationalization, and Migration: Ideologies and Realities of Global Transformation

Jonathan Friedman

There is a rapidly growing dominant representation of the state of the world, one that is consistent with the experiences of many academics, professionals, and more so of media elites, international bureaucrats and diplomats. This is a representation of a world on the move. The emergent representations of such groups are based on the emergent identities of such groups. The cosmopolitanism that has become a central feature of much recent discussion and discourse, I shall argue, is a positioned discourse, one that is based on the globalized or cosmopolitan circumstances of the producers of such discourse. It is the world seen from a certain vantage point. It is also the case that this vantage point is not particularly new, even if its saliency is historically variable. Freemasonry at the end of the 18th century and some versions of managerial New Age engage a similar repertoire of representations of the world. The purpose of what follows is to map these positions in relation to the material realities of globalization, and migration.

Globalization is often represented as the New Age, a post-2000 era in which the all the posts shall be passed as we enter the end-zone of a new world, a global world, postmodern, post-national, and hybrid. This is based on a certain experience of movement among intellectuals and among other elites. Before we were local, but now we are global. The evolution of the world is one from the less to the more inclusive. This experience is certainly real for those who indulge it, but it can not be a sufficient basis for generalization about the world. That is, there is no reason why the experience of some should be conflated with the experience of all. And, of course, the evolutionary emphasis in much of this discourse can easily be countered. We need only compare the current period with the world at the end of the last century (see below).

Let us take a step backward here and ask some questions. Is the globalization of the world a recent phenomenon as often assumed? Is everything really so different today? Have territorial identities and cultures really vanished from the earth? In much of the discourse the answer is normative. There are, they admit, plenty of nationalists and ethnics and indigenous radicals around, but they have got it all wrong! They haven't caught up with progress! And *progress is globalization*, the formation of a global village, and the village is no longer a village but a world city. And this city is an ecumene of cultural cut-'n'-mix, a coming together of the world's cultures under a single urban roof.

There is another approach to the global that is not bound to evolutionary assumptions. Nor is it so caught up in the categories that are commonly employed to describe the world, but, rather, maintains a healthy distance to them. We might begin by suggesting that there is plenty of evidence to suggest that globalization is neither a necessary stage of world history, nor a phenomena that is particularly new. While there is much debate on this issue, there is also an emergent and well founded argument that the world is no more globalized today than it was at the turn of the century. David Harvey who has done much to analyze the material bases of globalization puts the information revolution in a continuum that includes a whole series of earlier technological time-space compressions. Hirst and Thompson go much further in trying to de-spectacularize the phenomenon.

> Submarine telegraphy cables from the 1860s onwards connected inter-continental markets. They made possible day-to-day trading and price-making across thousands of miles, a far greater innovation than the advent of electronic trading today. Chicago and London, Melbourne and Manchester were linked in close to real time. Bond markets also became closely interconnected and large-scale international lending—both portfolio and direct investment—grew rapidly during this period. (Hirst & Thompson 1996, 3)

Foreign direct investment which was a minor phenomenon relevant to portfolio investment reached 9 percent of world output in 1913, a proportion was not surpassed until the early 1990s (Bairoch & Kozul-Wright 1996, 10). Openness to foreign trade was not markedly different in 1993 than in 1913. In the 1890s the British were very taken with all the new world products that were inundating their markets (Briggs & Snowman 1996), cars, films, radio and x-rays, and lightbulbs.

> As in the late-20th century trade was booming, driven upwards by falling trans-port costs and by a flood of overseas investment. There was also migration on a vast scale from the Old World to the New.
>
> Indeed, in some respects the world economy was more integrated in the late-19th century than it is today. The most important force in the convergence of the 19th-century economies ... was mass migration mainly to America. In the 1890s, which in fact was not the busiest decade, emigration rates from Ireland, Italy, Spain, and Scandinavia were all above 40 per thousand. The flow of people out of Europe, 300,000 people a year in mid-century, reached 1 million a year after 1900. On top of that, many people moved within Europe. True, there are large migrations today, but not on this scale. (*Economist* 20 December–2 January 1997–78, 73)

Recent surveys of globalization have also tended to point to the early years of this century as the peak period of modern migration and of globalization in general. After a period in which migration was primarily from North to South in the 19th century, there is a reversal as well as a large scale horizontal movement of population at the end of the century. In the forty years from the 1880s about 30 million Europeans alone migrated to the United States and Australia. While total migration figures today are much larger, they are not larger as a percentage of the national populations involved (Held, *et al.* 1999).

This was a period of instability, to be sure, of enormous capital flows, like today. It was also a period of declining British hegemony and increasing British cultural expansion. Britain had become the world's banker after having been the world's workshop and there was a growing literature concerning the growing issue of the rentier classes and of an emerging financial capitalism. Britain had no enemies as such, except those that it was helping to create by its own export of capital. Arrrighi argues on the basis of historical research that massive financial expansions have accompanied all the major hegemonic declines in the history of the European world system.

> To borrow an expression from Fernand Braudel (1984: 246)—the inspirer of the idea of systemic cycles of accumulation—these periods of intensifying competi-tion, financial expansion and structural instability are nothing but the 'autumn' of a major capitalist development. It is the time when the leader of the preceding expansion of world trade reaps the fruits of its leadership by virtue of its commanding position over world-scale processes of capital accumulation. But it is also the time when that same leader is gradually displaced at the commanding heights of world capitalism by an emerging new leadership. (Arrighi 1997, 2)

This line of argument has been central for the kind of historical global systemic analysis that we have engaged since the mid-1970s. If our argument dovetails with Arrighi here, it is due to a certain equifinality of research results and not a mere theoretical similarity. In this model East Asia should be the next center of the world system, but many are arguing today that what historically appears as a periodical globalization may be becoming a permanent state of affairs (Sassen 1997; Friedman 1996, 1997). According to proponents of a certain approach to globalization, we are witnessing a real evolutionary process toward the formation of a global informational economy as distinct from the former industrial based "world economy":

> A global economy is something different: it is an economy with the capacity to work as a unit in real time, or chosen time, on a planetary scale." (Castells 2000, 101)

The informational economy is not a post-industrial economy but an economy in which dominant economic activities, including industrial production, are subsumed by information technology. This is thus, a model of technological evolution. It might well be that information technology has brought with it a new organizational framework, that it is a kind of technological revolution, but in productivity terms this does not seem to be the case (Gordon 1999). Instead we might speak of an increase in the velocity of economic transactions, especially financial transactions and the vastly increased ability to move financial instruments across the globe. But how this change articulates with the cyclical processes of the system is not clear. We might argue that as a result of this speed up the cycles of accumulation may have so decreased in periodicity so as to make geographical shifts in hegemony a mere short lived tendency rather than a process that can be realized. This should not detract from acknowledging the degree to which East Asia has grown to a dominant economic position. It might even be argued that the current crisis is a result of precisely this region's rapid growth in a period of stagnating or shrinking real world markets for commodities.

The purpose of starting with all of this is to set the stage for a perspective. Globalization has occurred previously. It does not necessarily indicate that we are entering a new era in evolutionary terms, and it is certainly structurally comprehensible in terms of what is known about the world system. Globalization is a structural phenomenon in the terms set out here. In economic terms, it refers primarily to the decentralization of capital accumulation. The unification of the world in technological terms is a process that is financed by decentralizing capital investment, not by some autonomous cultural or even technological process. And while it certainly generates a global perspective for those who travel along the upper edges of the system, there are other processes that are equally global in terms of their systematicity, but exceedingly local/national/ethnic/indigenous in terms of their constitution. This is the crux of the problem: the current situation is one which is producing both globalized and localized identities. Now in sociological terms both of these phenomena are local. Globalization is in fact a process of local transformation, the packing in of global events, products and frameworks into the local. It is not about deterritorializing the local but about changing its content, not least in identity terms. A cosmopolitan is not primarily one who constantly travels the world, but one who identifies with it in opposition to his own locality. That is why so many working class border crossers in the world are so blatantly innocent of such an identity. They are less interested in celebrating their border crossing than in avoiding precisely the borders which are so deadly dangerous in their lives. The true cosmopolitans are, as always, members of a privileged elite, and they are not so in objectively cultural terms, if such terms make any sense, but in terms of their practices of identity. It should also be noted that our contemporary cosmopolitanism is quite different than the internationalism of previous decades. The latter was not so much a question of the gathering of cultures, but of the goal of a common humanity as a single species under the banner of a common goal, the creation of a new world order of social justice.

The approach suggested in this discussion is one in which globalization is not an evolutionary stage, the movement toward a new world, but a particular configuration of the world system which is a phase in a larger cycle of expansion and contraction. This would explain the very rapid rise of East and Southeast Asia to major actor status in the world, representing today, still, the fastest growing and perhaps the most important region of the world economy, in spite of the recent crisis. And the recent crisis itself might possibly be accounted for by the massive buildup of capital in Asia, an area that has accounted for well over half of the worlds growth in manufacturing over the past twenty years. Such rapid growth is dependent upon larger world markets for its expansion and as the latter during this same period were experiencing shrinkage there was bound to be a problem sooner or later. It is also the case that this enormous flood of investment was increasingly shifted into speculation which could only worsen the situation. Just as the US crash triggered the larger European crisis in 1929, the Asian crisis could have triggered similar problems in the West and all the tendencies were there except for the systemic controls that hindered the spread of the crisis to other parts of the world. It is quite extraordinary in this regard that the *Economist* after years of acclamation for the East and Southeast Asian economies, their cultural and organizational advantages that we in the West would do well to emulate, did a complete turn about in the midst of the crisis, completely reversing the signs of the terms of a former discourse of fame to one of infamy,

> Most of the financial mess is of Asians' own making, and nowhere is this clearer than in South Korea. For years, the government has treated the banks as tools of state industrial policy, ordering them to make loans to uncreditworthy companies and industries. (*The Economist* 15–23 November 1997, 19)

As much as one may enjoy the masses of material that are published in this illustrious journal, it is apparently to the journalists advantage that they remain anonymous. This kind of reversal of discourse is to be expected from those who have their noses so close to particular realities that they have no perspective on the larger processes involved including those that produce their own understandings.

The historicization of globalization is important for the development of a truly global systemic argument since it provides evidence that all this has happened in some form in the past. This is not to say that there are not important differences, but that there are some fundamental properties of the world system that should not be forgotten and that it is from these properties that we can ultimately assess the current transformations of the world. Held *et al.* (1999) divide political economic perspectives into three, the hyperglobalizers, the skeptics and the transformationalists. The first, referred to above, believe in the progressive vision of a new global world beyond the nation state. The second criticizes this view, arguing that the world has not changed significantly. The third, most popular right now, is that the world system is transforming in significant ways. The transformationalists do not claim that we are moving beyond the nation-state, but that the state itself is being transformed. They avoid the high ground and prefer more complex models of what is happening. If there is a truly global system emerging, in the sense suggested by Castells (2000), one that moves beyond an international system to one in which integration on a global scale is far deeper and totalizing, then we have yet to see its manifestations.

The Contemporary Situation: Fragmentation and Globalization

The current transformation of the global system is one in which there is a combination of vertical and horizontal polarization, polarization between classes, and the fragmentation of populations into separate culturally defined and defended identities. We have tried to understand this process in terms of a simultaneous dialectic of indigenization on the one hand and cosmopolitanization on the other.

Fragmentation and Indigeneity

In global perspective, there is not that much disagreement today concerning the fact that the world is pervaded by a plethora of indigenous, immigrant, sexual, and other cultural political strategies aimed at a kind of cultural liberation from the perceived homogenizing force of the state. In a certain, perhaps perverted, sense this is as true of the new elites as of the regional minorities, but in very different ways. The rise of indigenous movements is part of this larger systemic process, which is not to say that it is a mere product in a mechanical deterministic sense. There are two very different but related aspects to this process. The social process consists in the disintegration of homogenizing processes that were the mainstays of the nation-state. This has led to increasing conflicts about particular rights and of the rights of "particular" people, a real conflict between individual versus collective rights and of the national versus ethnic. Cultural politics in general is a politics of difference, a transformation of difference into claims on the public sphere, for recognition, for funds, for land. But the differences are themselves differentiated in important and interesting ways, not least in relation to extant structures of identification. Both regional and indigenous identities in nation-states make claims based on aboriginality. These are claims on territory as such and they are based on a reversal of a situation that is defined as conquest. Roots here are localized in a particular landscape. There are important ambivalences here. All nationals can also be regionals and many nationals can identify as indigenous. All of this is a question of the practice of a particular kind of identity, an identity of rootedness, of genealogy as it relates to territory. It is in the very structure of the nation-state that such identities are prior identities. No nation can logically precede the populations that it unified in its very constitution. This, of course, is a logical and not an empirical argument. There is no guarantee that the nation-state did not itself generate regional identities. In fact much of the "Invention of Tradition" tradition consists in arguing precisely in such terms. Just as colonial governments created regional and state-to-be identities in Africa, so did nation-states create regional minorities at home. What is overlooked in this intellectualist tradition is the way in which identities are actually constituted. The latter consist in linking a matrix of local identifications and experiences to a higher order category which then comes to function as a unifying symbolic complex. The logic of territorial identity is segmentary. It proceeds in terms of increasing encompassment and it depends on a practice of creating of fields of security. It expresses a certain life-orientation, an intentionality, that cannot be waved away by intellectual flourishes.

The differential aspect of indigeneity is not a mere social struggle for recognition of difference. It is about the way difference must be construed and incarnated in real lives. There are extreme examples of this process that are expressive of the deep structures of the nation-state. It has led the Afrikaners of South Africa to apply for membership in the World Council of Indigenous Peoples. One of the most spectacular is the formation referred to as the Washitaw nation. The Washitaw according to Dahl (1997) are a self-identified tribe, inhabiting the Louisiana, Mississippi, Oklahoma area. They are black and are affiliated with the extreme right "Republic of Texas". They claim to be descended from West Africans who moved to America when the continents were still joined, i.e. before the Indians:

We are the aborigines—the dark-skinned, bushy-haired original inhabitants of 'so-called' north and south America (Muu, Afrumuurican). (Bey 1996, 4)

They have an empress who claims not only land but also an aristocratic descent for her tribe. Dahl shows that there are early references to Indians from the early-19th century that indeed describe the Choctaw as somehow different than their neighbors, but it is not clear that they were black. On the other hand, there are Black Indian tribes in Surinam who are descendants of runaway slaves and it is not unlikely that blacks may have been adopted into the Indian tribes of the area. What is more important is the fact that there is a local identity that may well be one that resulted from historical relations between Blacks and Indians, but that it has been transformed into a tribal identity in which the African is paramount and more indigenous (antecedent to) than the Indian. The structure of the identity is what is important here and its association with the Republic of Texas is significant. For such groups, the major enemy is the state; representative of the cosmopolitan and the anti-popular, oppressor of real people, imperial and necessarily intolerant of the kind of aboriginal difference represented by the Washitaw and similar organizations. Their political aim is control over territory and governmental autonomy. They make their own licence plates (as do certain Hawai'ian groups) and refuse the entire tax system of the United States.

The representation that is erected here is one whose logic is organized by the core structure of nationhood, a relation between cultural identity and territory opposed to the territorial or civil state which is associated with usurpers and conquerors. This kind of a structure emerges in conditions in which the state is clearly *not* representative of the people, or at least some of the people. Such conditions are variable, not only in space, but in time as well. The logic linking peoplehood and indigeneity to the constitution of the nation-state is the same kind of logic, one characterized as a structure of opposition. Kapferer (1988), in his discussion of Singhalese and Australian forms of nationalism suggests that Australia, as a variant of the modern nation-state, is one based on an absolute distinction between nation and state. The people identify as separate and subordinate to the state, which is perceived as a foreign body. This is, of course, the archetype of the colonial relationship. Australia is exemplary in that its history is one of a country that was not merely a colony, but a penal colony, peopled by the powerless and clearly not associated in an organic way with statehood, not any more than prisoners can be said to own the prison that they inhabit. Australia is pervaded by an ambivalence that is quite complex. The core of the country, the nation, is profoundly alienated from the state which it has periodically tried to capture. Its relation to both territory and empire places it in a fragile position. If its primary identity is established in relation to its main country of origin as a penal colony, it is also, by definition, an immigrant country. Not only alienated from the state, but even from nature, the latter is associated with the savage and uncontrollable outback that can only be conquered but neither appropriated nor understood (Lattas 1997). Caught between and opposed to the state, the Aborigines and new immigrants, this is a potentially volatile structure of identification that produces both primitivist and anti-primitivist ideologies. It may help account for a state-organized multiculturalism whose policy expressed in the government document, *Creative Nation*, is aimed at recreating a new national identity based on a notion of combined differences which are not weighted in any clear way, thus alienating both a significant core of Australians and the Aborigines as well. It might also help account for the particular racism directed against Aborigines, one that places immigrants and Aborigines in the same category of *threat-to-the-nation* (Blainey 1995). The other extreme is represented by relatively "homogeneous" countries like Germany and even more so the Scandinavian countries, where peoplehood, nature, and the state are fused, and in which the modern-state can be said to have been captured by the people, at least until quite recently. Now, of course, this is a historical process as well. In Sweden, the patriarchal structure was not imbued with a strong notion of representativity until the working class movements transformed its patriarchal organization into an anti-state of sorts.[1] Where the early patriarchal structure was one in which the ruling class attempted to own the people, its capture inverted this relation. This is of course more complicated, since the state itself is essentially a representative governmental body and not a class. The real conflict relates to the control of the state as a political instrument. The social democratic state, the "peoples home" became a power in itself, just as anthropologist Clastre's (1977) anti-chief. The latter is the transparent instrument of peoplehood, but also an instrument of violent control and leveling. Clastre's argument was not, of course, about the modern nation state, but about "primitive" society understood as an anti-state machine, one that indeed created chiefs, but which defined them as the locus of popular sovereignty rather than of chiefly power. The chief could never exert his own intentionality with regard to his subjects. He was, on the contrary, excluded from all decision making and more of a slave than a patron, a symbol of anti-power, a mere instrument of the sovereign population. The great disaster and mystery of history, for Clastres, is the way in which the relation between people and rulers became inverted, transformed into its proper sense in world history. While Clastre's Amazonian material does not clearly support his interpretation, the Swedish nation state-displays significant aspects of this "primitive" relation. The Swedish state reorganized much of social and economic life in striving to create the "good society" in the name of the people. This representativity was maintained until recently at the same time as state functions were defined actively as extensions of the will of the people. As Clastre and others have also pointed out, such a structure accords an enormous potential for the transformation of the state into an autonomous and self-directed organism. The practice of homogeneity in Sweden was successful largely because it resonated with local identities, but this does not detract from the structural violence involved in the formation of any state-based identity. The ruling class was, in important respects, and excepting here the nobility, an outgrowth of the "people". Indigeneity is only fragmenting when it is a separate identity within the state (as with the Saami).

The indigenous as a general form of intentionality is about rooting. In certain conditions it produces alternative identities aligned against the state. In other conditions it can produce extreme nationalism within the state. This accounts for the apparent paradox that the ideology of the New European Right is so similar to that of some indigenous movements. As a strategy it is more general than indigenous movements as such. Self-directedness is what makes such movements distinct. There is no logical way that national states and indigenous movements can co-exist without a change within the larger structure of the state itself, or by concluding compromises that simply accentuate the ambivalence in the situation. The articulation of indigeneity and the world system produces a whole set of new contradictions that are becoming salient in the current situation.

This simplified continuum is a continuum of positions in the global system as well as a continuum of logical variation. It is not a static or general typology but refers to an organization of identification that can itself change over time. The globalized identities of today are those that have stressed the superiority of hybridity and then of multiculturalism which, from their point of view, is an encompassment of difference, that depends on "being above it all". But such positions are only possible with reference to the nation state itself. They are those who define themselves as going beyond the nation state and who declare that the latter is a dying or dead institution and even blame it for the major ills of the world, usually summed up in the word, "essentialism". But this is merely one position in a spectrum of possibilities that I cannot explore here. At the other end of the spectrum is indigeneity itself. The relation between national elites and the nationalist position is highly ambivalent insofar as it is ideologically egalitarian at the same time that it is hierarchical in practice.

I suggested that the major operator in this continuum is the dynamics of class formation in the global system. Globalizers are those who identify with the top of the system while localizers tend to

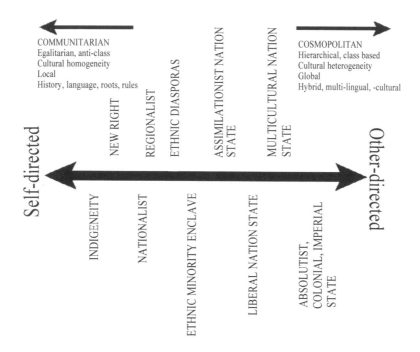

Figure 3.1. Continuum of identity strategies in the nation state

identify with the bottom. There is more to this, however, than mere identity politics.

Global Process and the Unification of Fragments Under Capitalism: The New Classes

In a recent and very important thesis, Elizabeth Rata (2000), has described what she refers to as the emergence of tribal capitalism. Her hypothesis is that a new class has emerged, a post industrial class, whose wealth and power are based in the new sectors of economic development, the media, Internet and other software sectors, and the professions surrounding these sectors This class is the bearer of a new ideology, one that, must at first oppose itself to old capitalist elites. This class occupies an ambivalent position, a combination of particular elite status and a universalistic ideology of equality used in the struggle against the old hegemonic class. This leads to the emergence out of a guilt complex typical for this class position of a bi-cultural ideology for New Zealand … the idea that We are all both White and Maori … we are special. This is noteworthy insofar as it captures the notion of hybridity that is common to many other elite ideologies, ie. Australia, Canada and among a certain similar cultural elite in the United States (not least academics). This is the global-orientation that I described above in relation to the establishment of globalization as an ideology. Rata traces the way in which this class ideology articulated with the strengthening of Maori identity via the establishment of a separate cultural project, language schools, a national cultural revival and then land rights and access to capital on established tribal lands. This is a movement from cultural identity to tribal property. The Waitangi Amendment Act established the tribes as corporate political and economic entities and later, the Maori Fisheries Commission became the means of transfer of property rights and funds for the establishment of fishing enterprises. The effects of jurid-ification were increasing potential conflicts within the tribes as people struggled to define their genealogical rights to means of production. The issue of exclusion vs inclusion with respect to such rights is an expression of the tendency to class division among the Maori. This is a theme that appears throughout the rest of the thesis and is interesting to compare to peoples such as the Sami in which access to Reindeer and herding territories is a basis of privilege that severely divides the population, even though the colonial history is somewhat different. The combination of tribal organization, capital accumulation and transfers of funds is important in understanding the way a local movement can become reorganized into the global system. The class structure that seems to be emergent is one in which those who control capital within the tribes introduce wage labor among lower ranked kin tending turning them into a subordinate class if these relations are reproduced. The second class division emerges between those with and without access to tribal property, more than half of the Maori who still inhabit urban ghettos. Rata makes use of Marxism and especially Regulation Theory to develop her thesis that there is a new form of accumulation emerging here, the "tribal capitalist mode".

There is a third process which Rata touches on as well, the forma-tion of a Maori middle class based on the control over specialized knowledge in the matrix linking the new National cultural class, referred to above, the cultural apparatuses of the state and the recon-struction of Maori society. These are intellectuals who played and continue to play key roles in the Maori movement, but also function as consultants to both tribes and government, as mediators and teachers. It is, of course, to be expected that intelligentsia should emerge within such movements and that they should become increasingly established as the movements become institutionalized. They, are, after all, the focal points for political unity and often political action as well, pivots in the competition for funding and rights. It would be a sign of incomprehension, not untypical of anthropologists, to critique such developments on the grounds that they deviate from the anthropologist's conception of traditional culture. Even the class aspect of this development is quite logical in terms of the process of integration itself. On the other hand, such divisions are bound to be sources of potential conflict within the emerging larger political community.

Verticalization, Fragmentation and the Social Transformation of the Global System

Verticalization, or class polarization, is a vector of the global system and it effects all of the forms of fragmentation that constitute the other major vector in the system. Ethnification and class formation are the paired processes that characterize this simultaneous development. The transformation of the nation state into a modern form of Absolutist state is an expression of the same process. The increase in clientelism in European States, and between the states and regions, and in the European Union as a whole, is part of the disintegration of the homogeneous nation state. The notion of a Europe based on regions rather than states is part of this and would transfer power to Brussels while undermining the relation between states and their subregions. Thus, the notion promoted by some of the cultural globalists, that we have somehow moved beyond the obsolete nation state and are entering a new world of the post-national, is a misconstrual of a more complex situation. While it is true that global capital exercises increasing power over national conditions of reproduction, this does not spell the end of the nation state as such, but its transformation, from a homogeneous entity in which common goals link the "people" and their state, to a separation of the state from the nation. The state itself, is becoming increasingly oriented to international capital flows, and to the regulation of such flows as they relate to conditions of maintenance of territorial economic units. The recent Asian crisis has made this resoundingly evident. George

Soros apparently lost over 100 million dollars in Asia, and he has, more generally, clamored for increasing international controls over financial flows.

> Although I have made a fortune in the financial markets, I now fear that untrammeled intensification of laissez-faire capitalism and the spread of market values to all areas of life is endangering our open and democratic society. The main enemy of the open society, I believe, is no longer the communist but the capitalist threat.... Too much competition and too little cooperation can cause intolerable inequities and instability.... The doctrine of laissez-faire capitalism holds that the common good is best served by the uninhibited pursuit of self-interest. Unless it is tempered by the recognition of a common interest that ought to take precedence over particular interests, our present system... is liable to break down. (Soros 1997: 45, 48)

This expresses a desire, at present being implemented by some states, for a stronger regulation of the conditions of equilibrium in the world market. Work by Sassen indicates that Nation State functions are increasingly shifting from national to international issues. This is what might be called the lift-off of the State. In Europe it is related in its turn to the emerging relation between nation states and the European Union. European governmental organs are not tied to constituencies as are national organs. They have experienced problems of corruption, in uncontrolled use of power, in inordinately high remunerations for their members, but this is also reflected in the many credit card crises at the national level: there is a general accountability crisis in the nation state which is expressed in declining respect for politicians who are considered increasingly to be a class with their own interests. Politicians, on the other hand, have in various ways, expressed their distaste for ordinary people whom they often accuse for being red-necked and nationalist. That this can occur in a country like Sweden is ample evidence of the forces involved. Carl Bildt, European Bosnia negotiator and leader of the Conservative party, has written that a European government is the ultimate solution for the continent and that its form could well take a form reminiscent of the Hapsburg Empire. Similar statements have come from social democrats and others. Sweden, which is officially multicultural, has, in a government bill, stated categorically that Sweden no longer has a common history since there are so many different immigrant groups present on Swedish soil (where does that put the United States or Canada?). The bill goes on to formulate a new structure for the state that moves clearly in the direction of a plural society, based on the association of different cultural groups.

There are tendencies in the media elite and in the state to classify any opposition to this planned transformation as racism. The overall impact of the transformation of the global system is one that places the state in a new kind of vortex of global forces, one where it becomes a focal point for an association of different groups rather than the representative of what one comedian has called "that special interest group, the people". This structural tendency is one in which the political class and the other cultural elite class factions identify increasingly with the global, in which, as has been said of the American situation,

> They have more in common with their counterparts in Brussels or Hong Kong than with the masses of Americans not yet plugged into the network of global communications. (Lasch 1995: 35)

Now the state, transformed in this way, becomes the focal point of certain distributions of favors, funds and positions to an increasingly fragmented nation state. The clientelism to which I referred above is very much the product of this transformation. Regional, immigrant and indigenous minorities all become subject to this changing field of forces. The field tends to create new elites that move within the global sphere, ranked lower than the real big-shots, since they are clients to the real sources of power and money. They may have global spheres of their own, like the World Council of Indigenous Peoples and they may sometimes mingle with higher ranked elites, but they are primarily local clients in the global mesh of neo-feudal dependencies.

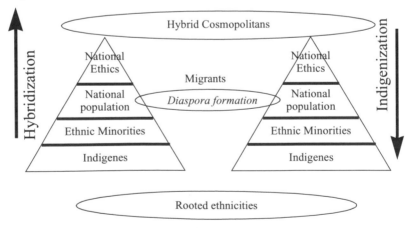

Figure 3.2. The dialectics of hybridization and indigenization

The rise of indigenous movements was part of a general process of transformation in the world system one in which the weakening of the Western nation state took the form of the rise of cultural politics. This was, as suggested, at the start, part of a common decline in hegemony which was also expressed in a rapid increase in economic globalization. Whether this is a temporary or permanent change cannot be determined here because the general periodicity of accumulation has increased, because globalization has become more rapid, cheaper and increasingly institutionalized. It has, in any case, produced major transformations of class relations; the emergence of a new cosmopolitan elite or congeries of elites that have been sucked into the globalization process and who are the producers of globalizing representations of the world, understandings that challenge the very existence of the nation state and proclaim a new post-national era at the same time as fragmentation and cultural conflict are more pervasive than ever at lower levels of the system. The articulation of verticalizing and fragmenting process produces the paradox of class division at all levels, including movements that begin in urban ghettos.

Globalization and the Disintegration of Territorial States

The unification of fragments discussed above is a one in which fragmenting identities are integrated into global circuits of both accumulation and political elite formation. There is, however, another major process that links global network formation to a process of disintegration of the state. This consists in the proliferation of global operators, from doctors without borders to the myriad of subcontracting NGO's that live on global tax money and funds, but also the rapidly developing array of mafias, military mercenary firms, that are involved in some of the worlds three largest trades, arms, people and drugs. While these networking organizations have very different intentions and goals, they combine to create a powerful decentralizing effect on the world state system. Many state functions are farmed out to such organizations and there is often collusion between state functionaries and representatives of such organizations. This is particularly evident in those world zones characterized by weak or weakened state structures. In Eastern Europe many political functions are sub-contracted out to NGO's that are charged with the development of "civil society", "democratization", health care etc. In the West this is also evident in certain sectors where privatization has been on the increase in health, transport, and other sectors, also a process of devolution of state functions, most often to multinational companies. This process links local state functions and practical operations to global operators transforming certain welfare functions into tax farming operations. The logic of the welfare state is eliminated in this devolution. The notion of a society "taking care" of itself via its state is replaced by an individualized relation to various capitalist activities. The emergence of what has been called "humanitarian ideology" (Hours 2000) has been implied in a veritable industry of humanitarian organizations whose stated ideals are often contradicted by the actual organizational requisites and ensuing practices that are entirely oriented to the maintenance of organizations rather than the solution of "humanist" problems. Even European states have been profoundly involved in the process of fragmentation of Third World territories. France's relation to Africa, often referred to under the rubric *Francafrique*, an organic totality of clientelistic power has witnessed the formation of private territories governed by various French ministries in collusion with multinational oil companies (former state companies like scandal saturated Elf) mercenary firms providing security (such as Executive Outcomes[2]) and local officials who are integrated into transnational payrolls. All this has led to the proliferation of ethnic-territorial warfare fueled and propelled by international interests (Reyna 2003). The recent publication of work by Verschave (2000) on the French-African relationship has led to a lawsuit by three African heads of state against the author.

This aspect of globalization is tantamount to the fragmentation of territorial states insofar as it implies the appropriation of functions, regions, peoples and their incorporation into *other* projects organized by sub-national yet transnational organizations. As a structural phenomenon it cannot be reduced to such phenomena as global criminal networks or NGO's. The Chiapas movement was successful in large part because of its ability to exploit the internet and international news media. The Hawaiian indigenous movement sports one of the top ten home pages on the internet. The transnational accumulation of resources, financial, political and cultural is in itself a fragmentation of the larger territorial unit.

Migration as a Total Social Phenomenon and a Global Systemic Phenomenon

In terms of the framework I have sought to outline here, migration cannot be understood in itself as one particular phenomenon, an "ethnoscape" or field of population movement. Its characteristics are expressions of the larger context which define its nature and conditions of operation. The global refers to the distribution of conditions of existence in the world arena and the way such conditions determine the transformations of life worlds, intentionalities and structures. The expression "total social phenomenon" (Mauss 1969) refers to the holistic context of practices that are often, by abstraction, reduced to one of their aspects alone. A perfect example of this is found in the globalization literature, not least in anthropology which, given its preoccupation with cultural and social specificities, ought to have been able to overcome this problem. This is the reduction of culture to demography. It is often said that it is the movement of people in the world today that has led to their loss of rootedness. Their very "footlooseness", a physical term, is the cause of what is described as diaspora formation. This in its turn is linked, for example, and strongly so, in the work of Appadurai, to globalization on one side and to its consequences, the transgression of national borders, as well as the transcendence of the nation state whose demise is immanent, after a period of violent resistence, thus freeing us all to live in a new transnational world. All of this is highly reductionistic in the worst materialist sense. Migration, in the sense of the mere movement of people, does not in itself imply cultural flow. It is necessary to grasp the entire process in social and cultural terms in order to make real sense of it. The reasons for movement, the intentionalities of movement are all quite specific just as their conditions can be accounted for in global terms. Movement itself is transnational, but only if there are nation states and borders of a particular kind to cross. The transnational is logically dependent on the prior existence of the nation state and cannot be said to transcend the latter. The truly post-national would in such terms correspond to a more extensive global form of governance. Once borders are crossed, the identification of the process in terms of a relation between host and newcomer must be examined in its totality. Even if we ignore the vast issue of the legal structures of membership, of citizenship, there are the more general issues of the actual social forms of integration/non-integration, from assimilation to enclavization. This depends on the relation between subjects and the larger migratory process, and it depends on the way in which groupness is practiced and constructed (also a practice). If these phenomena are understood as practices and not as stable or fixed realities then stability itself is a product of a practice of stabilization, the maintenance and reproduction of particular structures of social reality. Practices are specific and in this sense can be understood as cultural, but they are also historically specific and thus historically variable. I have tried in previous work to demonstrate the importance of a long term historical understanding of the transformation of such practices (Friedman 1994). It might, for example, be suggested that for the Western nation state there are a variety of overlapping forms of integration that differ in space as well as in time, real social integration, which is not the same as formal state-defined integration. There are interesting contrasts among different states, for example, between France and the United States in the first quarter of this century as expressed in Durkheim's student Halbwachs' visit in the 1920's to Chicago where he discovered that ethnicity was major academic issue in a country of immigrants. He contrasted immigrant America with his own France where such issues did not exist, presumably because France was not an immigrant society. But the hard statistics of physical movement were, of course, quite the contrary since France was in this period at least as immigrant dense as the United States (Noirel 1996:13). The difference was in the practices of identification of others, in terms of a continuum of French civilization rather than ethnically specificor absolutely different identities. But such issues are also historically variable within the same nation state. In most of the West during this century there has been a strong assimilationist ideology in which it has simply been assumed that immigrants become integrated into their host societies, thus joining another national project than their own. The attractiveness and political force of integration has been a historical variable in the history of the nation state, one that is sometimes overlooked by its observers in any one period. Sociologists and political scientists following World War II were very busy calculating how long it would take for all ethnic differences to disappear. The generally accepted scheme of integration in the United States was one leading from immigrant status, to the formation of ethic minorities through a variety of economic and then cultural assimilation processes to the emergence of "symbolic ethnicity" (Gans) in which the ethnic was reduced to certain ritually salient activities in an otherwise assimilated population. Then suddenly in the mid-seventies it became apparent that the entire process had gone into reverse.(Esman 1977) Ethnicity was on the rise and in a big way. It might well have been "symbolic" ethnicity but it carried the promise of re-identification, re-rooting. The re-awakening included, first regional movements, then national obsessions with pre-modern roots, then indigenous and finally migrant

populations. All of this shift led to a self-evident aura of multiculturalism in a world where, a decade earlier, such notions would have
been unthinkable.

I first encountered the phenomenon in Hawaii in the late 70's.
Here a people that had been more or less erased from the ethnographic map of the world, not least by anthropologists, began to
reappear in force. The Hawaiian movement for the re-establishment
of a culture, a social life and control over territory began to emerge
and was successful in ways that would have been unpredictable in
terms of a static understanding of the categories that existed several
years previous. Indigenous movements throughout the West in the
same period produced new attempts to create autonomy within the
nation state. Regions had already done similar things in Europe and
national populations were following suit. Thus, re-identification had
become and still is a formidable phenomenon. This is not so much a
question of actual life forms, although it may well resonate with
them, but with the formation of social identities.

The process has continued in Western Europe and has been
accompanied in Eastern Europe by violent forms of disintegration
and fragmentation in which cultural identity has become a major
source of violent mobilization. In Africa, the disintegration of the
post-colonial state has led to a similar kind of ethnification. Even in
Indonesia, where rapid growth had either crushed or assimilated
difference, the latter has returned with a vengeance in the current
economic crisis.

The current crisis in Western European states with respect to
immigration is about the structures of the nation state form itself,
especially in its welfare state variety. France had a higher level of
immigration in the 1920's than it does today, but there was an
unquestionable context of assimilation that was absolutely dominant in the earlier period. Today this ideology no longer works, not
as the result of an evolution to a higher state, but because real
marginalization and segregation have created conditions in which
economic integration is limited except as low paid temporary work
and where the formation of ghettoized existences has also strengthened the process of enclave formation. There are of course
individuals who get out and their numbers vary as they always
have, but there is a significant core of those who do not leave their
own groups and instead construct worlds apart. Such worlds may
or may not be diasporic, depending very much on other factors
related to family structure, authority, and the nature of social reproduction in such groups. In research done in Sweden one finds the

kind of territoriality that Schiffauer discusses in his contribution to this volume, youth that identify, not genealogically or with their so-called mixed, hybrid situations, but with place as such. Latin American youth are often associated with this kind of localization. They are weak on diaspora and strong on neighborhood identification. They thus enter into a struggle over social space, especially where they reside but often in the town centers as well. Hakka Chinese with whom we have worked are almost oblivious to the national public space. They live in a world of kinship that spans the globe, where the diaspora is the true place of their existences. We note that this is very much a matter of intergenerational control. In one case where children began to become too attached to *place* and did not want to learn to write Chinese the transnational clan was called to a meeting and this family was forced to move to another town by the larger collective.

The argument of the first part of this paper is that there are major configurational transformations in process in the contemporary period. These transformations are expressed in part by the current globalization of capital as well as the ideological capitalization on globalization by emergent elites. The consequent weakening of the nation states has in its turn led to fragmentation and a logarithmic increase in cultural politics. The nation state has also become increasingly polarized in class terms, upper classes have seen enormous increases in income while lower classes have either faced declining or unchanging incomes combined with increasingly flexible work or absolute unemployment. Now as large scale immigration in this period has been introduced into this declining mobility it can be hypothesized that conflicts might well emerge, that immigrants would find it difficult to integrate at the same time as increasing numbers of nationals were themselves being excluded. This is potent fuel for the fires of fragmentation, and the issue cannot be reduced to the question of immigration as such. It is the articulation of social and cultural fragmentation, class polarization and immigration that is the volatile mixture. The emergence of conflict is here a question of particular thresholds, a variable that is specific to each particular locality.

The forms that migration take in periods like this tend to be associated with the ethnification process in general. For any particular stream of migration understood as a temporal phenomenon we can speak of the following interlinked processes.

A. integration/assimilation

  1. This refers to the movement of individual subjects from the world of the migrant group into the world of the host group. It takes numerous forms but it always consists in the appropriation of a new reality by the subjects involved. Often this can only function in transgenerational terms. This appropriation may consist in a re-identification with the host social world or it may consist, as is common in most Western societies of a division between an ethnic or specific cultural sphere that remains private or relegated to the subgroup and a national public space. Ordinary social life is here part of the majority society but certain events and occasions that mark specific identity are kept separate.

B. enclavization

  2. This refers to a number of processes within which alternative worlds are constructed and maintained in practice. Diasporic formations are largely ethnifications of the migration process itself where a series of cultural, economic and social relations are maintained transnationally. But such transnational relations may be replaced by a practice of reterritorialization and an identification with place appropriated as minority territory. Concepts such as "insertion" are state discourses that are common in multicultural politics and refer to the management of the same tendency or its institutionalization. The result of the articulation of state multiculturalism and enclavization is the division of the social field of the nation state into separate largely endo-social sectors. This tendency has been discussed under the rubric of pluralism and plural society (e.g. Furnivall 1948) and has clear colonial connotations.

These two categories which contain a number of subcategories are themselves products of the articulation of migration and state structures in particular historical conjunctures. In previous work on the modeling of the results of such processes we arrived at the following two tendencies, to be understood in terms of a larger continuum of variation.

The identification process that orders such models is one that occurs in the complex field of emergent alternatives within the national arena itself. We limit ourselves here to the variants of Western nation states, and it should be noted that this is not a universal phenomenon. In societies structured by more pluralist or

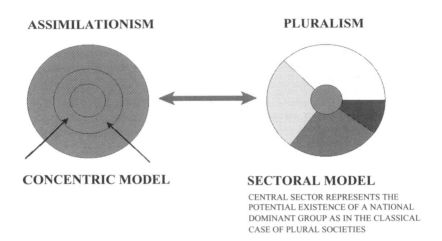

ASSIMILATIONISM

PLURALISM

CONCENTRIC MODEL

SECTORAL MODEL

CENTRAL SECTOR REPRESENTS THE
POTENTIAL EXISTENCE OF A NATIONAL
DOMINANT GROUP AS IN THE CLASSICAL
CASE OF PLURAL SOCIETIES

Figure 3.3. Models of ethnic integration

pluralizing vectors the results are quite different. In countries like India the process of integration depends traditionally on the caste organization itself, so that immigrant groups of traders (Parsees) just as tribal groups of the periphery could be directly integrated into the larger system. Such systems as all plural polities have often been successful in integrating cultural difference in the form of ethnic hierarchy and it might be suggested that it is the hierarchy itself that provides the social framework of integration as such. Nation states are, on the contrary, based on individualization, the destruction of intervening sodalities between state and subject and a tendency toward egalitarianism. Such tendencies have and apparently still are structurally incapable of accommodating a high degree of explicit cultural division in the sense of ethnic or any other culturally based group formation. Plural societies are also organized around the differential relation of corporate groups to the state. In such cases the notion of nation state does not really apply. Many of the states of the third world are territorial polities that are only nation states in the formal sense, one imposed by international organizations, but their internal structures are quite different than those upon which the concept has usually been based. In the development of the European Union one might also speak of a potential new political formation, closer to that of older imperial structures, which, as we have indicated, are capable of accommodating plural situations because their elites tend not to be identified with any particular population and stress their own cosmopolitanism. Some politicians, as we have noted, have already begun to compare the EU to the Habsburg Empire as an organization that was truly multicultural even if it is lacking in the usual democratic accountability. These may be two sides of the same coin. In this discussion we have limited ourselves to the nation state order. And it is in the social field of the nation state that the variations which we discussed above can, I think, be correctly situated as processes of structuration of identity in the practical social sense of the word rather than as mere symbolic representations. The relation between integration within the ethnic group as opposed to the larger nation state is depicted in a simplified way below. The diagram is meant to suggest the basic contours of the simultaneous relation between the two levels.

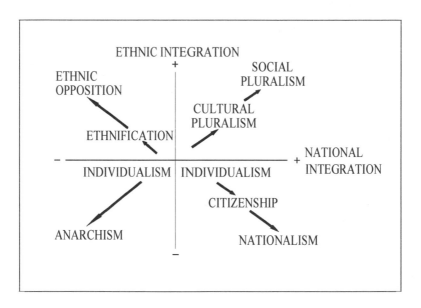

Figure 3.4. Ethnic and national integration

In the approach advocated here, migration as a total social phenomenon needs to account for changing forms of identification in host societies as well as changing forms of migratory identifications and their articulation. The fact that a given procent of a population pursues strong diasporic strategies or, on the other hand, exits from the group and becomes integrated in the larger national arena is part of a reality that must be grasped in all its variations. It does not imply that the diasporic relations are irrelevant but that they are not to treated as cultural essences embodied in individuals. On the contrary they must be understood in their social structural and dynamic contexts. It is in this sense that the global field also becomes crucial since there are clearly periods of ethnification, as in Europe and the United States today that have superceded (not in any evolutionary sense) formerly modernist and nationalizing tendencies. It is these tendencies that lead to the conflictual situations that have become so rampant in large parts of Western Europe and the United States, tendencies that are comparable if not necessarily similar to other processes of ethnification in Africa and Eastern Europe.

Conclusion

I have tried to argue for a contextualization of the question of migration processes in terms of the more general changing configuration of political structures and forms of identification in the global arena. Periods of large scale migration must be understood as historically specific to particular phases of the larger system, not least, those of shifting hegemony. The degree to which such migration leads to new conflict is also a function of the state of the structures of incorporation and exclusion at that particular historical moment. And within the global context, the specific forms of social practice of migrating and host populations, which are also historically variable, must frame our understanding of the final results of such processes. We live in a period of rapid social and cultural fragmentation in parts of the world, in Eastern Europe, in Africa and to a lesser degree in Western Europe and the U.S. and a simultaneous consolidation and nationalization in other parts of the world, East Asia and Southeast Asia (excepting Indonesia for reasons spelled out in the model). The fate of migrants in such a world as well as their strategies and even the causes of their movement, as in the case of the explosive increase of refugees must be placed within these larger socio-cultural and political economic contexts if we are to understand them clearly and if we wish ultimately to try and address the often excruciating problems involved.

Note

1. It should be noted, however, that the patriarchal state was strongly oriented to the "people" and to the formation of a national unity of an organic type based very much on the responsibility of the national elites toward the people. The very notion of "people's home" was a conservative party concept.

Part Two: MIGRATION AND NEGOTIATIONS OF IDENTITY: LOCAL AND TRANSNATIONAL STRATEGIES

*Cosmo*politans are Cosmo*politans*: On the Relevance of Local Identification in Globalizing Society

Werner Schiffauer

In this paper I want to challenge a proposition that is expressed in the idea of this conference and which—it may be added—is very much a consensus in the international debate. It reads: "Immigrants increasingly have greater difficulty and less interest in identifying with the places to which they migrate" (Friedman 1999a, 1).

This proposition is based on the assumption that the transformation from Fordian to Post-Fordian economics (i.e. information based economics) had a negative impact on the assimilative potential of industrial states: With regard to *economy*, the decline of heavy industry reduced the capacity for integration of immigrants into the labor force. This resulted in new forms of inclusion and exclusion and the formation of superfluous classes (Dubet & Lapeyronnie 1994).[1] The *political* consequence was the declining importance of the classic "integration-machines" like labor unions and labor parties. All this resulted in a growing division of society which had dramatic *cultural* consequences, the most important of which is the radicalized segregation of educational system, setting apart the schools of the rich and the schools of the poor. This cultural division of society was furthered by the development of communication technology. The easy availability of television programs produced in the country of origin and new possibilities of direct communication across countries facilitated direct contact with relatives and acquaintances back home and thus reduced pressures for cultural assimilation. The combination of all these factors had structural consequences for the relation between immigrant minorities and dominant society. The assimilation process seems to have slowed down and migrants seem to establish themselves as more or less permanent diaspora communities. These develop their own patterns of cultural dynamics by creating stable political, religious, economic, and social networks with diasporas elsewhere as well as with the country of origin. In this scenario the gap between immigrant community and host society widens; while at the same time inter-diaspora relations between communities intensify.

At first glance it appears that this situation is prone to bring forth two types of transnational migrant identity. The first is a communal, reassertive identity. By re-inventing culture or religion, a diaspora community develops a representation of itself and stresses its categories of sameness to diasporas elsewhere. This often goes hand in hand with a strong emphasis on boundaries both with regard to the majority as well as with regard to other ethnic and religious communities. The claim to shared values makes possible empowerment and mobilization for collective action (see for example Schiffauer 2000). The other type of transnational identity appears to be extremely individualistic (see for example Schmitt-Hornstein 1995). Whereas communal identities emphasize a positive belonging to an ethnic or religious group and stresses boundaries, the extreme individualists define themselves primarily negatively and reject boundaries. They tend to voice statements like: "I am neither X nor Y, I am I." These individualists are sometimes characterized as cosmopolitans who enjoy plurality and heterogeneity, and as "prone to articulate complex affiliations, meaningful attachments, and multiple allegiances to issues, people, places, and traditions that lie beyond the boundaries of their resident nation-state" (Vertovec 2000).[2] Thus the new situation of migration seems to bring forth two polar types of collectivities: A radicalized communal identity merging the individual with a (transnational) collective, and a radicalized individual identity, stressing the independence from all kinds of collective identities. What seems to be difficult in a transnational situation is the development of an "integrated" identity, balancing in a meaningful way the aspirations of the individual and the demands of the society he or she lives in. The field seems to be divided between communalists who reify identities and draw boundaries that stress transnational loyalties on the one hand, and "homeless" cosmopolitans emphasizing no loyalty at all on the other.

In this case the consequences for a national civil society would be grave. Civil society is based on the basic acceptance of heterogeneity and would be threatened by a rise of fundamentalist or communalist tendencies. However it also relies on a generalized commitment to society. One cannot build a civil society either with reassertive boundary drawers or with evasive individualists.

This scepticism towards the new migratory situation and its consequences (which is most clearly articulated by conservative communitarian philosophers) would be justified, if there would be nothing but community or oneself for the migrants to identify with. I want to show, however, that the statement I quoted in the beginning—"Immigrants increasingly have greater difficulty and less interest in identifying with the place to which they migrate"—is empirically not true. While it is true that immigrants have greater difficulty and less interest in identifying with the *nation* to which they migrate, the very opposite is often true with regard to the place to which they move. I want to show that this has an important impact on the processes of identity formation. My argument in fact consists of three parts: 1) Under the surface of transnational identifications migrants develop strong local ties to their place of residence; 2) This type of local identification usually complements other possibilities of identification like descent or religion but sometimes also competes with them; and 3) Local identification means a chance for civil society—in particular in times of globalization and growing migrant population. Although I restrict myself in the following to the individualist fraction of the transnationals (because they are more articulate on this issue), the argument might also hold true for the communalists.

I refer to immigrants of the second generation living in Berlin. Before going into the case it may be helpful to sketch briefly some particularities of the German situation. One crucial fact is that there is no symbolic space defined for migrants in the German national discourse.[3] This again is related to the strong emphasis on culture, which characterizes the German discourse on citizenship. It is a widely shared opinion that migrants should adapt (which mostly means assimilate) to German culture before they are granted citizenship.[4] There are complex historical reasons for this emphasis on culture. An explanation would have to consider the particularities of German nation building in the 19th century and the related idea of the *Kulturnation*. But also the early the loss of the colonies in 1918 meant that Germany did not have to deal with decolonization after World War II and therefore never had that special category of immigrants from former colonies; rather it had to integrate millions of German refugees from Eastern Europe. The ethnic cleansing during

93

National-Socialism and the loss of the German East with a strong
Polish population after World War II meant that post war Germany
turned out to be the ethnically the most homogenous German state
in history. All that led to the development of a latent but strong
ethno-cultural identity in the Federal Republic. Immigrants were
and are naturalized all the time (laws permitted that), but due to the
strong culturalist encoding of citizenship, naturalization became
easily viewed by both sides as a kind of conversion, and migrants
were often hesitant to apply for it. Because of the comparatively
greater difficulties with regard to political integration the ground for
the development of diasporic identities seems to be more fertile in
Germany than elsewhere in Western Europe.

After these general remarks let me now turn to the concrete case.
I want to start with a quotation taken a from group interview, which
was conducted in 1997, with young immigrants from Sri Lanka,
Turkey, Greece, Kosovo-Albania, Lebanon, and Croatia, living in
Berlin.[5] In the course of this interview Dimitra (19, Greek nation-
ality, high school-student, born and raised in Berlin) said:

> Relatives at home do not accept anything which happens here in Berlin, and
> they see everything in an unfavorable light. It's really drastic. I cannot commu-
> nicate with people there, ordinary people I mean. And many of my relatives are
> conservative, extremely conservative. And I feel at home (*zu Hause*) in Berlin.

Statements like that come up in very different settings. Let me quote
just one other example I came across recently:

> I am a Berliner. Not because I was born here—no, but because my whole life
> took place here. My friends, my family, my education, my career, my catastro-
> phes, and everything that happened. I know the problems of this city, its positive
> and negative sides. That's why I am a Berliner. (Aziza A., rapper)[6]

All statements concerning identities are of course contextual; we
define who we are always in relation to some specified other. The
group interview quoted above was conducted in Germany and the
interviewer was an ethnic German. The participants thus defined
themselves in Germany *vis-à-vis* a German. When emphasizing the
fact that she was a "Berliner", Dimitra mentioned however first her
relatives at home who disapproved of everything happening in
Berlin. It is very likely that this disapproval went hand in hand with
a criticism directed at her that she had become "German". It was
pointed out by different participants in the interview that this
criticism was not only voiced by relatives in the country of origin but

also (and even more so) by their parents in Germany. There was a common complaint that parents are quick in interpreting all kinds of activities of their children as "germanizing". This reduction of complexity by the parents is quite understandable; it results from fears widespread among members of the first generation to become alienated from their children in a foreign environment. This fear makes them screen the activities of the second generation for signs of *germanization*. Defining oneself as Berliner thus answers to an ascription of being German by relatives and parents. On a first plane it thus reads: "No I am not a German but I am a Berliner."

The insistence on an identity as Berliners answers to yet another dimension of ethnic stereotyping. The participants in the group interview were all students at the *Otto-Hahn-Gesamtschule* in the borough of Neukölln in Berlin. Teachers at this school like in other German schools tend to make a clear distinction between migrants from the South and the East and migrants from the West and the North. The former are depicted as the "immigrants" ("Ausländer") proper: They come from the poorer regions of the world and are primarily perceived as "problematic." The teachers tend to interpret actions of their students or their respective parents (e.g. a refusal to participate in school trips) not as attempts to cope with a structurally difficult situation, but rather explain them as "Islamic conservatism" or "traditional mentality". So the statement might also be interpreted as saying: "No. I am not an *Ausländer*. I am a Berliner."

In order to understand better this importance attached to Berlin we should discuss in some more detail some aspects of the process of identity formation among immigrants of the second and third generation. The double ascription as *germanized* by parents and as *Ausländer* by Germans creates a complex problem of acknowledgment. The compromises the young immigrants make when attempting to grow up as a Turk/Greek/Tamil in Germany tend to be misinterpreted by the parents as attempts of becoming German and by teachers as sticking to a Turk/Greek/Tamil background (and rejecting the necessity of integration). Needless to say that both *Ausländer* parents and German teachers have only a very stereotypical knowledge about each other. Even more important is the normative issue. Both worlds tend to depict each other as problematic: In immigrant families, Germany is associated with broken homes (German children are supposedly thrown out of the house by the age of eighteen), sexual libertinage, alcohol and drugs, and Nazism and violence. The Germans portray the immigrant families as backward, authoritarian if not oppressive, violent, and hostile to women. So the immigrant children growing up in Germany find themselves in many situations in which one important aspect of their existence is devalued.

Many immigrant children in some phase of their life develop the strategy to defend German "culture" *vis-à-vis* their parents and their respective "home" culture *vis-à-vis* the Germans. But due to the rather stereotypical knowledge of these worlds about each other, the children find themselves trapped in the situation that when they say the truth, a wrong message comes across. This is a very painful situation. Even if they are linguistically competent in two languages, migrant children cannot translate from one context to the other because everything said is interpreted in terms of distorting preconceptions. In such a situation they are forced to represent themselves in a systematically distorted way so that at least part of the message gets across. Muslim girls in order to defend their families against preconceived notions of rigidity and authoritarianism were observed to argue in the classroom that they had the same liberties like all other girls, which on face value was not the case (Mannitz 1999, 302).

In a situation of mutual misrepresentation one would expect the dominant culture finally to win. In this case the migrant youth sooner or later would adapt to the majority culture and thus find a solution for his/her difficult situation. In fact the person to whom we owe the best account of such a situation, Eva Hoffmann, solved her problems in this way. She had moved with her parents from Poland to Canada in the fifties. In a very precise language she describes the feeling of loss of reality and powerlessness, which comes with such a situation. The title of her book *Lost in Translation* neatly sums up the problem I am trying to describe here. However, very few young immigrants finally end up identifying with the majority culture in Germany. The reason is discrimination, a reality many immigrant youths become painfully aware of during puberty. The timing of this realization of discrimination has psychological but above all sociological reasons. At this age, young immigrants move out of the rather protected spheres of family and school into wider society and experience rejection. This experience makes identification with Germany very difficult because it now has the sting of identification with a society that rejects them. The resulting conflict can express itself in a variety of ways: Aggressiveness, depression, and identification with radical opposition groups.[7] The confrontation with discrimination means that young Turks growing up in Germany are thrown back to the group from which they wanted to break away, and they are shown that they are undesired by the group to which they wanted to belong.

They thus have to come to terms with a situation that is in itself contradictory.[8]

It is in this situation that statements like "I am a Berliner" are to be read. They show the possibilities of a positive identification beyond ethnic and/or religious categories that often inflict pain. Let us now explore closer what it means to identify with a city.

First of all the identification with a city can be read as a refusal to be identified with national and ethnic categories. To identify with Berlin, Paris or New York means exactly *not* to identify with Germany, France or the United States. In the same group interview another participant remarked: "You cannot feel as a German ... typically German is somewhat repulsive. I mean I don't even know what is typically German." To identify with a city also means a refusal to be reduced to the ethnic background or to the place where one is born. It thus is a very outspoken criticism of *germanization* by the parents or the exclusion as *Ausländer* by the German society. But it seems to me that it also entails a criticism of categories like "hybridity", "plural identities", "hyphenated identities". All these concepts take the ethnic viz. national as the ultimate point of reference. A plural identity like Turko-German is conceived of as a composite of several (generally not more than two or three) basic identities. To state, "I am a Berliner", however, means a quality of its own. It is a positive claim to belonging.

To identify with Berlin is more than to just identify with the particular quarter where you grow up. It is not by chance that the young migrants quoted above state that they are "Berliners" and not just "Kreuzbergers", although they might prefer to live in Kreuzberg rather than in other parts of Berlin. The identification with Berlin is possible because big cities develop their own brand of cultures. The fact that world-cities are complex, heterogeneous and diversified entities exactly does not imply that they are amorphous. This is reflected in an anthropomorphous terminology. Cities, so it is said, have a character, a "personality" (or an image). What is meant with statements like that is that they might change constantly—but there are patterns of changes, ways of dealing with change, certain rhythms, certain beats (Schiffauer 1997). Under certain circumstances we can get addicted to it. "[Big Cities] embody certain ideas, opinions and attitudes, norms and values. They are no empty pages but narrative spaces, containing certain stories (of important persons and important events), myths (of heroes and demons), parables (of virtues and vices)" (Lindner 1999). Or to put it yet differently: Cities are places where strangers meet—but these meetings can take place in very different ways with different cities, corresponding to their specific culture of public spaces (Schiffauer 1997a). Because cities have a particular character we can develop very strong emotional ties to our "own" city, be it London, Paris, or Berlin, we can love it and be proud of it. And even more, there is the experience that cities have a certain influence on the habitus of their inhabitants. As one Kurdish lady put it: "I dressed up much more in Stuttgart than in Berlin. Stuttgart is just more *chic*. It was impossible to run around there like they do here." In a way you become a "Berliner" a "New Yorker" or a "Parisian" while living in these respective places.

In fact this identification can be very pronounced. I know immigrants who expressed that they could not conceive of living anywhere else than in Berlin. Or take the following quotation of a young migrant who described his vacation. The first days in Turkey, he told me, were "like in a dream"—he was feeling immediately at home and completely at ease. "But then comes a time, a day—and you want to return to Germany. Because you live here. You start to think of Berlin, of your friends, the girls or what else. The discotheques, something that is fun, a hobby or something" (Schiffauer 1985, 166). It is clearly homesickness that is expressed in these lines. Statements like that render absurd notions of the migrant as a no-where man or bound only to transnational identities. The construction of the cosmopolitan man, who develops "habits of mind and life" through which he or she can end up anywhere in the world and be in the "same relation of familiarity and strangeness" to the local culture, and, by the same token, "feel partially adjusted everywhere" is just not true. Ethnic, religious, or cosmopolitan transnationalism can, and does more often than not, go hand in hand with strong feelings of belonging. Transnationalism is clearly something else than translocalism.

Let me add some anthropological considerations. The anthropological principle that is referred to here is "locality"—a principle of group formation that is opposed to descent (ethnicity) or religion (ideology). The three principles each have a value in their own right and cannot be reduced to each other. In contrast to descent (ethnicity) or religion (values), locality seems to be a rather "superficial" principle of integration as it has a strong aesthetic dimension. Locality means identification with a landscape. The solidarity it brings forth is based on sharing space rather than sharing values or ancestors. This has strong sensual connotations—sharing a space means sharing smells, sounds, tastes, and rhythms. We refer to a landscape through physiognomic knowledge. We appropriate it by moving in it and we start to identify with it when we detect structures—favorite places, favorite routes, favorite stores. This *is* superficial—as it is concerned with the surface rather than the essence. But in a way (as among others Marcel Proust has shown), it is also more basic and elementary. We have an aesthetic relation to our environment before we have a conceptual one—and when we start to reflect about childhood and belonging, we discover very soon that it is this type of visual, olfactoric, auditive relation to our environment which is essential.

This is of course true for all kinds of landscapes, for rural landscapes as well as for small towns and big cities. It is, however, with regard to big cities that the specific character of local identification becomes more apparent. Rural landscapes and small towns are not necessarily homogenous with regard to ethnic and/or religious affiliation but they are rather clearly structured. This implies that the principles locality, descent, and religion get easily conflated. A region or a village easily gets identified with one particular ethnic or religious group. This is far more difficult or even impossible in a cosmopolitan environment where things are unclear and fluid. It is in a constantly changing, complex, and heterogeneous cosmopolitan landscape where local identification emerges most clearly as a principle of its own. It is there were, we can develop love of a heterogeneous place with its characteristic sounds, lights, smells. This is not necessarily the love of heterogeneity: We still can prefer to stick exclusively with our own kind but we do so it in a special setting which has its own atmosphere and its particular qualities. This type of aesthetic identification creates a relationship with social spaces that are not integrated on the basis of values. It is an identification that takes the shape of a specific biography, a biography "of catastrophes and everything that happened".

In practice conscious attempts are often made to conflate these different principles of group formation (and with it, of constructing belonging, identity and solidarity): Nationalist thinking, for example, can be described as the attempt to merge the principle of locality with descent and/or ideology. It is not by chance that classical nationalist imaginary always referred to the peasant landscape (where conflation was easier) and rarely to the big city (where it is hardly possible). But there were of course also conscious attempts in big cities to colonize the local in the name of ethnicity/descent of religion/ideology. All of us know that locality sometimes lost this battle of principles. Cosmopolitan cities like Sarajevo, Belgrade, Beirut, Belfast, and others could be easily added, broken apart on ethnic and/or religious lines. And of course this was also the case with Berlin in the 1930s. But exactly the same cities also prove that locality (and the identification with a city) is not just a phenomenon of secondary importance to descent or religion: The spirit of cosmopolitanism, the love of a place in all its heterogeneity, has a certain tenacity. It can be defeated from time to time, but it certainly reappears sooner or later. Locality is a potential but not necessary an actual source of identification. Its realization requires representational efforts.[9] Sensual experience is only the "raw material" for an identification with a city. In order to become effective it has to be expressed in one way or the other. It has to be objectified in stories or pictures. Art plays a crucial role in this process. It finds expressions for the volatile and hardly tangible atmosphere, which results from the coexistence of heterogeneous elements. One might mention Hubert Selby's Brooklyn, Godard's Paris, or Zaimoglus' Hamburg as examples.

In my opinion there is a great potential in this type of local identification, because aesthetic integration is in a way both superficial and basic. It allows integration/loyalty/ solidarity without conformity. It is therefore particularly attractive for the migrant. In a situation in which he easily gets lost in translation the love to the city in which he lives serves as a positive anchoring. It is, after all, the place where he lives his life; where he goes to school, falls in love, marries, where his children grow up. It becomes his own place, inseparably tied up with his biography. This allows for identification without suppressing opposition. The cosmopolitan is not the homeless person having his identifications everywhere except in the place where he lives as nationalist (and often anti-Semitic) propaganda have tried to suggest. The existence of local identification shows also that the communitarian position, which sees value integration as the prerequisite for loyalty and solidarity, is simply not true. We can identify with a city, can be proud of it, boast about it, without sharing the values of the great majority of our co-citizens. The love for one's place allows for integrating society without integrating value systems, because it is *here* where we want to make the best out of our lives (including that of our children). *Cosmo*politans (in the sense of *Weltbürger*) are in fact cosmo*politans*—inhabitants of world cities.

Notes

1.   At the moment at least I seems to be more than doubtful whether the growing importance of the service sector provides enough jobs to counteract this tendency.

2. To call them cosmopolitans makes sense because of the political implications of this term. It allows us to conceive bilinguality and the competence to move in different spheres as an asset rather than a deficit.
3. It is telling that history books only reserve a very passing note for migration (Schiffauer *et al.* 1999, 58 ff).
4. A comparison with France is telling. France also articulates strong demands on assimilation but not in the name of a (particular) culture but in the name of (presumably global) civilization. The French discourse invites migrants to participate in a cosmopolitan project and thus assigns a symbolic space for them.
5. The interview was conducted by Sabine Mannitz in the context of the research project, State-School-Ethnicity, financed by the Volkswagen foundation. The results are published in Schiffauer *et al.* 1999.
6. Although I restrict myself to the discussions of immigrants to Germany I might mention that similar statements are also heard in other contexts. Take the following example from Keya Ganguly: "Being a child of Indian immigrants, I find it very difficult to identify myself with that sort of ideology of difference, especially since the identification might occur at another level. For instance I choose to be identified with Philadelphians rather than with Indians from Bombay" (Quoted in Schmidt-Hornstein, forthcoming).
7. For a precise description of a conflict resolution of this kind see Schmidt-Hornstein (1995). See also Tertilt's (1996) excellent study of a Turkish gang in Frankfurt am Main.
8. I showed elsewhere that this type of problems is not restricted to "cosmopolitans" but that they also explain the attachment to communalist groups (Schiffauer 1999).
9. The same holds true for the other two principles of solidarity. Loyalty can be based on descent and religion but does not result by itself in solidarity. Relatives who meet feel some obligation because of the feeling of amity, but we know that this is just a basis and no guarantee for solidarity. It is a claim, but it has to be actualized and brothers sometimes become the fiercest enemies. The same holds true for religion.

CHAPTER 5

"Dwelling in Displacement": On Diasporization and the Production of National Subjects

Helmuth Berking

Diaspora is everywhere. Since the early 1970s we have been witnessing an ongoing process of semantic homogenization concerning all kinds of phenomena related to the large-scale movement of people. Where once there were "ethnic minorities", "overseas communities", "labor migrants", "exiles", and "refugees", today, it seems, there are "diasporas". The language of diaspora, historically positioned and more or less restricted to the in part violent expulsion, in part voluntary movement and territorial reset-tlement of Jewish, Greek, and, finally, Armenian communities, has meanwhile gained momentum not only in the academic discourse but even among those groups that have until now not defined themselves in these terms. When movement more than settlement, routes more than roots, "homes away from home" take center stage, "dwelling in displacement" (Clifford 1997, 254) becomes a common feature in a globalizing world. As a descriptive, but also highly normative concept, aimed at exploring a particular social condition of globality, the discourse on diaspora is intimately interwoven with or even based on attempts at theorizing cultural globalization in general and post-colonialism in particular. Only within this context does diaspora reveal its multiple meanings.

In conceptualizing the transnationalization of commodities and people, of financial and cultural markets, of loyalties and collective identities, theories of globalization share three basic convictions (Berking 1998). They usually construct two separate territorial logics by differentiating a global "space of flows" from a more traditionally located "space of places" (Castells 1996, 378); they break with the longstanding and foundational isomorphism between territoriality, identity, and culture (Appadurai 1996a); and they find in the thesis of the end or at least a significant loss of the nation-state's sovereignty a common ground. Seen from this perspective, diaspora appears to be a perfect fit. It articulates transnational forms of sociation and solidarity, displays de-territorialized cultural identities, and challenges the principles on which nation-states rest. In short, these new and old societal formations represent both globalizing forces from 'below' and the strict opposite of state-organized societies; their designated other is the nation-state, which is, to quote Arjun Appadurai, "on its last legs" (*ibid.*, 16).

In sketching in this background, I would like to revise the prominent but solely negative role assigned to the nation-state. Bringing the state back in means exploring whether nation-states themselves do not play a particularly crucial role in creating, maintaining, and policing transnational spaces inhabited by diasporic communities, and if they do so, how this might affect common images of diasporization. This is not to suggest that diasporas are purely context-driven formations. However, their context-generating capacities are not exclusively grounded in transnational space. They are also highly dependent on local configurations of power, that is, on the particular institutional constraints of their host societies and, as far as they exist, their homelands, both of which are organized as nation-states. Therefore, and contrary to the global framing of transmigration, I will depart from a traditional point of view by describing some institutional constraints that societies organized as nation-states impose on their migrant populations. Then I will briefly characterize diasporic locations within this framework in order, finally, to seek out the "sense of possibility" diasporas may release in terms of promoting alternative modes of sociality and identity. The main frame of reference will be US society, which until not too long ago was perceived as a highly successful example of the way multiculturalism can be implemented—a powerful image that has circulated around the globe, though structurally it was built on and into the racial particularities of American society (Bourdieu & Wacquant 1999). This interplay of institutionalized racism and multiculturalism, however, offers some promising insights into power configurations to which local diasporic groups are subjected to and must respond.

A central problem of multiethnic nation states poses itself in creating a categorical order capable of producing national subjects and identifying those subgroups that are subject to societal discrimination. In an effort to secure equal opportunities for its ethnic and religious communities, US state administrations compile "race and ethnicity related data", which, as in our case, legitimate the adoption and implementation of anti-discrimination legislation and affirmative action. Yet, once set in motion, these programs' unintended side-effects increasingly motivate, via the distribution of material advantages, exactly those ethnic group formations against which the programs were initially devised. The ethnic dilemmas are all too visible. If state administrations do not intervene, the rate of discrimination and racist and ethnic exclusion will actually rise. Yet because the state itself intervenes via strategies of positive discrimination, the state necessarily violates the basic principle of equality, which then, in turn, is even more vehemently subject to legal enforcement by the majority population. In short, through its intervention the state creates a social reality in which society is divided precisely according to those racial criteria,[1] which its "therapy" sought to abolish. "A legal construct, that was indebted to the color-blind equality principle, actually led in the US, at first involuntarily but then quite pointedly, to the strengthening of color consciousness with the devastating effect of at least in part extremist reciprocal ethnocentric closures, and without on average improving the social conditions of blacks (or other positively highlighted minorities)" (Brumlik & Leggewie 1994, 439).

Federal regulations force Americans to identify themselves as "Caucasian," "Afro-American", "Native American", "Hispanic" or "Asian-American and other Pacific Islander". The wording has always been controversial (Lee 1993), because it remained the secret of the census bureau why East Indians, Pakistanis, Japanese, and Chinese, for instance, should all find themselves quite arbitrarily in the category of "Asian". And yet this institutional arbitrariness of bureaucratic categorization, fostered by racial violence and daily experiences of discrimination, brought a hitherto unseen pan-Asian identity formation into life (Esperitu 1992; Jusdanis 1996), a macro-ethnic umbrella under which all the groups that were previously seen as distinct, now identified racially as Asian, began to accede to a state-imposed identification. Associations like those of Asian-American students, businesses, and media add institutional strength to a macro-ethnic politics of identity aiming at self-empowerment within the ethno-racial landscape of US society.[2] Similar processes of macro-ethnic identity formation can be observed among the different Latino/Hispanic populations, which leads Mike Davis to speak of US Latinos, who "are already the fifth largest 'nation' in Latin America", as a "Latin American Nation" (Davis 1999, 9). The crucial question mark, however, applies to 'common bonds'. What are the ties that bind, that undermine, or even replace ethnic identities in favor of pan-ethnicities? They are first of all negative ones driven by formative experiences of ethnic exclusion and similar locations within the racial and class hierarchy of US society. They are therefore to a certain extent also local ones, limited to the historical conditions of the dominant culture in and against which they appeared. It seems at least questionable whether a "Pan-Asian" identity that arose in the US will retain its particular symbolic value in a different symbolic universe.

An interesting change in the racial nomenclature of US society occurred 1997. To catch up statistically with the growing segment of "halfies",—the number of children from "interracial families" grew between 1972 and 1990 from 500,000 to over two million—"mixed people" can now declare themselves as members of more than one race (*New York Times*, November 8, 1997, A 20). The child of an African-American and a Japanese woman, for instance, would check both Afro-American and Asian, a novelty which evoked the sharp protest of civil rights groups which fear that this "double counting" could entail a premeditated manipulation of the size of minority groups and thus manipulation of redistribution practices concerning material and symbolic resources.

The significance of these few examples seems to be threefold. They show, first, that the entire institutional system of American society, including public consciousness, and extending down into the tiniest pores of everyday life, is permeated by racial and ethnic categorizations. Second, they demonstrate the power of institutions to "make", to invoke ethnic groups. *Nota bene*: It is the institutional arrangements of the state that actually encourage ethnic groups to organize as collective agents.[3] Third, they also suggest that the race-based nomenclature is beginning to loose touch with reality. It actually requires some sociological imagination to come up with what is supposed to happen statistically with the children of the halfies' children.

Thus far the focus has been on incentives of state policies that initiate ethnic group-formation processes via imposed identifications and the distribution of material and symbolic advantages from above. This dynamics is complemented and even accelerated by tendencies of ethnic closure from below. During the last decades migrant communities have been fundamentally changed insofar as their interest politics are organized no longer around "assimilation" but around "cultural self-determination". Not "adaptation" but "recognition" marks the focal point on which a new politics of ethnicity is based.

Roughly, one can distinguish between three types of migration. First, there are those men and women who leave their country of origin for a limited time and return home at the end of their contractual obligations; since they are socially and linguistically isolated in the host country, intercultural exchange does not play a significant role in their case. Guest workers in Germany, for instance, could be considered the typical embodiment of this structure of migration.

In the second place, there is the classic form of migration in which people leave their homeland for ever in order to become rooted in a new world (Portes & Rumbault 1996; Rumbault 1991). This type of migration follows fixed patterns keyed to the geopolitical traditions of the receiving countries. The former European colonial powers are the preferred destination of those whom they once colonized. The US, which in the mid-1980s took in a remarkable 19 percent of global migration, is the choice of those national populations with which the US has foreign and economic, though not always peaceful, policy ties (Sassen 1996, 79). Migrants usually find in the country of reception an already existing, socially and spatially segregated "ethnic community" which, as a kind of transition mechanism, enables them to take their first steps on the new terrain and facilitates cultural assimilation. Despite their being a fixed institution that represents neither the old nor the new, but a specific "in-between", the ethnic communities (the Little Italies, Pilsens, and Germantowns) are not the obvious and self-evident ends of the journey. These communities are instead inhabited by those transitionals, who separate from the community in accordance with the degree of economic success they have achieved, in order then really to "arrive" in the country of arrival. Here the famous three-step formula from migrants to ethnics to nationals finds its fundamentum in re. But the three-generation issue was solely restricted to the white majority culture. It never worked for blacks, nor does it apply for the new 'colored' immigrant populations (Portes 1996). If the transfer between ethnic community and host society is inhibited or even prevented by xenophobia or racist exclusion, those strategies aimed at ethnicization and socially and spatially motivated ghettoization almost automatically start to bite.[4]

The third type of migration is the old diasporic one, but now transposed to mark the making and remaking of transnational locations and to carry the hopes and the burden implied by globalization from below. "Diasporas", notes Khachig Tölölyan, "are the exemplary communities of the transnational moment" (Tölölyan 1991, 4). Attempts to construct an ideal type (Safran 1991; Cohen 1997) draw heavily on Jewish diasporic experiences. The defining features, then, would be: dispersion from an original homeland, continuous attachment and identification with and support of the (imagined) homeland, experiences of exclusion from the dominant culture of the various host societies, and a sense of community and collective identity that transcends territorial confinement. But the language of diaspora itself cannot be confined to an ideal construct, so the term 'diaspora' nowadays is applied to all ethnic groups living outside their territories of origin (Tölölyan 1996). Special attention is given to the transnational quality of sociation, which rests on the peculiar sociospatial significance of the fact that diasporas are located simultaneously within particular states and outside of any particular state (Faist 2000; Portes, Guarnizo & Landot 1999; Smith & Guranizo 1998).

Diasporas can neither be reduced to epiphenomena of the nation-state nor seen as appendices of global capitalism (Anthias 1998; Clifford 1997; Hall 1990; Gilroy 1993; Cohen 1997; Mitchell 1997). They are regarded as part and partners of those transnational networks in which social life is contextualized both "here" and "there" and in which multiple loyalties and identities are constituted and maintained against the nation-state's construction of national subjects. Transnational connectedness, that at least is the assumption, breaks the typical binarism of minority and majority societies, strengthens the resistance "against an oppressive national hegemony", (Clifford 1997, 255) and creates those "diasporic public spheres" (Appadurai 1996) that are perceived as non-state power sources in transnational spaces. There is by no means an important moment of power gain and self-empowerment that derives from transnational location. But does the transnational so easily and unconditionally translate out into the transethnic, as some authors assume (Clifford 1997; Brah 1996)? Again, what are the ties that bind the new agents of diasporic space? Transethnic solidarity? Why, then, is "home" such an overused metaphor in diasporic discourse (Anthias 1998)? There is hardly any empirical evidence indicating that the Turkish diaspora, for instance, transcends the borders of ethnicity with respect to the Kurds. And the scepticism as to whether Black Muslims or nationalistic "expatriate Greeks" do not represent more of a new form of ethnic particularism than transnational identities is not easy to dismiss (Anthias 1998, 567). Floya Anthias' insightful evaluation of diasporic discourses has shown the risks inherent in neglecting the interplay of class, gender, ethnicity, and nation by simply ascribing community status to various ethnic groups identified by their place of origin. Diaspora, she concludes, cannot replace the problems of ethnicity, because diaspora "itself relies on a conception of ethnic bonds as central, but dynamic, elements of social organization" (*ibid.*, 576).

The image of diaspora as one that undermines the ethnic spectacle, however, also loses its contours if one bears in mind that the "age of transnationalism" is at the same time a period of continued, if not historically forced, "nation-state building processes". (Glick Schiller, Basch, & Szanton-Blanc 1997, 135). It is not only individuals and groups abroad that may be actively engaged in the production of national subjects in their countries of origin. States as well respond to "their" populations living outside their national borders and seek to organize "their" diaspora as a nation-state project by dissociating step-by-step political membership from territorial presence.

The Indian diaspora, for instance, extends from Sydney to the Silicon Valley and is intertwined in diverse and direct ways with the political and religious disputes in India and its host countries. At the same time, the Indian state seeks to encourage reinvestment in India by bestowing on the population living outside its territories the special status of "non-residential Indian", rewarded by tax breaks, property rights, freedom of travel, and government loans (Appadurai 1996a, 45fn). Elections in the Dominican Republic are won through the support of 'lost Dominicanyorks', a term that refers to the fact that New York's Dominican diaspora transfers home more than $1 billion per year. This has led to proposals for a change in the constitution geared to enabling the diaspora to win seats in the home parliament. Like Colombia, the Dominican government grants its diaspora dual citizenship and active voting rights "at home". The Mexican government has for decades used its "program for Mexican communities abroad" to pursue a successful "global nation policy" (Smith 1997, 199) that is directed in particular at the Mexican-American communities and goes hand in hand with the extension and the active support of transnational organization structures—a strategy which increases the power of both sides. While the Mexican state expands extra-territorially, for instance, through the active creation of "its" diaspora, which probably will be allowed to vote in presidential elections scheduled for the year 2000 (*ibid.*, 205), the transmigrants are gaining direct influence in the decision-making processes of state administrations in their regions of origin via financial and political-organizational engagement in a huge array of local development projects. The annual transfer of approximately 8–10 billion "Migra-dollars" seems to be the financial backbone of rural Mexico and Central-America as a whole (Davis 1999, 27).

These examples could be extended indefinitely. More relevantly, what is articulated in these diasporic public spheres appears to be the contours of an institutionalization of modes of political membership that clash with demands of inclusion and identity in societies organized as nation-states and their own, traditional distribution of citizenship.[5]

Beyond the overdetermined representation of diaspora as a new transnational form of interaction that negates all ethnic and racial identity politics, we are called on to rediscover the active and quite successful role of the states of origin, regularly enforced by transmigrant populations themselves, in including their population "abroad" politically, economically, and culturally in the process of nation-state formation "at home". With the dissociation of membership and territorial belonging, however, the principle of territorial sovereignty on which the "classic" nation-states typically rest looses its foundational value. A different process of state formation, operating from a position "of dependent development" (Smith 1997, 203), here comes into play, one which necessarily collides with the "First World's" institutionalized production of national subjects based on territoriality, sovereignty, and identity. What we are dealing with are not only diasporas but also at least two contradictory nation-state projects meeting in very conflicting ways in the field of diaspora. While the countries of origin are expanding extraterritorially by de-territorializing political membership, the receiving countries are stepping up the pressure aimed at assimilating and securing the loyalties of their migrant populations. Diasporic locations at the same time represent both: they are arenas in which states compete over re-definitions of membership and civil rights, and they are go-betweens which mediate these conflicts and are thus capable of creating something new,[6] precisely because of their lived experience as a societal formation simultaneously located "here" and "there". It is exactly this permanent and institutionally secured in-betweenness that provides the scope to resist, at least partly, the assimilating pressures exerted by national cultures.

Within the framework of the receiving state the institutional environment of a local diasporic group can be displayed as follows. To be realistic, we would have to include here all interactive practices and exchange channels with which a local diasporic group is involved concerning other diasporas from the same state of origin.

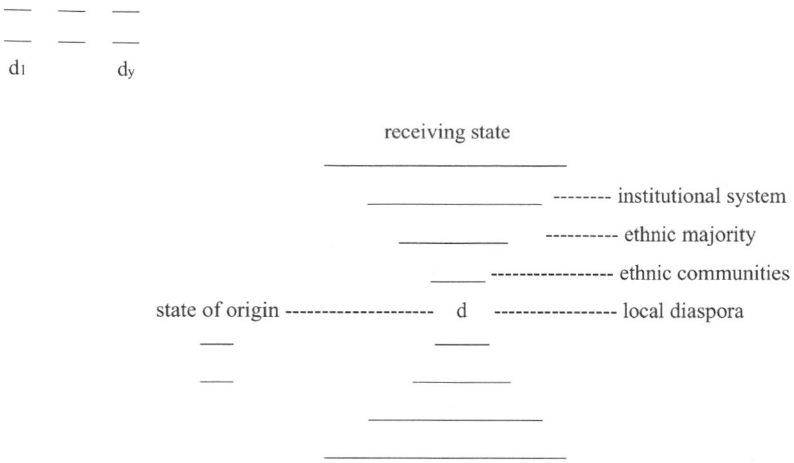

d_l d_y

receiving state

-------- institutional system

---------- ethnic majority

----------------- ethnic communities

state of origin --------------------   d   ----------------- local diaspora

Figure 5.1. The institutional environment of a local diasporic group

The realization that nation-states play a special role in the formation of transnational space necessarily implies that the constellation
in which a "politics of ethnicity", now so relentlessly imposing its
mark on US society (Brumlik & Leggewie 1994, 438), will assume an
altered form. The dynamic of ethnicization, which so far has been
localized in the specific interaction between state administrations
and ethnic minorities on the one hand and strategies of ethnic
closure between these groups on the other hand, is now additionally
reinforced through intervening third parties. Not only institutional
racism from above and ethnicization from below but also ethno-
national mobilization "from outside" provide the "framework" in
which a self-fulfilling politics of ethnicity can come to the fore. It
would, however, be negligent to characterize the sociocultural and
economic connections that transmigrants maintain with their countries of origin merely as effects of ethno-national mobilization of the
states of origin. The experiences of ethnic exclusion and racial
discrimination made in the recipient countries are counteracted by
experiences of status gain and heightened opportunity to win influence in the local communities of origin (Goldring 1997, 180). In
short, their place of origin allows individuals and groups, in their role
as emigrants, all that is systematically denied to them in their role as
immigrants.[7]

Another condition that to a certain extent determines action
orientations of local diasporic groups can be defined as the power
effects of the respective dominant culture. In the multicultural

universe of US society not all ethnicities carry the same symbolic value. "Black" and "White" form the extreme positions of a hierarchical order within which each ethnic group must "locate" itself in relation to all other ethnic groups, just as the group itself is relentlessly "located" by others. Mexican-Americans, for instance, find themselves "below Americans of European origin, above African-Americans and Puerto Ricans on the East coast ..., and in a variable and sometimes competitive position in relation to other Latinos, Asian-Americans, and African-Americans in other parts of the country" (Goldring 1997, 182). In New York, Mexicans tend to distance themselves from African-Americans and Puerto Ricans by defining themselves as "not black", while they are defined by the dominant society as "not white" (*ibid.*). The vanguard of this ethnically stratified hierarchy, however, is made up by the whites who, in their position as dominant ethnic group, have remained peculiarly underexposed in analytical terms (Doane 1997).

From the perspective of the sociology of knowledge, this analytic blind spot has to do with the dominance of hegemonic ethnic groups insofar as the latter control those symbolic resources which have historically always limited knowledge production concerning "race and ethnicity" to minorities and subordinate groups. The status of the "ethnic" therefore remains structurally bound to evocations assigned by the majority society, which does not apply these terms to itself. That the British in India or the French in Algeria have never been addressed as an ethnic minority (King 1997, 140) exemplifies the close interaction of dominant position and ethnicizing identification that continually aims at the classification of others. Like the Germans in Germany, white Americans in the US do not perceive themselves as the dominant ethnic group. But it is exactly this systematic negation of their own ethnic identity that is both a result of their dominant position and the presupposition for maintaining the dominance of the dominant ethnic culture. "Hidden ethnicity" is the term American sociologist Asley Doane proposes to grasp the transposition of ethnic forms of sociality into generalized and thus "normalized" ones (Doane 1997). If this is the case, then cultural pluralism as the classic argument of multiculturalists, assuming as it does that the co-existence of a multiplicity of identities would clearly break the dominance of dominant national cultures, looses some of its ground.

Throughout the history of the United States the symbolic borders defined by belonging to the dominant ethnic group have repeatedly shifted in direct response to inter-group conflicts. English settlers formed the crystallizing core of that Anglo-American identity, which step-by-step, at first through the inclusion of Protestants, then of all European Americans, was widened to embrace the macro-ethnic category of Americans of European origin. If one follows the empirical findings, ethnic self-identifications either play no role or only an arbitrary one for this group. While almost all whites can name their European ancestors, this sense of heritage is of a more or less individual nature. The 'favor' and the privilege bestowed by whiteness in the United States or Germanness in Germany consist in transcending the common routines of daily discrimination and race-based stigmatization. "To be white in America," Robert Terry laconically notes, "is not to have to think about it" (cited in Doane 1997, 379).

A further neutralization effect emerges when cultural orientations of the dominant ethnic group take on the normative force of the factual and are for this reason no loner perceivable as the symbolic power sources of a specific ethnic identity. One only needs to bear in mind that the institutional system of US society is unmistakably marked by Anglo-American standards in order to focus one's view on the quite distinct behavior requirements that this institutional order demands of its members. It is such shifts, reinforced through already achieved transpositions from ethnic to national identity, that pave the way for these mental constructs, which Michael Banton has characterized as "minus-one ethnicity", namely the conviction that dominant cultures and their members represent not ethnic but general or even universal principles of sociality (Doane 1997, 380). Today there are primarily two complementary figures of argument, which serve to secure the dominance of the dominant culture. The former idea of ethnicity as a traditional residue is being replaced by an image of ethnicity as part of a foreign culture; and the negated ethnicity of the dominant ethnic group is declared to be the paradigmatic norm for minorities.

That identity politics of ethnic groups are perceived as elements of foreign cultures outside their nation-state territory has to do with the significant character of diasporas as transnational locations, but also with the extraterritorial expansion of the states of origin already mentioned. The normative expectations of majority society, then, aim at normalizing culturally distinctive practices within the given institutional framework. The second and complementary strategy places its trust in the symbolic power of that "hidden ethnicity" which again and again has proven itself, as noted by Bourdieu, as a "power for the implementation of power". It is precisely to the degree to which the ethnic identity of the dominant ethnic group has shrunk to the symbolic form of individual heritage/ancestry in the self-perception of the group that it becomes possible and opportune to define ethnicity generally as a problem of individual origin. "Thus, the vision of American society," states Asley Doane, "becomes one in which ethnicity is reduced to ancestry, and all members must conform to an institutionalized (and hidden) dominant group identity" (Doane 1997, 385). From the norm-setting perspective of dominant groups, the social problems, then, no longer prove to be outcomes of ethnic or racist discrimination but can be dealt with as a habitual incapacity of the members of ethnic groups to behave in accordance with societal norms.

Such observations should, however, not lead us to forget that the dominance of dominant ethnic groups is always relative and depends structurally on the mobilization and power potentials of 'subordinate' groups. Though nation-states take their part in constructing transnational spaces, the power rate is definitely rising in favor of diasporas. These formations criss-cross the inclusion requirements of dominant cultures. They are culturally not assimilable; and at least in nation-states under the rule of law, they cannot be discriminated against legally without giving rise to international repercussions. In short, diasporas are not governable from the outside and precisely in this sense they may actually represent locations in which alternative orientations running counter to the dominance of dominant cultures can take on the character of reality in the long run.

Raymond Williams once proposed understanding the history of socialism as a history of a multiplicity of local and localized forms of protest and resistance that hold their own against the dominance of dominant cultures, in order finally to condense, beyond the local contexts of signification, into a generalized alternative idea of society. The interesting part of this picture, I believe, lies in linking the creation of commonly shared or 'universal' orientations and values to the context-generating power of local practices. It is the multiplicity of "militant particularisms" that finally calls forth generalized alternative orientations.[8] With respect to diasporas, this means that the latter should be perceived not as an end in themselves but as a strategic place where the potential of local particularisms may generate alternatives to the dominant mode of producing national subjects. But to actually follow up on this point of view, it would be necessary to pay far more attention to the very local conditions under which diasporic groups produce their particular localities. It is by no means said that "dwelling in displacement" is tantamount to dwelling in resistance or that state-imposed identifications translate out into transcultural identities. The history of diasporization always needs to be narrated in transnational contexts, but at least until further notice it is bound to be played out in societies organized along the lines of the nation state.

Notes

1. This dilemma is constantly reiterated in the social sciences as well. To analyze ethnic and racial categorizations means not only to reproduce the ethnic nomenclature of a society but also to add some symbolic value to it. Social scientists who study ethnicity have to realize and recognize the fact "that to study it is to bring it continually into being" (Banks 1996, 189).

2. Ulf Hannerz (1974) has convincingly shown why and how ethnic self-empowerment within the history of the US was always intimately intertwined with economic interest group formation.

3. In an attempt to overcome the flaws of purely actor-centered perspectives, the "New Institutionalism" (Powell & DiMaggio 1991; Brubaker 1994) focuses its attention on the context-generating power of institutionalized settings to start out by generating collective actors. The ongoing ethnicization of US society cannot be understood without reference to the framing of institutional racism.

4. Racist exclusion seems to be an obvious cause for triggering ethnicization. But state imposed and institutionalized frames of 'multiculturalism' and 'cultural pluralism' can and do evoke similar effects.

5. Citizenship is a highly contested research site. While Saskia Sassen (1996) uses the term "economic citizenship" to analyze the impact of economic globalization on democracy, Nick Stevenson (1998) experiments with a concept of "cultural citizenship" to open up a horizon of "cultural cosmopolitanism". See also Jasemin Soysal's (1994) attempt at developing the new constellation from citizenship and human rights regimes, proposing the term "postnational membership".

6. The typical perception of diasporas as a kind of undercover organization of foreign forces by receiving states misses systematically the range of political fragmentation and is exactly this fragmentation that limits the opportunity structure of sending states to control their diasporas abroad. With respect to these limitations of symbolic power games, one could state that diasporas cannot be successfully dominated from the outside.

7. This particular tradeoff between discrimination abroad and heightened status at home seems to be limited to labor migrants.

8. David Harvey (1997, 26) reintroduced this concept of Raymond Williams with respect to communities.

CHAPTER 6

Migration, Identity Negotiation, and Self-Experience

Katherine Pratt Ewing

Modern law gives rise to a proliferation and naturalization of identities, creating and policing many of the categories that individuals are obliged to take up as identities. In the past few decades, identity has also become a key term in the "identity politics" that have erupted as a political issue in many parts of the world. In conflict after conflict based on identity politics, it is often the presumption on the part of participants and/or observers that such identities are rooted in a distinctive "culture" that must be preserved and defended. This idea of a fixed culture and the fixed identities that have emerged from it is itself a product of a recent global discourse that is played out in the media and has roots in certain older anthropological approaches that named cultures, drew boundaries between societies, and presumed that "cultures" were timeless traditions that needed to be studied before they "disappeared" under the pressures of modernity.[1]

Similarly, official policies that constitute ethnic, racial, and other identities also contribute to the essentialization of ethnicity as primordial or natural, thereby maintaining "minorities" as different from members of the dominant "culture". With respect to public and official discourses, the fixing of identities is a basic means by which the state contributes to the ordering of the social world. State authorities bestow identities through law, public policy, and routinized practices in everyday arenas as, for example, when a teacher in a German public school has each child in her classroom hold up a card naming "their" country for a class photo, so that a child born in Berlin whose grandparents come from Turkey is designated "Turkish". Specific laws—whether they be laws imposing restrictions on non-citizens or on certain classes of citizens, or even affirmative action legislation intended to enhance the rights and opportunities of minority groups—are statements embedded within a broader discourse that is also manifested in everyday practices that those labeled "ethnics" must regularly live with. Immigrant populations are defined by their collective identities and are referred to overtly as "ethnic minorities". As Soysal has pointed out in writing of the Netherlands, recent government measures "are designed to provide a bridge between migrant groups and Dutch institutions, which are presumed to be in natural disparity" (Soysal 1994, 50). This policy, a kind of social work approach, creates and naturalizes difference by bestowing identity, in the same movement by which it seeks to bridge difference.

Though most anthropologists present and past would question the validity of a static, bounded notion of culture, it continues to be taken up in one form or another in the name of preserving one's heritage as a basis for political struggle across the globe among groups seeking social rights, political voice, economic opportunity, and meaningful lives. At the same time, scholars, after focusing intensively on issues of identity with respect to ethnicity, race and gender, have begun to question the usefulness of "identity" as an analytic category. It is now generally recognized that such identities are not primordial and essential, though individuals inhabiting such identities or assigning such identities to others may claim them to be. Or, to put it another way, despite this scholarly questioning of identity as an analytic category, identities do exist in public culture and the social world; they are reified symbols and markers of social position and cultural difference that are embodied in individuals within specific social and political contexts. But an individual need not be the bearer of a single identity. One of the difficulties for governments that try to organize their populations in terms of discrete groups based on identity, as well as for social movements that strive to mobilize people on the basis of a common identity, is that individuals take up multiple, crosscutting identities. Common gender, for instance, may unite people organizing for women's rights, while at the same time ethnicity and race issues drive them apart. The issue of multiple, shifting, and negotiated identities is particularly salient for immigrants and minorities. Studies addressing the problems of "assimilation" of minorities often begin with the premise of fixed identities, as in the case of "Turks" in Germany, who continue to be identified as Turkish even when they are among the second or third generation to live in Germany. Along with the premise of identity as a fixed attribute often follows the

implicitly normative conclusion that such descendants of immigrants are likely to experience some form of identity confusion if
they cannot clearly identify themselves as either Turkish or
German. But if we instead begin with the premise that a single,
fixed identity is not the cornerstone of self-experience, it is
possible to focus instead on the fluidity of identity. As the individual moves from one arena to the next and from one set of
discursive practices to another, we may expect to see shifting identities, particularly if that individual occupies a radically different
structural position within each arena, as is often the case for those
who inhabit a minority identity. By the same token, ideologically
and bureaucratically imposed identities may or may not be taken
up as a subject position by the individual in a straightforward or
predictable way.

The question thus becomes: how, to what extent, and in what
situations do individuals inhabit and negotiate such reified identities? In this chapter, I consider how individuals manifest multiple
identities, ask whether such multiplicity entails corresponding shifts
in self-experience, and suggest that we can specify situations where
the phenomenon of identity is not relevant or salient. I argue that
the experience of identities—the specific ways and the extent to
which they are taken on as "self"—depends in part upon the positioning of the individual as subject within a discourse that
constitutes a specific identity such as ethnic minority—process of
"identification", which are shaped by relations of power, authority,
solidarity, and emotional connection between the individual and
those others who bestow or deny identities.

Recently those studying identity as a political and cultural issue
have begun to consider the individual as the subject of identity negotiation and as a locus of multiple, even conflicting identities.[2] Paul
Gilroy (1993a), for instance, in his studies of modern diaspora, has
focused on "identifications" or "affiliations", rather than on fixed
identities, as ways of belonging. Stuart Hall has moved in a similar
direction. He has gained considerable recognition for his efforts to
characterize the experience of racial identifications among minorities in Britain. He has also questioned the nature of the subjectivity
that underpins the political process, recognizing the need to move
away from conceptions of the political subject and political action
based on a unified identity and the rational calculation of interests
(Hall 1995, 63). He addresses both of these issues—the experience of
racial identity and the nature of the political subject—by focusing on
the process of "identification", a concept that allows him to

destabilize the popular notion of fixed identities that is often at the heart of ideologies associated with identity politics. In his use of the concept of identification, Hall creates an uneasy synthesis encompassing, on the one hand, an approach to political ideology and popular discourse inspired primarily by Foucault and Derrida and, on the other hand, what Hall calls a "cautious step" toward Freudian psychoanalysis.

I find much that is congenial in Hall's approach to the problem of identity. In particular, I agree that looking at the process of identification in relationship to multiple, inconsistent ideologies is an extremely useful strategy for understanding how the subject negotiates identity and maintains multiple, often conflicting identities, a problem that has occupied me for a number of years. Hall defines identification very broadly as the moment when the subject takes a position from which to speak and is thus temporarily, but only temporarily, constituted by an ideology or discourse. In Hall's words: "By identity or identities, I mean the processes that constitute and continuously re-form the subject who has to act and speak in the social and cultural world" (Hall 1995, 65). From Foucault he adopts the proposition that the speaking subject is never outside representation but is discursively constituted within and through webs of power (Foucault 1978; 1984); from Derrida he takes the premise that when we speak, meanings are only momentarily fixed and are continually sliding as social situations (and power relations) change (Derrida 1978), and that the logic of identification involves a conjunction of socio-political and unconscious processes (Hall 1995, 65). In this sweeping juxtaposition of approaches, Hall does bring a sophisticated theory of signs and of the discursively constituted subject into clearer focus within debates about the nature of identity. But he focuses primarily on the instability of discourse and leaves the role of unconscious processes in identity formation undeveloped. I suggest that the concept of "identification" as Hall and others such as Paul Gilroy use it encompasses several processes that must be distinguished and articulated if we are to have a well-developed theory of identity formation and negotiation. Exploring these processes of identification requires taking the appropriation of psychoanalysis a cautious step further than Hall has done.[3] A more careful exploration of the process of identification is an important step in promoting a fuller understanding of the immigrant experience that goes beyond popular but superficial notions of identity such as that of "hybrid" or "halfie".

Contextualizing Shifting Identities

In an earlier paper (Ewing 1990) I have argued that people can be observed to project multiple, inconsistent self-representations that are context-dependent and may shift rapidly. These representations can be thought of as reifications of experience, reflexive efforts to articulate and objectify the fluidity of subjective experience. As I put it then:

> When we consider the temporal flow of experience, we can observe that individuals are continuously reconstituting themselves into new selves in response to internal and external stimuli. They construct these new selves from their available set of self-representations, which are based on cultural constructs. The particular developmental histories of these self-representations are shaped by the psychological processes [and the experiences] of the individual. As a result of these processes of self-reconstitution, an external observer may see shifts in self-presentation of which the participants in an interaction are unaware. These self-representations are accompanied by changes in other attitudes and in emotional state. (Ewing 1990, 258)

In that paper I also stressed that inconsistencies in these shifting self-representations stem in part from inconsistent cultural premises that are the stuff of cultural argument.

Hall, drawing on Derrida's and Foucault's theoretical language, has described what he calls identities in rather different terms. Nevertheless, there are significant parallels between his model of identities and my model of self-representations:

> I understand identities as points of suture, points of temporary attachment, as a way of understanding the constant transformations of who one is or as Foucault puts it, 'who one is to become'. You only discover who you are because of the identities you are required to take on, into which you are interpellated; but you must take up those positionalities, however, temporarily, in order to act at all. Identities are, as it were, the forms in which we are obliged to act, while always knowing that they are representations which can never be adequate to the subject processes that are temporarily invested in them. Identities also have histories, within the discourses which construct or narrate them, and they are going to be transformed.
>
> ... In the same way, you have to take a position in order to say anything, even though meaning refuses to be finally fixed and that position is an often contradictory holding operation rather than a position of truth. (Hall 1995, 64-65)

In each of these models, dialogues contain rapid, even unintentional shifts in premises about the nature of the immediate situation. Frequently, the speaker juxtaposes contradictory positions without attempting to integrate them. In other cases the speaker makes some effort at synthesis or integration, whether in the past or in the current conversation. Narrative often plays an important role in this process of integration.

Given the parallels I have highlighted, what is the relationship between what I have called "self-representations" and what Hall calls "identities"? Are we simply using different words for the same thing? I argue that these concepts should be distinguished. A key difference in emphasis between the two quoted passages is that Hall stressed the discursive histories (public discourses that constitute the subject) of identities to which individuals are temporarily attached as subjects, while I stressed the personal histories of the self-representations that the individual takes up. I would limit identities to articulated self-representations—those that have been taken up into discourse. Hall also implied that identification is a self-conscious process, while I emphasized that the individual may be quite unaware of shifts in positioning.[4] But at the point when the speaker not only looks back self-reflexively, but also attaches a label to the subject position they have occupied, that label becomes an identity.

Thus, much of the time, I argue, we do not speak from specifiable identities. The apparently all-pervasive importance of identities stems from a global discursive shift in the late twentieth century away from a discourse of assimilation associated with the vision of the modern nation-state as the basic constituent of a global and political social order to a discourse of multiculturalism and the associated spatial juxtaposition of culturally diverse groups whose members defend their particular "identities" and cultural practices in specific social contexts and a variety of political arenas, not all of them nationally or territorially based. I will demonstrate in the following sections the loose and fluid relationship between the identities that an individual explicitly inhabits as a subject position in such public arenas, self-representations that may be more implicit, and the processes of unconscious identification.

Slippage in the Discursive Constitution of Identity

A key aspect of the process of taking up identities is its fluidity: the meaning of one's statements and the position from which one speaks are in flux, identities are constantly shifting, and they move in and out of focus. We can see this fluidity in meaning at the level of public discourse—the level that Hall stressed—with respect to the meaning and discursive history of the headscarf among Turkish Muslim women. The headscarf is a highly visible identity marker that has been the focus of contestation in the media, the courts, and other public arenas not only in Turkey but also in several European countries. The decision to wear a headscarf is an explicit assertion of identity, but the discursive meaning of this identity is not fixed. It shifts not only with respect to specific moments in time, but also with respect to location—whether within Turkey or in a diasporic setting such as Germany, or even more precisely, at one specific university or another, in one neighborhood or another, and also with respect to the immediate interlocutors in a specific situation. The decision to cover, as a "conscious" Muslim woman in urban Turkey, was an unusual one in the early 1980s during the headscarf controversy (see Olsen 1985; Ewing 2000a), when women began to contest a ban on headscarves in state buildings that had been in place since the 1920s. The women who took on this identity at that time formed a vanguard of the Islamist movement in Turkey. Wearing a headscarf to school was perceived by others as active political protest, whatever the intentions of the wearer, and such women were interpellated or given the identity of "radical Islamist" in public discourse. When I was in Istanbul in 1995, I spoke with a number of women who had adopted the headscarf in the 1980s. Several of them expressed an experience of sharp disjunction between this externally imposed identity as political activist and their identities and self-representations as they experienced them among other covered women and practicing Muslims.

But the meaning of the headscarf as a sign and, hence, the identities of covered women are in constant flux as the political situation changes and as the social situation of each individual woman changes. Given the political vicissitudes of Islamization and the headscarf issue in Turkey, young women who decide to cover themselves may or may not face active and absolute prohibitions at their high schools and universities and, when they do join the movement, they are likely to become part of a sizeable yet close-knit community of like-minded students at their school or university. Covering is for many a way of belonging and of managing the conflicts and anxieties associated with moving to a big city for study or work.

This headscarf struggle is relevant for migrants and the children of Turkish migrants in Germany and the Netherlands. Because the headscarf has become a clearly focused sign of identity that also embodies an explicitly articulated position of resistance to what is portrayed as the illegitimate authority of the Turkish state, it readily becomes an aspect of identity to covered women in Germany and an important element of the meaning to them of living in Germany, where they are generally allowed to wear headscarves unimpeded. A 21-year-old covered woman who had lived her whole life in Berlin, for instance, was familiar in great detail with several films made in Turkey that offer models for how a young woman comes to realize that being covered is the only way to really experience God. But in these films each personal realization is placed within the context of a struggle against state-sanctioned secularism and against the banning of headscarves in universities. She had attended a talk given at one of the Turkish mosques of Berlin's Islamic Federation by a covered speaker who had experienced the struggle first-hand, and she had seen images of sit-down protests that are broadcast on news programs from Turkey. She had imagined what she would do if faced with a choice between education and her headscarf in her university and clearly identified with the activists she had seen.

The meaning of the headscarf in countries such as Germany, the Netherlands, and France is also shaped in public discourse within these countries, most explicitly in the courts. Here, too, these meanings and associated identity constructions are publicly contested and differ from one country to the next. In secularist France, which strictly bars religious activity in state schools, the headscarf was officially defined as a political symbol of "fundamentalist Islam", thereby justifying the banning of the headscarf in state schools and bestowing the identity of fundamentalist on a girl who tries to wear such a headscarf to school. In Germany, where religion, in contrast, has a constitutionally mandated place in the classroom, the wearing of a headscarf has for the most part been defined in terms of freedom of individual religious expression. Its meaning as an identity-marker has, therefore, been officially designated as and limited to "Muslim" in most classroom settings. But even in Germany, local fear of politically radical undertones has emerged in cases of covered Muslim women who have sought unsuccessfully to teach in state schools and have challenged their dismissals in the courts. In such cases, an argument has been made by some observers that the headscarf is primarily an ideological symbol that should not be imposed on children in the classroom, a position similar to that taken by the French government (see Ewing 2000b).

But in everyday classroom settings in Germany, the headscarf does not always serve to foreground even a Muslim identity. For most ordinary classroom interactions, "identity" of one sort or another needn't always be salient. The Turkish-German covered woman described above, who was so ready to think in terms of the

politics of the headscarf when speaking about Turkey, tried to articulate an actual absence of identity as bestowed by the headscarf (or
at least an identity quite different from that of "other", as was
marked by Turkish politics) by describing the reactions of her classmates when she first began to wear the headscarf, just before she
entered sixth grade. She said that, in that transition from fifth to sixth
grade, her classmates, who were of diverse backgrounds, did not
change in their behavior toward her—she did not suddenly feel like
a different person when interacting with them. By the end of sixth
grade, she said that classmates hadn't remembered that she had ever
not been covered. In this story she sought to articulate her sense that,
even with a visible marker of identity such as the headscarf, her classmates did not in everyday interaction constitute her in terms of this
categorical identity, but rather in terms of her unique histories with
each of them. These interactions would encompass the range of often
implicit representations of self and other such as "friend", "smart
girl", etc.

Inhabiting Discursive Identities

Despite the power and authority of the state and public culture to
impose identity, such identities, even when accepted, may not be
fully inhabited. The formation of new nations in the immediate
postcolonial era was accompanied by policies intended to create
citizens with a "national" identity, with governments trying to
replace local identities with national ones, a process of indoctrination
often accomplished through techniques such as universal education
(with a curriculum that includes "civics" courses in schools, and
through the constitution of a militarized, male national identity
through the draft (Altinay 1999)—intended to be a total experience
that molds the body and the psyche at all levels, leaving no gap
between identity and self experience.

Clearly, the rise in the salience of ethnic identities within and
across the borders of nation-states has already demonstrated the
failure (or the erroneous premises) of such efforts to constitute
national identity as a core identity: a discourse of fanatic loyalty to
one's "motherland" or "fatherland" sounds rather hollow and
anachronistic today. Nevertheless, with the dramatic rise in migration across national borders in recent decades, there have been
agonizing national debates and the emergence of a literature on the
problems of dual citizenship (e.g. Miller 1998; Shevchuk 1996; Spiro
1997). Dual citizenship is presumed to be a challenge to the logic of

national identity, with its expectation of an undivided loyalty on the part of citizens who have internalized this identity.

Not surprisingly, at the most "official" level of one's passport or passports, citizenship may not shape identity in contexts much beyond the visas one must obtain when traveling or the immigration lines one has to wait in when trying to enter a country. It is not a matter of competing identities and loyalties. For many immigrants faced with a choice of nationality, the key issue is not identity but opportunities for or constraints on sheer physical, bodily mobility and action. In the present era, models of identity that presume a strategic, rational actor do seem to apply to the citizenship decisions that many migrants face. Having been labeled a specific ethnic minority, families and individuals are subject to constraints on their mobility that they respond to strategically. Further, government policies on citizenship and immigration may shape people's actions in unexpected ways that would seem to be quite divorced from the issue of identity at together.

For example, with the new law in Germany regarding citizenship, individuals are now in a position to (and are forced to) make a choice about being a Turkish or a German citizen. Many families have responded strategically and as individuals to this opportunity with little apparent concern for identity issues. Consider the following Kreuzberg family, long-term residents of Berlin: the grandparents, after spending several years in Germany (having brought their teenage children with them in the 1970s) returned permanently to Turkey a few years ago, leaving all their children and grandchildren behind in Germany. They wanted to continue to be able to visit their descendants, but as Turkish citizens they had been forced to visit Germany every six months or lose their visiting rights altogether. Two trips a year were more than they found convenient. With the new citizenship law, they opted for German citizenship, so that they would not have to visit as often. Though this choice may also limit their options or rights in Turkey—such as the ability to own land—personal networks and relationships of trust provide ways to work around such constraints.

Other members of the family also opted for German citizenship because they knew that they would be able to move more freely with a German passport than a Turkish one. The one exception was the family's 21-year-old son. He decided to remain a Turkish citizen because he does not want to serve in the German military. The ironic consequence of this choice is that he, the only family member to remain Turkish, is the one member of the family who will not be able even to visit Turkey, because if he did, he would be subject to the Turkish draft. This young man clearly does not see military service as a desirable rite of passage into full national identity, in either country.

A conversation with a group of teenage, covered Muslim girls at a mosque in Kreuzberg in Berlin further demonstrates the low salience of national identity, but also how the specific meaning of "German" national identity excludes these girls from taking on the identity of "German". All of the approximately 12 girls I spoke with were born in Germany and expressed no intention of ever moving to Turkey. Within the context of a larger conversation, we began a discussion about the issue of identity with my question about whether they saw themselves as Turkish or German. One girl gave the "hybridity" answer to the issue of national identity, saying that she was "50-50". Another said, "Nationality cannot be changed—it is Turkish. I have a Turkish passport." But another girl immediately responded, "I want to get a German passport, but my parents are Turkish, so I have to wait until I am 16. You have more rights with a German passport." And another added, "It makes no difference if someone is Turkish or German. The important thing is living in peace and freedom." Because of restrictions on wearing a headscarf in Turkey, they all concurred that peace and freedom are possible in Germany, but not in Turkey. For most of them, choice of the passport is explicitly a matter of what will give them more rights and opportunities, just as for the family I described above. The girl who said that the label "Turkish" or "German" makes no difference focused, not on identity, but on the unimpeded practice of everyday life, where, ideally, one is not forced to look back at one's actions and self-consciously label them in terms of identity.

But what about the girl who said that nationality cannot be changed? Clearly, she was wrong with respect to the passport issue (and was immediately corrected by another girl). To interpret her statement, it is important to note that it was uttered, not within the context of the passport discussion, but in the context of the idea of being "German". In contrast to American citizenship, Germanness is an identity that is not simply a matter of living within the territory of the German nation-state, and the bestowing of German citizenship occurs in very different ways among different ethnic groups, instantiating the particular principles of German identity, which are rooted in an idea of ethnicity through "blood" that excludes anyone who carries an identity of "Turk". It is not a matter of language: these girls are fluent German speakers, while many people from other countries who have automatically become "German" citizens cannot speak German. Given this discourse of Germanness and associated immigration policies, inhabiting a German identity in this sense of German blood is not possible for these girls, whether or not they acquire German passports or become culturally German. But in another context—for example, at an airport immigration desk—they may inhabit unproblematically a German identity.

The identity of people in the position of these girls is also not a matter of being "50-50", except in the context of our abstract discussion in the mosque or in academic and popular discourse about hybridity (Bhabha 1993; Werbner & Modood 1997). Even if the celebration of hybridity in academic discourse and in the media has created a new form of identity to be taken on—one that creates new expressive possibilities in cinema and literature and in other specific contexts—hybridity is no more a totalized, fully inhabitable or fully adequate form of identity than are the ill-fitting labels of "Turk", "immigrant", or "German". If and when one identity or another is taken up and experienced as "self", is always a matter of social context, goals and constraints.

For those concerned with issues of national identity and loyalty, evidence of such strategic decision making may well be disturbing. But for those who are suspicious of emotionally charged nationalism and the xenophobia it may generate, the apparent absence of such sentiment may be welcome and suggests a kind of "cosmopolitanism" that is recently being celebrated (see van der Veer, Schiffauer, this volume). Sahlins has accused approaches to culture and identity that presume such strategic motivation of ignoring "cultural structuration" of difference, which he sees playing out in "an expanding segmentary scheme, involving the objectification of ethnic-cultural entities on regional, national, and international lands", based on ordering principles that are manifest in epitomizing symbols but that do not normally rise to consciousness (Sahlins 1999, 409). But the primacy of strategic thinking in the taking up of national identity would suggest that many immigrants do not experience national identity from within such a cultural structure.

On the other hand, for some Turkish immigrants—though only some—religious identity is another matter, and the symbolic organization of Muslim identity vis-à-vis non-Muslim identity may take on the sort of dyadic structuration that Sahlins describes. This kind of deeply resonating structure of signs is projected in the media from both sides. For instance, while in Berlin, I watched a Turkish film, *Danimarkali Gelin* [*Danish Bride*] (Diriklik 1993), that was given to me by a covered Muslim woman born in Berlin. The film portrays a worldly Turkish Muslim who meets a young Christian woman in Europe. They decide to marry, and she converts to Islam for the marriage. They move to urban Turkey, where they live in close contact with his family. Though her national and cultural difference is at first foregrounded by her light blond hair, it is rapidly pushed to the background by the total absence of any other cultural difference—most unrealistically, she speaks totally fluent Turkish. The plot revolves around the European bride's increasing devotion to the proper observance of Islam and the tensions this produces within the groom's Muslim but minimally observant family. There is a moment in the film that depicts precisely the kind of dyadic structuration with its strong emotional charge that Sahlins is talking about: One evening a young Turkish niece is playing and, in play, gets on her knees and folds her hands in imitation of Christian prayer. The bride's response upon recognizing this posture is to hold her hand to her mouth and rush from the room, as if she is about to vomit. In contrast, she "naturally" feels an inner compulsion to become an increasingly devout, covered Muslim woman (at which point the blond hair that had made her stand out as different disappears beneath the headscarf). The intentions of this highly didactic film are transparent. In projecting the inherent rightness of being a proper Muslim, it minimizes the significance of national and cultural difference but creates two absolute dichotomies: between Islam and Christianity on the one hand, and between devotion to Islam and corrupt secularism on the other. The bride has been depicted as fully inhabiting the identity of Muslim. In the non-Muslim imaginary, this gut-wrenching form of identity inhabiting is experienced as something to be feared. It reduces the non-Muslim to nauseating other.

There are people who inhabit identities in this way, at least temporarily or in specific contexts.[5] Both media and scholarly attention tends to focus on such identities, as in the popular media phrase, "Islamic terrorist". Among anthropologists, Werner Schiffauer (1999) has conducted ethnographic interviewing among second generation Turkish-German young men caught up in the Islamist community of Cemaleddin Kaplan, which in the 1980s saw itself as the spearhead of an Islamic revolution aiming to replace Turkey's secularist government with an Islamic regime. Schiffauer found that such young men, though cosmopolitan in background, with exposure to multiple cultures and sophisticated educational training, consciously rejected a cosmopolitan identification because of their experience of discrimination, while also rejecting the lifestyle of their parents' generation and overt identification with their parents.

This taking up of a clearly defined and bounded identity thus involves managing conflict and inconsistency by rejecting competing identities that are organized in terms of a structure of oppositions. This is a very specific way of organizing multiple, inconsistent identities that is by no means characteristic of most Muslims today. In getting to know even devout covered Muslim women in Berlin, I found that most had not organized their identities in this way and, instead, moved quite fluidly through a German environment.

Identities and Self-representations

Though clearly a sharp distinction cannot be made between "identity" and "self-representation", I am using the term identity to refer to the assumption of categories that are explicitly articulated by the individual and others, in part because they are constituted in public discourse such as the law, popular culture, and ideologies. Identities would, then, include such categories as "woman", "educated person", "Turk", "immigrant", "hybrid", etc. Self-representations and self-experience must, of course, include one's identities but also one's affective, historical, and bodily relationships to such identities. One can speak from a position that presumes such attitudes as, "I feel stupid", or "my parents embarrass me", or "I feel out of place here". These are self- experiences and representations based on contextually specific patterns of interactions with others, though they can also tie into discursive constructions of identity as, for example the categories "smart" and its covert or euphemistically articulated opposites such as "slow", "stupid", "ordinary", that are identity-producing labels readily attached to children in school settings. The power of such identity labels comes both from the associative links, overt and covert, that are made between such labels and ethnic identity, and from how they coincide with existing self-representations.

The explicit labeling of identity in schools often occurs in the everyday practices of teachers, whose attitudes as authorities have an impact on self-representations of the children they teach, as in the example I mentioned above of a class picture taken of ten year olds in a German public school in the Kreuzberg section of Berlin. In this photograph, the children all held identifying cards. The cards displayed, not their names, but the country of each child's supposed origin. Of the 20 or so children, four were labeled Deutschland, one

Bosnia, and the rest Turkei. This concrete identification occurred despite the fact that virtually all the Turkish children were born in Berlin and potentially held German citizenship. In the Netherlands, schools that have an almost exclusively minority population are often labeled "black" schools. To an American eye and ear, such practices display a blatant lack of sensitivity to issues of difference and discrimination, accustomed as Americans are to a public discourse in which identity differences are in many situations studiously ignored in silence.

But the American strategy of silence may shape self-experience and self-representations in ways that are just as insidious and even more difficult to resist than are explicit identities and labeling, as studies of self-fulfilling prophesies (Jussim 1986) and the "expectancy model" (Miller & Turnbull 1986) suggest. According to this model, holders of stereotypic beliefs and expectations treat others in ways that result in the others' conforming to those expectations (see Nuckolls 1998, 167).[6] Such studies suggest that covert identity labels can be taken on as self- experience through implicit communications on the part of these teachers.

Another Turkish-German woman I talked with had grown up in Berlin, was in training to become an elementary school teacher, and was working toward her MA from Technical University. Her recent education classes had led her to reflect on her own elementary school experiences. She described how the classes had given her a new perspective on the feelings of inferiority that she has experienced as a child in school. She now realized that teachers had in many situations made it clear that they did not expect her to do as well in language arts courses as her "German" classmates, despite her native fluency. Her reaction had been to prove that she could do as well. Nevertheless, she hadn't been fully aware as a child that she was being treated as "Turkish", an identity with the attributes of ignorance and poor school preparation attached to it, but had instead experienced the discrimination as a personal judgment, that she partially internalized as a self-representation.

The experience of such identities—the specific ways they are taken on as self- representations—depends in part upon the significance of the authorities by whom they are bestowed. Freudian-influenced models of the mind suggest that fantasies of order and authority are a key component in the organization of the ego or self, articulated in concepts ranging from Freud's "superego" to Lacan's "Symbolic Order". Althusser (1971) and more recently Zizek (1989) have sought to link up these intra-psychic images of authority, as well as the dynamics of desire, with political processes, creating models for the structure of political fantasy. Such images of order and authority, based on both fantasy and practical experience, are an important aspect of self-experience and are profoundly shaped by one's social positioning, class, and personal history. Such experiences of the self *vis-à-vis* images of authority may actually be inconsistent with one's adult identities, creating intra-psychic and interpersonal inconsistencies and even conflicts that may be difficult to resolve or manage. I argue that "identity" and the concept of shifting identifications as Hall formulates it should be distinguished from the issue of self-experience as constituted through implicit identifications. For members of an ethnic minority, the field of images of authority may be very complex and particularly fraught with images that are not only inconsistent but also contradictory. Individual members of such a minority may draw on different strategies to negotiate an array of identities, for example, by renouncing one or more identities while ideologically embracing another, as in the case of the teenager who rejects a Turkish identity altogether or who rejects German culture and takes up a radical Muslim identity (see Schiffauer 1999), or by contextualizing and tightly compartmentalizing inconsistent identities. Whatever strategy is used, implicit self-representations may be organized quite differently. They may actually cross cultural boundaries that separate one marked identity from another.

To illustrate this, I will briefly summarize the situation of a Turkish-Dutch woman whom I first met in The Hague four days after she had run away from her husband. Her story of the events leading up to her dramatic departure reveals both her long-term strategies for negotiating identities that were radically disjunctive and the stresses that caused her strategies to break down. In addition, because I met her at a time of crisis, more implicit aspects of her self-organization—by which I mean the organization of her self-representations—were more visible than they might otherwise have been in more settled times.[7]

Nergis was 23 years old, the daughter of a Turkish "guest worker" whom I met in The Hague four days after she had run away from her husband. Engaged at age 11 to a cousin still in Turkey, Nergis had, by her own account, been forced into an arranged marriage at age 18. The fight that precipitated her departure from her husband was the final round in a long-term dispute over money. Educated in Dutch schools (in the later years of her education, her determination to continue studying was at odds with her parents' wishes), Nergis had a professional job, while her husband, an illegal immigrant brought to the Netherlands for the marriage, was an unskilled laborer. Thus in one world, she was a young Dutch professional in a well-paying job with a promising future. In another, she was structurally powerless—an ethnic Turk and new mother whose daily life was tightly constrained by her husband and family, who themselves lived on the margins of Dutch society. She and her husband had sent money that she had earned to her in-laws in Istanbul to buy an apartment for them. One of the conditions that Nergis had insisted upon was that the apartment be in her own name, since she had paid for it. The fight erupted when her husband informed her that they would not put the apartment into her name. When she protested, her husband said to her, "Who are you that you think they should put it in your name?"

In her story of leaving her husband, Nergis articulated a frustration with her self-experience as a "money machine". In her description of the fight, the "money machine" stands in implicit contrast with her own desire to be recognized as someone who earns money in her own right and who owns property. Her professional status and income give her an identity as an autonomous individual, a professional woman, and a property-holder. Her husband spoke from a different discourse, in which the family collectively controls resources, including those of adult sons, and the husband is officially the sole authority and decision maker, the representative of the family to the outside world. In this frame of meaning, she is a wife who should be guarded and protected.

Nergis had compartmentalized two distinct identities, dividing her time between these worlds for many years, but her marital situation and her income had created a contradiction, turning her into a money machine. It was ultimately this contradiction, at one level a result of Dutch immigration policies that allow immigration only for the spouse of a resident, that pushed her to disrupt the balance she had achieved: her husband and family wanted to exploit her earnings while denying her the power and respect that she felt should accompany her ability to earn.

But other aspects of Nergis' situation offer a balance to the notion that the self is constituted by the identities conferred through the gaze/judgment/power of the other or by a discourse such as the law in any simple way. Nergis has not been fully constituted in an identity as an autonomous, individual self by a bourgeois legal discourse, nor has she been located as a Turkish girl who is naturally different from the Dutch, fully inhabiting the identity of protected wife. Nor does she simply jump between incommensurable worlds, and never in our conversations did she articulate her identity in terms of "50-50".

As evidenced by her description of her school and professional career, Nergis had always been a powerful person within her family's world, though occupying a subject-position or identity that was very subordinate. In her early years of schooling, she had managed to transfer out of what she called a "black" school, forming alliances with teachers who recognized her academic potential and lobbied on her behalf. At home, she would push her parents to accede to her wishes and pull back just before they retaliated by setting limits. Strategically, she hadn't pushed to get a full university education, because she had feared that they could prevent it, leaving her with nothing. "I let my mother know how much I didn't want this marriage, but at a certain point, I hid my objections because I was afraid that if they thought I wouldn't go through with it, they would prevent me from continuing in school." When during her teen years marriage arrangements would escalate too much and her resistance became more overt, her parents would threaten to take her out of school: "Then I would submit and be quiet about my feelings." The decision to accede to the marriage had thus been a product of strategic negotiations, in which her parents and her fiancé agreed to let her finish the training program that she had selected as a shorter alternative to the university, allowing her to continue to attend classes even after marriage.

She told stories of her mother resorting to magic in order to win Nergis over to the idea of this arranged marriage. Though Nergis resisted her mother's wishes, she nevertheless shared her mother's world in the telling of these stories, which emphasized Nergis' ability to disrupt the magic rather than a stance debunking the whole idea of its effectiveness. The premise was that magic works but can be escaped through careful and clever maneuvering. Projected in many of her stories, including this one, was a self-representation as smart, clever, and resourceful, in this case, within a culturally Turkish setting of evading magic. This self-representation also carried into her depiction of her ability to choose a practical and feasible career, and in her descriptions of her effectiveness on the job. It thus transcends the boundaries between her two identities as Turkish wife and Dutch professional. Nergis also described several powerful people in her life, including her grandmother, her parents, the *imam* at the mosque (who sided with her mother in trying to convince her to accept the marriage), her teachers, in elementary school, and her boss. The self-representations she maintains exist in relationship to these others yet, like her image of herself as clever and resourceful, also cross the cultural divide. For instance, another self-representation that had been a powerful factor in her submission to the marriage was that of "good girl", which she had wished to preserve. When she was describing her late adolescence, she contrasted herself with her best friend and with other young women who had run away with men or who had gotten involved in activities defined as "corrupt" by the Turkish community. To maintain this identity as a good girl, she had let there be a discrepancy between her parents' view of her and her "feelings". Similarly, she mentioned several times how people in the community thought it was an ideal marriage, because she always went along with things in public. When she left her husband, she temporarily let go of this image of "good girl", though she was later able to reclaim it when, following divorce, the conflict with her family was resolved. But this representation was important in her approach both to school and to work, where she had formed such positive relationships with her teachers and her boss that she was able to enlist their help in contesting her parents' wishes: Her teachers had supported her move to a more distant but academically superior school, and her boss (and his wife) had offered her a place to stay when she left her husband and got thoroughly caught up in the drama of hiding her from her husband and family.

To give another example of how an implicit self-representation might not be associated with a discursively articulated identity, I turn to the example of a young woman whom I knew quite well in Pakistan and in the United States after she had moved there upon her marriage. I knew her well enough that I presume to be able to read between the lines of her explicit utterances because of our shared experiences. At certain points in our interaction, she expressed fantasies of how she would help support her parents that, along with other evidence, I interpreted as a manifestation of a long-standing self representation involving the fantasy of being a son (sons are highly valued in Pakistan, and the fact that she was a second daughter had been quite explicitly a disappointment to her parents when she was a small child).[8] This fantasy was a position from which she spoke, to use Hall's terminology. Yet it was one that she would never acknowledge overtly—being a son was not one of her "identities" and, given the organization of her gender identity, could not be acknowledged as a desire. But my presence as a professional woman offered her an opportunity for an explicit fantasy that was a kind of compromise solution. She identified with her image of me as a professional woman—an image that could have become an articulated "identity" had she pursued it.

Identification and Identities

I have already discussed the often loose connection between identities and self-representations. We inhabit discursive identities only partially and intermittently. Hall has chosen the term "identification" in order to characterize this fluid relationship between discursively constituted identities and the subject or agent in order to emphasize its processual nature. Though Hall also suggests that he is taking into account Freud's usage of the term identification, identification is a very specific process in Freud's theory. In "Mourning and Melancholia" (Freud 1957), identification with a loved "object" is a response to loss: Libidinal attachment is replaced by introjection and a narcissistic investment in the identification. Identification is thus a process, often unconscious, in which the subject in some manner becomes like the lost object. It is quite different from identity understood as a discursive position in Hall's sense. Though Hall does allude to Freud's association of the process of identification with loss and ambivalence (Hall 1997, 3), I do not see that this aspect of identification is integrated into his approach to identification. With identification in Hall's sense, the process involves a direct, temporary assumption of a subject position by the speaker who stands in relation to a discourse. Freud's process of identification, in contrast, always involves an ambivalent relationship with an image or fantasy of a significant other. In the case of the Pakistani woman who unconsciously identified with the image of being a son, loss is a central aspect of this identification, though it could not be described as identifying with the image of a lost loved one. One could say, rather, that she identified with her parents' unfulfilled desire and their image of loss for failing to have a son; in Lacanian terms, she intensely desired to be the object of their desire by identifying with this image. Taking into account this dimension of loss and its powerful affective charge moves considerations of identification and their relationship to the taking up of identities beyond the rather limited explanatory realm of strategic, pragmatic calculation.[9]

Considering the role of unconscious processes in identity formation does not mean reducing all to an underlying "psycho-sexual" dimension. The activation of desire is an important component of the process of assuming an identity, as Zizek (1989), drawing on Lacan, has explored in his work on the role of unsatisfiable desire in advertising and politics. But it is difficult to ponder the problem of identity without also coming around to issues of self-esteem and recognition.[10] Werner Schiffauer (1999), for instance, in his research among second-generation Turkish-German youth (a conflict-ridden "identity"), has suggested that a struggle for recognition motivates many of these youth to identify with radical Islamist groups. Schiffauer is using a psychologically based explanatory model, though its emphasis on recognition is phrased in terms that are more Hegelian than Freudian. His work suggests that issues surrounding the process of identification are central and that the relationship between culturally labeled identities on the one hand and, on the other hand, self-representations that have a history within the family and other settings of individual development is a problematic one for many of these youth.

During the course of development, the individual unconsciously identifies with aspects of significant others and takes on their specific attributes.[11] This is not simply a process of discursive representation, but includes mimesis—not only conscious, expressible imitation but also imitation in ways that both subject and object imitated may be unaware of—as a vitally important component. It is a process by which the subject develops self-representations, but these self-representations may or may not become explicit identities that the person may articulate discursively. As a next step, through a condensation of images—the superposition of several images in a process akin to metaphor (see Freud 1953)—the individual may attach a discursively constituted subject position, an "identity", to an already existing, perhaps implicit, self representation (with all of its associated affects and memories).

Issues of power and authority, which I have argued shape how identifications are taken up, come up most saliently in Freud's work with respect to his concept of "transference". This concept can also be used to characterize how representatives of the state or leaders of a social movement may be experienced as objects of fantasy. In the classic psychoanalytic transference in a clinical setting, a person experiences toward someone in his or her current environment thoughts and feelings that originally applied to an object of an attachment in childhood. Freud stressed transferences of various aspects of the child's experiences of the parents, though such objects of fantasy need not be limited to images of the parents. In a process of metaphorical condensation, the subject assimilates the image of one person to the image of another. While Freud exposed unconscious aspects of transference in a clinical setting during the process of psychoanalysis, demonstrating transferences that his patients were not aware of, this process of transference occurs at a more overt level all the time and is an important element of social interaction. For instance, in Schiffauer's story of an Islamist young man who strongly identified with the Islamist leader Cemaleddin Kaplan, Schiffauer suggested that this identification involved transference of the boy's identification with his grandfather onto the leader.

This metaphorical process of condensation and the "transference" of a fantasy image of, say, an authority figure onto a new person can readily cross the boundaries between identities, even when the individual negotiates these identities by strictly compartmentalizing them. We can see outlines of this process in Nergis' stories. Nergis "identifies" with the benign authority figures in her life, experiencing her relationships with her teachers and, later, her boss, in images similar to certain aspects of her relationships with her parents. I expect that if we had gone into more detail about the ups and downs of her school experiences, some of her teachers would also have sounded like the controlling, restrictive side of her parents that was foregrounded in our conversations because of the overt conflict she was in the midst of. Her tales of skipping school to be with her friends, for instance, suggest a strategic defiance very similar to her stance in resisting her parents' plans for her marriage. The reenactment of such patterns in very different social contexts creates personal consistencies across the cultural divide maintained by ethnicity. Conversely, inconsistent representations of self and other happen even within the home. Such phenomena affect and shape the ways an individual inhabits a discursively constituted identity, making an analysis of identity in terms of concepts such as "hybridity" inadequate.

Conclusion

There is one more methodological point that should be emphasized when examining processes of identification as points of interpellation with respect to public discourses on the one hand and as the history of an individual's self-representations on the other. In interpreting a person's utterances and action as an identity from which the person is speaking, it must not be presumed that an utterance is univocal for a specific moment in time and that it temporarily fixes a meaning and an interpellation that may at the next moment shift. Rather, much of the fluidity of identity comes from the fact that an utterance may be doing multiple things at once. Furthermore, these simultaneous multiple acts may be mutually inconsistent. Some of these inconsistencies, however, may move toward resolution through narrative—through telling stories. Narrative, more than simply being the way identity is expressed, is, due to its particular attributes and structure, a point of intersection between unconscious processes and identity negotiation.

In most social situations, many identities may be activated at once. It is in polarized situations when individuals are perceived, not in terms of a complex array of potential identities and relationships, but rather as embodying a single, fixed identity—an ethnicity or a race—that the potential for discrimination and even violence is greatest and more rigid strategies of identity maintenance may be resorted to. A possible strategy for overcoming the Turkish-German divide in Germany is not necessarily for those identified as Turkish to simply "assimilate" by shedding markers of identity that make them different from Germans, but rather for their multiplex identities to be recognized in public discourses.

Notes

1. However, see Sahlins (1999) for an insightful challenge to this particular "post-modern" critique of classical anthropological theory. Sahlins points out that earlier anthropological theorizing did, in fact, recognize the inconsistency and fluidity of cultures. On the other hand, I would argue that the notion of culture as it has been taken up politically frequently does have the quality of static tradition, if only as a form of strategic essentialism.
2. "Identity" first emerged as a theoretical concept focused on the individual. Within psychology it was elaborated most notably in the work of the Freudian-inspired ego psychologist Erik Erikson (1980) and within sociology in the work of G.H. Mead and Cooley (see Cerulo 1997; Strykes 1992). Erikson, strongly influenced by cultural anthropology, was concerned with the cultural shaping of identity, while work inspired by Mead and Cooley, what is often called "microsociology", focused on how interpersonal interactions shape individual identity and sense of self. But those studying ethnic and political identity generally approach it, not from the perspective of the constitution of individual identity, but with a focus on discursive processes or on collective identity as a property of groups.
3. This is something that Hall may have been understandably reluctant to do given academic politics and the resistance to anything psychological that characterize many social scientists. At one point Hall alludes to what the "unconscious processes" actually include but only by attributing the characterization to a respected colleague rather than to Freud: "what Jacqueline calls psycho-sexual processes." (Hall 1995, 64) This is actually a far narrower take on what constitutes unconscious processes than even most psychoanalysts would accept today.

4. Hall's emphasis on the temporary and partial nature of identities taken up in a self-conscious fashion is reminiscent of Gayatri Spivak's (1990) concept of "strategic essentialism", meant to identify an explicitly political strategy of resistance for minorities. Hall's own position as a spokesperson for black minorities and champion of a "black" popular culture has itself involved strategic academic writings; his emphasis on the partial, fluid, and contradictory quality of one's identities is no doubt autobiographical.

5. Beginning with the psychologist William James, there has been scholarship devoted to identity transformations that accompany religious conversion, and the joining of religious movements and this phenomenon may be a special way of inhabiting an identity. But it is not generally applicable to the way most people inhabit even religious identities on a day-to-day basis.

6. In an experimental study of self-fulfilling prophecies, Rosenthal and Jacobson (1968) induced teachers to believe that some of their students, selected at random, were gifted. Following this intervention, this group of students was more academically successful than their classmates.

7. For a more detailed account and analysis of this woman's story, see Ewing (2001).

8. See Ewing (1990) for a more detailed discussion of this case.

9. This is a criticism that has been made of the work of identity theorists. Sahlins (1999), for instance, has decried the "functionalism" of such work. He would put forth, instead, an emphasis on how "structure" imbues identity markers with a Durkheimian sacredness, which I take to mean an affective charge erupting from collective effervescence. I don't see this explanation as incompatible with one that focuses on more individually specific sources of affect, since the symbols in terms of which identities are reified are multivocal, imbued with multiple layers of meaning, as Victor Turner (1967), in trying to synthesize Durkheimian and Freudian approaches, so brilliantly articulated.

10. Freud attempted to explain self esteem and what he called "narcissism" in terms of a model of libido turned back on itself, but subsequent theorists, including psychoanalysts, have suggested that self-esteem, ego formation and identity issues, are a distinct "strand" of development and see problems with self-esteem as being based on "deficit"—a lack of self-regulating mechanisms—rather than on conflict, which is at the core of Freud's model.

11. Within psychoanalytic circles, especially among ego psychologists such as Hartmann (1964) and Erikson (1980), "identification" was considered to be the fundamental process by which the ego is formed.

CHAPTER 7

It Is Not Where You Are From, It Is Where You Are At: Place-Based Alternatives to Diaspora Discourses[1]

Arif Dirlik

I reflect below on some questions raised by recent controversies in US politics concerning Chinese political and espionage activity. The questions I am interested in are those that bear upon Americans of Chinese descent, who have become implicated almost inevitably in conflicts involving two states, the one representing their society of origin, the other representing the society of their arrival, residence, citizenship, and/or birth. Three questions are foremost in the discussion: the question of anti-Chinese racism, the complexities introduced into the question of Chinese-American identity by new patterns of migration, and the possible complicity in fostering racial representations of Chinese-Americans of putatively progressive discourses of globalization. It is the last question, however, that is the focus of my attention, as it is relevant to a consideration of how to resolve the problems presented by the first two questions. These questions obviously are relevant most immediately to the US, although they may have some bearing also on other societies where pressures from immigrant populations are forcing a reconsideration of questions of national identity and sovereignty.

My goal in this discussion is pedagogic in a fundamental sense: how to bring issues related to a new world situation into teaching activity; hopefully to stimulate progressive visions rather than visions that serve past or present configurations of power. I am equally concerned, at a more existential level, with our responsibilities as educators on how to deal with Chinese-American students who are puzzled by their cultural identities, when those identities include so many sensitive issues. Having analyzed the contemporary world in all its material and cultural complexity, how do we go convey to our students our sense of how to live in it, cope with it, and take sides in it? The answers are not abstract, even if the problems are. And they depend not just on identities, which are enormously complex, but also on self-identifications. The question is how to think through the implications and consequences of different self-identifications. Not a particularly new question, but one that seems to be entrapped presently between globalization and national identity, as if they set the limits to thinking about self-identification. Thinking places may be one way out of the entrapment. History, which may imprison or liberate depending on how it is used, may be another.

In early March 1999, a Chinese-American scientist of Taiwanese origin, Wen Ho Lee, was dismissed from his position as researcher in the Los Alamos laboratory on suspicion of having leaked nuclear secrets to People's Republic of China scientists. No formal charges were brought against Lee, as the evidence against him was entirely circumstantial: that he had travelled to the People's Republic of China (PRC) to attend scientific conferences, and spoken with Chinese scientists. Lee may have been a victim of real or contrived anti-Chinese feeling in the US congress, where Republicans seem to have discovered in the China threat an issue with which to harass the Democratic administration. The circumstances of his dismissal nevertheless have had a chilling effect on Chinese-Americans, especially the many Chinese-American scientists in US universities and government service, who perceive in the unofficial charges against Lee a threat that retaining ties to their place of origin will bring them under similar suspicion (Butterfield & Kahn 1999). Edward Liu, a San Francisco attorney, has described the suspicions against Lee as "guilt by ethnicity" (Liu 1999, 2). The demoralizing effect of the case has been such that Energy Secretary Bill Richardson had to reassure scientists of Chinese origin that the government would not permit "racial profiling" in its workplaces (*Los Angles Times* 12 June 1999).

The anxiety created by the Wen Ho Lee case might not have been so severe were it not for the fact that it followed on the heels of, and in some ways issued from, an earlier scandal concerning PRC involvement in American politics. This was the scandal over Democratic Party fundraising, centering around John Huang, another US citizen of Taiwanese origin, but eventually including a number of colorful, if shady, Chinese immigrant businessmen with names such as Charlie Trie and Johnny Chung. When Huang was charged with corruption on the grounds that he raised funds from foreign sources, the Democratic National Committee proceeded immediately to canvas all contributors with Chinese names to ascertain whether or not they were foreigners, turning a run-of-the-mill case of political corruption into a racial issue. The Committee's action reactivated the long-standing assumption that anyone with a Chinese name might in all probability be foreign, reaffirming implicitly that a Chinese name was the marker of racial foreignness. What followed may not have been entirely novel, but seemed quite logical neverthe-less in terms of contemporary diasporic "networks" (perhaps, more appropriately in this case, "webs"). John Huang's connections to the Riady family in Indonesia which surfaced quickly not only under-lined the probable foreignness of Chinese contributors, but also suggested further connections between Chinese-Americans and other Chinese Overseas that seemed to be confirmed by revelations that several other Chinese-American fundraisers, or contributors, had ties to Chinese in South and Southeast Asia, who in turn had business relations in the People's Republic of China. Congressional investigation further uncovered ties between Chinese-American contributors to the Democratic Party, and business people from the People's Republic with close ties to the military who had been active in acquiring advanced technologies from US companies. Before long a petty corruption case was to turn into a case of possible conspiracy that extended from Beijing, through Chinese Overseas to Chinese-Americans. These earlier findings have contributed both to lending credibility to the charges against Wen Ho Lee, and to the effects it produced among Chinese-Americans. The latter, it would seem, have become pawns in internal politics in the US, and the intrusion into American politics in recent years of growing hostility between the US and the Peoples Republic of China.

At one, and the most superficial, level, the implication of Chinese-Americans in threats to US national sovereignty and security may be viewed as a product of the legacy of anti-Asian racism that goes back to the 19th century, and continues to dominate political and popular thinking in the US despite professions of multiculturalism that have assigned to Asian Americans a privileged place in American society as the "model minority". Politicians who have pursued these cases with a vengeance, and their counterparts in the media who have done so much to publicize them, would no doubt deny that there is anything racist in their concerns for national security issues, and that they consciously target Chinese-Americans in their inquiries. Yet there is something obviously hypocritical in the assumptions that guide their inquiries. There may well be more than a grain of truth to the conviction that the government of the PRC may have engaged in activities to influence American politics, and sought one way or another to obtain technological/military information from the US On the other hand, influencing policy elsewhere (including in the PRC), to put it mildly, is a regular practice of the US government itself. And foreigners or natives lobbying to influence US foreign policy is an integral part of the functioning of the US government, of which the most prominent instance over the years may be the influence of the Jewish population in the US on shaping US policy toward Israel and the Arabs. If racism is not exactly the right word for it, that does not change the fact of discriminatory practices toward certain groups viewed to be alien or hostile to American national interests. And it so happens that in this case, the group involved is identifiable by certain physical and cultural markers (e.g. names) that usually serve racial identification. Given the history of attitudes toward Asian-Americans in the US, such discrimination is difficult to distinguish from racism plain and simple. For six decades, Chinese were barred from immigration to the US on the basis of their supposedly immutable characteristics, which represented a blurred admixture of cultural legacies and phenotypical endowments. During World War II, in what may be the most egregious case of racism toward Asian-Americans, Japanese-Americans, including those who were American by birthright, were forced into a US version of concentration camps. During the Korean War, with the US at war with the newly established People's Republic of China, Chinese in the US came under FBI supervision, even though many of the Chinese in the US were hostile to the People's Republic for a variety of reasons. With such a historical legacy, it is indeed difficult to escape the impression that in the present case, too, a racial unconscious is at work both in the condemnations of the PRC, and in the association of Asian-Americans with PRC activities. Not the least difficult aspect of the problem is the manner in which allegations concerning Chinese activity move easily from the activities of individuals to suspicion of the group as a whole.

This view is superficial not because it is wrong or misplaced, or because of its identification of racism as a root-problem of American society and politics, but because in its historicism it overlooks the very real problems presented by a world situation where the almost uncontrolled, and uncontrollable, movements of people have indeed made it nearly impossible to distinguish differences within the same ethnic group—say, between a fourth generation American of

Chinese descent and a newly arrived Chinese immigrant, whose political loyalties still are directed toward the country of origin. The loyalty of Chinese-Americans to the country of their origin is not an entirely new phenomenon. As early as the first decade of this century, Chinese in the US were courted by, and responded to, various political factions competing to overthrow the government of the Qing Dynasty (Armentrout-Ma 1990). During World War II, Chinese-Americans enthusiastically supported the Republican Government in China against the Japanese invasion, even lending their support to the incarceration of their fellow Americans, the Japanese-Americans (Weici & Shaosheng 1991, 20–31). In the 1960s, a younger generation of Chinese-Americans threw their support to the government of the PRC, whose revolutionary anti-colonial activities resonated with their own sense of being an "internal colony" in the US. Viewed in this perspective, the report that Chinese-Americans in San Francisco recently received Premier Zhu Rongji with enthusiasm, some of them referring to him as "our Premier", may not be too surprising.

Nevertheless, the issue of political loyalty is a complicated one. If Chinese-Americans have been concerned with the fate of China in the modern world, the wars, revolutions, and divisions that have marked the history of 20th century China have also divided them deeply, not to speak of the geographical, cultural, and social divisions that they have brought with them to the US (and elsewhere). The idea that all Chinese-Americans may be grouped around certain cultural and political loyalties is a ludicrous one, as is apparent with any close examination of Chinese-Americans, and their historical experiences, in the US and elsewhere. If some Chinese-Americans may see nothing wrong with John Huang collecting Riady money, others have voiced their protest against the channelling of "foreign money" into American politics.

The problem lies elsewhere: the rather impressive increase in the numbers of cmigrant Chinese, especially with the easing of restrictions on emigration in the PRC, and accompanying it, the increasing audibility of calls for a Chinese identity regardless of time and space that, ironically, nourishes off Chinese visibility in economic activity around the world, but especially in the so-called Pacific region. The number of Chinese in the US, kept low for decades by exclusion and subsequent immigration restrictions, has expanded rapidly since the passage of the Immigration Law of 1965, from 237,000 in 1960 to over 800,000 by 1980 and over 1,200,000 by 1990. And the numbers keep increasing. Along with the change in sheer numbers, there is a change as well in the composition of the immigrants from the majority of working people of peasant origin in the first century of immigration to educated, and wealthy, immigrants from urban areas around East and Southeast Asia. Perhaps more importantly, whereas in 1960 American-born Chinese made up 61 percent of the population, by 1980 the situation had been reversed, so that 63 percent of the population consisted of new immigrants. The increase over the last decade in the number of immigrants originating from the PRC also has added in many cases a group that is more self-assertively nationalistic in its commitments to China, to the point where they often come into conflict with earlier Chinese immigrants (Linter 1999).[2] Add to this the so-called "astronauts", who fly back and forth across the Pacific, often with homes on either side, whose "flexible citizenship" (Ong 1999) does not point to any clear national affinity, and the complexity of the situation is evident. Under the circumstances, the term "Chinese-American" itself has become quite problematic, as is evident in the increasing preference of many in recent years for the alternative term, "diasporic Chinese".

The latter term derives additional plausibility from the reconstruction of Chinese networks that nourish off the flourishing economies of East and Southeast Asia in which migrant Chinese have played an important part, not just in Southeast Asia but especially, in recent years, in the People's Republic of China. A by-product of this economic empowerment has been the emergence or newly acquired prominence of business and academic organizations that are devoted to facilitating intra-diasporic activities of one kind or another across national boundaries. Not the least important of these activities is to produce out of the variety of emigrant experiences a common diasporic culture, which already has resulted in a cultural nationalism, providing fertile grounds for the rediscovery of "Chinese" identity among scattered populations of Chinese around the world who long had assumed the coloring of the environments in which they lived.

All this, of course, is quite consistent with the so-called trend toward globalization. What the new situation presents is the increasing visibility of a diasporic ethnicity, or transnation (Basch, Glick-Schiller, & Szanton Blanc 1994), that feeds off intensified cultural activity, which is in turn empowered by globalized economic activity that has brought prominence to Chinese populations. It is this situation that presents a new kind of problem that is no longer containable or explainable through earlier legacies of racism. It is not necessary to deny the persistence of anti-Asian racial attitudes in the

US to suggest that the John Huang and Wen Ho Lee cases have dimensions that derive from this new situation, rather than merely representing the most recent instances of a century and a half of anti-Asian racism. When Chinese-Americans, however we may wish to define them, themselves insist on the construction of diasporic networks that extend from Washington, DC to Beijing, charges of conspiracy along the same network acquire a new kind of plausibility; although they are none the less hypocritical for that reason, as I shall elaborate below, as the networks may extend in either direction. The attorney from San Francisco, whom I have cited already, observes accurately that,

> When the pendulum of US-China relations swings upward, diasporic Chinese overseas, by virtue of their dual identity, backgrounds, and language skills, are viewed positively as "bridges", to liaise with the homeland, and to close the cultural divide between the homeland and their adopted country, and vice versa ... On the other hand, in this latest downswing of the pendulum in US-China relations, our "bridging" role has now become a liability and an object of suspicion, mistrust, and disloyalty. Where contacts, liaisons, developing "guanxi" in the past were desired, now the potential "fifth column" tag attaches. (Liu 1999, 3)

It is an accurate statement, yet one that misses its own implications: that the one image may be complicit with the other even though they seem to be opposites. The statement is also one that is problematic for its definition of "home", as I will elaborate below, as well as, in this particular case, its reference to a "dual identity", as Edward Liu himself is a Chinese-American by way of the Philippines, a historical trajectory that is erased in the US-China juxtaposition, and the reference to the "dual identity". It is possible that similar oversights played a part in the activities of John Huang and Wen Ho Lee, which suggests that the most immediate issue, and a highly sensitive one, is the possibility of Chinese-American complicity in the fertilization of long-standing racial attitudes in the US.

This is what is overlooked in most of the globalization discourse, preoccupied as it is with Eurocentrism and Eurocentric racism, the decline of the nation-state, and the emergence of transnational diasporic populations and cultures, and is oblivious, for the same reason, to the fact that changing global relationships do not signify an end to relationships of power, and that the new discourses that have emerged to articulate a new global situation, while they may forcefully repudiate earlier power relationships, may nevertheless be complicit with, or contribute to, new configurations of power. Most serious is the obliviousness of globalization discourse to the persistence of territorial states, still insisting on being nation-states despite all the current hype about globalization, and to the need to account for the globalized movements of people within a context of power relations defined by state-to-state relationships. Globalization discourse is quick to point to the increasing porosity of national boundaries, and even the imminent demise of the nation-state, over-looking that while globalization has created problems for earlier conceptions of the nation-state, the alleged porosity of state bounda-ries remains more in the realm of wishful thinking than in the realities of a geopolitical situation where border conflicts seem rather to be on the increase. Borders that may be porous for certain activi-ties, say capital flows, moreover, do not show the same porosity when it comes to movements of people. It is arguable even that globaliza-tion, rather than creating the mythical global village, may also serve to expand the reach of the territorial state through not just economic means but also in the import and export of human beings; migrant populations such as the Chinese may promise an increasingly unified world, but evidence so far suggests that, within the context of compe-tition between territorial states, they are likely also to be placed in the service of national powers that seek to project their interests globally, and therefore are subject to the vagaries of changing relations between such states—as the statement by Liu suggests—however one-sidedly, as it overlooks the contradictory relationships within the so-called Chinese diaspora, as well as the contradictory relationship of diasporic Chinese to their "homeland". It may be impossible, needless to say, to project state interests globally without also exporting conflicts over politics and culture, which is also a charac-teristic of the contemporary scene, where those supposedly of the same national origin nevertheless are deeply divided by social and ideological conflicts. But in either case, it is silly to think that globali-zation and the power of the territorial state of necessity represent a zero-sum relationship where the success of one must represent the demise of the other.

Rather than address this crucial contradiction, globalization discourse offers a utopian, evolutionary portrayal of the world in which movements of people are in the process of eroding national boundaries, promising a global social and political reorganization, and seeks to explain new conflicts as hangovers from the past, rather than as products of the very contradictions of globalization—which is one more reminder of its kinship with earlier modernization discourses. Perhaps even more seriously, globalization discourse as it applies to migrant populations, which I will describe here as diaspora discourse, contributes to the very cultural reifications that it is intended to overcome, and is complicit in the foregrounding of ethnic/racial conceptualizations of the world. This is the problem that I would like to examine below in somewhat greater detail.

The reconceptualization of Chinese Overseas in terms of diaspora or transnationality responds to a real situation: the reconfiguration of migrant societies and their political and cultural orientations. But diaspora and transnationality as concepts are also discursive or, perhaps more appropriately, imaginary; not only do they have normative implications, but they also articulate relations of power within populations so depicted, as well as in their relationship to societies of origin and arrival.[3] Diaspora discourse has an undeniable appeal in the critical possibilities it offers against assumptions of national cultural homogeneity, which historically has resulted in the denial of full cultural (and political) citizenship to those who resisted assimilation into the dominant conceptualizations of national culture, were refused entry into it, or whose cultural complexity could not be contained easily within a single conception of national culture. Taking their cue from Paul Gilroy's (1996) concept of "double consciousness" with reference to the African diaspora, Ong and Nonini (1997a, 12) write of Chinese in diaspora that "they face many directions at once—toward China, other Asian countries, and the West—with multiple perspectives on modernities, perspectives often gained at great cost through their passage via itineraries marked by sojourning, absence, nostalgia, and at times exile and loss."

This critical appeal, however, also disguises the possibility that diasporic notions of culture, if employed without due regard to the social and political complexities of so-called diasporic populations, may issue in reifications of their own, opening the way to new forms of cultural domination, manipulation, and commodification. To quote Ong and Nonini once again, "there is nothing intrinsically liberating about diasporic cultures" (1997a, 325). In pursuit of their interests, diasporic Chinese elites have collaborated with despotic political regimes, pursued exploitative practices of their own, and have utilized the notion of "Chineseness" as a cover for their own class interests. The danger of reification is implicit in a contemporary culturalism which easily loses sight of the distinction between recognizing autonomy to culture as a realm of analysis versus the rendering of culture into a self-sufficient explanation for all aspects of life; therefore rendering culture once again into an off-ground phenomenon available to exploitation for a multiplicity of purposes.

Moreover, since much of the discussion of culture and cultural identity is mediated by the new discipline of "cultural studies", there has been a tendency to carry questions and findings concerning one group of people to all groups similarly placed, in effect erasing considerable differences in the experiences of different populations through the universalization of the language of cultural studies. In either case, the erasure is the erasure of the social relations that configure difference within and between groups and, with them, of historicity.

The linking of Chinese-Americans to diasporic Chinese and the government in Beijing has provoked charges of racism among Asian Americans and their many sympathizers. Racism is there, to be sure. But is this racism simply an extension of the historical racism against Asian-Americans, or does it represent something new? If so, is it possible that at least some Asian-Americans have been complicit in producing a new kind of racist discourse? The question is fraught with difficulties—chief among them shifting responsibility to the victim—but it must be raised nevertheless. My goal in raising the question is not to erase racism, but to underline the unprecedented depth to which race and ethnicity have become principles of politics, not just in the US but globally. If the Democratic National Committee used Chinese names as markers of racial foreignness, is it possible that the government in China, or some Chinese transnational looking for recruits, might do the same? INS agents at the US-Mexican border, upon finding out the Turkish origins of my name, have stopped me for a special search. On account of the same name, I have been approached by Turkish "grassroots" organizations mobilizing against condemnations of Turkey for its activities against the Kurds, or its refusal to acknowledge the Armenian massacres. The name does bring a burden, but the burden is the ethnicization and racialization of politics, which is open to all for exploitation.

The new consciousness of diaspora and, diasporic identity cutting across national boundaries, is at least one significant factor in this racialization of politics in its current phase. The linking of John Huang, Chinese Overseas, and the Beijing government, I would like to suggest here, has been facilitated by the new discourse on the Chinese diaspora that, in reifying Chineseness, has created fertile grounds for nourishing a new racism. The idea of diaspora is responsible in the first place for abolishing the difference between Chinese-Americans and Chinese elsewhere (including in China). In response to a legacy of discrimination against Chinese-Americans, which made them hesitant even to acknowledge their ties to China and other Chinese, some Chinese-Americans and their sympathizers have been all too anxious to reaffirm such ties, in turn suppressing the cultural differences arising from the different historical trajectories of different Chinese populations scattered around the world. The anti-assimilationist mood (expressed most fervently in liberal "multi-culturalism") itself has contributed in no small measure to such cultural reification by a metonymic reduction of the culture of the Other to "representative" ethnographic elements or texts divorced from all social and historical context, that may then serve purposes of self-representation by the diasporic population, or self-congratulatory consumption in the carnivals of the society at large. While in much of contemporary diaspora discourse the preferred term for representing difference is culture, the question of culture, to quote Gilroy, is "almost biologized by its proximity to 'race'" (1996, 263). *Because* of the fact that the very phenomenon of diaspora has produced a multiplicity of Chinese cultures, the affirmation of "Chineseness" may be sustained only by recourse to a common origin, or descent, that persists in spite of widely different historical trajectories, which results in the elevation of ethnicity and race over all the other factors—often divisive—that have gone into the shaping of Chinese populations and their cultures. Diasporic identity in its reification does not overcome the racial prejudices of earlier assumptions of national cultural homogeneity, but in many ways follows a similar logic, now at the level not of nations but off-ground "transnations". The "children of the Yellow Emperor" may be all the more of a racial category for having abandoned its ties to the political category of the nation.[4]

Let me add a note of clarification here. In taking a critical stance toward the notion of diaspora, I am not suggesting that Chinese-Americans should therefore renounce ties to China, or other Chinese Overseas. The question is how these ties are conceived and articulated, and whether or not they erase very significant historical differences among the Chinese populations in different locations around the globe. I will illustrate again by reference to the John Huang case. Professor Ling-chi Wang of UC-Berkeley, who alerted and informed many in the US about the case by gathering and electronically disseminating information, played a very important part in publicizing the case. Over the past year, Professor Wang's communications have ranged widely from the John Huang case to the election of Chinese officials around the country, from defense of the People's Republic of China against various allegations to reportage on anti-Chinese activity in Southeast Asia. Now, a discursive field that covers all these elements appears at first sight to differ little from what I have been calling diaspora discourse, motivated as it is by bringing together information on Chinese regardless of place. What disrupts this field, however, is its unwavering focus on concrete problems of its immediate environment. Professor Wang was quick from the beginning to distance Asian-Americans from "foreign money", drawing a national boundary between Chinese here and Chinese donors of campaign funds from Southeast Asia (Wang 1997). The communications throughout have stressed issues of class and community, distinguishing community interests of Chinese-Americans from the activities of transnationally oriented diasporic Chinese with economic and political interests of their own. And this electronic discourse has remained focused throughout on the issue of campaign finance reform in the US, as campaign corruption rather than the color of money has been defined as the basic problem. In other words, the discourse, while ranging transnationally, has been quite grounded in its immediate environment. This, I think, is what distinguishes it from the diaspora discourse the way I understand that term here.

In its failure to specify its own location *vis-à-vis* the hegemonic, self-serving, and often financially lucrative reification of "Chineseness" in the political economy of transnationalism, critical diaspora discourse itself has fallen prey to the manipulation and commodification made possible by cultural reification, and contributes to the foregrounding of ethnicity and race in contemporary political and cultural thinking. There has been a tendency in recent scholarship, publication industry, and arts and literature, for instance, to abolish the difference between Asians and Asian-Americans. In scholarship, contrary to an earlier refusal of Asian Studies specialists to have anything to do with Asian-American Studies, there have been calls recently to integrate Asian-American Studies into Asian Studies, which partly reflects the increased prominence of trans-Pacific population flows, but also suggests the increasingly lucrative promise of reorienting Asian-American Studies in that direction. Publishers' catalogs, especially those devoted to "multiculturalism" and ethnic relations, freely blend Asian with Asian-American themes; and it is not rare to see these days a catalog in which *Woman Warrior* is placed right next to *The Dream of the Red Chamber*. A film series on "Asian-American film" at the University of North Carolina mysteriously includes many more films from Asia than from Asian-America; either due to the imaginary China of its China specialist organizer, or to increase the appeal of the series, which may not matter much as the ideological effect is the same.

Moreover, and more fundamentally, within the context of flour-ishing Pacific economies (at least until very recently), some Asian-Americans—most notably Chinese-Americans—have been assigned the role of "bridges" to Asia, a role which they have assumed readily for its lucrative promises. The metaphor of "bridge" as a depiction of Asian-Americans is not quite novel. In a recent dissertation that analyzes with sensitivity Asian-Americans' relationship to the Chicago School of Sociology, Henry Yu (1995, 162–189) argues that in their association with the Chicago sociologists, second generation Asian Americans internalized an image of themselves as "bridges" between American society and societies of origin in Asia, advanta-geously placed to serve as cultural interpreters. The advantage, however, came at a heavy price. The condition for successful service as "bridges" between cultures was marginality; it was their status as "marginal men" who existed between two societies without belonging fully to either that enabled the status of cultural inter-preter. As one such "marginal man", Kazuo Kawai, wrote:

> My decision to be an interpreter has improved my relations with both races. I am happy because I don't try to be a poor imitation of an American. I am happy because I don't vainly try to be a poor imitation of a genuine Japanese. I am simply what I am. I don't try to imitate either, so I am never disappointed when I find myself excluded from either side. (Quoted in *ibid.*, 184)

Kawai, of course, was not qualified to be a cultural "interpreter" in any serious sense of the term. While he was Japanese by birth, he was American by upbringing and culture, and his claims to access to Japanese culture were forced on him by alienation from American society, which excluded him, necessitating an imaginary affinity with his parents' society of origin. The notion that someone who did not belong to either society was for that very reason qualified to serve as cultural interpreter between the two glossed over fundamental problems of cultural orientation—which seems to have escaped both Kawai and his Chicago School mentors. Be that as it may, what is important here is that the metaphor of "bridge" between two societies was ultimately a product of alienation from a society that refused to recognize him as anything but a foreigner.

While the latter may not be the case in any obvious way presently, the metaphor of bridge nevertheless continues to invoke the foreign-ness of Asian-Americans. Much more so than in the case of those like Kawai, a diasporic identification may be a matter of choice rather than necessity. Contemporary "bridges", moreover, are most prominently economic brokers rather than cultural interpreters. Nevertheless, there is a racialization at work when diasporic populations, regardless of their widely different cultural trajectories internally, are expected to bridge the gap between places of arrival and places of origin by virtue of presumed cultural legacies that are more imagined than real. Thus Ronnie C. Chan, the chairman of the Hang Lung Development Group, a Hong Kong real estate company, urges Chinese-Americans in Hawai'i to become "bicultural" so as to serve as bridges between Chinese and US business, telling them that, "We all need our cultural roots, but put them away for a while and become truly bicultural" (Quoted in *Hawaii Herald Tribune* 18 June 1998, 1). Roots in this case take precedence over history; so that Chan urges Chinese-Americans not to learn to be Chinese again, but learn to be Americans!

The economic emergence of Chinese populations across the Pacific may be the single most important factor in the cultural rehomogenization of Chineseness. The most significant by-product of this economic emergence may be the recent Confucian revival, which attributes the economic success of Chinese (in some versions also of Japanese and Koreans), without regard to time or place, to the persistence of "Confucian values"; which were viewed earlier as obstacles to capitalism, but have been rendered now into the source of everything from economic development to the production of "model minorities". As I have discussed this problem extensively elsewhere (Dirlik 1995), I will simply note here that this so-called Confucian revival reproduces within a context of transnationality the most egregious prejudices of Orientalism. It is also a transnational product itself, for its emergence in the late seventies and early eighties involved, at least by way of intertextual collusion, experts on Chinese philosophy, US futurologists, and authoritarian regimes in East and Southeast Asia. According to its more enthusiastic proponents, Confucian values of thrift, diligence, educational achievement, family loyalty, discipline, harmony, obedience to authority—a list that reads like a dream list of the ideal worker or employee—have been responsible for the unquestioning commitment of Chinese (and East Asian) populations to capitalist development. In the more socially-based versions of the argument, Confucian values owe their persistence to the central importance throughout Chinese societies of kinship and pseudo-kinship ties—themselves products of the social diffusion of Confucian values: the networks of *guanxi*, that distinguish the socially oriented capitalism of the Chinese from individualistic and conflict-ridden

"Western" capitalism. As with the Confucian argument, there is little sense of time and place in these social arguments, as if social relations and networks were not subject to change and fluctuation. The net result is a portrayal of Chinese where, networked through *guanxi* and driven by Confucianism, Chinese around the world are rendered into a "tribe", in the words of the Pacific visionary Joel Kotkin (1996), committed to a relentless search for wealth. These same networks, needless to say, also make Chinese into ideal "bridges" with Asia.

Some of this argumentation, where it is promoted by Chinese scholars or leaders, no doubt draws upon a newfound sense of economic power and presence to reassert a Chinese identity against the century-old cultural hegemony of Eurocentrism; that utilizes earlier Orientalist representations to turn them against claims of Euro-American superiority. Nevertheless, they have been attached most prominently to questions of economic success, with a consequent commodification not only of the so-called Confucian values, but of Chinese as well. To quote from a recent piece by the same Joel Kotkin, "With their cultural, linguistic, and family ties to China, Chinese-American entrepreneurs like [Henry Y.] Hwang are proving to be America's secret weapon in recapturing a predominant economic role in the world's most populous nation" (1996, 25). Never mind the problematic question of "cultural and linguistic ties to China" on the part of many Chinese-Americans, it may not be very far from Kotkin's portrayal of Chinese-Americans as American economic moles in China to William Safire's depiction of John Huang as a Chinese political mole in Washington, DC.

The attitudes that lie at the root of these recent tendencies are not the less productive of racism for being produced by or sympathetic to Chinese and other Asian populations. They are also quite unstable, in that the sympathy itself may be subject to significant fluctuation, on occasion even turning into its opposite. This has happened to some extent with the recent so-called "economic meltdown" in Asia, with which "Asian values", among them Confucianism, once again lost their luster. It turns out now that "Asian values" have been responsible for creating a corrupt "crony capitalism" that inevitably led to economic breakdown.

Chinese populations are no less divided by class, gender, ethnic, and place differences than other populations. Not the least among those differences are differences of place and history. Reification of diaspora erases, or at the least, blurs such differences. As Appadurai has written of "ethnoscapes",

The central paradox of ethnic politics in today's world is that primordial (whether of language or skin color or neighborhood or kinship) have become globalized. That is, sentiments whose greatest force is their ability to ignite intimacy into a political sentiment and turn locality into a staging ground for identity, have become spread over vast and irregular spaces as groups move, yet stay linked to one another through sophisticated media capabilities. This is not to deny that such primordia are often the product of invented traditions or retrospective affiliations, but to emphasize that because of the disjunctive and unstable interaction of commerce, media, national policies and consumer fantasies, ethnicity, once a genie contained in the bottle of some sort of locality (however large), has now become a global force. (Appadurai 1990, 15)

While the globalization of ethnicity is no doubt bound up with abstract forces that contribute to global restructurations, it is important nevertheless to draw attention to agencies engaged actively in inventing traditions and producing retrospective affiliations. If differences of history and place are erased by the shifting of attention to a general category of diaspora (which I take to be equivalent to Appadurai's "ethnoscapes"), it is necessary to raise the question of whom such erasure serves. There is no reason to suppose that the government in Beijing (or, for that matter, Taiwan) is any more reluctant than the government in Washington or US transnational corporations to use diasporic Chinese for its own purposes. On the other hand, both from a political and an economic perspective, some diasporic Chinese are obviously of greater use than others, and in turn benefit from the erasure of differences among Chinese, which enable them to speak for all Chinese (Kwong 1997, especially Chapter 5). Reconceptualization of Chinese populations in terms of diasporas, in other words, serves economic and political class interests (it is not accidental that the Chinese-American John Huang was connected with the Riady family, which made him useful in a number of ways).

Diaspora discourse does not provide an answer to the question that I posed at the beginning: how to deal with this new situation in coping with everyday life. While the diasporic imaginary is obviously capable of disrupting a world conceived in terms of nations as homogeneous entities, or even transgressing against the borders of nation-states, diasporas themselves may serve as sources of new identities in only the most off-ground reified sense. Diasporic consciousness has no history; indeed, its claims may be sustained only in negation of history and historicity. This consciousness, whether in its homogenizing or hybrid forms, may serve the purpose of cultural projects of various kinds; it is much more difficult to imagine what progressive political projects it might produce, unless it is qualified with a consciousness of place.

Criticism of diasporic consciousness need not imply an urge to return to the nation with its colonial, homogenizing and assimilationist ideology. While recent critiques of the nation have introduced new insights, they often fail to address the question of who stands to benefit the most from the erasure of national boundaries. Whatever its colonizing tendencies may be, the nation is still capable, properly controlled from below, to offer protection to those within its boundaries.[5] It is not very surprising, therefore, that those Chinese-Americans devoted to social issues and community building should be suspicious of the claims of diasporas, or the questioning of national boundaries. In this case, too, place consciousness is a fundamental issue, for it leads to a different conception of the nation; bottom-up rather than top down (Chatterjee 1997).

To raise the question of places is to raise the issue of difference on a whole range of fronts, including those of class, gender, and ethnicity. It is also to raise the question of history in identity. Identity is no less an identity for being historical (is there any other kind?). Contrary to a hegemonic cultural reification or a whimpering preoccupation with the location of "home", which seem to have acquired popularity as alternative expressions of diasporic consciousness, what is important is to enable people to feel at home where they live.[6] This does not require that people abandon their legacies, only that they recognize the historicity of their cultural identities, and that those identities are subject to change in the course of historical encounters. In the words of the Indian writer, Farrukh Dhondy, "what makes people is not their genes, is not their nostalgia, it's their interactions of daily existence" (Quoted in Jussawalla 1997, 32). Identity is not merely a matter of a cultural given, it is also a matter of identification, which includes a determination of what and where "home" may be.

The historicity of identity is by no means transparent, since history itself makes sense in terms of its social locations. One of the prominent phenomena of our times is the fragmentation of history into a number of seemingly irreconcilable spaces, most importantly ethnic spaces. The proliferation of histories without any apparent connections to one another, or that consciously repudiate such connections, has led to the substitution for history of heritage, as David Lowenthal puts it, or more pessimistically, a condition of "schizophrenic nominalism", in Fredric Jameson's words, that has deprived history of all temporal and spatial meaning (Lowenthal 1995; Jameson 1991).[7]

Such negative evaluations stem at least partially from the break-down of a Eurocentric temporality that provided coherence, but only at the cost of repressing other histories than its own. The breakdown of history may be viewed, from a less pessimistic perspective, as the assault on a hegemonic history of the previously repressed, who have now returned to visibility to demand a presence for themselves. The challenge is how to create new unities out of this fragmentation, which may be a precondition for achieving a more democratic unity to transcend an earlier illusion of unity that could be sustained only through a hegemonic history. A further, and crucial, question is where to locate this new history or histories? The effort no doubt has to proceed at more than one location; but one location that is indis-pensable, I think, consists of places.

Diasporas are dispersals from some remembered homeland, from some concrete place, which after the fact is conceived in terms of the nation (at least over the last century), although concrete places of origin retain their visibility even in their incorporation into the language of the nation or of diaspora. The dispersed also land in concrete places in the host society which, too, is captured in national terms, even if the very fact of diaspora if nothing else disturbs efforts to define nation and national culture. Ling-chi Wang (1991, 199–200) tells us that one Chinese metaphor for the diasporic condi-tion is "growing roots where landed" (*luodi shenggen*). While a prejudice for the nation makes it possible to speak of "national soil", and demands assimilation to some "national culture", rootedness as a metaphor points inevitably to concrete places that belie easy assumptions of the homogeneity of national soil or culture. Kathleen Neil Conzen (1990, 9) writes of German immigrants to the US that, "... as change occurred, it could proceed without the kinds of qual-itative shifts implied by the familiar notions of acculturation and assimilation. Culture was more strongly localized—naturalized in the literal botanical sense of the term—than it was ethnicized, and the structures of everyday life, rather than being assimilated to those of some broader element within American society, responded to the transforming pressures of modern life on a parallel trajectory of their own." The statement points to both the concrete place-basedness and the historicity of diasporic identity. James Clifford (1997) uses the metaphor of "routes" to capture the spatio-temporality of cultural identity; I will describe it simply as "historical trajectory through places".[8] Encounters in places traversed involve both forgetting and new acquisitions. The past is not erased, therefore, but rewritten. Similarly, the new acquisitions do not imply disappearance into the new environment, but rather the proliferation of future possibilities.

What attention to place suggests is the historicity of identity. The "assimilation theory" to which Conzen objects presupposed dehistoricized and placeless notions of culture; assimilation implied movement from one to the other.[9] One could not be both Chinese and American, but had to move from being Chinese (whatever that might mean) to being American (whatever that might mean); hence failure to become "fully American" could produce such notions as "dual personality", which precluded being American, as well as suggesting that such an identity represented the degeneration of the components out of which it was formed. The very formulation of the problem precluded what from our vantage point would seem to be an obvious answer: that it is possible to be Chinese without being like other Chinese, and it is possible to be an American without being like other Americans. In either case, the history traversed makes a crucial difference in the formation of new identities that unite and divide in new ways.

Ironically, contemporary critiques of assimilation theory, to the extent that they ignore place and history, end up with similar assumptions. Multiculturalism may evaluate hybridity differently than an earlier monoculturalism permitted, but it nevertheless retains similar culturalist assumptions (some notion of Chineseness conjoined to some notion of Americanness to produce a hybrid product). And since culturalism still runs against the evidence of difference, it is still potentially productive of the reification of ethnicity and, ultimately, race. If diasporic reification erases the many historical legacies of the past, hybridity disallows the future. Without a clear account of how different "hybridities" may be productive of new cultures, hybridity in the abstract points merely to an existence between cultures frozen in time.

On the other hand, place consciousness is quite visible in Asian-American literary texts. The inhabitants of these texts move through ethnic spaces out of choice or necessity, but the ethnic spaces are themselves located in places with a variety of co-habitants. The classic example may be Carlos Bulosan's *America Is In the Heart*, which literally traces the author's movements from place to place, starting in Philippine places, and then up and down the US West coast. Place-consciousness is most readily evident in contemporary Asian-American literature in the literature of Hawai'i—of writers such as Milton Murayama, Gary Pak, and Wing Tek Lum—whose forays into the histories of different ethnic groups share in common a language that marks them as irreducibly Hawaiian. Another example, especially interesting because of the deep contrast between the author's literary output and his more formal discussions, is that of Frank Chin. Chin's literary works are quite attentive to places, and to the historicity of Chinese American identities. On the other hand, when the author turns to formal discussions of identity, his representation of Chinese identity match the most egregious reifications of an earlier Orientalism. This itself may be revealing of a gap between depictions of concrete everyday life, and an imagined ethnicity constructed very much in the course of daily life, but lifted out of it to be represented as an identity that transcends history. The contrast raises interesting questions concerning the ways in which transnationalization and diasporic consciousness may affect a place-based understanding of ethnicity.

The insistence on places against diasporic reification has consequences that are not only analytical in an abstract sense. It draws attention, in the first place, to another, place-based, kind of politics. One of the dangerous consequences of undue attention to diasporas is to distance the so-called diasporic populations from their immediate environments, to render them into foreigners in the context of everyday life. Given the pervasiveness of conflicts in American society that pitch different diasporic populations against one another, rather than retreat behind reified identities that further promote mutual suspicion and racial division, it is necessary to engage others in political projects to create political alliances where differences may be "bridged", and common social and cultural bonds formed to enable different populations to learn to live with one another.[10] A Chinese living in Los Angeles has more of a stake in identifying with his/her African or Hispanic-American neighbors than with some distant cousin in Hong Kong (without implying that the two kinds of relationships need to be understood in zero-sum terms). Following the logic of the argument above, I suggest that place-based politics offers the most effective means to achieving such ends. Place-based politics does not presuppose communities that shut out the world, but refocuses attention on building society from the bottom up.

Radical (perhaps unrealistically radical)[11] as a place-based politics may seem, it is unlikely to fulfil its radical promise unless it also challenges the hegemony of the global imaginary that utopianizes transnationalism. My use of places is somewhat different than in discussions of the "local" in some postcolonial literature, which tends to view places in isolation from the larger structures that inform them and the categorical allegiances (such as class or gender) that enter into their constitution. The reassertion of place that I am suggesting could hardly be accomplished, therefore, without challenging those larger structures, and working over such categorical allegiances. Without reference to structures, the notion of historicity itself readily disintegrates into a jumble of empirical phenomena with no meaning outside themselves. To speak of places presently is to set them against the new global or transnational imaginaries, with their fetishism of a dehistoricized developmentalism and placeless spaces.

Liberal multiculturalism seeks to make room for different cultures, but with a hegemonic containment of difference within the structures of capitalism assumed to offer a common destiny for all, which perpetuates fundamental hegemonies under the new require- ments of broadened cultural tolerance. Culturalism without history may serve to divide (as it does); it may also serve to consolidate hegemony. It may not be too surprising that we witness exactly such a hegemonic unity at the level of transnationalized ruling classes, whose claims to cultural difference are negotiated with the assump- tion of common interests, while the same culturalism is often manifested in deadly conflicts among the population at large at the ground level. The return to history from culture is important precisely because it may serve as a reminder of how people at the level of places are not just divided by different cultural legacies but also united by common histories and interests without which those differences themselves may be incomprehensible. What need to be resolved at this level are different memories; not just histories remembered differently but also histories remembered jointly.

History is important for another reason than the possibilities it offers for resolution of past and present differences. Released from a hegemonic containment within contemporary structures of power, the recognition of different pasts inevitably invites the possibility of envisioning the future differently. The historicization of cultures—the recognition of different historical trajectories—may have a crucial role to play in opening up a dialogue over different futures. Political projects that account for the different historical possibilities may fulfil their radical promise only if they prove capable of imagining alternative futures as well.

The other consequence is also political, but within the context of academic politics, for there is a pedagogic dimension to realizing such political goals. It is rather unfortunate that recent ideological formations, backed by the power of foundations, have encouraged the capturing of ethnicities in "diasporic" American or cultural studies. In the case of studies of Asian-Americans in particular, the most favored choices these days would seem to be to recognize Asian-American Studies as a field of its own, to break it down into various national components (Chinese, Japanese, Filipino, etc.), or to absorb it into American or Asian Studies. Political premises and goals inform each choice. Asian-American Studies as a field is under attack from the inside for its homogenizing implications, as well as its domination by some groups over others. Breaking it down, however, does not offer any readily acceptable solution, as it merely replaces continental homogeneity by national homogeneities; why should there be a Chinese-American rather than, say, Fuzhounese American Studies? And why stop at Fuzhou?

On the other hand, absorbing Asian-American Studies into either Asian or American Studies would seem to achieve little more than bringing it as a field under the hegemony of the study of societies of origin or arrival. On the surface, American Studies would seem to be an appropriate home for Asian-American Studies, as Asian-American history is grounded in US history, which continues to be the concrete location for Asian-American experience. On the other hand, it is also clear that Asian-American history extends beyond the boundaries of US history, and by virtue of that has special requirements—chief among them language—that are not likely to be accommodated with ease within the context of American Studies as presently organized. These needs have prompted some scholars to advocate some kind of a merger between Asian and Asian-American Studies. After all, Asian Studies would benefit from greater awareness of Asian-American populations, which might complicate notions of Asia with beneficial results. At the same time closer integration with Asian Studies would bring into Asian-American Studies a closer grasp of societies of origin, as well as a disciplinary training in languages, which may be necessary for more sophisticated scholarship; as is indicated by the growing number of Asian-American scholars who have extended the boundaries of Asian American Studies. I am thinking here of scholars such as Yuji Ichioka, Him Mark Lai, Marlon Hom, Sau-ling Wong, and Scott Wong, to name a few, who have produced works that have enriched the field by using non-English language sources.

Dialogue between the different fields is not only desirable, therefore, but is necessary. Mergers are a different matter. The reasoning underlying these proposed mergers is full of pitfalls, especially when viewed from the perspective of politics. Absorption of Asian-American into American Studies *prima facie* would perpetuate the hegemonies that do not disappear but are in fact consolidated under the guise of multiculturalism. The case with Asian Studies is even more problematic, as the justification for it is fundamentally diasporic, with all the implications of that term that I have discussed above. One of the most important characteristics of Asian-American Studies, as of all the ethnic studies projects that were born of the political ferment of the 1960s, was its insistence on ties to community projects. This was a reason that, for a long time, Asian Studies scholars disassociated themselves from Asian-American scholarship, for such explicit ties to political projects made the field suspect in terms of scholarship (which, of course, did not apply to scholars of Asia with ties to other kinds of political projects, respectable because of their ties to power). The new interest of scholars of Asia in Asian-American Studies may be attributed to something as mundane as the lucrative promise of a field in demand all of a sudden due to the explosion in the numbers of students of Asian origins. I suspect, however, that what makes the association tolerable is the respectability Asian-American Studies has acquired as it is transnationalized, or diasporized, achieving respectability at the cost of alienation from its radical political projects. It may be noteworthy here that a panel in the recent annual meeting of the Association for Asian Studies ("Crossing Boundaries: Bridging Asian-American Studies and Asian Studies") "bridges" the gap not by addressing Asian-American issues, but by including in the panel Evelyn Hu-De Hart, the only participant recognizable as a serious scholar of Asian-America (to be distinguished from being Asian American). Judging by the titles of the papers listed, the panel reveals little recognition of the integrity and coherence of Asian-American Studies as a field with its own problems and paradigms, not to speak of the intellectual and political implications of those paradigms.[12] The claim to "bridging" the two fields, as with most occasions informed by that particular term, rests on the assumption of some vague diasporic unity across the Pacific. The danger (and the quite real possibility) here is the disappearance into some vague diasporic field of problems specific to Asian-America.

If education has anything to do with politics, and it does have everything to do with it, the wiser course to follow in overcoming ethnic divisions would be to reinforce programs in Ethnic Studies, which initially had as one of its fundamental goals the bridging of ethnic divisions and the pursuit of common projects (based in communities) to that end. Ethnic Studies since their inception have been viewed with suspicion by the political and educational establishments, and suffered from internal divisions as well. Whether or not these legacies can be overcome is a big question, embedded as they are in the structures of US society and academic institutions. The irony is that while Ethnic Studies might help ideologically in overcoming ethnic divisions, it is not likely to receive much support unless inter-ethnic political cooperation has sufficient force to render it credible in the first place. The ideology of globalization, of which diasporic ideology is one constituent, further threatens to undermine its promise (and existence). Here, too, place-based politics may have something to offer in countering the ideologies of the age.

Notes

1. Since this essay was written, I have discovered an essay written by Paul Gilroy (1990/1991) with the same title, "It Ain't Where You are From, It's Where You are At: The Dialectics of Diasporic Identification." I welcome the coincidence, which is a reason for keeping the title of this essay as it is.

2. The article by Linter (1999) deals mainly with Southeast Asia. There has been a reluctance in the US to speak about earlier and new generations of immigrants.

3. This double aspect of the concept is investigated in several of the essays, especially the editors' introduction and epilogue, in Ong and Donald Nonini (1997).

4. Lynn Pan (1990) refers to the propensity of many Chinese Overseas to think along racial or, at the least, biological lines, in evaluating Chinese success in business.

5. For a defense of the nation from what may seem to be a surprising source, see Sub-Commandante Marcos (1999).

6. I am referring here to the title of a conference held in early November 1997 at New York University, "Where is Home?" (previously the title of an exhibition on the Chinese in the US). The preoccupation has its roots in a particularly narcissistic and manipulative offshoot of Cultural Studies. The "yearning" for home need not be a consequence of such narcissism. Feroza Jussawalla, a writer of South Asian origin, defends her case for "home" in response to the oppressive refusal of the society of arrival to recognize genuine political and cultural citizenship to the ethnically, racially, and culturally different even after generations of residence in the new "home", which indeed has been the experience of many. On the other hand, I find implausible her alternative that, "the answer is to assimilate and yet to keep our distinctness, our senses of nationality" (Jussawala 1997, 36).

7. Jameson's pessimism is related to a yearning for an earlier class politics of socialism. He describes the contemporary fragmentation of history with the same vocabulary that he uses to describe the new social movements: as having emerged from the "rubbles" of an earlier unified and coherent history and politics. This yearning does not allow him to see the progressive potential of the new "rubble."

8. I may note here an aspect of the contemporary dissatisfaction with history for supposedly ignoring questions of space out of a preoccupation with questions of time. While this may be a legitimate criticism for certain kinds of histories, such criticism itself seems to be more concerned with 19th-century historicism and conceptions of history than with the actual practice of historians. To this historian at any rate, the concept of historicity as a concrete concept is inseparable from location in time *and* space-within a *social* context—to complete Soja's (1996) "trialectics".

9. Henry Yu (1995, 185–188) argues that the Chicago sociologists de-historicized the experiences of their "oriental" subjects by rendering into static universal categories what were stages in their life histories.

10. The divisive effects of diasporic discourse as I approach it here are similar to the divisive effects of the idea of a "model minority".

11. The difficulties are obvious, but then we do not seem to have too many choices. For a sensitive discussion of the difficulties involved in what she calls "transversal politics" (a term coined by Italian feminists), see Yuval-Davis (1997). I have discussed the problems and the possibilities at greater length in Dirlik (2001).

12. A concomitant roundtable discussion subtitled "Where Do Asia and Asian America Meet?" may have been more promising, with the participation of Gail Nomura and Scott Wong.

CHAPTER 8

Cosmopolitan Options

Peter van der Veer

It does not seem very difficult to draw a picture of the cosmopolitan person. Recently, this has been done by the anthropologist Ulf Hannerz and his description fits one's expectations: "... genuine cosmopolitanism is first of all an orientation, a willingness to engage with the Other. It entails an intellectual and esthetic openness toward divergent cultural experiences, a search for contrasts rather than uniformity". (Hannerz 1996, 103). The picture, drawn by Hannerz, refers to enlightened intellectuals and foremost to the anthropologist. It is a very flattering image, an ideal to aspire to. The counter-image is that of the parochial person, tied down by the narrow confines of 'local' life, and therefore simply not interested in different people, different customs. Cosmopolitanism is often seen as a liberating alternative to ethnic and nationalist chauvinism. However, one does want to ask what intellectual and aesthetic openness entails and on what terms one engages the Other. When one turns one's attention to the colonial period, one cannot deny missionaries or colonial officers a willingness to engage with the Other. In that connection I have always understood Johannes Fabian's *Time and the Other* (1983) with its emphasis on the 'coevalness' of the Other as a profoundly missionary book, theologically interpreting why the missionary and the anthropologist have difficulties to 'recognize' the Other. Anthropologists are not that different from missionaries and colonial officers, since they all share an enabling condition of engagement, namely Western imperialism. In this paper I want to examine first cosmopolitanism as a trope of colonial and secular modernity. After that, I want to briefly explore what a postcolonial cosmopolitanism might look like.

The cosmopolitan as an intellectual, who is not limited by the local culture of his place of upbringing, is a trope of secular modernity. In gender terms the cosmopolitan is obviously a man; an individual who has the ability to live anywhere and the capacity to tolerate and understand the barbarism of others. The trope comes up in English in the early-19th century, a period marked by the simultaneous expansion of imperialism and nationalism. These two historical formations belong together, since the nation-state emerges within an expanding world-system (van der Veer & Lehmann 1999). Their intimate connection is already expressed very well in Adam Smith's thinking about the tension between the fiscality of the state and global free trade. It is in the context of his writing on political economy that in 1848 John Stuart Mill refers to capital becoming more and more 'cosmopolitan'. Cosmopolitanism is the Western engagement with the rest of the world and that engagement is a colonial one which simultaneously transcends the national boundaries and is tied to it. Instead of perceiving cosmopolitanism and nationalism as alternatives, one should perhaps recognize them as the poles in a dialectical relationship. The importance of imperial migration for nationalism is perhaps clearest in the 'pioneer' nationalisms of the Americas and some of the later nationalist movements in Europe, Asia, and Africa (Anderson 1991; van der Veer 1995). But more generally, it is important to consider the development of cultural nationalism in Western Europe in the context of empire building (Said 1993). National culture in Britain, for instance, nationalizes the imperial encounter and reflects upon the mission of the nation in the empire, while cosmopolitanism is based upon the possibilities of encounter as given in empire (Baucom 1999; van der Veer 2001).

In Daniel Lerner's classic *The Passing of Traditional Society* one finds the argument that Western modernity has depended principally on "the mobile personality"—that is, on a type of person eager to move, to change, and to invent. Lerner argued that empathy defined the mobile personality, and he glossed 'empathy' as "the capacity to see oneself in the other fellow's situation" (Lerner 1958, 50). In a fascinating comment on Lerner, the Shakespearean scholar Stephen Greenblatt suggests that what Professor Lerner calls 'empathy', Shakespeare calls 'Iago'. The connection is the idea of improvisation; that is "the ability both to capitalize on the unforeseen and to transform given materials into one's own scenario" (Greenblatt 1980, 225). The basis of empathy is thus the power to get into the life world of the Other and transform it. Such power is neither good nor bad, but it is also never completely disinterested.[1]

Secularity is a characteristic of cosmopolitanism. Liberal thinkers, from John Stuart Mill to Ernest Gellner, tend to assume that religious affiliation restricts the believer to the absolutist claims of religion and condemns him to intolerance. Colonizing modernity therefore disclaims its roots in a Christian, European past and claims a cosmopolitan openness to other civilizations. However, this is an openness to understanding with a desire to bring progress and improvement, a cosmopolitanism with a moral mission. This is quite explicit in such projects as British utilitarianism, French 'mission civilisatrice', and Dutch 'Ethische Politiek'. There is not the desire to spread Christianity, but the desire to spread the morality of the modern nation-state, the cosmopolitanism of the colonial empire.

A further understanding of that quality of 'empathy' and 'improvisation' that the cosmopolitan as a mobile personality possesses is perhaps reached if we look at the problem of cultural translation. Translation is the activity in which the cosmopolitan in his open engagement with the Other has to excel and it shows exactly that some languages are weaker than others. Talal Asad has argued that, "because the languages of third world societies are seen as weaker in relation to Western languages (and today, especially English), they are more likely to submit to forcible transformation in the translation process than the other way around. The reason for this is, first, that in their political-economic relations with third world countries, Western nations have the greater ability to manipulate the latter. And, second, Western languages produce and deploy desired knowledge more readily than third world languages do" (Asad 1993, 190).

If we speak of translation we, of course, understand that this implies a conversion of a conceptual framework into another, which is more powerful and thus more universal. Difficulties of this sort have been discussed at length by the anthropologist Rodney Needham (1972). He points out that most languages do not have an equivalent for the English "belief". In a fascinating book on translation and conversion in Tagalog society in the Philippines in the late-16th century Vicente Rafael (1993) has argued that conversion (changing one thing into something else) is synonymous with translation (changing one language into another). The language of the Other had to be converted into a language, which could carry the holy message. The indeterminacy of translation creates a field of interaction, which is riddled with anxiety.

The issue of translation and conversion not only raises the question of the power of languages, but also that of differences in colonial trajectories and languages of conquest. There are considerable differences between being colonized by the Spanish, the Portuguese, the French, the British, or the Dutch. By having Spanish as the colonial language one enters into colonial cosmopolitanism in a quite different way than when one is conquered by the British. A colonial language, like Spanish, can be used as a medium of resistance against American hegemony in Latin America, while it becomes at the same time a significant rival in the heartland of Global English, the USA.

The cosmopolitan person is not only a translator, but also a spy who commands more languages than the people he spies upon as well as the ability to translate their languages into the language of the rulers. It is the ultimate colonial fantasy, well expressed in Kipling's writings, that the colonial hero has a perfect grasp of the language and the customs of the 'natives', the 'locals', but still in his crossing over remains true to himself and returns to his own world where he uses his acquired knowledge for the improvement of colonial rule. Interesting enough, westernized natives in the colonized areas were not considered to have the ability to cross over, but are ridiculed as impostors, as wogs.

Undoubtedly, the best Dutch realization of the cosmopolitan as spy has been the Christian Snouck Hurgronje (1857–1936), one of the greatest Orientalist students of Muslim Law. In 1884 he went to Jeddah to study the Haj and in 1885 he converted to Islam to be able to enter Mecca. He was financially supported by the Dutch colonial ministry, which needed information about Muslims from the Dutch Indies who stayed in Mecca. Not only the Dutch, but also all colonial governments had a theory that Muslims all over the world might unite in a 'pan Islamism' which would be a serious threat to colonial rule. Mecca would play a crucial role in that worldwide conspiracy. Snouck's expert knowledge on the Aceh Muslims in Mecca made him later a perfect political advisor for Muslim affairs in the Dutch Indies. His policy advice became crucial in the military campaign of the Dutch to repress a Muslim rebellion in Aceh, the bloodiest episode in Dutch colonial history. The question whether Snouck had been really converted to Islam and had secretly married in the Dutch Indies with one or two Muslim wives is still hotly debated in Holland. I recently heard from a historian in Leiden, where Snouck is revered as the patron saint of Oriental Studies, that it was considered to open Snouck's grave to see whether he had been buried in the direction of Mecca. Whatever the results might be of this far-going empiricism, to all parties in this debate it is clear that Snouck had been a truly cosmopolitan man (van der Veer 1995a).

Cosmopolitanism is thus not only a trope of modernity, but more specifically of colonial modernity. It is therefore ironic to see the celebration of a cosmopolitanism, rooted in colonial modernity, in some postcolonial writing. Especially the American literary critic Homi Bhabha is quite exuberant in his description of the possibilities of migrant populations, of subjects "formed-in-between": "Such cultures of a post-colonial contra-modernity may be contingent to modernity, discontinuous or in contention with it, resistant to its oppressive, assimilationist technologies; but they also deploy the cultural hybridity of their borderline conditions to 'translate', and therefore reinscribe, the social imagery of both metropolis and modernity." (Bhahba 1993, 6) In my view, however, Bhabha does not find a contra-modernity, but precisely a modernity that invites intellectuals from the post-colony not only to receive and imbibe it as in a Macaulayan project of educating the natives, but to become agents in its reproduction after the demise of the colony-metropole divide. The racial distinction between natives and metropolitans has become obsolete and is replaced with the notion that anyone can be cosmopolitan, as long as one remains open, mobile, and improvising.

The celebration of hybridity, syncretism and multiculturalism in postcolonial studies needs to be critically examined (van der Veer 1997). Bhahba's claim that one can bring newness into the world, that one can reinvent oneself when one is writing literature from the cultural interstices, is a conceit of the literature-producing and consuming world. Literary texts are the very sites of self-fashioning in modern, bourgeois culture. Literature has replaced religious texts as a source of elevated reflection about the nature of the self. Salman Rushdie's literary work, which is taken as a prime example of cosmo-politan writing by Bhabha, takes part precisely in this replacement of the religious by literary secularity. What is remarkable in Rushdie's work is the extent to which it feeds on Indian culture and Muslim and Hindu religious traditions. It translates these materials for a Western audience in precisely the way Stephen Greenblatt describes Shakespeare's Iago.

My argument, so far, has been that cosmopolitanism is best understood as a form of improvisation and translation that charac-terized colonial modernity and that has insinuated itself in the multicultural hybridity celebrated in postcolonial literary studies. My suggestion is that the cosmopolitanism of the 19th and early-20th century can be 'provincialized', that is can be shown to be a 'view from somewhere' that is universalized through colonialism. To gain an understanding of a cosmopolitanism, that is character-istic for the postcolonial period, one should perhaps recognize the failure of the universalization of Western, secular modernity and examine the nature of new, global encounters and the cosmopolitan options that they enable. There are, at least, two ways of going about this. The first, which I reject, is based upon a recognition of the fact that the old cosmopolitanism was rooted in Western civilization and that it has failed to become truly universal. This recognition results in an attempt to revive pre-national, civilizational boundaries, which cannot be transcended by a universalizing project, but should result in a cosmopolitan, multicultural respect for difference. I am referring here to the civilizational theory of Samuel Huntington (Huntington 1996; van der Veer 1999). I will describe this argument in some detail and then proceed to an alternative, which I endorse, namely to try to understand cosmopolitanism by examining cosmopolitan projects in global cities.

Civilizations and Cosmopolitanism

If cosmopolitanism is a sign of Enlightenment universalism, one must come to the conclusion that the cultural resistances against it have not diminished, but increased. According to Samuel Huntington, "the great divisions among humankind and the dominating source of conflict will be cultural ... The fault lines between civilizations will be the battle lines of the future" (Huntington 1996, 22). Huntington argues for a new kind of cosmopolitanism that recognizes civilizational difference. He does away with the application of the term 'civilization' as a universalist Western standard to judge societies. He emphasizes the lack of universal standards and the existence of essential differences between civilizations that have their own normative standards. In his view there cannot be a universal civilization, since the central elements of any civilization, language and religion, do not show any sign of developing into one universal language or one universal religion (*ibid.*, 57). Religion is taken by Huntington to be the defining characteristic of a civilization and he points out that secularization does not seem to take place in most parts of the world.

Huntington also rejects the view that modernization means Westernization. He chooses thus the particularistic option in his use of the term 'civilization' and ends up with a set of irreducibly different, but modern civilizations, which together make up the world order. By recognizing civilizational difference and by abandoning the project of universalizing Western modernity, especially in terms of universal human rights, Huntington proposes a cosmopolitanism that is characterized by non-interference.

One way of interpreting Huntington's move to the civilizational level is to relate it to the perceived crisis of the nation-state under pressure of globalization. It is hard to deny that we witness in our times a significant increase in the speed and frequency with which people, goods, and information move across the boundaries of states. The question is to what extent and in what direction that fact transforms or replaces people's identification with their national culture. If 95 percent of the population increase will be in the poorest regions of the world one does not have to be a prophet of doom to predict that migration to the rich regions of the world has only just begun. Contrary to what one might think, however, migration may reinforce nationalism rather than weaken it. The question I want to raise here is the following: What role does religion play in the dialectics between national and transnational? World religions, by their very nature, transcend national boundaries. It is true for Christianity, Islam, Buddhism, and to a lesser extent, Hinduism that they have a message for mankind. They have, traditionally, been organized in a globalizing fashion to further worldwide expansion or, to put it in religious terms, missionization. Nevertheless, religion has been used in a great many cases to build national cultures. The tension between the local and the global, between the national and the transnational is therefore not at all novel for religions.

What can be argued, however, is that the transnational element in religion gets new possibilities thanks to the growth of transnational migration. In fact, we do see the flourishing of large transnational religious movements, such as Pentecostalism in Christianity, the Tablighi Jama'at in Islam, and the Vishwa Hindu Parishad in Hinduism. Interestingly, it is the Muslim movement that is, contrary to what Westerners would expect, avowedly apolitical and not aligned to nationalist politics. Worldly affairs do not matter directly for it. Its view is that the world will improve when every Muslim simply tries to be a good Muslim by fulfilling one's duties. However, this stance does have political consequences. Its message is for migrants a perfect defense against assimilation. In that sense the movement may come up strongly against the policies of some states. What we have here is a globalized movement that tries to create safe, communal havens for the faithful away from the influence of a globalized market culture. Despite the ubiquitous discourse on the universal community of Islam, the umma, there is a clear tendency of localization, of becoming involved in the politics of the nation-state in which one lives, when those politics (as in the case of veiling at school) affect one's communal life. One could see here one Islamic cosmopolitanism coming into conflict with secular (Christian) cosmopolitanism in a number of sites both in the Middle East (Turkey, Algeria) and Western Europe.

The Vishwa Hindu Parishad (VHP), on the contrary, has explicit political aims and is deeply involved in Hindu nationalism. It is directly allied to the Hindu nationalist party, the Bharatiya Janata Party (Indian People's Party). It is highly successful in India where it is the largest political force, but also among Hindu migrants in the US, the Caribbean, Britain, and South Africa or, better, wherever one finds Hindu communities in the diaspora. Again, it is fascinating to see here a Hindu cosmopolitanism that is posed as an alternative to a secular (Christian) one, which is exemplified by the VHP's criticism of the award of the Noble Prize to Amartya Sen as a Christian conspiracy.

The Pentecostalist movements, finally, are often deeply involved in the politics of national culture in the societies in which they are active. There is no evidence that processes of globalization and trans-nationalism impair the contribution of religion to the various nationalisms in the world.

Why did Huntington's theory get the attention it received? It is perhaps illuminating to examine the use that has been made of civilizational ideas, such as those of Huntington, in Europe. Huntington writes about the West in Atlantic terms, joining the US and Western Europe, but it is in Europe and especially in the Mediterranean region where the civilizational borders between Islam and Christianity are drawn.

When the Wall fell the discussion about the future of Germany was held between 'Wessies' and 'Ossies', forgetting—as usual—that Berlin, the new capital of unified Germany, is the third largest Turkish city in the world after Ankara and Istanbul. What indeed is the place of Turkey and that of Turkish citizens who reside in Western Europe? Is the border between Muslim Turkey and Christian Greece the significant one for a unified Europe and is this border internally reproduced as a boundary between secular Christian citizens and religiously minded Muslim residents? An affirmative answer to this question seems to be the implicit message of a summit of European Christian-democrats under the leadership of the then German Chancellor, Helmut Kohl. These Christian politicians want to deny Turkey membership of Europe since it does not belong to Christian civilization.

We have here the long-standing competition and enmity between Christian Europe and the Ottoman Empire, of which the Bosnian war, the Bulgarian troubles, the Kosovo crisis, and the tense relation between Greece and Turkey are the historical offshoots. It is fair, however, to remind oneself of the fact that there has not been an

Islamic military threat to Europe since the defeat of the Ottomans at the gates of Vienna in 1683. On the contrary, European powers have colonized large parts of the Ottoman Empire in the 19th century. The struggle has been won by the Western powers and it has led to the dismantling of the Ottoman Empire and the formation of a modern, secular nation-state Turkey. Nevertheless, the old question of the colonial period emerges again, but now in the metropoles of the former colonizing nations. Are people of other race, other religion capable of reaching the endpoint of civilizational evolution, European cosmopolitan modernity? To what extent can Muslims become modern; to what extent can they be equal to modern Christians? What we have here is a tension between the universal principles of the Enlightenment and their rootedness in Christian civilization. The Christian-Democrats want to put the struggle between secularist and fundamentalist Muslims in Turkey outside Europe without engaging the fact that that struggle also takes place within its own global cities.

Migration from Islamic countries is one of the political issues most alive in Western Europe. Despite all the political rhetoric in especially France and Germany the presence of large groups of Muslims, as in earlier period large groups of Jews, is a fact that will continue to disrupt any civilizational illusions one might have about the Christian West and the non-Christian Rest. The struggle is really for the acceptance of the stranger without desiring to obliterate him either by assimilation or by multiculturalism. There are differences in the world and, as Montaigne already observed, "each calls that Barbarism what is not his own practice". To live with each other's barbarism, without violence, in one and the same multicultural society is the challenge of the 21st century.

Although the issue of multiculturalism is not straightforwardly examined in Huntington's book, it does seem to motivate his entire project. As he puts it at the end of his book in the following, revealing passage: "Some Americans have promoted multiculturalism at home; some have promoted universalism abroad; and some have done both. Multiculturalism at home threatens the United States and the West; universalism abroad threatens the West and the World. Both deny the uniqueness of Western culture. The global monoculturalists want to make the world like America. The domestic multiculturalists want to make America like the world. A multicultural America is impossible because a non-Western America is not American. A multicultural world is unavoidable because global empire is impossible. The preservation of the United States and the

West requires the renewal of Western identity. The security of the world requires acceptance of global multiculturality" (Huntington 1996, 318). This ideological message deals with a real issue, faced not only by the United States, but also by a great number of other societies, namely multiculturalism versus cultural assimilation. This issue cannot be solved, however, by projecting multiculturalism out of domestic politics onto the stage of world politics.

Cosmopolitanism and Global Cities

Nowadays we find the cosmos in the polis and often it looks like chaos. In other words, the postcolonial cities of today show a massive deprovincialization of the world or, one may say, a new cosmopolitanism. While the old cosmopolitanism separated colony and metropole spatially and intellectually, metropoles now show a full spectrum of immigrants from everywhere. Clifford Geertz expresses this with his usual rhetorical flourish:

> As the entanglements of everybody with everybody else have grown in recent times to the point where everyone is tripping over everyone's feet and everyone is everyone's face, its disruptive power, its capacity to induce doubts in those who think they have things figured out, taped, under control, rapidly increases. We live in a bazaar, not a cathedral; a whirl, not a diagram, and this makes it difficult for anyone anymore to be wholly at ease with his or her own ideas, no matter how official, no matter how cherished, no matter how plated with certainty. (Geertz 1994,169)

There are a variety of responses to this situation. One of them is indeed non-interference or even indifference. Hannerz (1996) argues correctly that this attitude is not cosmopolitanism, since it is the attitude of sticking to one's own, of the hedgehog rather than of the fox. As we have seen, genuine cosmopolitanism in his view is a willingness to engage with the Other and we have already analyzed and critiqued what the terms of engagement are under colonial conditions. The question, again, is what are the conditions and terms of engagement in today's global cities. In an essay on the cultural role of world cities Hannerz uses, approvingly, a quotation from V.S. Naipaul as his motto: "Cities like London were to change. They were to cease being more or less national cities; they were to become cities of the world, modern-day Romes, establishing the pattern of what great cities should be, in the eyes of islanders like myself and people even more remote in language and culture. They were to be cities visited for learning and elegant goods and manners and freedom by all the barbarian peoples of the globe, people of forest and desert, Arabs, Africans, Malays" (Quoted in Hannerz 1996, 127; Naipaul 1987, 141–142). Again, we see here that the cultural engagement is perceived as an attempt to uplift the "great unwashed", now constituted by groups of very different cultural backgrounds. Naipaul is, of course, one of the great believers in a universal civilization, rooted in the Enlightenment, and not at all sympathetic to the persistence of backward cultures, predominantly of what he perceives as an anti-rational religious kind. He is a representative of the cosmopolitanism analyzed in the beginning of this paper. But is this the only possibility of engagement in the global city?

We see in global cities predominantly a cultural engagement within the context of a politics of immigration (Holton & Appadurai 1996; Hansen 1999). These cities are a product of the increased mobility of capital and labor and they are the sites of new notions of membership, solidarity, and violence. Particularly interesting are the new social movements, which mobilize outsiders to gain access to housing, property, sanitation, health services, education, childcare, employment, and protection. The established respond to these claims by developing more and more elaborate security measures, creating walled enclaves in the city. Ghettos, ethnic neighborhoods, enclaves are the conditions of engagement in the global city. Gender and communal identities are newly constructed in the encounter with the Other, which is often anonymous and indifferent, but sometimes violent when spatial markings of identity are violated. Nothing is fixed and settled in the urban space. Outsiders today are the established of tomorrow and the demands of the globalized network society prevent a reflexive life planning for most people except a tiny elite (Castells 1997).

Much of the cultural engagement in the global cities in the world is reactive to the enormous dislocations of modern flexible capital and labor. People do try to build enclaves of communal identity and stake their claims to ownership of the city violently. Their engagement with the Other is not necessarily pleasant. Nevertheless, I believe that it is in these urban arenas that new sources of the self, in religious, gender, and political terms, develop. If we are looking for a postcolonial cosmopolitanism it is the global city we have to examine. I, for one, do not want to be restricted by Baudrillard's description of postmodern culture as immediate and bland, transparent and fast-moving … a blip on the screen, impelled by commercialism, without depth, without place. In fact, locality is produced by global forces and the global city is a very real domain in which cosmopolitanism as a pattern of inclusion and exclusion in the public sphere emerges. Especially, transnational movements which help migrants to cope with the conditions of migration and labor flexibility, such as the Tablighi Jama'at in Islam, do not simply build religious enclaves, safe havens of the self, but are creatively developing new religious understandings of their predicament, entailing an encounter with the multiplicity of Others on their own terms. It is impossible to simply call these movements closed, confined and confining, provincial as against cosmopolitan. They carry cosmopolitan projects, that is they engage the Other, but emerge from very different histories than that of the European Enlightenment.

Global cities are located everywhere, from Hong Kong to Rio de Janeiro, from Bombay to Los Angeles; they are not anymore the metropoles of colonial empires. The global imageries, which are at play in them, are just as multi-centred. I met a Pakistani taxi-driver in New York who was saving money to study Islamic science in Tehran and I am regularly traveling in airplanes with Hindu grandmothers who are located both in India and the US and connect their grandchildren with a culture, which is constantly negotiated in New York and San Francisco. The 19th century bourgeois project of cosmopolitanism is not anymore possible in the global cities of today. Since the differences are too substantial, the diasporic communications too frequent. As Pnina Werbner (1999) has recently argued about working-class Pakistani cosmopolitans, labor migration forges global pathways, routes along which Islamic and familial transnational worlds are constituted. One does not know what the postmodern, postcolonial cosmopolitanism will look like and perhaps we have to reject the term cosmopolitanism altogether when it continues to carry the meanings of the European Enlightenment and of colonialism. Whether we call the new engagements and confrontations in the global cities of the world cosmopolitan, global, or transnational is less important than to understand that the new global cities are the site of a number of very different projects of engagement with the Other, including Islamic, Hindu, Pentecostalist, environmentalist, gay, feminist, and others.

Notes

1. The reference to Lerner and Greenblatt are taken from Talal Asad (1993, 11–12).

CHAPTER 9

Parting from Phantoms: What Is at Issue in the Development of Transnational Television from Turkey[1]

Kevin Robins and Asu Aksoy

What tense do you want to live in?
"I want to live in the imperative of the future passive participle, in the 'what ought to be'."
That's the way I'd like to breathe. That's what pleases me. There is such a thing as mounted,
bandit-band, equestrian honour. That is why I like the splendid Latin "gerundive"—the verb
on horseback.

Osip Mandelstam

At the present time, there is considerable interest in the possibilities of transnationalism (Vertovec 1999). In this article, we want to explore some of the issues, with particular reference to transnational media, and to the creation of transnational cultural spaces. We want to consider to what extent it may be possible to move beyond the old media order, which was founded on what was predominantly a system of national broadcasting spaces. And we want to ask whether the logic of transnationalization might now bring into existence something that could be described as being, in some meaningful way, a new kind of media and cultural order—an order that would go against the national grain. Is it possible that an emergent order could be associated with a new ethos of multiculturalism or even cosmopolitanism? What would the institution of such a new order entail? We are very much concerned with the cultural possibilities that may be (potentially) inherent in the transnationalization process. And our concern will for the most part be with how these possibilities might exist in the particular context of the changing cultural space of Europe.

What we find in a great many contemporary analyses of the new media industries is a sense of anticipation and expectation about potential developments—there is a real concern with innovation. What is happening is generally understood in terms of a transformative shift from old to (supposedly) new communications technologies (satellite TV, cable)—in terms of a shift in technological paradigms—and this technological shift then tends to be associated with the idea of a positive transformation in cultural paradigms. Developments in media industries and cultures are regarded in terms of a progressive transition (almost evolution), in which an earlier paradigm, characterized by the organization of media cultures (and economies) on a national basis, is now being progressively replaced by a new one, characterized by a post-national organization. But, in our view, when it comes to articulating more precisely what new and positive possibilities might be anticipated, most of these analyses display a disappointing lack of imagination. If change is envisaged, it doesn't turn out to be something that we could call cultural innovation. Indeed, the rhetoric of the new often seems to conceal an underlying logic of cultural continuity and conservation—the national imaginary always seems to remain at its heart. Whatever their general enthusiasm, then, we suggest that these researchers and commentators on changing media paradigms fail to open up the question of just what it is that could be "new" about the new transnational media. There has been a reluctance, or an inability, directly to address the question of cultural innovation in the context of media transnationalism.

This question of cultural innovation is clearly not an easy one. There are great obstacles and difficulties in the way of re-instituting media culture. First, there is the problem of prevailing logics of cultural inertia or closure that continue to stand in the way of more cosmopolitan cultural arrangements. The old mentality of the national order is not easily overcome, as we shall go on to demonstrate; and it will not be at all easy to move beyond the national imagination and condition. Second, there is the problem of articulating what the potential of transnationalism might actually be. A critical transnationalism requires a commitment to the difficult task of elaborating new cultural arrangements and practices. What should be our starting point as we begin thinking about the possibilities of forging post-national—or perhaps they are better regarded as counter-national—dispositions and sensibilities in the context of contemporary developments in communications? On what basis, according to what values and objectives, might it be possible to institute a more genuinely transnational cultural order? And, in the context of this particular discussion, what kind of positive interventions might it be possible to make in the distinctive context of what Philip Schlesinger (1994) has called "Europe's contradictory communicative space"?

Our discussion in this chapter is intended as a contribution to the wider debates on the nature of any future transnational media and cultural order, and particularly a new European order. Its approach is different from that of the commentators and researchers whose agenda we have been (so far obliquely) criticizing, however. It does not seek to develop a general and abstract argument about transnational broadcasting spaces—and certainly not an argument predicated on technological transformation. The central concern, in thinking about what is possible, is with what is possible in relation to particular (transnational) cultures, at particular conjunctures, in particular circumstances. In the following discussion, we shall develop our ideas around one particular example or case study, that of Turkish transnational culture in the European space. It is our belief that, through the consideration of what is possible, at this particular historical moment, within the framework of what is defining itself as Turkish transnationalism, we may be able to address some of the broader possibilities that may be inherent in the processes of transnationalism. Indeed, we would go further and argue that the general issues can *only* be addressed when they are grounded in the particular dynamics and times of particular cultural configurations. The general issues are ones that we only ever know and experience through their particular manifestations, and through the particular opportunities or challenges they present to us—as with the distinctive issues raised by the Turkish example under discussion here.

Building on arguments in earlier articles concerning the dramatic transformations that re-shaped the Turkish national media scene in the 1990s (Robins & Aksoy 1997; Aksoy 1997; Şahin & Aksoy 1993), we shall briefly survey new developments in transnational broadcasting. Here it will be a question of identifying what particular cultural institutions and businesses are undertaking—their various and different strategies for transnationalism. We shall then go on to consider the significance of transnational Turkish media for the Turkish populations now living outside Turkey—the implications of television from Turkey for the cultural lives and identities of "Turks abroad". How are European Turks—of which there are many different kinds—implicated in the new transnational media they now have access to? The point is to establish how the specific conditions of Turkish cultural development have brought into existence a complex and diverse transnational culture—a culture endowed with its own particular and distinctive possibilities.

In exploring the nature of the new networks of transnational Turkish media and culture, particularly across the European space, we are especially concerned to explore what we regard as their real—but unrealized—transnational potential. First, their potential for the Turks themselves—we conceive this potential in terms of the critical interrogation of Turkish culture and identity, the challenge to taken-for-granted "Turkishness". But, second, their potential also for Europeans and for the European cultural space. For clearly these new Turkish media also have potential implications for the meaning of "Germanness" or "Frenchness" or "Europeanness". How, we have to ask, would we figure Turkish transnational media—and, by the same token, we could say Indian, Chinese, Maghrebi, Arabic, and a variety of other transnational networks -- into the meaning of a new European cultural order? It is our belief that an understanding of the changing nature of Turkish culture may actually help us to open up certain questions about the nature of European culture (see Robins 1996).

Our discussion of Turkish media and culture is grounded in our own experience of Turkish media and culture, in Turkey and in Britain. It is intended to convey a sense of the ordinariness of that culture, and of the potential that it has precisely because of that ordinariness. But we believe that it is necessary to explore the nature of this potentiality. So, as we move towards the end of our discussion, we shall become more committed to the gerundive tense of thinking. We shall reflect on the possibilities that (Turkish) transnational media might actually open up in the European space. We want to give some sense of what a transnational culture could amount to in the European context. It is in this cause, then, that we shall move towards the tense of the imperative of the future passive participle. We will set out our own sense of possibilities, in order to provoke others to think about what could be possible—possibly different—in (European) cultural transnationalism.

"Diasporic Media" and Transnational Culture

Let us begin by considering how the emergence of what has commonly been referred to as "diasporic media" is generally being approached now by communications researchers and analysts—for there does seem to be a rough consensus now about what is at issue. Most apparently, there is the evocation of techno-cultural change; the general inference is that the combined logics of globalization and technological revolution are now conspiring to produce significant cultural transformations. And what comes across is a positive commitment to the possibilities inherent in new global mobilities and in the creation of new migrant—or transmigrant—cultures across the global and European scene. But, at the same time, there always also seems to be a rather conservative undertow to this transnational cultural analysis. In the end, one is left with the sense that, actually, there are no meaningful changes in the way that transnational cultures can imagine and organize themselves. The analysis of transnational media remains grounded in the conventional ideal of community bonding and the sharing of a common culture. For, in the end, in spite of all the evocations of the possibilities inherent in global flows and mobilities, there seems to be a basic inability to move on from the core ideas and concepts of the national imagination. In the discussion of transnational futures, the fundamental reference point continues to be the stubborn and insistent idea of "imagined community" (Robins 1999).

So, for example, in their generally very interesting book on *New Patterns in Global Television*, John Sinclair, Elizabeth Jacka, and Stuart Cunningham (1996) are quick to point to the new ambiguities and complexities in identity associated with new kinds of global and local television. As an example of the new kind of multiple identities now available, they invoke a (hypothetical) "Egyptian immigrant in Britain ... [who] might think of herself as a Glaswegian when she watches her local Scottish channel, a British resident when she switches over to the BBC, an Islamic Arab expatriate in Europe when she tunes in to the satellite service from the Middle East, and a world citizen when she channel surfs on to CNN" (*ibid.*, 25). It is a good and suggestive illustration. But, having acknowledged the reality of "multiple social identities being overlaid in the individual subject", and, consequently, the necessity now for a "more pluralistic conception of audience identity" (ibid., 26), Sinclair *et al.* then draw back from the radical possibilities of this argument. For theoretical support, it seems that they can find nothing better than Benedict Anderson's concept of "imagined community". Thus: "Benedict Anderson's concept of 'imagined communities' has been one of the most influential tropes in theories of national consciousness for more than a decade, but as satellite television distribution transcends the borders of the nation-state, there is some value in applying it to the new audience entities which that process creates" (*ibid.*, 24–25). (A rather perverse judgment, we think.) Of central concern to their book, Sinclair *et al.* tell us, are "the imagined communities of speakers of the same language and participants in similar cultures which form the geolinguistic regions exploited by the media entrepreneurs, especially the diasporic communities of émigrés on distant continents" (*ibid.*, 25). The new, and potentially productive, complexities of transnational media cultures are ultimately denied, then, in a theoretical move that simply reduces all identity possibilities to being equivalent forms of belonging to that of imagined community.

In introducing a recent theme issue of *Javnost/The Public* concerned with "Globalization and Diasporic Media", Stefaan Verhulst (1999) makes the same kind of theoretical retreat. In what is again a very useful discussion, he too sets out to alert us to the novel processes associated with cultural globalization—processes that are considered to be associated with the progressive erosion of national borders. But precisely what kind of future is it that he is signaling when he evokes the idea of a cultural trajectory towards "emerging transnationalism" and the "de-territorialization of identities"? Well, the envisaged new order actually turns out again to bear a striking resemblance to the old one. What, in fact, comes across most clearly is the rather unaspiring, and uninspiring, belief, rather the argument, that "diasporic communications enable the existence of re-imagined communities" (Verhulst 1999, 31). Benedict Anderson's famous concept is again given a trial run in the context of a fascination with long-distance nationalisms—nations beyond their states—in the transnational era. The expectation is that transnational media will help globally-dispersed groups to form "new bonds of cohesiveness": "diasporic groups are now, with the tools of developing communications technology, working to maintain their identities, whether they are defined by religious fervor, ethnic pride, economic ambition, historic places of origin, by establishing supportive or interactive communities" (*ibid.*, 31). What seems most positive for Verhulst is that "electronic communications flows lead to a more immediate, less impeded, more intense and more effective form of transnational bonding" (*ibid.*, 30). New communications technologies are primarily valued, then, in so far as they work to sustain cultural cohesion and solidarity—the ties of (imagined) community—over global distances.

A further example of this kind of thinking about diasporic media is to be found in a widely circulated and well-received report on diasporic media written for the Department of Canadian Heritage.

Here Karim Karim (1998) is again initially motivated by a sense that there is something culturally new, and potentially innovative, about the combined emergence of digital technologies and global communications. He explicitly invokes the discourses of postcolonial studies, for example the idea of "third space", and suggests the possibility of the new media order bringing about new forms of "transnational citizenship" or "cosmopolitan democracy". But, in the end, the rhetoric of the new collapses before the resurgence of what is a more conservative, and far more insistent, discursive trope. In the end, it is again the discourse of national imagination that prevails. It turns out that the significance of the new media resides in their potential for maintaining "community links" (*ibid.*, 7) and enabling "community self-assertion" (*ibid.*, 4). Karim's concern turns to the ways in which diasporic media can sustain community cohesion and integration across the globe. Again, then, it is the national imaginary that becomes the central paradigm for thinking about the new transnational cultures and media. It seems, at one point, as if Karim might resist the conceptual allure of "imagined community". Thus, in considering the case of a transnational Indian community on the Internet, he notes that "this is not Benedict Anderson's 'imagined community' since it is extra-national, but it is, nevertheless, imagined" (*ibid.*, 15). But, despite this technical-geographical qualification, Karim in fact takes on board the substance of the "imagined community" concept, concerned as he is with the maintenance of at-a-distance cultural "commonalities" and "communal identity" (*ibid.*, 15). His report turns out ultimately to be simply an account of the institution of long-distance nationalisms. Diasporic communities are in the end conceived as "transnations" (*ibid.*, 4)—no other possibility ever really surfaces. In what is supposed to be an account of cultural transformation, we must surely be disappointed by the fact that nothing significantly new is allowed to emerge. Like the other media scholars that we have been considering, Karim ends up by subordinating the issues—and the potentiality—surrounding transnationalism to the old prevailing discourses of the national imaginary.

In sum, it seems to us that there are really two fundamental problems with what has now become the prevailing discourse on transnational media. The first problem concerns its understanding of television; its understanding of television, that is to say, as primarily a technology—with the consequent assumption that what is going on amounts to some kind of technological (or technological-organizational) revolution in the audiovisual industries. Against this

technological emphasis, we want to argue for the alternative conception of television, as an imaginary institution—in terms of a set of
dispositions and practices that, generally, command legitimacy,
adherence, and support. In the case of television, as many communications researchers have frequently observed, these dispositions
and practices have been very much associated with the reproduction
of the national culture and consciousness. This has made television
generally a conservative institution, screening the known and
familiar, and sustaining the pleasures of belonging, and continuously
affirming one's belonging, to the imagined community. Evoking the
religiosity of national attachment, Arnaud Viviant (1999, 3) likens
television viewing to participation in a holy mass. As an imaginary
institution, he maintains, television has involved a submission to the
social order—"the whole function of television in our society is to
absorb and to accept what is in the majority, to define and redefine
it endlessly, through all its shifts, its perpetual movement." From this
cultural-institutional perspective, it may be said that television has
developed a particular affinity with the national imaginary; and,
furthermore, that, in this cause, it has functioned as a conservative
force, committed to the confirmation and conservation of the imagined community. What we have to acknowledge is the inflexibility
and intractability of this particular imaginary institution, its inherent
tendency to resist both cultural change and cultural complexity.
When we come to consider the so-called new media (satellite and
cable television), we simply cannot make the assumption that they
will bring about change in the cultural order. If it is change that we
want, this must mean actively confronting the momentum of television as an instituted and embedded cultural reality. Rather than
relying on a technical fix, we have to consider just how—and
perhaps whether—television could be re-instituted as an imaginary
force.

A second, and perhaps even more fundamental, problem with the
discourses that we have been discussing takes us further into the
question of how they tend to think about questions of culture and
identity. The problematical thing is that culture and identity are only
ever conceived in terms of, and in the context of, "imagined communities". We may note, for example—and it is certainly not an
irrelevant example here, in the context of this article dealing with
Turkish transnational television—the status that the Kurdish television station, MED-TV (now known as Medya TV), has assumed in
many of these discourses (see, e.g. Karim 1998, 12). The point about
MED-TV is that it represents a late assertion of the right to

combined nationhood and statehood. As Amir Hassanpour (1998, 53, 66) has observed, MED-TV has actually been about "sovereignty in the sky", about the creation of a cultural space in which "viewers experience the citizenship of a state with its national flag, national anthem, national television, and national news agency". MED-TV offers perhaps the most potent expression of what, it seems, is also being looked for and valued in all the other examples of diasporic television: the maintenance of (national) community bonds over distance. The problem for us is that everything is reduced to being about the relations of imagined community. This concept, which has historically been so much associated with the imagination of national culture and identity, has now become (paradoxically) accepted as the theoretical basis for thinking about transnational or post-national developments.

This concern with imagined community seems to us especially perverse among scholars and commentators who are clearly interested in thinking about cultural transformation and potential alternative cultural formations—about the new dynamics of globalization, transnationalism, post-colonialism, and so on. It is perverse, we maintain, because the idea or concept of "imagined community" cannot provide us with the intellectual means to explore new or alternative cultural trajectories and possibilities. Indeed, we would suggest that the idea of "imagined community" actually works to inhibit thinking on these difficult issues. It stands in the way of conceiving and articulating a cultural and political project beyond the limitations of the national cultural imagination. In our view, the mobilization of this master concept in fact reflects a contemporary intellectual inertia—we might even say a certain intellectual laziness—in confronting what is at issue in contemporary cultural change. Within this discursive framework the question of culture and identity is reduced to the question only of belonging—with national belonging serving as the model for all types of belonging. There is no scope then for elaborating alternative (in the sense of more cosmopolitan) cultural projects. No intellectual space is provided for thinking about cultures in terms of the ever more complex possibilities—in terms of heterogeneity, encounter, transformation, mobility—that contemporary societies are now constantly throwing up. The fundamental problem is that, within the diminished imaginary universe of "imagined community", any consideration of what might be new and energizing in contemporary cultural transformations is foreclosed from the very outset.

Having made clear our difficulties with the prevailing discourses on "diasporic media", we turn now to a consideration of how we might begin to think alternatively about media and cultural transnationalism. This must involve recognition of the tenacity of imagined community—and, therefore, of the real difficulties that confront us in trying to think our way from a national to a new transnational imaginary in media cultures. Possibilities will not emerge automatically out of the development of the media themselves. It is a question, rather, of our capacity to invent more complex and more accommodating discursive spaces. Such a capacity really depends on our ability to identify where there may be transformations or contradictions within existing broadcasting cultures that might just open up possibilities—however small—to then be further worked on and elaborated. More ambitious projects depend on our ability to first redescribe—against the grain of imagined community—what is going on (for better and for worse) in actually existing media systems.

Transnational Television from Turkey: The Real Life of Imagined Community

So what, we shall now ask, has been happening in the recent transnationalization of television from Turkey? What can we say about the cultural implications of these transnational developments, particularly with respect to the sense of a Turkish imagined community? And, most crucially for us, where can we find possibilities of a counter-national kind in these Turkish developments?

First, we have to consider just what is available to Turkish populations living across the European space. In its TV listings, the Frankfurt edition of *Hürriyet* (the largest-circulation Turkish newspaper in both Turkey and Europe) gives program information on ten main channels. A few others are also available. So, at present, it is possible to receive around twelve channels from Turkey via satellite dishes (and around thirty in total with digital reception equipment, which few Turks possess at the present time). We may classify the available (analogue) channels thus:

- TRT-INT—This is the service provided by the Turkish state-broadcaster, the Turkish Radio and Television Authority. Available since 1990, this channel has been the most accessible, as it has also been available on cable systems in certain European countries (Germany, Switzerland, Holland, Belgium, Austria, Denmark). TRT-INT has been the organization that has been

most actively and strategically involved in transnational broadcasting. Among all the Turkish channels, TRT-INT has
produced the greatest amount of programming aimed specifically
at the European Turkish audience—at one point 50 percent of its
programs were produced in Europe, though financial restrictions
have meant that dedicated programming is now somewhat less.
TRT's programs strongly reflect the "official" state culture,
projecting what is regarded as an ideal image of the republican
nation (and practicing extensive cultural censorship in the same
cause, too).

- KanalD, Star, ATV, Show TV, BRT—These are all family-
oriented commercial channels. Even in Turkey, their origins are
quite recent (early 1990s), but, among Turkish audiences in
both Turkey and Europe, they have rapidly established themselves as the mainstream channels. We might note here that
these commercial channels were originally what we might call
accidental transnationalists. They came into existence in
Turkey itself as pirate broadcasters, transmitting their programs
by satellite from Europe (Robins & Aksoy 1997), and it was also
possible to pick up these signals in Western Europe. Show TV,
KanalD, and ATV have all experimented with dedicated European channels (involving predominantly Turkish output,
combined with just a small amount of local material). These
channels make available a very different kind of programming
than TRT-INT—they have a more metropolitan image.
Programming combines global styles and formats with the kind
of ("impure") local Turkish popular culture that TRT has
always disavowed.

- Kanal 7, TGRT, Samanyolu—These channels had their origins
as religious channels. In the early days (the early-1990s), they
were perceived as being at the forefront of Islamic revival—what
one journalist then described as "the television offensive of the
Islamists" (Cemal 1993). Programming was of a pious nature,
projecting an ideal Islamic version of Turkish culture. More
recently, both TGRT and Samanyolu (STV) channels have
compromised with commercial values—particularly TGRT,
which has now become more like a mainstream channel. Kanal
7 had—and still has—a reputation even among secular Turks for
the quality of its news and documentaries output.

- NTV, CNN Türk, Cine 5, Kral—These are more specialist
channels. NTV and CNN Türk are 24-hour dedicated news
channels. Cine 5 is a subscription channel. It had the franchise on

Turkish Premier League football until the 1999–2000 season, and now it specializes in movies. Kral is a music channel, aimed at young people.

One possible understanding of the development of transnational television from Turkey might be in terms of how it is serving to extend the imagined community of Turks across the European space (and beyond). Those who feel sympathy for the fate of migrant Turks, cut off from their "homeland", might feel that it is a good thing for them to be virtually reintegrated into their "own" culture. More intolerant observers will complain about the way in which Turks have retreated into their own cultural ghetto. In both cases—from the perspective of sympathy and of complaint—what is assumed is that these new channels offer the possibility now for the maintenance of national identity and culture—"in diaspora". But we want to oppose this often taken-for-granted idea that Turks—in Turkey and in Europe—are watching something called "Turkish television". We think it is important to resist this undifferentiating image of Turkish television. What we want to stress, and take account of, is the degree of pluralism that has been introduced into Turkish media culture.

This is important because the pluralization of the airwaves has now made it possible for competing versions of Turkish culture to co-exist. The availability of many different channels from Turkey may in fact be sensitizing many Turkish viewers to the complexity and contradictoriness of cultural processes. What may actually become more apparent to Turkish audiences—if not to the European observers of those audiences—is the fictional nature of the imagined community project.

Turkish media culture was once the domain of TRT alone. It was the domain in which TRT projected the national fiction of the ideal community of Turks. TRT still continues to operate as if this were the case. This has been particularly so in its transnational activities. In recent years, the state broadcaster has been undertaking a conscious project to extend the imagined community of both Turkish and Turkic peoples. It initiated TRT-INT to reach Turks in Europe, and also in Australia and New Zealand, and now the US, and also started a service called TRT Avrasya directed at the Turkic populations in the former-Soviet republics of Central Asia (Aksoy & Robins 2000). TRT has been very concerned to bind the "Turks abroad" into the national project. A senior producer in TRT makes clear the agenda:

When the Turkish population living abroad began to grow, then the fear that we might lose them came to the forefront. In Europe, and especially in Germany, it was felt that the new generation was drifting away from Turkey. In response to this, in order to strengthen people's ties with Turkey, more programs were made in the early nineties that targeted them, those living abroad. (Interview with Hasan Çakır, Ankara, 26 November 1999)

TRT's agenda has been centered precisely on the kind of transnational bonding and community links that researchers on "diasporic media" have been drawing our attention to (though we don't think that this kind of long-distance nationalism is what these commentators can be thinking of when they evoke the comforts of imagined community).

But now TRT no longer has a monopoly over Turkish media culture. Its programming is now only one of the possibilities on offer in what has become the newly diverse marketplace of Turkish media culture. The absolutely crucial development was the introduction of private channels in the early 1990s. For what the extremely rapid development of commercial television channels at that time did was to bring about a certain disordering of the national ideal—the "official" statist ideal of the Turkish imagined community. What the commercial operators undertook was the task of bringing into existence a new kind of cultural identity, against the grain of the "official" identity. For audiences up until that moment of broadcasting transformation, "Turkish" television had been synonymous with TRT, and meant nothing but TRT. The new commercial interests had to establish their own distinctive image as Turkish channels. What they succeeded very rapidly in doing was to create alternative kinds of "Turkishness"—new kinds of "Turkishness" to compete against the "official" national identity projected by the state broadcaster. As the media executive and consultant İbrahim Altınsay remarked to us, "Whilst TRT was a reflection of those in power, private broadcasting became a reflection of the people. It was instrumental in thinking about what meant to be Turkish" (Interview, Istanbul, 14 July 1994).

In seeking to institute itself as a reflection of the people, commercial television helped to make possible a new cultural politics of Turkishness. Because they started out as pirate operators, the commercial stations could avoid censorship and put on the screens the kinds of images and stories that TRT could never have permitted (Robins & Aksoy 1997). Their aim was to create an entirely new audience culture, and they believed that they could best do so by directly attacking the old taboos that had kept TRT-style Turkish culture straight-jacketed. Pretty much everything that had previously been a forbidden subject suddenly became visible and accessible. All those—we may call them the official untouchables—who had been censored in the old state culture of television—Kurds, Alevis, members of religious sects, women with headscarves, radical feminists, transvestites, gays, *arabesk* performers (*arabesk* was deemed to be a decadent musical form)—paraded through new-style current affairs debates, talk shows, and entertainment programs.

İbrahim Altınsay went as far as describing what happened when the new commercial channels burst onto the scene as a "civilizing process": "The private broadcasters defied everything that had been censored by TRT. Private broadcasting meant the emergence of a civil culture in Turkey ... It was a period of self-discovery ... Television became an important source for seeing alternative ways of being and living" (Interview, Istanbul, 14 July 1994). Without making exaggerated claims, we may say that private television channels played a significant part in undermining the hold of the "official" culture, which had for so long kept the "unofficial" side of Turkish cultural life repressed. What they helped to create was a far more liberal cultural environment, one in which sensitive issues around the nation, identity, religion, and so on, could be more openly debated. They were an important part of a process in which Turkey became a more multi-vocal society.

What we want to emphasize, then, is that the "official" imagined community of TRT no longer exercises its monopoly over the airwaves. The advent of the commercial channels served to open up a bigger—a more encompassing and a more accommodating—cultural space. The key point that we want to make is that this process has had very important implications for the televisual mediation of imagined community among Turks—implications that have to do with a certain de-fictionalization of Turkish media culture. First, we would suggest that the proliferation of commercial channels, with their more metropolitan take on Turkishness, has meant that the "official" version of Turkish identity has been in some way relativized. There are now competing images of Turkish reality on the screens. TRT's has become one interpretation of what it is to be a Turk, but only one among other possible interpretations, and no longer the privileged one. TRT has lost its authoritative position. As Hasan Çakır puts it, "A sizeable proportion of the Turkish audience in Germany trusts TRT because it is a state institution, and another sizeable proportion does not believe it because it is a state broadcasting institution" (Interview, Ankara, 26 November 1999). Now that they have the possibility to watch alternative news programs, audiences are in a better position to assess the accuracy or objectivity of the state broadcaster, and to judge its reliability. We may say that the fictional nature of its cultural universe has now become apparent to viewers who watch TRT's programs.

Second, with respect to this process of de-fictionalization, we may say that the alternative channels and sources—the commercial chan-nels—have also introduced a new kind of programming that has far less investment in the high fiction of "official" imagined community. This relates to the point, made above, that rather than seeking to reflect the interests of those in power, the private operators sought, for what were good commercial reasons, to address the Turkish people. They were concerned not with the fictional Turkish culture that was the invention of the "official" ideology, but with something more closely resembling the sociological reality and diversity of ordi-nary Turkish people. On the commercial channels, it became possible for all kinds of previously disavowed groups and individ-uals—what we referred to as the untouchables of the official culture—to make themselves seen and heard through the screen. What the "official" culture thought of as the "dark face" of Islam, for example, suddenly became ubiquitous on the television screen, and, through this ubiquity, simply ordinary (Öncü 1994). Generally, what the new channels succeeded in doing was to connect their audiences to the previously obscured ordinariness of Turkish society. "We discover that those we formerly saw as superior to ourselves are ordi-nary just like us," as Aydın Uğur (1996, 61) puts it. "When we see that the members of a cultural group we had negative impressions of, and even feared and resented, actually have weaknesses, emotions, etc., just like us, the expectation of a threat attributable to them diminishes." Turkish commercial channels connected, in a radical way, with the long-repressed banality of the culture. Ayşe Öncü (2000) puts it very well when she says that the ordinary and banal "enter[ed] the universe of argument and scrutiny, becoming part of the struggle for representation against the fixities of orthodoxy." She adds "the banal undergoes a 'change of state' when unformulated experiences acquire voice and visibility, entering the established world of political order, to become potentially 'subversive'."

What should be clear is the inadequacy of the idea that "the Turkish diaspora" watches something called "Turkish television", and in so doing becomes unproblematically drawn into the embrace of Turkish imagined community. What we are saying is that the current mythologization of Turkish television culture needs to be turned into a sociologization. Only within a sociological discourse, does it become possible to see the real diversity and complexity within the institution of Turkish television, which now exists across different cultural registers. We want to emphasize the importance of engaging with this complex institution of television in terms of the conditions of its real existence, at this very particular historical conjuncture—of engaging with the real life of the different Turkish populations in Europe, rather than with the homogenizing fiction of Turkish imagined community that is often projected onto them by non-Turkish researchers and commentators on the "diaspora" (as well, of course, as by the Turkish state). As Turkish people engage with the de-fictionalization of their culture, Europeans (researchers, commentators, politicians) should be supporting their re-negotiations. They, too, could be looking at Turkish media for what is ordinary and banal—and subversive.

Peculiarities of the Turkish

We are signaling the significance of the new diversity and complexity in Turkish media culture at the present time. To consider the possible implications of this pluralization, we need now to go on to situate this account of the new media scene in the context of what is happening more broadly to Turkish culture and identity—in Turkey and in Europe—at this particular historical moment. In seeking to identify the peculiarities of the Turkish example, one cultural development that we have to recognize is the strong re-assertion of Turkish nationalism (Poulton 1999). At the same time, however, what we have been witnessing, over the last decade or so is the emergence of a new identity politics in the culture (Ayata 1997). There have been articulations of a new and emergent agenda around cultural diversity and difference—expressed in terms of religious, ethnic, and linguistic identities, but also, as Turkey has become increasingly open to global economic forces, in terms of new consumerist and lifestyle identities. A certain contestation is occurring, in which contrary forces are competing over the contemporary meaning of Turkish culture and identity—a contestation between a closed idea of Turkishness (the state idea) and more open and plural possibilities (the ones we have associated with the processes of de-fictionalization).

There is evidently a powerful conservative force in all cultures, a force that constantly seeks to instate cohesion and stability as the norm, denying or disavowing the reality that all cultures are always bound to change—to change, as Tzvetan Todorov (1997, 6) puts it, "because culture does not exist in isolation, because groups are numerous, because the individuals within each group are numerous." But this force of continuity is not absolute. At particular times and in particular circumstances, cultures are reminded that they are made up from elements that are numerous, and that they are, therefore, susceptible to change. They become aware—perhaps it is only for a brief historical moment—that the cultural community they imagined as being eternal in fact turns out to be only provisional. Immanuel Wallerstein draws attention to this fundamental provisionality of all cultures when he poses the question "Does India exist?" "Just to pose the issue this way is to invite ridicule," he says, "but it also points up the arbitrariness of all statements about India's (or anyone else's) 'culture'. India's culture is what we collectively say it is. And we can disagree" (Wallerstein 1991, 133–134). As they have become much more aware of what we might call their constitutive numerousness, Turks—in Turkey and in Europe—have also become more aware of this provisional nature of cultural identity. At this particular historical moment, Turkish culture is more fluid than it has ever been. Turks are involved in a process of re-negotiating their identities. And the Turks in Europe are involved in an even more complex process of negotiation, positioning themselves in relation to both their "homeland" and the European nation-states in which they happen to live (Kastoryano 1996). What is at issue is whether it will be possible for them to establish new forms of cultural association, ones that are more accommodating than those of the nation-state community.

We are only saying that certain possibilities have become more evident at the present time, not that they will be realized. (Of course, for them to ever be realized, it is always necessary for us to explore and to articulate the conditions of possibility.) The conservative forces in the society are extremely powerful; the forces that disavow pluralism and change. In considering the possibilities of transformation, we have to consider what stands in the way of change. First, there is the resistance thrown up by those who feel threatened by any possibility of cultural re-institution. (In the final part of this discussion, we shall consider a second obstacle, which is the profound difficulty of actually conceiving society on an alternative basis.) Of course, there is bound to be resistance from "within"—from the Turkish state and the institutions of the "official" culture—and we need not really go into that at any length here. More interesting, and perhaps more problematical, is the resistance to change coming from where one might have expected more sympathy—from the European side. Identities never exist in isolation, never create their trajectories only from resources within. "Turkishness" now is not a matter for the Turks alone. The European attitude towards cultural developments among Turkish "minorities" is also extremely important and influential. What we want to reflect on now is the European context in which the new transnational Turkish cultures are developing—the changing relational space in which Turkish and European (German, in particular) cultures encounter each other. How have observers and commentators in Europe sought to understand and to respond to recent developments in Turkish media and culture?

Put simply, the answer must be that the Europeans are obstacles to change. European reactions to the new Turkish media stand in the way of any kind of Turkish cultural revisionism. In the European response, it seems as if the issues can only be framed from the point of view of national cultures ("the Turk")—as if no other cultural arrangement were conceivable. In part, no doubt, this is because of a basic ignorance about the complexity—the internal numerousness—of Turkish populations. There is no awareness of the existence of Alevis, or of the differences between various Muslim groups and communities, or of disagreements between a wide range of secular interest groups. In this respect, the European attitude reflects what Dubravka Ugrešić (1998, 239) describes (in the context of Eastern Europe) as an attitude of "innocent-indifferent ignorance"; as far as most Europeans are concerned, Turkey is, to borrow her term, a "mental empty space". It is simply and sadly assumed, on the basis of an attitude that ranges between rank arrogance and bored disinterest, that Turks are all the same (all the same kind of problem, that is to say).

But it is not just a question of cultural ignorance or unawareness. We also have to take into account the complex and compulsive workings of the mentality of imagined community among Europeans. What is at issue is how the "host" culture chooses—or feels itself driven—to cope with its migrant "minorities", its own foreigners. Significantly, the "host" country is likely to receive its migrants as an imagined community, addressing them on the basis of an imagined national homogeneity (Rigoni 1997, 52–53). To some extent this is a function of bureaucratic-administrative convenience, but it also represents what we may regard as an identity strategy on the part of the "host" culture. We might see it in terms of a projective mechanism—a kind of collective act of projective identification—in which, say, the German host seeks (needs?) to project a *Volk*ish identity onto the Turks, in order to both experience and justify the existence of its own German *Volk*ishness. Through the image it forms of the other as an imagined community, the "host" nation brings into focus its own imaginary unity and coherence. This way of relating to the others within (or of just dealing with their presence) works to provide a certain kind of identity support. It makes it possible to achieve a certain (though always provisional) narcissistic comfort—and to keep at bay (what always remains as) a more foundational discomfort. It is a strategy that works in some respects, but one that always remains grounded in a basic fear, haunted by the constant sense of having, in some way or other, to control or manage the other's cultural presence. There are always the times when the presence of the "other" imagined community within suddenly comes to seem unacceptable and intolerable.

Recently, we have seen such resentment expressed in the considerable offense that has been taken against the development of the new transnational Turkish media culture—a cultural development that seems to indicate the more assertive presence of this particular other imagined community (one that could be more easily tolerated when it remained a silent minority). In Germany particularly, there has been a profound discomfort with Turkish satellite television, at times amounting to even a panic. This discomfort has manifested itself in arguments about the disloyalty of Turks towards the "host" culture—with the image of Turks as ungrateful and disrespectful guests. In stronger versions, it has been seen in terms of the failure of the integration project. Wilhelm Heitmeyer has famously described this as a process of "dis-integration". Among Turkish youth, he has argued, there is now an "identity crisis", a crisis that arises because these young people are increasingly caught in "a balancing act, a conflict of loyalties, between the norms and demands of 'their' culture, or at least the culture of their parents and grandparents, on the one hand, and the values and expectations of the German majority and of their German peer group, on the other" (Heitmeyer *et al.* 1997, 17). Turkish popular culture, including television and pop music, is listed among the factors responsible for the "acculturation stress" among Turkish youth. The assumption that is then commonly made is that, in order to resolve this conflictual dilemma, young Turks are likely to turn exclusively to—to take refuge in—Turkish media and the Turkish cultural space. The basic assumption is clearly that loyalty, in the case of migrants especially, can only be singular. In choosing to watch Turkish television (in choosing the inevitable, it seems), the Turkish migrants give evidence of their essential (seemingly inescapable) Turkishness. By the same token, they seem to be making it quite clear that they do not, and can never, really belong in the German cultural domain (thereby seeming to restore its imagined purity back to the German people).

Heitmeyer's represents an alarmist discourse—a discourse mobilizing the image of parallel societies, societies in disjuncture. There are other, less sensationalist versions of this argument concerning Turkish television as a threat to integration, including ones from the Turkish community itself. These accounts regard transnational Turkish broadcasting as giving rise to cultural enclosure and sequestration. Thus, Cem Özdemir, a member of the Green Party, and the first member of the German Parliament with Turkish origins, says:

> I wish that satellite dishes hadn't been invented. The number of Turkish families watching German television has decreased. In a lot of families only Turkish channels are being watched. There is very little about German society to be found on these channels. We know for a fact that watching or listening to channels which are not in German leads to the gradual deterioration of the language of the foreigners who live here ... It's a natural right for people to use, and to not want to forget, their own language. But in allowing this to happen, we are also bringing problems to this country [Germany]. (Quoted in Karakullukçu 1999)

In this discourse, too, we find that the issue of media consumption is framed in either/or terms. There is the same sense that, when they make their choice between Turkish and German channels, Turks will display their cultural weakness and make the wrong choice. Again, though this time out of understandable feelings of concern about the difficult position of Turkish migrants, there is an anxiety that Turks will fail to integrate. The debate around satellite television remains caught up in the inclusionist/exclusionist logic of imagined community.

Not all commentators see the new consumption of Turkish media products in such a bad light, however. Some are intent on dispelling the alarmist and anxious scenarios that have been proliferating. They want to put forward more positive accounts of the new transnational media order, drawing attention to what they regard as its virtues, and emphasizing the opportunities that may be opening up, rather than the problems. We would argue that these accounts do have a greater hold on the complexity of contemporary media transformations, permitting them to make a more balanced judgment about what is actually going on. There are two kinds of argument within this more critical perspective: one that essentially shares the same assumptions as the problem-oriented approaches that we have just been considering, but which then goes on to draw quite different conclusions (associated with a multiculturalist agenda); and another that comes up with a more nuanced and optimistic account of what is happening in the Turkish communities on the basis of a fundamental disagreement with those basic assumptions (associated with a more civic cultural agenda). In both cases, the idea of a radical failure of integration is directly challenged—though still significantly, we want to emphasize, from within the discursive frame of imagined community.

The first argument accepts the point that Turks prefer to watch Turkish television. But it maintains that this is not something we should be alarmed about. In fact, watching television "from home" can serve as a confidence-building measure for the migrant community. There is an element here of the argument that was prevalent in Germany in the 1970s and 1980s—the argument that "ethnic minority media" were good for providing "orientation-help" for immigrants, and that they helped to build "a bridge back to the homeland" (for guest workers who would presumably one day go back to that homeland) (Kosnick 2000). But, more recently (as it has become more apparent that the guests are staying on), the discourse has developed in terms of a multiculturalist argument (in the style of Charles Taylor) that, in the multi-ethnic societies of today, the way forward is through a "politics of recognition". From this perspective, the consumption of Turkish media may be seen, to use Jörg Becker's formulation, as only a temporary "moment of dissociation", and one that will, in the longer term, actually "help the identity of the other to be willing and able to become and remain integrated" (1996, 47). Thus, the consumption of Turkish media may not be about retreat and isolation, but may be regarded as "a positive and welcome process of humanization" (Becker 1997, 8). Dissociation is actually thought to be a functional moment in the integration process, affording Turks the necessary self-confidence and self-regard to become (human?) members of German society.

The second of the more positive accounts of migration and media consumption takes a rather different tack. Where the previous approach recognized that the Turks were watching their own "ethnic" programs, but then argued that there is nothing wrong with this "ethnicization" of the media landscape, the second approach actually rejects the idea of a Turkish preference for programs "from home". Thus, the Zentrum für Türkeistudien in Essen recognizes that "exclusive consumption of media in the language of the homeland will be regarded as a lack of willingness to integrate on the part of the foreign population" (1997, 13). But the evidence of its own audience surveys is then revealed to demonstrate "that the thesis of one-sided influence in media consumption" is not actually tenable. Turks watch both Turkish and German programming (and when they do not watch German programs it is for reasons of linguistic incapacity, especially among older persons, rather than because they are unwilling to). Not guilty, then, is the verdict from this more sympathetic perspective. Alec Hargreaves comes up with similar findings from research that he has conducted, and comes to the same basic judgment. In considering how Turks in Germany consume television output, he thinks in terms of cultural "hybridity", arguing "as the range of available channels widens, there is a tendency for individual viewing patterns to become more hybrid rather than locked within narrow monocultural confines" (1999, 12). But this idea of hybridity never really takes off in an argument that remains essentially implicated in the idea of imagined communities ("hybrid" simply means the watching of both Turkish- and German-language programs—which? how?—by an undifferentiated group called "the Turkish minority"). While there is the suggestion that "minorities are acculturating in several directions, i.e. adapting to diverse sets of cultural norms", the formulation then shifts back to make the argu-ment that particular circumstances have worked "to produce somewhat slower rates of acculturation among Turks than among Maghrebis in France" (*ibid.*, 2, 10; on Maghrebis, see similar argu-ments in Hargreaves & Mahdjoub 1997). It is a more complex analysis than that of the Zentrum für Türkeistudien, but it is still grounded in the basic ideas of minorities and of integration within a nation-state (in this case, civic) framework.

We return to the fundamental problem that the prevailing discourses on Turkish transnational culture and media take the idea of "imagined community" as their preeminent reference point. In the end, the imagination of transnationalism always turns out to be a national imagination. What becomes increasingly clear is that the terms that are available to describe what is now going on in the cultural world are simply inadequate.[2] In writing this chapter, we feel that we have been constantly struggling with (and against) an exhausted language—"diaspora", "ethnic community", "transna-tional community", "imagined community", "re-imagined community", "homeland", "minority", "integration", "ghettoiza-tion", and so on. We have been painfully aware of how restricting this language is. There is nothing to describe the world other than the language of the past -- nothing to open up its inherent possibilities, nothing to register what might be different about the future.

About an Interlocutor

Only reality can call to life another reality.

Osip Mandelstam

Finally, we come to consider the second of the difficulties that presently stand in the way of a counter-national cultural order. For, there is not just the problem of resistance to change, but also the sheer difficulty of shedding the national vision and of conceiving a different kind of order. At this point, we have to take our discussion again beyond the particularities of our Turkish case study, to open up some broader arguments about the meaning of transnationalism. Time to move the argument into the gerundive. We are concerned with how we might begin to think ourselves beyond—which means to think outside of—the enclosing space of the national imaginary (and we certainly do not underestimate the real difficulties in such an endeavor). It is a question—to use Christa Wolf's (1997) compelling image (applied in the German context)—of "parting from phantoms". Can we recognize the phantom relations and the phantom encounters—both within and without—that contemporary national cultures and identities implicate us in? Can we consider exorcising these phantoms that our imagined communities have become and, as Wolf puts it with deceptive simplicity, "get real" (*ibid.*, 302)?

What we actually have to deal with is what we might call the relational culture of imagined community. In this relational culture, a fundamental distinction is made between our relation to those within (with whom we share a mutual recognition of sameness) and all the others—those outside our community of fate, with whom we share little or nothing. In the first case, the social relations are grounded in a culture of intimacy and trust. As Eric Ringmar (1998, 542, 545) has argued, modern political culture was founded on a familial basis—or in terms of a public sphere that was "as intimate and true as the interaction taking place in a company of friends": "Modern man was the interior man, and interior man could only reveal himself if public relations were intimate relations. The intimate political community was called a nation, and the nation soon came to be seen as the only political entity which really could command our allegiance." From the perspective of this intimate bond, "outsiders" or "foreigners" could only be regarded with suspicion. "Intimacy is possible only between some," as Ringmar (*ibid.*, 545) notes. "There can be no 'we' among strangers since it is difficult to identify with people very different from ourselves." According to this kind of thinking—what Abdelmalek Sayad (1999) describes as "state thinking"—strangers are seen only as an essential threat. When they appear within "our" community as migrants or refugees, it can only be as a fundamentally disturbing presence, confounding the order that was predicated on a clear separation of inside and outside. The second kind of social relation of the imagined community is the relation with those who can't belong, those we can't understand, and with whom we could never be intimate. At best, they can only be regarded as guests, and they are expected to behave as polite guests. They have to "behave and conduct themselves according to what the code of etiquette drawn up by the local masters teaches and expects" (*ibid.*, 9). What we have is an imaginary organization of the world that is elaborated entirely from the perspective of the local, in terms of an order in which the local (this or that particular nation state) is at the center, marginalizing all the rest.

This is how an imagined community exists. We would argue that imagined communities cannot exist and think otherwise. There are two modalities between which any imagined community is permanently oscillating. There is that which draws on the pleasures of intimacy, celebrating what is familiar, and organizing the collective narcissism around all that is held in common. This is the confirming culture that is usually invoked in affirmative accounts of imagined communities. Then there is a quite different modality, evoked very well by Peter Sloterdijk. The nation is also, in his words (1998, 12), "a hysterical and panic-stricken information system, one that must constantly excite itself, make itself stressed, even terrorize itself and throw itself into a state of panic, in order to impress itself, and to convince itself, as a community of stress held in suspense, that it really exists." In this modality, the nation is a kind of panic machine, constantly mobilized against everything "alien", everything that seems to threaten its integrity and well-being.

There is something very problematical about this cultural condition of the imagined community. No doubt we can all immediately agree that the second of these modalities is deeply disturbing, with the hostility and fear that is expressed towards the others, branded as "aliens". But we would also argue that the intimate modality is equally problematical, with its underlying assumption that "the only people we really trust [are] people who in one way or another are like ourselves" (Ringmar 1998, 545). There is something disturbing about a culture and politics grounded in intimacy and self-enclosure. The imagined domains of both the alien and the intimate are equally problematical, and there is something fundamentally impossible about a cultural order that exists between these modalities (even though it has historically been possible for imagined communities to hold them in unproductive tension and to survive the deep stresses that are induced by this cultural condition).

In a great many discussions of imagined community, where it is felt that readers might mistakenly think that these kinds of community are simply imaginary (i.e. fictional, make-believe), the point is made that they are, in fact, very real (i.e. real in their effects). Perhaps it is now time for the point to be made that this division of the world between "us" and "them", "intimates" and "aliens", is indeed profoundly imaginary (fictitious, mythological). The discourse of imagined community is a discourse of phantom abstractions and phantom relations (with both intimates and aliens). This point is made in order to oppose the idea that we should, or should want to, draw now on the idea of "imagined community" to think about transnational or "diasporic" cultures and media.

What we have tried to argue in this chapter is that there are new developments in the European space which begin to go against the grain of imagined community, and that we must try to grasp what it is that is new about them. Thus, Michel Wieviorka (1998, 74–75) notes that "as the notions of assimilation and integration become more and more inadequate, ... it is more and more difficult, and less and less necessary for various minorities to slip into them." It is now possible to live alternatively, as a member of a diaspora: "a diaspora offers a chance to belong to several frameworks that are not all enclosed in the envelope of the national community" (*ibid.*). Amin Maalouf (1998, 12) makes the argument that we should no longer think of cultural identities as ascribed at birth. Identity changes and is transformed through the course of a lifetime, such that we should now think in terms of "composed identities". In the context of changing political cultures, Yasemin Soysal (1997, 511) observes that now "solidarities are shaped beyond national boundaries, and the referent is no longer the national citizen". Counter-national forms of membership are about "legitimating individuals' participation and imbuing them with 'actorhood' independent of membership status within a particular nation-state" (*ibid.*, 512). We are beginning to be in a position to think of what is going on in the world in other-than-national ways. To be in a position to recognize that, in so far as a particular "vision" of the social world is imposed through the principles of its "di-vision" (Bourdieu 1980), then through other, more complex, forms of division, it may be possible to come up with alternative visions. How, then, is it possible to conceive of spaces (in our case, the wider European space) according to a genuinely transnational vision?

To part from phantoms would be first to give up the imagined security of imagined community, to recognize the community of stress at the heart of its imagined coherence, and to acknowledge all those who now live in the European space in terms of their complex and differentiated realities. Only by acknowledging the reality of the migrant presence in Europe—addressing the Turks and others on the basis of a genuine reciprocity—can the European nation states "get real". For, as Osip Mandelstam (1977, 64) put it, with characteristic insight, "Only reality can call to life another reality". It would be a question of recognizing the others as interlocutors (to borrow Mandelstam's term). For Mandelstam, to relate to an interlocutor is to accept a certain distance, and to accept and to value that distance on the basis of the alternative kind of communicational possibilities that it opens up. The distance of separation is important: "If I know to whom I speak, I know ahead of time how he will regard what I say, whatever I might say, and consequently I shall manage not to be astonished by his astonishment" (*ibid.*, 63). With the interlocutor at a distance we enter into a relationship of mutual respect and revelation—a transformative relationship. Jacques Rancière has inflected Mandelstam's profound insight in a more political direction. Taking up Mandelstam's concern for the indeterminacy of the interlocutor ("the unexpectedness of his or her countenance"), he helps us to think beyond the imagined pleasures of imagined community. "An interlocutor is not a 'partner'," Rancière makes clear. "And the advances of democracy have always been due to improvisation by unprogrammed actors, by surplus interlocutors: a noisy crowd occupying the street, a silent crowd crossing their arms in a factory and so on" (1995, 103). Rather than conceiving them in terms of imagined communities, might we not see the migrant populations such as the Turks as being such kinds of unprogrammed actors in the new European space? What if we were to welcome their cultural presence, and to anticipate the possibilities they have brought, as surplus interlocutors in Europe now? That would be something.

Much of the contemporary debate on diasporic media has been concerned with a supposed technological transformation, which is then associated with the development of what are regarded as new kinds of transnational communities. We have argued that what is being thought of as new turns out in fact to be far from it. It turns out to be about no more than the re-animation, now on an expanded basis, of the national ideal of imagined community. Against this conservative vision, we have sought to think through some alternative possibilities. The discussion of alternative possibilities must be grounded in a recognition of the complexities of particular cultures, taking into account what might be achievable at particular historical conjunctures. It should also aspire to the creation of alternative kinds of cultural arrangement to those that have prevailed in the era of imagined communities. What we are suggesting is a discussion that seeks to open up a cosmopolitan perspective to new cultural and media developments in Europe now. It should be a cosmopolitanism that is committed to the value of cultural encounter; that recognizes that all cultures live by exchange (a truth which national communities have always worked hard to disavow), and that seeks thereby to know the conditions under which cultures can be creative (Abel 1999). It should be a cosmopolitanism committed to the possibilities that are inherent in the acts of translation between cultures. We are far from saying that such a cosmopolitan order is easily achievable. It is clear that belonging to an imagined community remains a powerful and compelling identity choice. In the realm of the media, we must be attentive to the long-instituted affinity between television culture and the national "group illusion" (Dorra 1996) But to formulate an alternative to the inert and groupish mentality of imagined community—to go with "the verb on horseback"—at least gives us a measure by which to gauge its poverty as a cultural choice. And without the positing, at least, of an alternative, we will never succeed in parting from our phantoms, and in creating meaningful cultural and political alternatives in what has become the phantom abode of Europe.

Notes

1. This chapter is based on research conducted within the ESRC Transnational Communities Programme—Award L214252040, Negotiating Spaces: Media and Cultural Practices in the Turkish Diaspora in Britain, France, and Germany.

2. Though we are now seeing some efforts to clarify the vocabulary we use to describe global migrant cultures. Thus, in the context of our particular concern with Turkish migrants, Riva Kastoryano (1999) has discussed the relative

merits of calling them a "diaspora" or a "transnational community"; Isabelle Rigoni (1997) has debated between "diaspora" and "network". Stéphane de Tapia (1994) has linked the idea of "diaspora" to that of "networks" and "migrant flows". In an interesting discussion, Thomas Faist (1999) has rejected the idea of "diaspora" in relation to Turkish populations, preferring to think in terms of "a transnationalized and segmented cultural space".

Part Three: CITIZENSHIP AND BELONGING: POLITICAL AND LEGAL REGIMES

CHAPTER 10

Migration, Belonging, and the Shrinking Inclusive Capacity of the Nation-State

Michael Bommes

Samuel Huntington's vision in the early 1990s of a "clash of civilizations" was met with significant public resonance and for migration research this was another occasion to underline its political meaning and importance. Again it seemed to become obvious that migration, culture, ethnicity, and conflict are linked in an inseparable manner. If the clash of civilizations appeared evident somewhere then it was the case of international migration (Bade & Bommes 1996). The supposition of a nearly automatic linkage is certainly problematic in scientific terms. But this caused no harm for migration research in organizational terms but rather provided new opportunities for funding and institutionalization in a general social context of fears caused by the rapid changes after 1989.[1]

Conflicts resulting from migration were increasingly seen as an outcome of the multiplication of different cultures in one country. Countries in Europe like Germany, the United Kingdom, the Netherlands, or Switzerland came to be described as multicultural societies (in the plural!) and they were advised to pay attention to this "fact" combined with the expectation that even if there is no road to multiculturalism without social conflicts, there is no viable alternative to tolerance as a device for the interaction of cultures either (Leggewie 1990).

The formula of the "multicultural society" has been criticized in many ways (Radtke 1990; Hoffmann-Nowotny 1996; Nassehi 1997). But it seems that meanwhile the framing of the consequences of migration as multicultural has lost much of its mobilizing potential for science and politics alike. Some countries like the

Netherlands or Sweden have become much more cautious in basing their policies on the diagnosis of the emergence of a multicultural society (Entzinger 1998; Ring 1998). It also became obvious that the term "multicultural" is used in very different ways in countries like Canada, the US, Australia, or Germany related to the different political traditions and backgrounds of dealing with immigration. More policy oriented sciences like political science and education, but also political philosophy (Taylor 1993; Kymlicka 1995) were fascinated for a while by the political debates about "multicultural society" and took part in them. It may be interesting to note that sociology remained distant and was not quite convinced by the appropriateness of the concept.

If one interprets Huntington's thesis of "the clash of civilizations" as a—certainly problematic—proposal to understand recent globalization processes, it is worth noting that majority of the contributions of migration research to the political and scientific debates about globalization are rarely linked to the debates on multicultural society. Instead "transnational migrations" are identified now as a central part of ongoing globalization processes (Glick Schiller, Basch, & Blanc-Szanton 1995, 1997a; Portes 1995; Pries 1996, 1997, 1998). "Multiculturalism" had been observed in the frame of the nation-state. It was described as a challenge for the efforts of cultural homogenization typically undertaken by nation-states (Gellner 1988). "Transnationalism" seems to be the key term for migration research when participating in the globalization debate. It stresses that the various forms of transnational migration and the emergent social networks need to be understood as part and expression of the general loss of centrality and sovereignty of the nation-state.

It could be argued that many of the recent proposals, which deny the continuing importance of nation-states, are premature and unconvincing (Bommes 1999). Insofar as research on "transnational migration" is based on these assumptions, it inherits some of the problems linked with them.[2] But the aim of this chapter is different. It is based on the distinction between the empirical relations referred to by multiculturalists and transnationalists on the one hand and their conceptual and theoretical tools us. Concentrating on some of the empirical phenomena reflected as multicultural or transnational, it will be argued that these phenomena can be interpreted as indicators of the shrinking inclusive capacity of national welfare states—without combining this with a premature prognosis about the end of *the* welfare state.

I.

Observers of multicultural society and of an emerging transnationalism share in different ways the proposition that central structural elements of the nation-state are running through a process of erosion. The multiplicity of cultures seen as a result of migration indicates the growing cultural heterogeneity of the population living within state territories. This questions the old program of the nation-state, i.e. the creation and/or the safeguarding of the cultural homogeneity of the population. In a different mode, transnationalism refers to the emergence of social structures which result from enduring migration flows and links, i.e. networks and organizations which stabilize such links and make them in this way transnational, links that transcend the borders of nation-states in a permanent manner. Transnationalism underlines at the same time the shifting strategies of migrants who start to orient themselves to these transnational structures of social opportunities. As a consequence of this, the nation-state, and its classical aim of "social integration", loses some of its centrality as a frame of social orientation.

For a theoretical interpretation of some of the social developments indicated by multiculturalism and transnationalism, a historical contextualization and reminder is useful. From the World War II until roughly the end of the 1980s, the large migration movements in the European immigrant countries, the US, Canada, and Australia—these movements included refugees and expellees, labor migrants, postcolonial migrants, and family migration—were met by a remarkably high level of provision of the affected national welfare states and relatively successful and effective programs of social integration (Hollifield 1992; Soysal 1994). In various countries, the social integration of migrants was initially politically unintended, but this did not seriously affect the common outcome best summarized by Hammar (1989, 1994). The majority of migrants were endowed with civil, social, and partly also political rights to an extent, which was formerly seen as a privilege of citizens. In this way they became what Hammar has called "denizens". In this context, the multiplication of cultures in an empirical sense, i.e. the immigration of individuals from different cultural backgrounds and the related multiplication of forms of life, was not necessarily combined with multiculturalism in the social sense that cultural differences and the ethnic and national meanings ascribed to them became a dominant mechanism for the allocation of social positions. In other words, culture and ethnicity were not socially dominant mechanisms for the creation of minorities.[3] The expanded welfare state after the World War II possessed enough capacity—at least in Europe, Canada, and Australia—to provide chances of social inclusion for migrants in a way that devalued to a significant extent ethnic and national forms of social closure.

The constellation of the 1970s and 1980s came to an end as a result of the political changes after 1989, the immigration of refugees and asylum seekers, new labor migrants, ethnic migrants like Jews and the Ethnic Germans from Eastern Europe, the growth of ethnic and national conflicts in the former socialist countries and in former Yugoslavia, and last but not least as a result of the shrinking interventionist capacity of national welfare states in the context of political, economic, legal, and scientific globalization and European integration. But what precisely in the field of migration has changed so dramatically and in what way docs the welfare state encounter limits that justify the assumption of fundamental shifts indicated by the formulas of transnationalism and multiculturalism? In order to discuss this, it is necessary to outline briefly the specific role of national welfare states in modern society for the political regulation of migration and its social consequences. This will provide the background for a theoretical interpretation of recent social changes.

II.

The modern nation-state is defined by the execution of sovereignty over a territory and a population. As Swaan has shown this was, right from the start, linked with the emergence of the welfare state (Swaan 1988). By means of providing chances of participation in the social realms of the economy, law, health, or education (i.e. as a welfare state), the nation-state created the social preconditions for a process in which former subjects became political citizens—a process in which the inclusion of the whole population into the political system as individual citizens and the claim of political sovereignty over these could gain legitimacy and universal validity. The welfare state became the central instance in modern society which moderated the relation between the principle of universal access to and inclusion in the social realms of the economy, the law, education, health, or politics and the reality of social exclusion.

The universalism of inclusion in modern society means that nobody should be excluded from claiming economic, legal, or educational provisions if he or she fulfils the social preconditions for any of these claims—e.g. one can participate in education if one is perceived as educable; one can participate in the economy if one gains access to monetary means; one can participate in law if one knows how to act on behalf of one's own rights. But this does obviously not imply that inclusion empirically succeeds.

One pivotal condition for this is the access to membership roles in organizations and to the income that is earned by fulfilling these roles, i.e. through labor. Finding employment in modern society means to offer competence and specific services to an organization in exchange for payment (and other rewards). The chances for individuals to gain access to the functional realms of the economy, law, health, or education are mediated in many ways by organizations. Organizations (firms, administrations, hospitals, courts, universities, etc.) engage individuals as members by formally specifying the conditions of participation. As a particular type of social field, organizations rely on the formal definition of membership that distinguishes between members and non-members. By engaging individuals as members, *organizations* distribute conditions and chances for inclusion and exclusion in other social spheres. Recruitment of personnel, the allocation of positions, and careers in organizations are linked with the distribution of money, reputation, and influence or—in the words of Bourdieu—economic, cultural, and social capital. Organizational memberships based on careers and the corresponding conditions of engaging individuals open up and mediate differential chances for individuals to obtain services and resources as consumers, patients, clients, pupils, electors, etc.

The organizational procedures for allocating positions and incomes are one central frame of reference for *welfare state* policies which aim to increase and especially to secure the transferability of chances, i.e. to assure that organizational membership does equip individuals with the necessary means and rights that provide options for participation in the social realms of the economy, education, law, health, politics, and the family.[4] Historically the welfare state became a mediator which tried to reduce barriers to participation and access to the provisions of the different social realms and to provide resources to transcend these barriers, e.g. by means of education, money, legal advice, health care, etc. These measures can be understood as efforts to secure the openness of social systems for individuals.

Welfare provided by the nation-state had right from the start a territorial index. The provisions of welfare states initially addressed only citizens, i.e. those individuals who were recognized by the state as belonging to its own territory. Nation building in Europe took place as a process by which a population was transformed into a unitary nation, a people ("Volk"), on a politically defined territory (Koselleck 1992; Brubaker 1992).[5] The nation may have been defined in rather ethno-cultural or political terms (like in Germany or France), but in the historical context of competitive state building processes in Europe, "the common welfare of the people of the nation", of "the community of national citizens" evolved as the general frame of reference for the state (Bommes 1999).

III.

One main result of this European tradition of nation-state building was the constitutively tense relation between immigration and the national welfare state. The efforts of welfare states aim at the mediation of social participation for their citizens. But organizations and the differentiated social realms of society do not allow for social inclusion on the basis of the distinctions and criteria preferred by nation-states. Inclusion and exclusion in the economy, education, law or health, but also in formal organizations do not correspond to the political distinction of belonging or non-belonging to the nation. In addition to this, migrations are not just the outcome of politically unwanted processes, but are to a large extent politically initiated or induced, like in the case of the labor migrations of the 1960s and 1970s, the different forms of ethnic migration, or contract labor migration.

Situated in the frame of the national welfare state, experiences of social exclusion provoke the question of why exclusion hits those belonging to the nation and not primarily those who do not so belong. Why are foreigners or new immigrants recruited by organizations if major parts of the indigenous population are unemployed? Why do immigrants participate in provisions of health and education and why do they gain entitlements at a time when the general capacity of welfare states to provide is shrinking? State borders that transcend migration induce a tendency to replicate the distinction between those included and those excluded as a distinction between the nation/people and the residual population inhabiting a state territory. This articulates the political expectation that both distinctions should classify the same group of individuals.

This tendency intensifies when it becomes clear that national welfare states with a shrinking capacity can—for various reasons—only regulate but not control, hinder or reverse immigration. For example, the labor migrations of the 1960s and 1970s had been politically initiated on the premise that the states can keep control over these migration processes and their consequences. But various political efforts to reverse these immigrations were confronted with self-created legal barriers, which were one consequence of the inclusion of "guest workers" into the social insurance systems of the welfare state (Hollifield 1992; Bommes 1997). In the case of family migration, international and national law limits the control capacities of states. In the case of refugees and asylum seekers, states have obligated themselves by international and national laws. Concerning internal migration inside of the EU, the member states have lost most of their interventionist capacity even if these migrations—as in the case of so-called freedom of services—undermine persistent national welfare regimes (Eichenhofer 1996, 1997; Santel & Hunger 1997).

To put it more systematically, the tendency to replicate the distinction between inclusion and exclusion as a distinction between the nation (people) on the one hand and immigrants (foreigners) on the other hand is structurally based in the claim of national welfare states to regulate the social realms of the economy, law, education, or health under the premises of providing welfare for their citizens and to secure chances for social inclusion into these realms. This tendency had only minor relevance from the 1960s to 1980s, a context in which a high level of welfare was combined with a political restriction on international mobility based on the East-West-confrontation. In this context and as a result of a progressive differentiation between politics and law, migrants in Western Europe had become denizens. Until the end of the 1980s, the subject of migration policies in Europe were mainly the social consequences of the immigration of the 1960s and 1970s and related programs of social integration on the one hand and efforts to strictly limit the numbers of refugees and asylum seekers on the other hand. For a number of reasons, it seems that such a policy, which included the immigrants into expansive programs of welfare, was part of a singular phase due to the specific post-war constellation.

The enforced globalization processes after 1989 and the growth of supranational forms of governance significantly eroded the constitutive principal of territoriality of the welfare state[6]—and made its fragility even more visible. No matter if politically initiated, allowed, tolerated, or forbidden, migration is the attempt to realize legally or illegally the chances of social inclusion opened up to individuals by processes of globalization. These attempts affect all states even if they declare that they are not immigration countries and do not want any immigration. Germany, the principal country of immigration in Europe, is a telling example of this.

IV.

Countries like Germany react to the process of loss of control over access and residence in state territory by diversifying and specifying their immigration regulations. They introduce new forms of border control and highly differentiated distinctions among migrant groups; they level resident permits and social entitlements and construct different paths of access to citizenship. One result of this diversified treatment of migrants through the national welfare state is the constitution of differentiated migrant populations. This ought to be obvious by a simply glanicng at the different migrant categories found in Germany.

(1) *Refugees, Expellees, and Ethnic Germans.* These groups of migrants in Germany after World War II had the unlimited right to immigrate since they counted as Germans for historical reasons reaching back to the state building conflicts of the 19th and 20th centuries. Since 1990 with the end of the unification process (for the first time the identity of population and territory has been accomplished and politically declared), the right of access for ethnic Germans to German territory has been successively reduced and finally limited to those born before 1993. The migrant category of Ethnic Germans, which had been a rather privileged one for reasons of national belonging, will be closed in the future—more precisely, in 2010. This change can be seen as part of the readjustment of the German concept of citizenship. In 1990, 1993, and 1999, amendments to the foreigner and citizenship laws installed legal access for labor migrants and their children to German citizenship. The restrictions on the legal status of Ethnic Germans can be interpreted as one part of the strengthening of territoriality as a criterion for the granting of citizenship on the one hand and of the weakening of the *ius sanguinis*-tradition on the other hand.

(2) *Labor Migrants and Their Families.* After their recruitment and settlement (which proved to be politically irreversible), they have become a normal client group of the welfare state and its programs of social integration, even if their position on the labor market exposes them to higher risks of poverty and exclusion (Geißler 1996). One consequence of the irreversible settlement process and the

inclusion into the welfare system has been the opening up and successive improvement of options for naturalization for these migrant groups since 1990.

(3) *Family Migrations.* This category circumscribes a potential of migration, which can be politically regulated but not avoided. Family chain migrations make use of a right that has only been established in modern society as a result of the institutionalization of the nuclear family, i.e. the right of each individual to found a family and not to be separated from it. Based on this, individual migrants transfer options of geographical mobility to the members of their families and in this way open up access to diversified chances for social inclusion. This holds true independently from the question of whether migrant families can rely on the legal protection offered to the family if they themselves form nuclear families. Migration policies that limit and control the foundation of families react to these implications but meet legal limits strengthened in countries like Germany by the constitutional protection of the family.

(4) *Asylum Seekers and Refugee Migration.* Since the end of the 1970s, asylum and refugee migration have been increasingly perceived as a problem of maintaining territorial sovereignty as well as institutionalized difference between the people and the population. In reaction to the worldwide growth of refugee and asylum migration since the early 1980s (Opitz 1997), European welfare states have restricted the conditions for granting asylum or refugee status and weakened the residence status of these groups. The harmonization of asylum policies in the frame of the Schengen and Dublin treaties and their implementation in the EU, the introduction of the category of so-called safe (third) countries, the strict visa requirements for migrants from most non-EU countries, and the enforcement of the political regulations of international transport—all these measures have had the effect that member states of the EU have to a large extent regained control over access to their territories (Joppke 1997). They have lowered the number of refugees since the beginning of the 1990s without breaking national or international law by making it extremely difficult for migrants to reach their territories independently from the issue of whether they are legitimate refugees, asylum seekers, or migrants in search of employment.

The way rich welfare states like Germany subvert national and international refugee law corresponds to the political regulations concerning the options for social inclusion and entitlements for refugees and asylum seekers. The refugees' choice of place of residence and freedom of movement is restricted, and they have no access, or only highly controlled access, to the labor market. Health protection and public assistance are reduced to minimum standards. In this way the welfare state tries to reduce the social participation of refugees and asylum seekers to a standard that allows it to accomplish its administrative procedures and at the same time limits the refugees' life options to a minimum, thus visibly preserving its provisional character (Bank 2000).

(5) *Seasonal or Contract Labor.* National welfare states are not without some capacity to control migration. For political reasons, they still allow for migration, e.g. in the form of seasonal or contract labor (Hönekopp 1997). The striking element of these forms of migration is their highly organized and regulated character. The residence status of these migrants is by law strictly and irreversibly limited, and such migrants are not included in the welfare provisions of the state. These regulations aim to preserve labor migration as an instrument of labor market policy while limiting the possibility that seasonal and contract laborers accrue irreversible legal and social entitlements, like the former "guest workers", The welfare state operates in a way that keeps up a threshold of inequality and the distinction between "the people" and "the population".

(6) *Undocumented or Illegal Migrants.* These groups are defined by their effort to avoid confrontation with the state and its attempts to ascribe a legal status. States like Portugal, Spain, or Italy, which have only recently become "new immigration" countries, have reacted to illegal immigration with several offers to legalize the status of the immigrants, but these initiatives have failed to a large extent (Santel 1995). In Germany this has never been tried; instead a stronger focus has been put on rigorous border controls and greater efforts to forcibly send migrants back to their countries of origin.

This short listing of different migrant categories clearly shows that the effort of national welfare states to preserve the politically constitutive distinction between the population and the people is what creates the various forms of migration and the differences between migrant groups, their legal status, and entitlements. The classification of migrants in these categories depends not on the qualities of the migrants themselves[7] but is a result of the modes of distinction and ascription on the part of the state.

V.

The way states differentiate migrants and define their options for social participation have structured in a peculiar way the empirical results of migration since World War II. This has become visible in the course of the 1990s as the expression of a creeping practical erosion of the core program of the national welfare state—i.e. the "integration" of its citizens and of the legally residing migrants into "society". We note here that this also undermines the traditional perspectives of migration research, which focus on the integration or assimilation of migrants and presuppose (mainly implicitly) the welfare state as a central frame of reference.

The political program of integrating migrants has not been explicitly overturned. Even if a country like Germany has until recently refused to be an immigration country, "the integration of legally resident foreigners" has remained on the agenda, parallel with attempts to hinder the stabilization of the residential status of other migrant groups like refugees, asylum seekers, contract and seasonal laborers, foreign students, and illegal migrants. The enduring validity of the program of integration for ethnic migrants, former labor migrants, and their families is politically emphasized even in the context of the reduced welfare capacity of the state.

Beyond these efforts to differentiate kinds of migrants in the allocation of welfare provisions, there are a growing number of social groups who lead their lives in ways which include recurrent transnational migrations or which are embedded in social contexts structured by such migrations, their related organizational forms, and the corresponding forms of state intervention. Because of these developments, migration is more difficult to describe in a plausible way as "an enduring move to another (national, MB) society or region of a single or a number of individuals" (Treibel 1990, 21), as it is put in a standard textbook on migration sociology. It seems that the state is losing in these constellations its central position as a frame of reference for the activities and orientations of a growing number of migrants. Again, this can be argued for along the lines of the different politically created migrant categories. We refer again to Germany as our main example.

(a) Based on the background of their national belonging, until 1990 welfare state programs treated Ethnic Germans as if they had lived their lives within the territory of the state. They became a part of "the German people" because they were made socially invisible as a migrant group through extensive welfare programs (Bommes 2000). These programs have been heavily reduced since the beginning of the 1990s, and the migration category "Ethnic Germans" has been successively closed. But this has not changed the fact that ethnic Germans, once immigrated, are seen as part of the state population; their "social integration" is still seen as a political duty. The nation-state remains the frame that defines this type of immigration. With the introduction of freedom of movement in the former Soviet Union and its successor states, however, migration networks have evolved which organize constant back and forth migration and maintain access to transnational resources. A trade in documents testifying descent and German belonging has emerged, as well as schools teaching the German language—both descent and belonging on the one hand and German language proficiency on the other are decisive preconditions for the official acknowledgement of "Germanness" and for the right of immigration as an Ethnic German. These developments could be interpreted as mere transitional phenomena, but they also form a context for the building of more enduring social structures.

(b) *Labor migrants* who immigrated within programs of state recruitment in order to realize chances of inclusion in the labor market form a second category. As a function of the length of their employment, they gained welfare and residence entitlements, followed by the political granting of naturalization combined with the expectation that they would finally be "fully integrated into the society (the community of citizens)". From the perspective of the welfare state this can be interpreted as a normalization of the results of this phase of immigration. The denizens finally become full citizens.

(c) *Second and third generation labor migrants and Ethnic Germans arriving after 1990* are confronted with high barriers to inclusion and the corresponding risks of exclusion, especially from the labor market. It is due to the specific risk faced by these generations that they strongly depend on the education system and its mode of distributing certificates and career chances in order to realize chances of inclusion in other social realms. Their parents are not in a position to mediate access to attractive jobs since they were recruited themselves for the less well-paid and structurally weak jobs. But at the same time the resources of migrant children for competition in the education system are not very extensive.

(d) Next to refugee and labor migrations, *family migrations* have become the most important source of migration in all immigration countries. They establish durable relations of migration between regions of origin and destinations. These family migrations and corresponding chain migrations constitute one major context for the crystallization of transnational networks and communities (Glick Schiller, Basch, & Blanc-Szanton 1995; Levitt 1998a; Müller-Mahn 2000). Continuous migrations themselves, and the networks, requirements, and opportunities linked with them, produce occasions for the emergence of organizations that provide the necessary political, legal, religious, health, cultural, and economic resources. Placed both in the context of origin and destination, these structures succeed in gaining a self-reliant character. "Transnationalism" of this kind obviously does not imply that the nation-state becomes irrelevant. Rather the way migrants—but not only migrants—start to orient themselves and their lives to the structures of social inclusion offered by these organizations and networks centered around migration, gain more and more continuity (Levitt 1998a, 1998b; Müller-Mahn 2000; Pries 1998).

Family migration and the resulting structures are especially relevant to the attempts of welfare states to preserve the difference between "the people" and "the population". The transnational structures of inclusion resulting from this migration open up paths of mobility for undocumented or illegal migrants, but they also provide multiple new opportunity and career structures for migrants transcending those of the immigration context (Müller-Mahn 2000). In this way, transnational organizations and networks also provide some compensation for migrants equipped with only weak welfare entitlements. For those migrants participating in transnational relations, the frame of the national welfare state successively loses some of its relevance. Consequently, the distinction between citizens and foreigners, the people and the population, is devalued. Transnational organizations, networks and bonds of loyalty along ethnic lines open up chances of inclusion alternatively to or beyond the welfare state. The state may be instrumentalized, but it is neither the origin nor the central frame of reference for those social relations crystallizing around migration.

(e) The immigration of *asylum seekers and refugees* is politically restricted in the way outlined above. Caused by civil wars, ethnic cleansing, or political repression, this type of migration relies on the availability of support networks organized around familial, ethnic, or regional bonds (like in the recent cases of the Bosnians, the Croatians, the Serbians, the Albanians, or the Kurds). The social and political restrictions, combined with the legal status as a refugee or asylum seeker, direct these migrants as well to the transnationally organized chances of access to income, finance, employment, transport, law, health and politics.

(f) If welfare states allow for the competition of foreign workers in the labor market in a highly organized form as in the case of *contractual and seasonal labor*, this not only induces the creation of organizations using the politically constructed difference between contract labor and free labor. This type of contract labor migration forms the context for new types of "commuter" migration networks for labor and trade (Morawska 1998).

(g) The number of *illegal or undocumented migrants* is difficult to assess, but this type of migration is the backside of the attempts at control by the national welfare state. Illegal migration is one result of the heightening threshold for immigrants from non-EU countries. Illegal migration takes on different forms (e.g. overstayers or clandestine immigration). But it makes especially visible the enormous extent to which national welfare states intervene politically into the opportunities of inclusion in the different social realms and their organizations and how strongly these states try to avoid the inclusion of non-citizens even where citizens do not take up such opportunities.[8] One central aim of the control and exclusion of migrants is the attempt to keep up the standards of social inclusion protected by welfare states and to hinder the undermining of these standards through unregulated immigration. However, under the conditions of globally increased chances of territorial mobility for individuals who can use existing migratory networks and worldwide operating organizations providing human smuggling for cash (Kyle 1998), welfare states attempts' to control migratory flows of create chances of social inclusion that are based on illegality.

Illegal migrants do not necessarily lead socially segregated lives. They do not live beyond the organizations regulated by the state but the domains of their social participation are hidden to the state and its efforts of control. In various areas of production and services all kinds of illegal employment evolve. Not only various organizations or private households are interested to preserve this employment because of the low wages in return for intensive and effective labor, but also a large proportion of the migrants themselves are interested in keeping up these relations since illegality itself provides their chances for social inclusion. Their competitive advantage or "Standortvorteil" on the relevant markets for labor and services is illegality, the bypassing of welfare state regulations. The threshold of inequality kept up by welfare states, successfully ignored by organizations and private households, changes into a chance of social inclusion for migrants. Their attempts to gain an income are not organized by the standards of equality and distribution typical of welfare states. In this way the effort of welfare states to keep up the difference between the people and the population and to privilege their citizens produces a paradoxical effect: the emergence of an area which seems to gain its dynamic precisely from these political efforts to hinder further immigration. This, in turn, works as the precondition for the reciprocal interest that develops between organizations and private households and illegal immigrants. The effort to keep up the welfare threshold in relation to external threat leads to a differential distribution and inequality on the inside. It feeds the growth of an illegal population and related social forms of organization and networks as part of the erosion of the welfare state frame of reference.

We can sum up by saying that the cases (c) to (g) provide evidence that the national welfare state is losing some of its centrality as a frame in the double sense that either the efforts of various migrant groups to realize chances of social inclusion are less and less oriented by the program of the welfare state, i.e. "integration into the society", or that migrants are excluded from this program in any case. In Germany only two migrant groups were principally addressed by this program: (1) Ethnic Germans as members of the national community were made part of the people by making them socially invisible as a migrant group; and (2) labor migrants of the "guest worker" period were first included in the welfare state and finally offered options of naturalization as the final step of their "full integration into the society". This can be interpreted as an attempt to re-normalize the relation between the population and the state by changing legally resident migrants into citizens. They are expected to be politically loyal in exchange for welfare provision and for belonging to the community of legitimate welfare receivers.

In contrast, a growing number of individuals (for whom the welfare state offers only limited perspectives or exclusion) orient themselves to the social structures and options linked with transnational relations and to the ethnic, regional or familial bonds of loyalty that they entail. Family migration and other forms of migration, including illegal migration, do more than limit the sovereignty of national welfare states over control of their territories. The resultant social structures suggest the forllowing question: If a growing part of the population in a state territory no longer aims to become part of the collectivity of citizens,[9] what will the effects be on national welfare states which have historically regulated the relation to the territorial population by transforming that population into "the people" and by maintaining the distinction between the people (their citizens) and the population?

The structural consequences linked with transnationalism make clear the historical improbability of the political project of the national welfare state, i.e. the effort to distinguish the people and the population living on its territory, to supervise this difference, and to keep it small. A rather large difference between the "core population", the community of the citizens, and the "residual population" of migrants of all kinds has become normal, and as a result the difference itself becomes precarious. The internal differentiation of the "residual population" into various migrant categories thus indicates two things: a shrinking capacity of control and provision of the welfare state, as well as a shift in the nature of the political inclusion of individuals into the nation-state. Questions of political inclusion are successively separated from questions of emphatic belonging to a national community legitimating related claims of "integration into the society" by means of the welfare state. This is the internal side of the loss of sovereignty of the nation-state. In the future, the state may no longer be able to pursue the program of full integration of all individuals subject to its authority. The classical program of the welfare state, "social integration" (which had been addressed to the former "guest workers" and their families) is no longer maintained in the same way. The inclusion of the "guest workers" was based on the presumably unrepeatable expansion of the welfare state during the 1960s and the 1970s.

The political devaluation of the semantics of community on the level of the state corresponds to the emergence of new identities below or beyond the state and its borders. Such identities may be articulated ethnically, regionally, or locally—it is left to parts of the population to create their own identities. The relevance of these parts of the population for the state is redefined mainly in administrative, legal, or policing terms. This indicates one of the meanings of those processes that have been discussed under the headings of "multicultural society" and "transnationalism." The emergence of ethnic identities is no longer entirely or mainly structured by the orientation or refusal to belong to national welfare states. These identities organize loyalties and chances of access less centered around states. The ethnic, multicultural, or transnational "milieus" signal and to some extent also allow for the retreat of the state from the political project to integrate nationally the population on its territory. These "milieus" articulate the shrinking capacity of the welfare state. The other side of this process is the social redefinition of those who belong to the remaining collective of legitimate welfare recipients (Bommes 2000).

Migration and the emergent identities linked with them make visible some of the social preconditions of participation in the functional realms of society and its organizations. They stand at right angles to the political system and its peculiarity of being segmentarily differentiated in space. It may turn out that the formula "integration into the society" was mainly part of the political semantics of a national welfare state, which was historically prevalent for a short period of time—sovereign only in an era in which the identification of society with the nation-state could gain socially persuasive power.

The debate about "multicultural society" still shared this identification of society with the nation-state. The nation-state was confronted with the assumption that the ongoing processes of cultural pluralization would force a correction of the presupposition that national homogeneity could be maintained as a political objective. "Transnationalism" does account for recent trends of migration, but even here the concept of national societies remains central. An alternative concept of the modern society which conceptualizes society as functionally differentiated world society (Luhmann 1997) allows us to interpret the transnational networks and organizations resulting from migration as part of globalization processes and as structural elements of a world society.[10] The national welfare state—the worldwide-established organizational form of politics in modern society—turns out to be an institution with specific conditions for functioning and specific limits with respect to its interventionist capacity. Its shrinking ability to foster social inclusion makes this evident. The consequence, however, is not that the national welfare state has become dispensable. The recent conflicts in former Yugoslavia are but one example that the nation-state remains, despite its reduced capacity to provide social inclusion—the central condition for the production of security and collectively binding decisions. Where the internal enforcement of the state and the political inclusion of the population fails, vital social preconditions for the functioning of the economy, law, science, health, education, and the family erode.

Notes

1. In Germany all the major institutes at the universities like the IMIS at the University of Osnabrueck, the INIIS at the University of Bremen, the EFMS at the University of Bamberg, or the "Institute for Interdisciplinary Research on Social Conflict and Violence" at the University of Bielefeld were founded after 1989 as an outcome of political conjunctures. They were not the result of a genuine long-term science policy.

2. By using the term "transnational", migration research tries to move away in a critical manner from the national frame of reference, which was (and is) central for classical migration research. In this frame, the social consequences of migration are immediately defined as the problematic of integrating individual migrants into a national society. Research on transnational migration demonstrates clearly that society cannot be identified with the borders of nation-states. However, many of these studies continue to describe migrants as moving between national societies in plural. One of the resulting problems is that individuals are seen as (partially) integrated in two or even more societies. Another objection is made by historians who deny that there is anything really new about "transnational migrations" which could not have been found already in earlier migration movements in history (see Lucassen & Lucassen 1997b: 23ff.; Gerber 2000).

3. For the US and Germany, see Santel and Hollifield 1998; for Australia, Castels 1996, 1998; for a comparative perspective on the US, Germany and France, see Hollifield 1992; and for Germany, see Bommes 1994.

4. Residualistic welfare states perceive the safeguard of transferabilities only in a limited sense as a political duty. The "conservative" type of welfare state, however, aims at the maintenance of the standard of living, whereas the "social democratic" type is based on the concept of "social citizenship" as interpreted by Marshall (see Esping-Anderson 1990).

5. Contrary to the development in Europe was the emergence of the people in the US a result of immigration. Consequently, immigration was never used in the same way to distinguish between those belonging to the nation and those who do not. Historically the existence of an immigration country like the US has itself provided a chance for social inclusion, and this made the emergence of a welfare state of the European type for the long term unlikely.

6. One effect of this is the reduction of the level of provision in a number of welfare states. For a comparative discussion of the perspectives of different welfare states see Esping-Anderson 1996.

7. Migrants need to take these categories into account. They have to decide how they will present themselves—e.g., as asylum seekers or family members—or to avoid it all by going illegal. It is not exceptional to find quite a number of migrants who move through all three statuses.

8. Partly because citizens can afford to do this, and partly because they are not allowed to use opportunities, because they imply the ignorance of welfare regulations concerning working hours, minimum wages, or social insurance.

9. This does not preclude naturalization. But naturalization cannot easily be taken as a sign for the "integration into the society", rather as making use of another social option which alleviates mobility.

10. This would allow us to account for transnational social structures resulting from migration in the 18th and 19th century, as Gerber (2000) argues quite convincingly.

CHAPTER 11

Beyond Sovereignty: *De-Facto* Transnationalism in Immigration Policy[1]

Saskia Sassen

Even as it continues to play the most important role in immigration policy making and implementation, the state has been transformed by the growth of a global economic system and other transnational processes. These have brought on conditions that bear on the state's regulatory role and its autonomy. Two particular aspects of this development are of significance to the role of the state in immigration policy making and implementation. One is the relocation of various components of state authority to supranational organizations such as the institutions of the European Union (EU), the World Trade Organization (WTO), or the international human rights code. A second is the de-facto privatization of various governance functions as a result of the privatization of public sector activities and of economic deregulation. This privatization assumes particular meanings in the context of the internationalization of trade and investment. Corporations, markets, and free trade agreements are now in charge of "governing" an increasing share of cross-border flows, including cross-border flows of specialized professional workers as part of the international trade and investment in services.

The major implication for immigration policy is that these developments have had an impact on the sovereignty of the state and, further, that the state itself has been a participant in the implementation of many of these new arrangements. The state has contributed to the formation of the global economic system and has furthered the consensus around the pursuit of economic globalization (see various chapters in Mittelman 1996; Sassen 1996). Both the impact on the state's sovereignty and the state's participation in the new global

229

economic system have transformed the state itself, affected the power of different agencies within it, and furthered the internationalization of the inter-state system through a proliferation of bi- and multilateral agreements.

Immigration policy is deeply embedded in the question of state sovereignty and the inter-state system. As a result it is no longer sufficient simply to assert the sovereign role of the state in immigration policy design and implementation; it is necessary to examine also the transformation of the state itself and what that can entail for migration policy and the regulation of migration flows and settlement. As I argue elsewhere (1999), it is becoming important to factor in the possibility of declining state sovereignty precisely because the state is a major actor in immigration policy and regulation. Nor is it sufficient simply to assert that globalization has brought with it a declining significance of the state in economic regulation. Why? The state has been a participant in this process and is the strategic institution for the legislative changes and innovations necessary for economic globalization as we know it today.

This may seem far removed from the question of immigration policy. But we need to expand the analytic terrain within which we examine the options for immigration policy making in the highly developed countries. And we cannot simply use the state as a background fact, a given.

One of the crucial issues in the transformation of the state that is relevant to immigration policy making has to do with the enormous work of legal innovation necessary for the formation of a global economy. The global economy is both a set of practices and a set of legal innovations within which to encase those practices (Sassen 1996). Economic globalization has created a new geography of power within which the state finds its sovereign power reconstituted, often diminished. And it has contributed to the formation of new legal regimes and much legal and policy innovation, much of it representing a relocation of authority away from the state.

Immigration policymaking in contrast, has suffered from a lack of innovation in most highly developed countries, with the exception of the work around the formation of the European Union and free trade agreements such as NAFTA and the Uruguay Round of the GATT. In the case of Europe, such policy changes as free movement within the Union and the shift of some immigration policy components to the European level, have required considerable innovation in international law. NAFTA and the WTO required the formation of specialized regimes for the circulation of professional services and other kinds of providers; this is likely to include individuals, particularly in the case of many professional services. These regimes within NAFTA and the WTO can be seen as containing a form of "migrant worker policy", albeit one addressed to highly specialized workers. Although they are supra-national regimes, private sector interests exercise growing influence.

These are the issues briefly discussed in this chapter. The organizing argument is that this reconfiguration has brought with it a *de-facto* transnationalism in the handling of a growing number of immigration issues, both domestically and internationally. This can take many forms: the shift of certain elements of immigration policy onto supra-national institutions in the European Union; the sharp increase in the extent and content of collaboration in the US-Mexico Binational Immigration Commisssion; the rapid increase in the use of international human rights instruments by judges adjudicating on immigration and refugee questions in both Europe and the US; and the already mentioned formation of a quasi-privatized regime for the circulation of service workers in the major free-trade agreements as part of the liberalization of international trade and investment in services. I consider these and other developments a *de facto* transnationalism because they are fragmented, incipient and have not been fully captured at the most formal levels of international public law and conventions, nor in national representations of the sovereign state. My argument is, then, that there is more on-the-ground transnationalism than hits the formal eye.

In order to develop this particular way of framing the evidence it is important first to bring some precision to concepts such as economic globalization and transnationalism and their impact on sovereignty and exclusive state authority over its territory. This is the subject of a first, very brief section, confined largely to states operating under the rule of law. The second and third sections focus on the constraints faced by the state in highly developed countries in the making of immigration policy today.

The State and the New Economic Regime

Two notions underlie much of the current discussion about globalization. One is the proposition that what the global economy gains, the national state loses, and vice-versa. The other is the proposition that if an event (from business transaction to a judiciary decision) takes place in a national territory it is a national event. In other words, dualism and geography (in a narrow territorial sense) are the hallmarks of this type of understanding.

But there is by now a considerable body of scholarship that has shown us that the spatiality of the global economy does not simply lie somewhere in the interstices between states (e.g. Mittelman 1996; Knox & Taylor 1995). To a good extent global processes and institutional arrangements materialize in national territories; even the most digitalized global financial market is grounded in a set of very material resources and spaces largely embedded in national territories. As has been said often, one of the key properties of the current phase in the long history of the world economy is the ascendance of information technologies, the associated increase in the mobility and liquidity of capital, and the resulting decline in the regulatory capacities of national states over key sectors of their economies. This is well illustrated by the case of the leading information industries, finance and the advanced corporate services. These tend to have a space economy that is transnational and is partly embedded in electronic spaces that override conventional jurisdictions and boundaries.

Yet, this is also a space economy which reveals the need for strategic sites with vast concentrations of resources and infrastructure, sites that are situated in national territories and are far less mobile than much of the general commentary on the global economy suggests. The excessive emphasis on the hypermobility and liquidity of capital is a partial account. We need to distinguish between the capacity for global transmission/communication and the material conditions that make this possible, between the globalization of the financial industry and the array of resources—from buildings to labor inputs—that makes this possible; and so on for other sectors as well.[2] Place is central to the multiple circuits through which economic globalization is constituted. One strategic type of place for these developments is the global city.[3]

As a consequence of this embedding of global processes in national territories, notably in global cities, one of the key features of the role of the state vis-à-vis economic globalization (unlike earlier forms of the global economy) has been to negotiate the intersection of national law and foreign actors—whether firms, markets or individuals. We generally use the term "deregulation" to describe the outcome of this negotiation. The problem with this term is that it only captures the withdrawal of the state from regulating its economy. It does not register all the ways in which the state participates in setting up the new frameworks through which globalization is furthered; nor does it capture the associated transformations inside the state (see Sassen 1996; see also, Smith *et al.* 1999; Olds *et al.* 1999; Biersteker *et al.* 2002; Drache & Gertler 1991).

Coding everything that involves the national state as an instance of the national is simply inadequate. The theoretical and methodological challenge presented by the current phase of globalization is that it entails a transcending of exclusive national territoriality and of the interstate system yet is implanted in national territories and institutions. Hence globalization directly engages two marking features of the nation state: exclusive territoriality and sovereignty.

Similarly, the emergent international human rights regime engages territoriality and sovereignty. What matters here is not so much the moral force of the idea, but the far more practical fact of a rapid multiplication of instruments available to judges and the build-up of case law where this applies, as in the US for example (e.g. Jacobson, 1996; Reisman, 1990). The key issue here is the fact that international regimes or codes, such as human rights, largely become operative in national courts. One could of course simply assert that in such cases we are dealing with what is ultimately a national institution. To do so means discounting even the possibility that the ascendance of such international regimes engages the sovereignty and territoriality of the national state. And since the multiplication of instruments and their growing use by national courts is a very recent development—unlike the concept of human rights—we must at least allow for the possibility that there are new processes afoot also in this realm.

In terms of sovereignty, the emergent consensus in the community of states to further globalization has created a set of specific obligations on participating states. The state remains as the ultimate guarantor of the "rights" of global capital, i.e. the protection of contracts and property rights. Thus the state has incorporated the global project of its own shrinking role in regulating economic transactions (Cox 1987; Panitch 1996). Firms operating transnationally want to ensure the functions traditionally exercised by the state in the national realm of the economy, notably guaranteeing property rights and contracts. The state here can be conceived of as representing a technical administrative capacity which cannot be replicated at this time by any other institutional arrangement; furthermore, this is a capacity backed by military power, with global power in the case of some states.

Deregulation and other policies furthering economic globalization cannot simply be considered as an instance of a declining significance of the state. Deregulation is a vehicle through which a growing number of states are furthering economic globalization and guaranteeing the rights of global capital, an essential ingredient of the former. Deregulation and kindred policies constitute the elements of a new legal regime dependent on consensus among states to further globalization. This manner of conceptualizing deregulation suggests that the duality national-global as mutually exclusive is problematic in that it does not adequately represent the work of national states in the implmentation of economic globalization.

While central, the role of the state in producing the legal encasements for economic globalization is no longer as exclusive as it was in earlier periods. Economic globalization has also been accompanied by the creation of new legal regimes and legal practices and the expansion and renovation of some older forms that bypass national legal systems. Among the most important ones in the private sector today are international commercial arbitration and the variety of institutions which fulfill rating and advisory functions that have become essential for the operation of the global economy.

These and other such transnational institutions and regimes do raise questions about the relation between state sovereignty and the governance of global economic processes. International commercial arbitration is basically a private justice system and credit rating agencies are private gate-keeping systems. Along with other such institutions they have emerged as important governance mechanisms whose authority is not centered in the state. They contribute to maintain order at the top, one could say.

All of this has had an impact on sovereignty and on the mutually exclusive territoriality that has marked the history of the modern state. This is an extremely complex and highly differentiated history that cannot be adequately described here. There is an enormously rich scholarship on this subject.[4]

There are two points I want to emphasize about this history here because they are relevant to the subject of this article, particularly the notion that we may need considerable innovation in immigration policy given today's major transformations. One of these points is the fact that at various periods of major transitions there was a coexistence of multiple systems of rule. This was the case, for instance in the transition from the medieval system of rule to the modern state.[5] And it may well be the case today in this period of transition to a global economy. As I will argue later, supranational organizations and regimes such as the General Agreement on Trade in Services (GATS) and NAFTA may well signal the strengthening of other non-exclusive systems of rule today. A second element in the history of the modern state that matters here is the fact of enormous contestation to the formation of and claims by central states (see Tilly 1975). Again I see this as relevant to the contemporary period in that it signals the possibility of regimes that go beyond state sovereignty or that involve far more developed instances of multilateralism notwithstanding strong resistance among policy makers and analysts to even the idea of such a possibility.

While these new conditions for transnational economies are being produced and implemented by governments and economic actors in highly developed countries, immigration policy in those same countries remains centered in older conceptions about control and regulation. One of the key obstacles to even beginning to think along totally different lines about immigration policy is the widespread conviction that any other approach than border control would lead to massive invasions from the Third World. Much general commentary and policy making wittingly or not tends to proceed as if most people in less developed countries want to go to a rich country, as if all immigrants want to become permanent settlers, as if the problem of current immigration policy has to do basically with gaps or failures in enforcement, as if raising the levels of border control is an effective way of regulating immigration.

This type of understanding of immigration clearly leads to a certain type of immigration policy, one centered on the fear of being invaded by people from less developed countries everywhere and hence on border control as the only answer. The evidence on immigration shows that most people do not want to leave their countries, that overall levels of permanent immigration are not very large, that there is considerable circulation and return migration, that most migration flows eventually stabilize if not decline (see Sassen 1999 for a review of the evidence on these issues). Making these the central facts about the reality of immigration should allow for a broader set of options when it comes to immigration policy than would be the case with mass emigration and invasion (see also, Isbister 1996).

Can the state escape the types of transformations described here regarding economic globalization, and the pressures towards transnationalism they entail, when it comes to a very different domain, that of immigration policy design and implementation?

Beyond Sovereignty: Constraints on States' Policy Making

In the case of immigration policy, states under the rule of law increasingly confront a range of rights and obligations, pressures from both inside and outside, from universal human rights to not so universal ethnic lobbies.

First, we see emerging a *de facto* regime, centered in international agreements and conventions as well as in various rights gained by immigrants, that limits the state's role in controlling immigration. An example of such an agreement is the International Convention adopted by the General Assembly of the UN on 18 December 1990 on the protection of the rights of all migrant workers and members of their families (Resolution 45/158).[6] Further, there is a set of rights of resident immigrants widely upheld by legal authorities. We have also seen the gradual expansion over the last three decades of civil and social rights to marginal populations, whether women, ethnic minorities, or immigrants and refugees.

In this context, the 1996 US immigration law, which curtails the rights of undocumented and legal immigrants, can be seen as a rejection of these international instruments. Nonetheless, precisely because these instruments exist the stage is set for at least some contestation. Indeed, some of the provisions restricting the rights of resident immigrants to welfare support have already had to be eliminated or diluted.

We have seen this contestation frequently in the long and arduous history of international human rights codes. The extension of rights, which has taken place mostly through the judiciary, has confronted states with a number of constraints in the area of immigration and refugee policy. For instance, there have been attempts by the legislature in France and Germany to limit family reunification which were blocked by administrative and constitutional courts on the grounds that such restrictions would violate international agreements. The courts have also regularly supported a combination of rights of resident immigrants which have the effect of limiting a government's power over resident immigrants. Similarly such courts have limited the ability of governments to restrict or stop asylum seekers from entering the country.

Efforts that mix the conventions on universal human rights and national judiciaries assume many different forms. Some of the instances in the US are the sanctuary movement in the 1980s which sought to establish protected areas, typically in churches, for refugees from Central America; judicial battles, such as those around the status of Salvadoreans granted indefinite stays though formally defined as illegal; the fight for the rights of detained Haitians in an earlier wave of boat lifts. It is clear that notwithstanding the lack of an enforcement apparatus, human rights limit the discretion of states in how they treat non-nationals on their territory. It is also worth noting in this regard that The United Nations High Commissioner for Refugees (UNHCR) is the only UN agency with a universally conceded right of access to a country experiencing a refugee crisis.

The growing influence of human rights law is particularly evident in Europe. It was not until the 1980s that the same began in the US, though it still lags behind.[7] This has been seen partly as a result of American definitions of personhood which have led courts in some cases to address the matter of undocumented immigrants within American constitutionalism, notably the idea of inalienable and natural rights of people and persons, without territorial confines. The emphasis on persons makes possible interpretations about undocumented immigrants, of a sort precluded if the emphasis were on citizens. (For a debate on these issues, see *Indiana Journal of Global Legal Studies* 2000). It was not till the mid-1970s and the early-1980s that domestic courts began to consider human rights codes as normative instruments in their own right. The rapid growth of undocumented immigration and the sense of the state's incapacity to control the flow and to regulate the various categories in its popula-tion was a factor leading courts to consider the international human rights regime; it allows courts to rule on basic protections of individ-uals not formally accounted in the national territory and legal system, notably undocumented aliens and unauthorized refugees.[8]

The growing accountability, in principle, of states under the rule of law to international human rights codes and institutions, together with the fact that individuals and non-state actors can make claims on those states in terms of those codes, signals a development that goes beyond the expansion of human rights within the framework of nation-states. It contributes to redefine the bases of legitimacy of states under the rule of law and the notion of nationality. Under human rights regimes states must increasingly take account of persons qua persons, rather than qua citizens. The individual is now an object of law and a site for rights regardless of whether a citizen or an alien.[9]

Finally, the numbers and kinds of political actors involved in immigration policy debates and policy making in Western Europe, North America, and Japan are far greater than they were two decades ago: the European Union, anti-immigrant parties, vast networks of organizations in both Europe and North America that often represent immigrants, or claim to do so, and fight for immi-grant rights, immigrant associations and immigrant politicians, mostly in the second generation, and, especially in the US so-called ethnic lobbies.[10] The policy process for immigration is no longer confined to a narrow governmental arena of ministerial and administrative interaction. Public opinion and public political debate have become part of the arena wherein immigration policy is shaped.[11] Whole parties position themselves politically in terms of their stand on immigration, especially in some of the European countries.

These developments are particularly evident in the case of the European Union.[12] Europe's single market program has had a powerful impact in raising the prominence of various issues associated with free circulation of people as an essential element in creating a frontier-free community; earlier EC institutions lacked the legal competence to deal with many of these issues but had to begin to address them. Gradually EC institutions wound up more deeply involved with visa policy, family reunification and migration policy all formerly exclusively in the domain of the individual national states. National governments resisted EC (and later EU) involvement in these once exclusively national domains. But now both legal and practical issues have made such involvement acceptable and inevitable notwithstanding many public pronouncements to the contrary. In brief, many aspects of immigration and refugee policy intersect with EU legal competence.

A key nexus here is the free movement of persons and attendant cross-border upholding of social rights as part of the formation of a single market. In practice the EU is assuming an increasingly important role and the fact that immigration is a long-term feature in these countries is slowly being acknowledged. The monetary and economic union requires greater flexibility in movement of workers and their families and thereby poses increasing problems for national immigration laws regarding non-EU nationals in EU member states. Although the third country national population is very small, politically they are an important issue. There is now growing recognition for the need of an EU-wide immigration policy, something denied for a long time by individual states.

In the case of the US, the combination of forces at the governmental level is quite different yet has similar general implications about the state's constraints in immigration policy making. Immigration policy in the US is today largely debated and shaped by Congress, and hence is highly public and subject to a vast multiplicity of local interests, notably ethnic lobbies.[13] This has made it a very public process, quite different from other processes of policy making.[14]

The fact that immigration in the US has historically been the preserve of the federal government assumes new meaning in today's context of radical devolution—the return of powers to the states.[15] Aman Jr. (1995) has noted that although political and constitutional arguments for reallocating federal power to the states are not new, the recent re-emergence of the Tenth Amendment as a politically viable and popular guideline is a major political shift since the New Deal in the relations between the federal government and the states. There is now an emerging conflict between several state governments and the Federal government around the particular issue of federal mandates concerning immigrants—such as access to public health care and schools—that lack mandatory federal funding. Thus states with disproportionate shares of immigrants are asserting that they are disproportionately burdened by the putative costs of immigration. In the US the costs of immigration are an area of great debate and wide ranging estimates.[16] At the heart of this conflict is the fact that the federal government sets policy but does not assume responsibility, financial or otherwise, for the implementation of many key aspects of immigration policy. The radical devolution under way now is going to accentuate some of these divisions further.

States are beginning to request reimbursement from the federal government for the costs of benefits and services that they are required to provide, especially to undocumented immigrants (Clark *et al.* 1994; GAO 1994, 1995). In 1994, six states (Arizona, California, Florida, New Jersey, New York, and Texas) filed separate suits in federal district courts to recover costs they claimed to have sustained because of the federal government's failure to enforce US immigration policy, protect the nation's borders, and provide adequate resources for immigration emergencies (Dunlap & Morse 1995).[17] The amounts range from US$50.5 million in New Jersey for Fiscal Year 1993 costs of imprisoning 500 undocumented criminal felons and construction of future facilities, to US$33.6 billion in New York for all state and county costs associated with undocumented immigration between 1988 to 1993. The conflict is illustrated by the notorious case of the state of California and its US$377 million lawsuit against the Federal government. District Court judges have dismissed all six lawsuits; some of the states appealed the decision The radical devolution under way now is going to accentuate some of these divisions further.

One of the questions raised by these developments concerns the nature of the control by national states in regulating immigration. The question here is not so much, how effective is a state's control over its borders—we know it is never absolute. The question concerns rather the substantive nature of state control over immigration given international human rights agreements, the extension of various social and political rights to resident immigrants over the last twenty years, the multiplication of political actors involved with the immigration question, and the variety of other dynamics within which immigration is embedded—some of which may be connected to foreign policies of the receiving states (Sassen 1999).

We can illuminate the issue of the substantive nature of the control by states over immigration with a twist on the zero sum argument. If a government closes one kind of entry category, recent history shows that another one will have a rise in numbers. A variant on this dynamic is that if a government has, for instance, a very liberal policy on asylum, public opinion may turn against all asylum seekers and close up the country totally; this in turn is likely to promote an increase in irregular entries.[18]

When Different Regimes Intersect

Immigration policy continues to be characterized by its formal isolation from other major processes, as if it were possible to handle migration as a bounded, closed event. There are, one could say, two major epistemic communities—one concerning the flow of capital and information; the other, immigration. Both of these epistemic communities are international, and both enjoy widespread consensus in the community of states.

The coexistence of such different regimes for capital and for immigrants has not been seen as an issue in the US while it has in the EU. The case of the EU is of interest here because it represents an advanced stage of formalization, and in this effort European states are discovering the difficulties if not impossibility of maintaining two such diverse regimes. The EU and the national governments of member states have found the juxtaposition of the divergent regimes for immigration flows and for other types of flows rather difficult to handle. The discussion, design and implementation of policy aimed at forming a European Union make it evident that immigration policy has to account for the facts of rapid economic internationalization. The EU shows us with great clarity the moment when states need to confront this contradiction in their design of formal policy frameworks.

The other major regional systems in the world are far from that moment and may never reach it. Yet they contain less formalized versions of the juxtaposition between border-free economies and border controls to keep immigrants out. NAFTA is one such instance, as are, in a more diffuse way, various initiatives for greater economic integration in the Western Hemisphere. Though less clearly than in Western Europe, these issues are also present in other regions with cross-border migrations. These are regional systems constituted partly as zones of influence of major economic or geo-political powers, e.g. the long term dominance of the US over the Caribbean Basin. What matters here is that to a good extent major international migration flows have been embedded in some or another variant of these regional systems. The quasi-transnational economic integration characterizing such regional systems produces its own variety of contradictions between drives for border-free economic spaces and border-control to keep immigrants and refu-gees out.

There are strategic sites where it becomes clear that the existence of two very different regimes for the circulation of capital and the circulation of immigrants poses problems that cannot be solved through the old rules of the game, where the facts of transnationali-zation weigh in on the state's decisions regarding immigration. For instance, the need to create special regimes for the circulation of service workers both within the GATS and NAFTA as part of the further internationalization of trade and investment in services. This regime for the circulation of service workers has been uncoupled from any notion of migration; but it represents in fact a version of temporary labor migration. It is a regime for labor mobility which is in good part under the oversight of entities that are quite autono-mous from the government. This points to an institutional reshuffling of some of the components of sovereign power over entry and can be seen as an extension of the general set of processes whereby state sovereignty is partly being decentered onto other non- or quasi-governmental entities for the governance of the global economy (Sassen 1996).[19]

The development of provisions for workers and business persons signals the difficulty of *not* dealing with the circulation of people in the implementation of free trade and investment frameworks. In their own specific ways each of these efforts—NAFTA, GATS and the European Union—has had to address cross-border labor circulation.

One instantiation of the impact of globalization on governmental policy making can be seen in Japan's immigration law Amendment passed in 1990. While this is quite different from how the issue plays in the context of free trade agreements, it nonetheless illustrates one way of handling the need for cross-border circulation of professional workers in a context of resistance to the notion of open borders. This legislation opened the country to several categories of highly special-ized professionals with a western background (e.g. experts in international finance, in western-style accounting, in western medi-cine, etc.) in recognition of the growing internationalization of the professional world in Japan; it made the entry of what is referred to as "simple labor" illegal (Sassen 2001, Chapter 9). This can be read as importing "Western human capital" and closing borders to immigrants.

Further, the need to address cross-border circulation of people has also become evident in free trade agreements in the less devel-oped world, notably in Latin America. (For more detailed accounts, including the original treaty documents, see Acuerdo de Cartagena 1991a, 1991b, 1991c; Leon & Kratochwil 1993; CEPAL 1994; Torales 1993; Marmora 1993; Stein 1993.) There has been a sharp increase in activity around the international circulation of people in each of the major regional trading blocks: Mercosur, the Grupo Andino, and the Mercado Comun de Centroamerica. Each one launched a variety of initiatives in the early-1990s on international labor migration among their member countries. This is in many ways a new development. Some of the founding treaties precede the flurry of meetings on labor migrations and the circulation of people. But it is clear that conditions in the early-1990s forced this issue on the agenda. When one examines what actually happened it becomes evident that the common markets for investment and commerce in each of these regions had themselves become activated under the impact of globalization, deregulation, privatization. It was the increased circulation of capital, goods and information under the impact of globalization, deregulation and privatization that forced the question of the circulation of people on the agenda.

In the case of the US and its major immigration source country, Mexico, it appears that the signing of NAFTA has also had the effect of activating a series of new initiatives regarding migration—a sort of *de facto* bilateralism which represents a radically new phase in the handling of migration between these two countries. It is worth providing some detail on these.

Not unlike what was the case in Latin America, we are seeing both a re-activation of older instruments and much new activity around the question of US-Mexico international migration. To provide better coordination between the two countries Presidents

Carter and Lopez Portillo established the US-Mexico Consultative Mechanism. This eventually led to the formation of the US-Mexico Binational Commission in 1981 to serve as a forum for meetings between Cabinet-level officials from both countries. It was conceived as a flexible mechanism that would meet once or twice a year. One of the early working groups formed was the Border Relations Action group, in 1981.

What is different since the mid-1990s is the frequency, focus and actual work that is getting done in the meetings of the working groups. NAFTA has further contributed to strengthen the contacts and collaboration in the working groups. Particularly active is the working group on Migration and Consular Affairs.[20] There are also disagreements between the two delegations that are discussed openly. Notably, the Mexican delegation is deeply concerned about the growing anti-immigrant feeling and measures in the US. The US delegation has agreed to work together to combat these developments. The Mexican delegation also expressed concern at the US proposal to expand and strengthen border fences to improve security in various locations. They emphasized both the negative effects of such a measure on the border communities and Mexican efforts to resolve the problems in the most troubled locations. Notwithstanding these serious disagreements, and perhaps precisely because of them, both delegations are convinced of the importance to continue this collaboration. With the elections of the current presidents, yet another place of collaboration has been launched.

Conclusion

All of these developments have the effect of: a) reducing the autonomy of the state in immigration policy making; and b) multiplying the sectors within the state that are addressing immigration policy and therewith multiplying the room for conflicts within the state. The assertion that the state is in charge of immigration policy is less and less helpful. Policy making regarding international issues can engage very different parts of the government. The state itself has not only been transformed by its participation in the global economy, but has of course never been a homogeneous actor. It is constituted through multiple agencies and social forces whose positions on the issue of immigration often diverge strongly from each other and also may change over time. Indeed it could be said (Mitchell 1989) that although the state has central control over immigration policy, the work of exercising that claimed power often begins with a limited contest between the state and interested social forces. These interest groups include agribusiness, manufacturing, humanitarian groups, unions, ethnic organizations, zero population growth efforts. Today we need to add to this the fact that the hierarchies of power and influence within the state are being reconfigured by the furthering of economic globalization.[21]

The conditions within which immigration policy is being made and implemented today range from the pressures of economic globalization and its implications for the role of the state to international agreements on human rights. And the institutional setting within which immigration policy is being made and implemented ranges from national states and local states to supranational organizations.

Why does this transformation of the state and the inter-state system matter for the regulation of immigration? The displacement of governance functions away from the state to non-state entities affects the state's capacity to control or keep controlling its borders. New systems of governance are being created. Increasingly they may create conflicts with the state's capacity to keep on regulating immigration in the same ways. Further, the transformation of the state itself through its role in the implementation of global processes, may well contribute to new constraints, options and vested interests. The ascendance of agencies linked to furthering globalization and the decline of those linked to domestic equity questions is quite likely to eventually have an effect on the immigration agenda.

The developments described here point to a number of trends that may become increasingly important for sound immigration policy making. First, where the effort towards the formation of transnational economic spaces has gone the farthest and been most formalized it has become very clear that existing frameworks for immigration policy are problematic. It is not the case that the coexistence of very different regimes for the circulation of capital and for that of people, is free of tension and contention. This is most evident in the legislative work necessary for the formation of the European Union. Lesser versions of this tension are evident in the need to design special provisions for the circulation of workers in all the major free trade agreements.

Secondly, we see the beginning of a displacement of government functions on to non-governmental or quasi-governmental institutions. This is most evident in the new transnational legal and regulatory regimes created in the context of economic globalization. But it is also intersecting with questions of migration, specifically temporary labor migration, as is evident in the creation of special regimes for the circulation of service workers and business persons both within the GATS and NAFTA as part of the further internationalization of trade and investment in services. This regime for the circulation of service workers has been separated from any notion of migration; but it represents in fact a version of temporary labor migration. It is a regime for labor mobility which is in good part under the oversight of entitites that are quite autonomous from the government. We can see in this displacement the elements of a privatization of certain aspects of the regulation of cross-border labor mobility.

Thirdly, the legitimation process for states under the rule of law calls for respect and enforcement of international human rights codes, regardless of the nationality and legal status of an individual. While enforcement is precarious, it nonetheless signals a major shift in the legitimation process. This is perhaps most evident in the strategic role that the judiciary has assumed in the highly developed countries when it comes to the rights of immigrants, refugees and asylum seekers.

Finally, the state itself has been transformed by this combination of developments. This is so partly because the state under the rule of law is one of the key institutional arenas for the implementation of these new transnational regimes—whether the global rights of capital or the human rights of all individuals regardless of nationality. And it is partly because the state has incorporated the objective of furthering a global economy, as is evident in the ascendance of certain government agencies, i.e. ministries of finance, and the decline of others, such as those linked to the social fund.

Because so many processes are transnational, goverments are increasingly not competent to address some of today's major issues unilaterally or even from the exclusive confines of the inter-state system narrowly defined. This is not the end of state sovereignty. It is rather, that the "exclusivity and scope of their competence" (Rosenau 1992) has altered, that there is a narrowing range within which the state's authority and legitimacy are operative.

There is no doubt that some of the intellectual technology that governments have and that allow them to control, i.e. Foucault's governmentality, has now shifted to non-state institutions. This is dramatically illustrated in the new privatized transnational regimes for cross-border business and the growing power of the logic of the global capital market over national economic policy.

These are transformations in the making as we speak. My reading is that they matter. It is easy to argue the opposite: the state is still absolute and nothing much has changed. But it may well be the case that these developments signal the beginning of a new era. Scholarship on mentalities has shown how difficult it is for people to recognize systemic change in their contemporary conditions. Seeing continuity is much simpler and often reassuring.

Official immigration policy today is not part of the explicated rules of the new game. Is this helpful in seeking to have a more effective and fairer long-term immigration policy in today's globalizing world?

Notes

1. This is a slightly modified version of an essay originally published as Sassen 1999b. The broader issues about the state and the global economy are developed in Sassen (1996) and about immigration in Sassen (1999).

2. Alongside the well-documented spatial dispersal of economic activities, new forms of territorial centralization of top-level management and control operations have appeared. National and global markets as well as globally integrated operations require central places where the work of globalization gets done. Further, information industries require a vast physical infrastructure containing strategic nodes with hyperconcentrations of facilities. Finally, even the most advanced information industries have a work process—that is, a complex of workers, machines and buildings that are more place-bound than the imagery of information outputs suggests. I develop this in Sassen (2001).

3. Global cities are centers for the *servicing* and *financing* of international trade, investment, and headquarter operations. That is to say, the multiplicity of specialized activities present in global cities are crucial in the valorization, indeed overvalorization of leading sectors of capital today. And in this sense they are strategic production sites for today's leading economic sectors. Elsewhere (Sassen 2001) I have looked at cities as production sites for the leading service industries of our time; one concern was to recover the infrastructure of activities, firms and jobs, that is necessary to run the advanced corporate economy. I focused on the *practice* of global control: the work of producing and reproducing the organization and management of a global production system and a global marketplace for finance.

4. This is a scholarship with a diversity of intellectual lineages: e.g. Ruggie 1993; Wallerstein 1988; Arrighi 1995; Jessop 1999; Rosenau 1992; Spruyt 1994. See Sassen 1996, for a discussion of this literature as it concerns the particular question under discussion here.

5. Thus, there were centralizing monarchies in Western Europe, city-states in Italy and city-leagues in Germany (see Wallerstein 1988). Further, even at a time when we see the emergence of nation states with exclusive territoriality and sovereignty, it can be argued that other forms might have become effective alternatives, e.g. the analysis in Spruyt, 1994, on the Italian city-states and the Hanseatic league in northern Europe.

6. It should be said that no developed country has signed this convention, mainly because they are unwilling to relinquish discretionary control over migrant workers. Yet the Convention does have moral authority and has served its purposes on various occasions in Europe, discussed later. The European Commission's 1994 Communication on Immigration and Asylum proposed that all member states ratify the UN Convention on workers.

7. And its weight in many of the Latin American countries is dubious. For a very detailed (and harrowing) account of the situation in Mexico, see Redding (1996). See also generally Sikkink (1993).

8. For instance, the Universal Declaration was cited in 76 federal cases from 1948 through 1994; over 90 percent of those cases took place since 1980 and of those, 49 percent involved immigration issues, and 54 percent if we add refugees (Jacobson 1996: 97). Jacobson also found that the term "human rights" was referred to in 19 federal cases before the 20th century, 34 times from 1900–1944, 191 from 1945–1969, 803 cases in the 1970s, over 2,000 in the 1980s, and estimated at 4,000 cases through the 1990s.

9. There is a whole debate about the notion of citizenship and what it means in the current context (See Soysal 1994; Baubock 1994; *Indiana Journal of Global Legal Studies* 2000; Isin & Turner 2002; Sassen 2002). One trend in this debate is a return to notions of cities and citizenship, particularly in so-called global cities, which are partly de-nationalized territories and have high concentrations of non-nationals from many different parts of the world (e.g. Holston 1996; Isin 2000; *Social Justice* 1993; Copjec & Sorkin 1999. The ascendance of human rights codes strengthens these tendencies to move away from nationality and national territory as absolute categories.

10. While these developments are well known for the cases of Europe and North America, there is not much general awareness of the fact that we are seeing incipient forms in Japan as well (see, e.g. Shank 1995; Sassen 2001; 1998, chapter 4). For instance in Japan today we see a strong group of human rights advocates for immigrants; efforts by non-official unions to organize undocumented immigrant workers; organizations working on behalf of immigrants which receive funding from individuals or government institutions in sending countries (e.g. the Thai Ambassador to Japan announced in October 1995 that his government will give a total of 2.5 million baht, about US$100,000, to five civic groups that assist Thai migrant workers, especially undocumented ones; see *Japan Times*, October 18, 1995).

11. Further, the growth of immigration, refugee flows, ethnicity, and regionalism, raise questions about the accepted notion of citizenship in contemporary nation-states and hence about the formal structures for accountability. My research on the international circulation of capital and labor has raised questions for me on the meaning of such concepts as national economy and national workforce under conditions of growing internationalization of capital and the growing presence of immigrant workers in major industrial countries. Furthermore, the rise of ethnicity in the US and in Europe among a mobile work-force raises questions about the content of the concept of nation-based citizenship.

The portability of national *identity* raises questions about the bonds with other countries, or localities within them; and the resurgence of ethnic regionalism creates barriers to the political incorporation of new immigrants.

12. There is a large and rich literature on the development of immigration policy at the European level. A bibliography and analyses on the particular angle under discussion here—limitations on the autonomy of the state in making immigration policy—can be found in Sassen (1999).

13. Jurisdiction over immigration matters in the US Congress lies with the Judiciary Committee, not with the Foreign Affairs Committee as might have been the case. Congressional intent on immigration is often at odds with the foreign affairs priorities of the Executive. There is a certain policy making tug of war (Mitchell 1989). It has not always been this way. In the late-1940s and 1950s there was great concern with how immigration policy could be used to advance foreign policy objectives. The history of what government agency was responsible for immigration is rather interesting. Earlier, when the Department of Labor (DOL) was created in 1914 it got the responsibility for immigration policy. On June 1933, President Roosevelt combined functions into the Immigration and Naturalization Service within DOL. The advent of WWII brought a shift in the administrative responsibility for the country's immigration policy: in 1940 President Roosevelt recommended it be shifted to the Department of Justice, because of the supposed political threat represented by immigrants from enemy countries. This was meant to last for the war and then INS was to be returned to the DOL. But it never was. It also meant that immigration wound up in Congress in committees traditionally reserved for lawyers, as are the Senate and House Judiciary Committees. It has been said that this is why immigration law is so complicated (and, I would add, so centered on the legalities of entry and so unconcerned with broader issues).

14. There are diverse social forces shaping the role of the state depending on the matter at hand. Thus in the early 1980s bank crisis, for instance, the players were few and well coordinated; the state basically relinquished the organizing capacity to the banks, the IMF, and a few other actors. It was all very discreet, indeed so discreet that if you look closely the government was hardly a player in that crisis. This is quite a contrast with the deliberations around the passing of the 1986 Immigration and Reform Control Act—which was a sort of national brawl. In trade liberalization discussions there are often multiple players, and the Executive may or may not relinquish powers to Congress.

15. In this light it is worth noting that in November 1995 a federal judge ruled large sections of Proposition 187 (passed by referendum in the state of California to be instituted in that state) unconstitutional, citing individual rights and the fact that "the state is powerless to enact its own scheme to regulate immigration," this being the preserve of the Federal government of the US.

16. An important study at that time by the Washington based Urban Institute (Clark *et al.* 1994) found that immigrants contributed US$30 billion more in taxes than they took in services in the early 1990s.

17. President Clinton's 1994 crime bill earmarked US$1.8 billion in disbursements over six years to help reimburse states for these incarcerations cots.

18. Increasingly, unilateral policy by a major immigration country is problematic. One of the dramatic examples was that of Germany. It began to receive massive numbers of entrants as the other European states gradually tightened their policies and Germany kept its very liberal asylum policy. Another case is the importance for the EU today that the Mediterranean countries—Italy, Spain, and Portugal—control their borders regarding non-EU entrants.

19. For instance, NAFTA's chapters on services, financial services, telecommunications, and "business persons" contain considerable detail on the various aspects relating to people operating in a country that is not their country of citizenship. For instance, Chapter Twelve, "Cross-Border Trade in Services" of the NAFTA (White House document, September 29, 1993) includes among its five types of measures those covering "the presence in its territory of a service provider of another Party" under Article 1201, including both provisions for firms and for individual workers. Under that same article there are also clear affirmations that nothing in the agreement on cross-border trade in services imposes any obligation regarding a non-national seeking access to the employment market of the other country, or to expect any right with respect to employment. Article 1202 contains explicit conditions of treatment of non-national service providers, so do Articles 1203, 1205, 1210 (especially Annex 1210.5), and 1213.2a and b. Similarly, Chapter Thirteen on Telecommunications and Chapter Fourteen on Financial Services contain specific provisions for service providers, including detailed regulations applying to workers. Chapter Sixteen on "Temporary Entry for Business Persons" covers provisions for those "engaged in trade in goods, the provision of services or the conduct of investment activities" (Article 1608).

20. The US Delegation for this group is chaired by the Assistant Secretary of State for Consular Affairs and the INS Commissioner.

21. For instance, an item on internal changes in the state which may have impacts on immigration policy is the ascendance of what Charles Keely has called soft security issues. According to some observers, recent government reorganization in the Departments of State, Defense, and the CIA reflects an implicit redefinition of national security. After the September 11, 2001 terrorist attacks in the U.S. we have clearly seen a re-narrowing of such national security concerns.

CHAPTER 12

Conflict and Transformation: New Forms of Nation-State Building in Iran, Afghanistan, and Tajikistan

Tschanguiz Pahlavan

Globalization and the Nation-State

It is generally believed that increasing globalization will lead in one form or another to the abolishment of the nation-states in the world. The present debate in Europe in defense of a federal Europe rather than a Europe of nation-states is actually strengthening the position of the "abolitionists" (*Le Monde*, 21 June 2000, 1, 15–17). They think there is no longer any necessity to preserve the existence of the present nation-states or to help newly independent political units reach the level of an integrated state structure within internationally recognized territorial boundaries.

Worldwide technological progress, global dissemination of information and media technology, international economic interconnections, and interdependency are considered the main elements supporting the idea that nation-states will sooner or later disappear from the world scene as useful or effective political and economic players (Pahlavan 1999, 399–518).

According to this approach, the responsibility for the world order will be or should be increasingly concentrated within the framework of the United Nations. Troubled areas of the world could be brought under control with the help of a military body attached to the United Nations. As a result, it would be appropriate to reform the structure of this world organization and its decision-making body (i.e. the Security Council).

This picture reflects the ideals and tendencies of the extreme globalists of our time. It is clear that all globalists do not follow the same line of thinking, but they are generally in favor of globalization and are not willing to accept the existence of the nation-state as a responsible body in the world of tomorrow.

Globalists generally oversee or ignore the concrete situations and experiences gained at the regional level. Moreover, the perfect model of the nation-state (in the view of the globalists) is that of the European experience. Even this model is in the process of disappearing due to increasing integration in the European community. Most globalists are resisting an evaluation of the new experiences and forms of the state building in non-European parts of the world. New efforts to reach national unity in non-Western regions are actually ignored or are not dealt with properly. New national states are being formed that are a combination of different ethnic, linguistic, and cultural groups. This is different from the principal European experiences based on one ethnicity, one language, or even one religion.

This chapter's main task is to examine the experiences at the particular regional level of Iran, Afghanistan, and Tajikistan in order to contribute to the present discussion, with no intention to generalize the results of such an approach to other places.

Specificities of the Region

By region, I refer here to only three countries—Iran, Afghanistan, and Tajikistan. This is naturally a very narrow sense of the greater region in which these three countries are located (Pahlavan 1992). I have chosen these three countries because they share close common cultural traditions and enjoy a number of cultural similarities. I do not intend, in this chapter, to become involved in a more complicated debate concerning various experiences at the level of the greater region, which deserves separate attention and analysis.

Iran, Afghanistan, and Tajikistan (hereafter referred to as IAT) have throughout history enjoyed common cultural, political, and literary traditions. Islam is the religion of the overwhelming majority of the people. In all three countries, Persian is the dominant language (in Afghanistan called "Dari", and in Tajikistan called "Tojiki"), which facilitates communication among the people living there and migrating from one place to another. Most importantly, they enjoy the same historical and literary background.

This commonality within the same civilizational framework did not prevent them from experiencing different political destinies, especially during the 19th and 20th centuries. Although Iran already had more or less internationally recognized borders, Afghanistan enjoyed the same position as a completely independent state only in the beginnings of the 20th century. The Tajikistan of today became part of the Russian empire, and in 1929 was organized as one of the Soviet republics. Only after the collapse of the Soviet Union could it declare its independence and become internationally recognized as an independent state. As a result, we are facing different levels of political development and various stages of state-building processes in these three countries.

Despite these differences in recent history, it is worth making a comparative analysis because of their cultural and historical similarities. All three of the IAT countries belong to the same civilization, are followers of various schools of Islam, and use Persian as their national language or lingua franca. Besides, political changes in the last two decades have brought them closer to each other due to Islamic uprisings or revolutions, wars, expanded migrations, and increasing communication among their governments and peoples.

By political development, I am speaking of the experiences gained in each state at the national level. Most of the political experiences of the IAT were, especially until the end of the 19th century, restricted to local areas and to ethnic or tribal entities. Even important events like the Afghan wars against Britain were carried out in particular local areas, through particular tribal warriors. They were not countrywide events and therefore not all inhabitants participated in these struggles. One might even say that the overwhelming majority of the people did not consider these wars to be directly concerned with their own life and property.

Rather than these more localized events, what is of interest to me are the events shared by all people in one country, or at least by a considerable majority of inhabitants, because I believe that such phenomena are able to lay the necessary foundations for creating a new solidarity that could be called "national".

The mere existence of a central power in one country does not necessarily create national solidarity among its inhabitants. The existence of central powers in some parts of the region is not equal to the existence of a nation-state, nor does it inevitably lead to the formation of one. Some of the central powers were established because of colonial rule and the need to negotiate with a body stronger than the local powers, or they become established because they were able to subjugate the small local groups in order to force them to pay taxes and obey their commands.

A nation-state, or a national state in some form, can be constituted only on the basis of the common experiences of the inhabitants of the country concerned. Even the formation of the central authority must be the outcome of a common experience in order to be able to function as a national element in the political destiny of the people.

Here, I shall deal with three main phenomena as "nationalizing elements"—a constitution, war, and migration. One might add other elements, but these seem to me to be the most important in the political shaping of the destiny of the people in the IAT countries. Though these three elements do not have the same value in each of the countries, on the whole, they together constitute forms of national solidarity that are worth examining comparatively.

Constitutions are the result of the joint experiences of a people in the form of revolutions, uprisings, or consensus among the various power holders in the countries concerned. As such, these constitutions shape the form and structure of the central administration governing the country on the basis of common rules and regulations.

In 1906, as a result of what is known as the Constitutional Revolution, Iran for the first time in its history became a constitutional government with an elected parliament. Although this development was repeatedly interrupted, the same constitution with minor changes remained valid until the Islamic Revolution of 1979.

The revolution of 1906 was the outcome of the joint efforts of people in many important parts of the country, as well as intellectuals and city-dwellers from various regions. "The people" wished to ban despotism and believed that they could attain national independence through a constitution and an elected parliament. Thus, it was generally felt that, with the passage of a basic law, they would be in a position to oppose the despotic rule of the Qajar kings and to prepare the ground for the people's participation in the power structure and political decision making.

The constitution of 1906, although not fully respected by the subsequent governments and was subject to a dynastic change in 1924, was considered the only legitimizing document in the country and remained valid as such until 1979. During the period spanning the First and Second World Wars, all the opposition forces, including the leftist anti-monarchy parties as well as nationalists, referred to this constitution to justify their demands and their actions. Precisely because of the opposition's attitude toward the constitution—either as an ideal or as a document to be revised or abolished—and their continual reference to it, it acted as legitimizing basis for national consensus.

It is noteworthy that despite all the political upheavals, unrest, and dynastic changes, the country has had only two constitutions, both of them outcomes of popular revolutions: the Constitutional Revolution of 1906 and the Islamic Revolution of 1979.

In Afghanistan, traditional legitimation of the power structure had been founded on a *Luya-jirga* (tribal assembly). From the third decade of the 20th century onwards, Afghanistan witnessed a number of constitutions, all of them approved at the top level and issued accordingly. They were not the result of popular movements. The first was approved by the king based on a proposal by an adviser. When the kingship was abolished and a republic was declared by one member of the royal family, Afghanistan entered a new phase in its history. This republic did not last long and was replaced by communists. In 1992 the Mujaheddin allied forces came to power in Kabul and ousted the communists from the government. Although various ethnic and religious groups took part in the Mujaheddin government, they were not able to agree on a new constitution.

From 1994, gradually the Taliban forces, backed by Pakistan, captured more than half of the country and finally the capital, Kabul, without being in a position to form a single comprehensive government. As a result, this country until very recently had two governments. The Taliban government was eventually recognized by only three countries in the region, whereas at the same time the government of the Mujaheddin enjoyed recognition as a member of the UN (Pahlavan 1999a).

Tajikistan's situation is a peculiar one. In 1924, it was a part of Uzbekistan. In 1929, it became a member republic of the Soviet Union. Only after the collapse of the Soviet Union did this country for the first time become independent and able to possess a new constitution. After a bloody civil war and the need for a new national consensus, the new constitution was approved by popular vote in 1999.

Constitutional movements in these countries demonstrate the desire of the people to form governments that allow different sectors of the society to gain access to the centers of power. This is still an ongoing process and far from complete. Disputes over the present Islamic constitution of Iran are one of the main issues dividing the government and the various opposition forces. Various minorities, as well as secular and religious sectors of Iranian society, are debating over a better form of government. They are not satisfied with the present religious state, which is based on a religious system of law. Afghanistan, because of a continuing civil war, is not in a position to agree upon a national constitution. Tajikistan, although having popularly approved a new constitution, has not been able to quiet the increasing discontent with the present legal system.

Despite all the controversies, it is obvious that constitutions are not mere formal documents. On the contrary, they are manifestations of trans-local sentiments and solidarities of different sectors of these societies in order to reach a countrywide (i.e. national) democratic form of central government subject to popular vote.

In the context of this chapter, war is considered a trans-local phenomenon. Therefore, wars fought at tribal or local levels are not considered here. As a trans-local, trans-sectoral experience, war should have an impact at the national level with mass participation from all over the country.

When different local areas, ethnic groups, and religious communities come together to fight for a common cause, they develop a transnational solidarity that extends far beyond the restricted local group. Such wars, especially those against foreign enemies, are important events leading to a sense of national, trans-local belonging. They can create such an attachment or strengthen the existing one.

Wars are the worst, most expensive, and bloodiest experiences for those involved. But they also induce participants to unite *vis-à-vis* an alien, external danger. War should not be considered an inevitable step towards nation building, but it might fulfill such a function in certain societies. Erich Maria Remarque (1999, 27–28) in his well-known anti-war novel writes that through war we become hard, rough, vengeful, and distrustful—qualities that were lacking prior to its advent. But the most important quality we acquire through war is a very stable and practical sense of belonging together—a sense of comradeship.

In the 20th century, two types of wars have occurred in the IAT—external and internal wars. In external wars, various sectors of people in one country fight united against a foreign enemy, such as in the Iranian war against Iraq or Afghanistan's war against the Soviet occupation. By internal wars, I mean civil wars such as the present hostilities within Afghanistan or the animosities between different local areas and groups in Tajikistan after 1992.

Whereas external wars strengthen the national unity, internal wars intensify existing deep-rooted hostilities within a society. Revolutions might be classified as internal wars, but since they give birth to a specific type of national solidarity, it would be appropriate to look at them separately. In the sociological sense, our only example of revolution is in Iran. In the other IAT countries (Afghanistan and Tajikistan), there have been no revolutions with mass participation to overthrow and replace an existing regime. Therefore, I will simply mention, in passing, the two Iranian revolutions of the 20th century.

During the 20th century, Iran experienced a number of upheavals or mobilizations with trans-local (i.e. national) effects—the Constitutional Revolution of 1906, the nationalization movement of 1951 against foreign control of the oil industry, the Islamic Revolution of 1979, and finally the eight-year war against Iraq. All these events brought the nation closer together, and different parts of the country took part in mass mobilizations, which were considered a matter of common interest. It is interesting to note that even minorities (ethnic and religious) participated in all these movements and trans-local changes. On the other hand, it is clear that because of these social and national uprisings all sectors of the society came together and experienced a sense of belonging to one nation. It is in this way that the sense of nationhood became strengthened. The war against Iraq's invasion is, in my opinion, the final stage of a long process of a modern nation-building process, which commenced at the beginning of the 20th century. This war, although carried out in the name of Islam, brought the overwhelming majority of the society together to defend their life and their country *vis-à-vis* a foreign enemy. It was a costly experience for Iranians. Although accompanied by serious errors of an inexperienced leadership, it nonetheless had an unprecedented influence on the formation of a unitary national identity.

In Afghanistan, the Jihad (Holy War) against the presence of Russian military forces was the first comprehensive national movement in the history of the country. Never before were all of Afghanistan's citizens in a position to unite around a common objective. Despite their differences, various Islamic sects (Sunnis and Shi'ites along with Isma'ilis), ethnic groups, and local areas took part in the Jihad and considered war as their highest objective. Religion helped them create an atmosphere of unity. They were able to put aside their disputes in order to push back their common enemy. People left their homes and local areas to join political and military organizations, which were functioning at a national level. As a result, trans-local movements and internal displacements brought various sectors of the society together and enabled them to enter into a broad nationwide solidarity.

Prior to the Jihad, citizens of Afghanistan rarely left their local areas and when they did so, it happened mostly on an individual basis. Trans-local movements as a mass phenomenon became evident only during the Jihad. The history of Afghanistan was not devoid of such phenomena, but movements were restricted to specific local areas and ethnic communities. Forced displacements were commonly carried out by one ethnic group against another. Naturally, such displacements were unable to strengthen or generate a sense of national, inter-ethnic solidarity.

In contrast, the Holy War against the Soviets was fought against a common enemy. Thus ethnic animosities were ignored or pushed aside temporarily. I would even say that this Jihad against foreign invasion was the first united form of action among Afghanistan's inhabitants. For the first time in its history, the country produced a national uprising to achieve a common goal. Because of this war, millions of people moved from one corner of the country to the other or were even forced to leave and seek refuge outside of their homeland.

When Mujaheddin forces came to power in 1992, they were able to form a government with the participation of different ethnic groups and religious communities. This government was a national government in the broadest sense. But since the roots of ethnic and religious hostilities were still alive, a new civil war, fueled from the outside, led the people of Afghanistan to a tragic destiny, which continues even to this day.

Although a civil war is generally considered a phenomenon of disunity, one might conclude that in similar situations, when a number of conflicting groups try to secure a share for themselves in the formation of the power structure and try to overcome the obstacles obstructing the forging of the nation-state, they have no other choice but to insist on their demands and their respective identities. As long as they were fighting against a foreign enemy, they were able to show unity. As soon as the foreign enemy disappeared, they immediately reverted to the underlying disputes over the kind of leadership to be instituted (in order to secure a place for the preservation of their identities in future governments). In this sense, even civil wars might be said to lead people to a new level of coexistence and national identity. In the case of Afghanistan, the civil war has been oriented toward the establishment of a new power structure. It has no secessionist character. In other words, this civil war, which has been carried out among different local areas, has not aimed at the dismemberment of the country. On the contrary, the conflicting parties have been trying to establish a multicultural, multi-ethnic state apparatus. It is the nature and structure of such a national state that has been the subject to disagreement.

Tajikistan has had a different experience regarding war and internal dispute. A new independent country with no experience in the field of international relations came into being after the collapse of the former Soviet Union. The state administration and the economy were completely controlled by the Russians. Even the communist party of Tajikistan was dependent on Moscow and had no real authority to act independently.

Although Central Asia has witnessed the presence of an ancient Tajik culture continuing into the present, the ethnic sensitivities of neighboring countries (supported by Soviet leadership) did not allow them to include all areas into the new Tajik republic established in 1929. Thus a small country approximately 90 percent mountainous was transformed into a new political entity. As a result, tensions within the new republic and in the region became from the very beginning an integral part of the state formations in Central Asia. No one was satisfied with the official boundaries set up by Soviet authorities.

After the dissolution of the Soviet Union, the Republic of Tajikistan encountered foreseeable local, political, and religious unrest. Each group tried to secure an appropriate place in the government and state administration for itself. Local powers in particular fought for their interests by mobilizing armed forces in order to preserve their control over local areas and to exercise influence in the structure of the administration.

After 1992, a number of political parties came into being, each attempting to shape the new identity of the country according to its own ideals. Islamists positioned themselves against secularists and communists. Parties tracing back the identity of the Tajiks to the ancient pre-Islamic Iranian empire actively participated in the political struggle against Islamists and former communists. Democratic slogans confronted technocrats of the old establishment. Everyone was struggling for a share of power and a place in the power structure. Thus, the country entered into an unprecedented civil war. Many were killed and thousands were forced to migrate.

Finally, peace talks were held with the support of the UN and a number of countries such as Iran and Russia. A new constitution, parliament, and presidential actions have brought the country to a delicate balance.

In recent years, particularly in the aftermath of the Soviet invasion of Afghanistan, the Islamic Revolution in Iran, the war imposed on Iran, and the breakup of the Soviet Union, many forces have been unleashed that caused new waves of population movement. The scale of these movements is unprecedented. Understanding this new development, its dimensions, and its ramifications requires deeper analysis in order to better grasp its true meaning.

Population movement and mass migration at the global level have been addressed in the context of refugee issues, and legal instruments drawn up for this purpose have mostly focused on the rights of refugees. The United Nations High Commissioner for Refugees (UNHCR) has pursued matters relating to refugees, concentrating on the human rights of refugees and the meeting of their basic requirements. But UNHCR has had to face new situations that were not the product of political events. There have been forced migrations of people in substantial numbers as the result of environmental or even cultural conditions. These complex manifestations of population movement have prompted analysts and researchers to conduct new studies and take into account not only the political dimensions but also cultural, social, and economic conditions.

Moreover, most studies on this subject to date have dealt with the issue of migration from one country to another, while in recent times internal displacement within one country has also become a major issue. Intensified efforts at border security and control have sometimes managed to stave the flow of migrants to neighboring or more distant countries. At the same time, internal displacement of populations has become an important form of population movement, which is different from political asylum and cultural or economic migration from one country to another. A new phenomenon that has not received adequate attention can also be added: population movement within a civilizational domain, a zone of shared culture.

Internal Displacement

When we speak of movements of populations within a civilization, we seek to focus our attention on population movements within a common and shared cultural ground. Even when population shifts take place within a given country belonging to a particular civilization, we want to have a better understanding of the vast transnational ramifications of this national phenomenon, of the link between internal and inter-civilizational population movements. At present when one speaks of internal displacement, it means displacements within the boundaries of a particular country. Internal displacement of populations is usually the product of internal feuding, ethnic clashes, forced settlements, and gross violations of human rights. In one of the reports of a conference in Colombo in 1995, the question of population displacement is quite thoroughly addressed (Internal Displacement Consultation on Refugee and Migratory Movements 1995, 2). According to this report, in 1992 when UNHCR began paying attention to this phenomenon, the number of displaced persons was close to 24 million. But in 1995 this number was estimated at 30 million, and today even more.

Even in 1995, the number of displaced persons was 10 million more than the refugee population, which was estimated to be about 20 million people. The same report adds that the number of displaced persons in Africa was 16 million, and in Asia more than the number presented in the Colombo Conference report. We can conclude that the real number of displaced persons in the world is more than 30 million people. Considering these numbers, we can suggest that population movement in general and internal displacement in particular is a global phenomenon, appearing in diverse regions of the world and even in Europe, which has been more stable but has been exposed to the consequences of the development unfolding on its periphery.

In 1994, UNHCR reported to the World Bank that about 10,000 people each day for the previous two years had been forced to flee their homes and cross national borders or face internal displacement as a result of civil wars and internal conflicts. Refusal by many countries to receive refugees and migrants has caused more people to settle inside their own country but far from their places of origin. Since internal displacement occurs within the political domain of a given country, it is covered by the laws of that country. Those who choose to go to other countries are generally given consideration for their potential to be classified as refugees and, if so classified, can receive international protection. But internally displaced persons are not in principle entitled to receive any assistance without the consent of their government, let alone those who want to change their legal status. This is particularly true if internal displacement occurs as a result of political strife within a country, and the ruling government and belligerent groups are hostile to displaced persons.

Providing aid and carrying out relief operations without the consent of political authorities is considered a breach of sovereignty.

The experience of Iraq and creating a security belt there were failures. Foreign interventions can also lead to violations of sovereignty and the undermining of the territorial integrity of states.

Although UNHCR admits that it has no special mandate for internally displaced persons, it emphasizes that there is no international organization that is directly responsible. UNHCR inevitably gets involved at the request of the Secretary General in situations arising out of internal displacement. In 1993, under increasing pressure to set boundaries for its mandate, UNHCR elaborated two criteria for its involvement in situations of internal displacement: (1) where the question of displacement has a direct relationship with refugees, especially when there is a linkage between return of refugees and the internally displaced population; (2) in situations where there is clear possibility that displacement will lead to a refugee situation; in such conditions UNHCR is bound to take preventive measures (*ibid.*, 4–5).

In fact, internal displacement is an internal issue, but since it erupts in different parts of the world it has taken on a universal or transnational global character. Another point that has not been taken into account to this day is the cultural and civilizational ramifications of displacement within a single civilizational realm. From this point of view internal displacement occurs at three levels—at the country level, within a civilization, and at the global level.

Furthermore, population displacement can be examined in terms of a larger set of inter-relations or as a separate or singular phenomenon. The former, which is the main theme of this analysis, takes place within the bounds of a cultural-geographical region, while the latter refers to movement outside of a cultural and civilizational zone. An example of the first type is the population displacement inside Afghanistan or two adjacent countries. An example of the second type is the displacement of the same people outside of this region to Germany, the US, etc.

Population displacement within the realm of Iranian civilization is not a new phenomenon. In the wake of the expansion of the Achemenid kingdom, Iranians settled in the newly conquered territory, resulting in the dissemination of their culture and religious convictions. The Achemenids did not solely emphasize their military presence. The Achemenid soldiers moved in their military expeditions along with their spouses, and land was allocated to solders in the conquered zones. The limited size of the populations meant that land was not given to soldiers solely through confiscation. New homesteads flourished. The Iranian aristocrats, following their Zoroastrian convictions, also considered it a moral duty to develop their lands. On the other hand, the majority of Iranians who were scattered throughout the kingdom were primarily urban settlers. They propagated Iranian ways of life in general, but were tightly united in their culture in small coherent groups.

Achemenid soldiers could stay longer in the expanded dominion of the kingdom, since they had their wives with them. Both farming and ethnically homogenous communities managed to endure in the newly conquered lands. The Zoroastrian priests also played an important role in this migration-colonization. They accompanied the military forces and settled where the soldiers chose to stay. Some priests lived with farmers and others with aristocrats. Historical evidence shows that these priests and settlers set up their houses of worship throughout the region. Today, it has become clear that Zoroastrianism has played an essential role in the religion and thought of the Hellenistic world.

It is also known that there were small communities of Zoroastrians in China during the Sassanid period. The number of these Zoroastrians increased with the Arab conquests, but there is not much information on this phenomenon. Iranians were in contact with different cultures and ethnic communities prior to Islam. This contact came about as a result of the expansion of empire, the migration of Iranians into new territories, and the inevitable acceptance of Greek forces in their territories (Boyce 1990).

During the Islamic period, the form of population displacement changed and was accompanied by the presence of Arabs and others in the territory of Iran. Iranians moved to other areas in the Islamic world. These types of population displacement continued until the Mongol invasion.

The invasion of the Mongols exposed the entire Iranian territory to destruction. In the 13th century, Mongols subdued large parts of Iran and forced large numbers of people, especially in Khorassan, to leave their homeland. They moved to different parts of the larger region, including Anatolia. During the Safavid period and in the 19th century, there were also migrations to Anatolia for commercial and religious reasons. Many Iranians who migrated to Ottoman cities managed to develop conditions for permanent settlement. During the Constitutional Revolution, many intellectuals migrated from Iran to Istanbul to avoid persecution by autocratic rulers.

In the 19th century, the number of Iranians in the domain of the Russian empire also increased, especially in the second part of the century. The defeat of Iran by Russia in the 19th century led to several migrations throughout the Russian empire. A major part of Iran fell into the hands of that empire and consequently large populations were separated from Iran. Many in Azerbaijan and Gilan went to the Caucasus and Central Asia in search of work. Statistics show that in 1899 more than 70,000 Iranians left for Russia, more than 60,000 went to the Caucasus, and more than 10,000 opted for Central Asia. These numbers are quite substantial as a proportion of the total population of the period.

Causes of Population Displacement in the Region

Developments and events occurring in the 1970s and 1980s gave rise to major population displacements. The Islamic Revolution in Iran in 1979 and the Soviet invasion of Afghanistan around the same time (December 1979) brought population movements into a new level. Displacements in Afghanistan first began inside the country then spread to the region. Population movements from Iran were mostly toward the Western world. There was also substantial migration to Turkey, although it was mostly a question of transit to other countries. Due to the difficulty of reaching their desired final destinations, however, many chose to settle in Turkey. The third wave of population movements in the region came as a result of the historical dissolution of the Soviet Union. When the Soviet Union broke up in December 1991, many believed that there would be a large influx of migrants to the West. But this did not occur, and instead there were massive movements of population within the territory of the former Soviet Union itself. Some other important events triggered population displacements in the region, including the invasion of Iran by Iraq, the Persian Gulf War, internal conflicts in Afghanistan after the victory of the Mujaheddin over the communist regime, the war between Azerbaijan and Armenia, internal strife in Georgia, and the war in Chechnya. In addition, economic and environmental factors greatly intensified population displacements.

All these events provide evidence that the region under review has historically experienced unprecedented population displacements, perhaps more severe than any other place in the world. These developments are unique both in terms of their scale and in their peculiar characteristics.

The aforesaid factors have caused new cultural, social, and political movements that will certainly leave an impact on the history of the region. What is crucial here is to ascertain the extent to which population movements are systemic rather than being blind and even random phenomena. In times of crisis, people usually seek refugee in the nearest safe haven. But population displacements may also display significant historical patterns. In some cases when a population enters a new social environment, it is absorbed by the more powerful forces and gradually loses its identity. The adaptive capacity of the new group will determine the degree of assimilation. In some cases, the new group may build a wall around itself and attempt to survive by relying on its own identity. In such cases the minority group either decays internally or gains relative advantages that make the larger group dependent on it, even commanding its respect. There is also the possibility that the new group may resort to crime in order to find a niche for itself. There is, finally, a particularly important and interesting possibility. This is where inter-group contact produces a kind of cultural relationship that opens the way to a new historical awareness. The case of Afghan refugees in Iran or population movements of Kurds in the region lying between Iran, Iraq, and Turkey are of this latter kind. There are, of course, other variations as well. Moreover, the economic, cultural, and political situation of the new homeland can greatly influence the dynamic of population movements. In migrant groups, prior knowledge of the new environment can also be influential.

In our Iranian civilizational zone, a number of major population movements have appeared. Some have homogenous historical affinities with Iranians and others, despite their cultural and historical differences, have had a significant impact on Iranian historical development. Afghanistan has much in common with Iran, but Russia has had a greater effect on Iranian destiny. Considering these characteristics, the following axes, among others, may be considered major and fundamental as well; Central Asia (especially Tajikistan), the Caucasus, and Afghanistan.

Massive and uncontrolled movements of millions of people as a result of the Soviet breakup comprise one of the salient features of this historical situation. According to UNHCR, political instability, economic insecurity, and ethnic conflicts in a vast region that were linked together mostly due to the presence of the Soviet Union brought about a massive wave of migration of people which has been unprecedented since the end of WWII. Although these population movements took place within the bounds of the Commonwealth of Independent States (CIS), they assumed greater dimensions, affecting neighboring countries and becoming a source of concern for the international community.

Population movements within the successor states of the former Soviet Union demonstrate that existing resources have not been adequate to meet these challenges. On the contrary, the inadequacies of the new independent governments aggravated the situation and undermined their efforts to bring about political and economic stability. Complex difficulties that emerged as a result of migration and population movement were the product of ethnic violence, political and cultural intolerance, economic hardships, and environmental degradation. This situation also gave rise to security and humanitarian problems that extended well beyond the geographical boundaries of the CIS countries. West, East, and Central European countries had to face influxes of illegal migration from the CIS countries. Countries like Afghanistan, Iran, and Pakistan had to receive migrants from Tajikistan.

The collapse of the Soviet Union was a major shock of the 20th century. This event not only caused major changes in global strategic alignments, but also presented new challenges to the entire region as well as within the Soviet Union. The future of the post-Soviet era is not very clear, but the possibility of severe political and economic shocks seems evident. The new independent states are trying to overcome major hurdles and take effective steps toward what they call state building. The fragile and transitory nature of their economies and polities is a salient feature at this phase, and this is combined with ethnic clashes and significant population movements.

Ethnic tension and population movement are not new to the region. In fact, the roots of current developments can be located in conflicts emerging during the formative days of the Soviet Union and even prior to that in the tsarist era.

The Soviet Union was a constellation of many nations and ethnic groups. Although it officially emphasized the principle of "free and equal participation" of all nations within the larger union, there was, in fact, a combination of serious contradictions and tensions among these nations. As Boris Yeltsin once said, the Soviet Union was the last of the great empires to disappear. This empire used autocratic and tyrannical means to secure its aims. The Soviet Union was almost equal in size to tsarist Russia. This vast land had eleven time zones and stretched 5,600 miles from the Baltic and Black Seas in the West to the Pacific Ocean in the East. The Soviet Union was also heir to the unresolved nationality and ethnic problems of the tsarist period, and it further aggravated the tense relationships among these nations. The complexity of these national problems manifested themselves in two forms. First, there was a vertical polarization between the majority Russians, who were culturally and politically dominant, and non-Russians who strove to set up autonomous states. The second form was horizontal tension among non-Russian peoples who inhabited adjacent areas and were affected by the "divide-and-rule" policy of Moscow.

When the October Revolution triumphed, theorizing about the nationality problems that were very common among the Bolsheviks gained new impetus. Lenin and the Bolsheviks knew well that the mere use of force could not keep the Russian empire from breaking up. For this reason, republics were founded in Central Asia that had, as the Bolsheviks claimed, an ethnic character. The same policy was also implemented in the Caucasus. In both places the artificial borders drawn by the central government paved the way for subsequent tensions. These borders were particularly arbitrary in Central Asia, where people called them the "dividing axe". Thus, in the Soviet Union, fifteen nations acquired ethnic republics with ethnic designations. Moreover, there were a number of ethnic groups that were given a substantial degree of autonomy.

The Soviet Union intended to gather diverse peoples around a single ideology that was represented as universal. Much effort was made to incorporate the republics into a single culture and social ideology. Economic progress in some of these regions was made possible, but at the cost of millions of lives. Some of the ethnic groups and a number of small national groups in Crimea and the Caucasus were forced to migrate to Siberia and Central Asia. Besides causing untold suffering, the forced migrations destroyed their ethnic character and, in some cases, even led to their total disappearance.

The death of Stalin mitigated some of the excesses, and many who had been forced to leave their homes gradually returned. But then the central government of the Soviet Union started encouraging White Russians and Ukrainians to migrate to non-Russian republics in order to serve as levers of pressure for Moscow's policies.

Russians and other Slavic peoples migrated to Central Asia, the Caucasus, and Baltic republics, especially to urban areas. The policy of the Soviet Union was based on encouraging migration under the pretext of achieving progress in the republics. This policy led to a further aggravation of tension. The Soviet Union tried to create conditions under which the migrant Russians could play a crucial role in local affairs. For this purpose, Russian language and culture were promoted in all republics. This policy was pursued from the time of Stalin.

The essence of the Soviet policy was to create "the Soviet People" around a Russian cultural nucleus. Thus, the Russians, who were themselves subject to severe oppression, enjoyed certain advantages compared to other peoples. Non-Russians had to learn Russian while few Russians needed to learn other languages. Since the birth rate among non-Russians was higher than that of the Russians, it gave rise to heightened concern among the migrant Russians and constrained the power of the Soviet planners and the military. These conditions caused greater migration from south to north in the 1980s. Although the Soviet government claimed that the problem of nationalities was resolved, with the advent of glasnost and perestroika by Gorbachev, ethnic tension erupted.

In early 1986, violence erupted in Nagano-Karabakh, a region that the Soviet government had placed under the jurisdiction of Azerbaijan in the 1920s, and led to the migration of 500,000 Armenians and Azerbaijanis. In the summer of the same year, local violence in the Farghanch Valley in Central Asia caused the expulsion of 60,000 Meskhetians from Uzbekistan and the Kyrgiz Republic.

The last census of the Soviet Union in 1989 showed that Russians constituted barely 50 percent of the 285 million population of the Soviet Union. This demonstrated the bitter truth to the Soviet leaders that their policies produced antithetical results. National sentiments became greatly visible in the entire Soviet Union. This census also revealed the extent of population displacement and assimilation and revealed the true situation of non-indigenous residents in non-Russian republics. According to the same census, although migration of Russians to the Ukraine and to the Baltic republics continued, Russians and other Slavs had moved out of Central Asia and the Caucasus since they saw no viable future for themselves.

In 1990, non-Russian populations sought to take matters into their own hands and achieve their national aspirations. In Central Asia and the Caucasus, the republics made new efforts to strengthen their political and national status. Waves of nationalism spread throughout Russia. With the coming to power of Boris Yeltsin, the empire entered a new phase of collapse. The coup in 1991 that was perpetrated with the support of the Communist Party expelled those who sought to preserve the former order, and the foundation of the Commonwealth of Independent States was laid in December 1991 (UNHCR Regional Bureau for Europe 1996).

Problems arising out of the collapse of the Soviet Union were not easily predictable. Neither the Russian leaders nor the Western countries expected to face such extensive and profound developments. Seventy years of Soviet domination had left behind such an impact that even the absence of the latter could not repair the situation. As a result, diverse ethnic groups with diverse "aspirations" were living together that in fact belonged to other nations in the immediate vicinity or even in more distant regions. Apart from the quarrel between Armenia and Azerbaijan that quickly turned into a war causing the death of thousands and displacement of hundreds of thousands of people, bloody conflicts also erupted in other areas that demonstrated the depth of potential and actual conflicts. It can be said with great certainty that the first ethnic conflict broke out in the northern Caucasus, in the Russian Federation in 1992. As a consequence of this conflict, thousands of Ingush and Pidgordony were expelled to northern Ossetia.

The Soviet Union claimed that the republics were created on the basis of the presence of single ethnic groups, but in all republics other ethnic groups were present to varying degrees. Many republics are indeed multi-ethnic and seek to integrate all ethnic groups around a single group holding political power. In Georgia and Moldavia, the situation degenerated to such a degree that it led to a war and substantial displacement.

In Tajikistan, population displacements began with the disintegration of the Soviet Union. Considering the complex social-political environment in Central Asia, it should have been expected that the collapse of the Soviet Union would result in widespread population displacements in various parts of the region. The Tajik civil war worsened the situation and gave rise to greater displacement. Some 60,000 persons crossed into Afghanistan, 200,000 into other Central Asian republics, and more than half a million were internally displaced. According to Tajik officials, the number of internally displaced reached 680,000 persons (UNHCR, CASAWAME 1997, 33; UNHCR, CASAWAME 1998, 25–26; UNHCR Regional Bureau for Europe 1996, 1).

At the end of 1994, approximately 600,000 persons who had moved to Russia were recognized as refugees or involuntary migrants. This is only one fourth of all the persons who have come to Russia since 1989. Russian statistics do not distinguish between refugees and forced migrants.

At the end of 1995, the total number of refugees and forced migrants reached approximately one million. At first, most of people came from Tajikistan, Georgia, or Azerbaijan. Although many Tajiks wished to move to Iran, the Iranian government did not open its borders to them. As a result, most of them had no other choice but to move to Russia, Afghanistan, and other Central Asian countries (UNHCR Regional Bureau for Europe 1996, 3).

Many observers believe that few tragedies are comparable to that which has befallen Afghanistan in the second half of the 20th century. The flawed nation-building policies of the pre-1979 era and Cold War politics created an intractable humanitarian problem. The official nation-building policy up to this time and even afterwards was based on Pashtunization of the society by ignoring the presence of many other ethnic groups in the country.

According to UNHCR reports, during the Soviet-Afghanistan war, more than 1.2 million Afghans perished, 300,000 were crippled for life, almost six million became refugees, while approximately two to three million were internally displaced as a result of fighting (*UNHCR, CASAWANE 1998a* 49, Appendix). Most of the Afghan refugees went to Pakistan and Iran (see Appendix A).

Iran has experienced a different development process. Many people left this country immediately after the revolution of 1979. But within the country there was an increasing number of Iranians who were persecuted because of their opposition to the regime. During the war with Iraq, there was a new wave of emigration. Most Iranian migrants preferred to go to the West, especially to the US, Europe, and Canada. There are also Iranian communities in Australia, Turkey, and other places. On the whole, it is estimated that approximately three million citizens of Iran have left the country during the past twenty years.

Iran was not only a country of emigration. It has been a country of immigration as well. A million Afghans, Irlei, and Kurdish refugees have immigrated. This is an important development that deserves to be dealt with separately.

Despite all the existing discontent in various parts of the world with the nation-state and nation-building processes, especially due to the increasingly despotic and extreme nationalistic behavior of autocratic rulers in a number of countries, there is also, in certain parts of the world, a strong tendency toward the formation of a new, or at least different, type of nation-state. This new type of central state is quite unlike the modern European model or experience, which is based on a single, homogenous group or built upon a core population or at least a strong process of assimilation. I would like to identify this new type of state as a "national-state" which is constructed on the principles of diversity. It is a kind of multi-ethnic, multi-cultural state although, as in the case of the region under discussion, there is a larger common cultural matrix. This national-state represents the diversity existing in the society and is the outcome of the historical development of the societies concerned. Without generalizing this phenomenon, I think it would be appropriate to pay attention to its development in the very region discussed in this paper.

The national-state is based on the common cultural, if not shared, experiences of the people concerned. Although comprising different types of ethnic groups, minorities, local areas, cultures, and languages, it is the incarnation of their coexistence. We might suggest that the fundamental fact of diversity within a common cultural matrix might force, even if it does not seem likely at present, this new type of state to be ethnically democratic in the long run.

The political development in the IAT countries is influenced by their respective political histories, especially during the past two centuries. Although belonging to the same cultural matrix, each of them has experienced a specific path of state building.

In all three countries, there are various ethnic groups and minorities striving for the preservation of their own cultural identity. But at the same time it is important to note that they do not strive for similar goals. Depending on their position in their respective countries and their historical experiences, these minorities and ethnic groups express concrete and specific demands regarding their status in the process of state-formation and development. Some of them have developed secessionist ideals, but most of them prefer to remain within the existing political structures while securing a proper place for themselves. They may only be able to preserve their identity by remaining within a circle of familiar cultures. In face of increasing globalization, they may have a chance to flourish in the realm of familiar cultures and value systems.

In the case of Afghanistan, wars have ruined the country and, despite all hostilities, the most important demand of various sectors of society, including the minorities, is to be recognized and to have a chance to participate in the process of political decision-making. Continuation of civil war has not changed that strong desire. On the contrary, it has strengthened it.

In the case of Iran, the main obstacle preventing minorities from attaining a sense of being equal and respected citizens is the ideology of state religion which is narrowly interpreted with the intention of excluding "other-thinking" Iranians from participation in decision-making and in the shaping of their destiny.

Whereas in Iran the Islamists rule the country by ignoring the majority of the people, especially the secular forces, in Tajikistan religious groups have been trying for a decade to secure a place for themselves in the state administration and local councils. They wish to be accepted as such and to be able to play a role in the political structure of Tajikistan.

Migration, among these neighboring countries, has played an important role in shaping "national identities" and the experience of belonging to the same polity. The combined strength of minority and national identities within a larger common civilizational realm seems to have led to a state form in which ethnic groups are major protagonists in the very definition of the nature of the state.

APPENDIX I.
AFGHAN REFUGEES POPULATION, 1980–1997
(AS OF 1 JANUARY 1997[1])

Year	Pakistan	Iran	India	Russian Federation
1980	400,000	200,000		
1981	1,400,000	500,000		
1982	2,375,000	800,000	3,000	
1983	2,700,000	1,200,000	4,000	
1984	2,800,000	1,500,000	5,000	
1985	2,900,000	1,800,000	6,000	
1986	2,700,000	2,000,000	6,000	
1987	2,873,000	2,221,000	6,000	
1988	3,156,000	2,700,000	5,000	
1989	3,255,000	2,900,000	5,000	
1990	3,272,000	2,940,000	8,000	
1991	3,185,000	3,000,000	12,000	
1992	3,077,000	2,900,000	10,000	
1993	1,627,000	2,700,000	11,000	12,000
1994	1,477,000	1,850,000	24,000	16,000
1995	1,053,000	1,623,000	22,000	17,000
1996	1,200,000	1,420,000	20,000	19,000
1997	1,200,000	1,400,000	19,000	20,000

[1] See *Second Regional Consultation on Refugees and Displaced Populations in Central Asia, South West Asia and the Middle East Asia, Ashagabat, 1998.*

CHAPTER 13

"Citizenship Light": Transnational Ties, Multiple Rules of Membership, and the "Pink Card"

Ayse S. Caglar

Introduction

It is 14 October 1997. Süleyman Demirel, the president of the Turkish Republic, is visiting Germany. In Rotes Rathaus, Eberhard Diepgen, the mayor of Berlin, gives a reception in Demirel's honor. The representatives of the Turkish community in Berlin, some German officials, as well as the Turkish protocol in Berlin are the guests. The hall is packed. First, Demirel addresses the invited guests. After the formal greeting, he addresses the audience as "my citizens". I feel a tension in the air. He pauses and then continues to convince the audience that this is not a slip, but he really means it. "Yes, you are first my citizens, then German citizens. You are our citizens and no matter what citizenship you take, you will remain as the citizens of the Turkish Republic."[1] His speech sets free a murmur in the room. I see smiling faces. I see faces and eyes being lit up. I see people with a contented look, turning to each other and nodding by their heads. Demirel is looking very pleased by the sight of the relaxed and smiling faces. With eyes wide open, I look at Diepgen standing one step behind Demirel. To my astonishment he is smiling too. Then I realize that this "communitas-like" atmosphere is ironically built on the desynchronization of the German and Turkish speakers in the room (namely, on the lack of simultaneous translation). With the German translation of Demirel's words, Diepgen's smile is wiped away at once. Now, he and some of the guests are not smiling any more. Diepgen looks astonished. His face has an expression of speechlessness. But the majority of the crowd seems not to care about the others. There is a mood of joy in the room. Demirel's speech gets a very warm applause. Completely ignoring what Demirel said, Diepgen sticks to his prepared speech. He tells us how the Berlin phone directory has two and-half pages of entries of the surname "Öztürk" (literally translated as the "real Turk"). "They are now part of Berlin's landscape, just like the numerous Berliners with Polish surnames are." Diepgen gets his applause too, though it does not seem to cheer him up. The party atmosphere continues for some of the guests. People are now indulging in small talk and enjoying the refreshments and the beverages served.

Contrary to Turkey, Germany does not officially recognize dual nationality, and this discrepancy is an important source of tension between the two countries with regard to the membership status of Turkish immigrants in Germany. In the Federal Republic of Germany, there are more than 2.1 million immigrants from Turkey. However, the rate of naturalization among Turkish immigrants is still very low. In 1996, the number of Turks who acquired German citizenship was 46,294. Although this figure is substantially higher than for 1990 and 1991 (2,034 and 3,529 respectively), it is still very low.[2] In 1997, Turkish immigrants who acquired German citizenship composed 1.85 percent of all Turkish immigrants. In Berlin the picture is not very different.[3] In 1997, only 6.8 percent of Turkish immigrants who were entitled to German citizenship were naturalized. Although the Turkish state allows dual citizenship, the German state does not. The new citizenship law in Germany (that came into effect on January 1, 2000) allows dual citizenship to the immigrant children born in Germany until they reach the age of 23.[4] Otherwise, there is the requirement to abandon one's birth citizenship upon naturalization in the German citizenship law. However, the Turkish state disregards this requirement in practice and as a policy encourages those Turks living abroad (especially those living in Germany) to apply for citizenship in their "host" countries so that they can enjoy full economic, social, and political rights in the countries of immigration. Meanwhile, it allows and practices the retention of nationality in the wake of foreign naturalization, even in countries where dual citizenship is not officially allowed. The consequence of the Turkish state's posture is that most of the naturalizations of Turkish immigrants in the countries in which dual citizenship is not recognized—Germany being such a country—result *de facto* in dual citizenship despite the host state's official position against it.

From this point of view, Demirel's talk was a diplomatic *faux pas*. However, this event is more than that and encompassed not only the tensions between the sending and receiving states, but also the sentiments surrounding citizenship issues and most importantly the role that states play in the formation and the reproduction of the processes which link immigrants and institutions across the borders of nation-states. In this chapter, I will examine a new category of membership designed by the Turkish state for its expatriates living abroad (especially in Europe) in two ways. I will first explore the interplay between this new status of membership and dual citizenship, and then disentangle Turkish immigrants' horizontal and vertical ties of citizenship and their flaws with regard to German and Turkish societies.

Transnational Social Fields

In today's world, increasing numbers of (im)migrants remain connected to their homelands despite their incorporation into the country of immigration. By means of a multiplicity of economic, social, cultural, and political ties immigrants, construct and reconstitute their lives simultaneously embedded in more than one society (Basch *et al.* 1994; Glick-Schiller *et al.* 1995; Vertovec 1999; Guarnizo & Smith 1998). Linear and cumulative migration theories, with their common assumptions of traditional patterns of immigrant adaptation, fall short of encompassing this border-crossing expansion of social space and the formation of "social fields" that connect and position some actors in more than one country. Transnationalism is a new analytical framework for viewing a "series of economic, socio-cultural, political, practical, and discursive relations that transcend the territorially-bound jurisdiction of the nation-state" (Guarnizo 1997, 5).

Transnationalism has been developed in an effort to describe and systematically analyze the phenomenon characterized by "triadic relationships". Triadic relations refer to the constant interaction and multiple relationships between groups and institutions in the country of settlement, in the country of origin, and among migrants located in different countries. They construe the main characteristic of transnational social spaces of migrants.[5] The transnationalism perspective brings the studies of migration and re-migration to a common trajectory where no clear paradigmatic distinctions are made between the sending and receiving countries or between migrants and returnees. Different arenas spanning the national boundaries enable migrants to remain active in multiple localities. The border-crossing social fields are the seedbed for the development of new subjectivities, new modes of political participation, and new relationships to localities.

Transnational formations are thought to be shaped under pressures from above and from below the level of nation-states. Although these distinctions are developed to capture the dynamic of power relations in transnational formations, in this division between levels above and below the nation-state, the role of states in the constitution and maintenance of social fields that cross borders somehow does not get its due importance. States influence the very nature of transnational actors, not only by providing the institutional environments within which they function (Krasner 1995), but also by their active policies designed for the re-incorporation of "nationals" abroad into the home market and the body politic more directly (Vertovec 1999; Levitt, 2000). With their continued cross-border activism, states have a constitutive role *vis-à-vis* transnational formations.

These border-crossing social fields transform many kinds of relations, including political relationships, in these arenas. They enable the actors to remain connected in terms of their political allegiance and participation to the countries of origin. However, what is at stake here is not a simple kind of political (and nostalgic) attachment to homelands, but the formation of a new mode of political participation in which membership and allegiances are shared across territorial divisions (Bauböck 1994). Dual citizenship which institutionalizes cross-border ties and membership in two different political entities establishes a fertile ground to explore the new transnational dynamic in political relations, participation, and the meaning of citizenship, as well as the constitutive role of the states in the transnational affairs of the immigrants.

Dual Citizenship

Rather than trading one political membership for another, immigrants remain connected to their country of origin in the wake of naturalizations. Today there is a surge in the number of dual nationals. The number of countries that make provisions for dual citizenship and tolerate dual citizenship is on the increase. Italy, Turkey, Colombia, and the Dominican Republic are recent additions to the group of countries (like Great Britain, Ireland, Switzerland, Greece, Israel, and El Salvador) that officially recognize dual citizenship (Spiro 1997). As it becomes more difficult for the nation-states to require and extract an exclusive relationship from its members, they increasingly waive the renunciation requirements of foreign allegiances for naturalization. Although some countries do not favor dual citizenship as a policy, they practice a complete toleration (like the US) (*ibid.*, 1413). This softening in state attitudes towards dual nationality is congruent with the changes in the international context *vis-à-vis* dual citizenship. The draft Convention of the Council of Europe in 1996 favors the retention of nationality upon naturalization in a foreign country (*ibid.*, 1457). This position is in strong contrast to the 1930 Hague Convention—which declared dual nationality not desirable and needed to be abolished—as well as the Convention of European States in 1963 on reduction of cases of multiple nationality (*ibid.*, 1449).

Dual citizenship is mostly the consequence of the interplay of the birthright citizenship rules of *ius soli* and *ius sanguinis* and mixed marriages (Spiro 1997; Hailbronner 1997). However, the major reason behind the explosive growth in the number of dual nationals in the last decade is the attitude of countries of emigration, which allows retention of nationality upon naturalization in the countries of immigration. An increasing number of states that have experienced out-migration lift constitutional restrictions on this matter to (re)incorporate their emigrants into their national market and polity (Smith 1999,10). Passing dual citizenship laws is one of the most important measures of these (re)incorporation strategies.[6]

For the countries of emigration that depend heavily on the stable remittances from their "nationals" abroad as well as on their lobbying activities, it is crucial to sustain these migrants' economic, political, and religious ties to their countries of origin. Dual citizenship is an important asset for the sending state. From this point of view, Demirel's talk—which at first sounds like a *faux pas*—should be evaluated within this general context. The hidden transcript of his talk was to underline or assure Turkish immigrants in Germany of the reach of the Turkish state beyond its territorial boundaries. In fact, he was directly addressing the anxieties of Turkish immigrants that hesitate to naturalize in Germany.

In Germany, the rates of naturalization for the groups that have access to dual citizenship are higher but still very low for those who are not allowed to have dual citizenship.[7] The most important reason behind Turkish immigrants' reluctance to naturalize is the expatriation requirement for naturalization in Germany. The immigrants insist on dual citizenship. The strong criticism of the new *Ausländergesetz* by Turkish immigrants and organizations also shows that dual citizenship is very high in their agenda.[8] Moreover, the fact that naturalizations rapidly go up among Turkish immigrants in other European countries that allow dual citizenship clearly indicates the strong correlation between naturalization rates and tolerance to dual citizenship.[9]

Instead of approaching this insistence on dual citizenship from within a framework of loyalty (which makes multiple loyalties an impossibility or a problem), it might be useful to focus on it from the perspective of the horizontal and vertical ties in the society which are closely related to the political governance capacity of the states involved. Citizenship entails a set of ties. As Faist (2000a, 23) very elegantly formulates, citizenship is the "institutionalization of the political syntax of social and symbolic ties". However, this set of ties cannot be reduced solely to a relationship between the individual and the state. It also encompasses substantial horizontal ties among the citizens. If citizenship refers to institutionalized and formalized ties of reciprocity, then immigrants' insistence on dual citizenship and their refusal to naturalize in the absence of dual citizenship in Germany hint at the particular nature of the ties of reciprocity between the immigrants and their fellow citizens in this country.

Citizenship Light: The "Pink Card"

Being aware of Turkish immigrants' abstinence from naturalization in the absence of a dual citizenship possibility, the Turkish state introduced some amendments to Turkish citizenship law (paragraph 403, Article 29). The aim was to encourage those Turks living abroad to apply for the citizenship in their "host" countries where dual citizenship is not officially allowed. The purpose of this amendment is very explicit in the bill that brought about the change (Genelge 1998, 1–2). In June 1995, the statuses of those who have to expatriate in order to acquire the citizenship of another country are redefined by Bill 4112. By having the permission to expatriate, the person in question becomes legally an "alien". What the new regulation does is to guarantee a bundle of rights to this new type (category) of "aliens" (ex-members). These ex-members are entitled to the "pink card" (*pembe kart*) which gives them access to a cluster of rights in their "home" country despite their official non-member status there (Cebecioglu 1995). The "pink card" was not conceptualized as a temporary solution to the low naturalization rates of a specific generation of Turkish immigrants. The children of the "pink card" holders are also entitled to this status (of "pink card" holder).

Although the "pink card" was accepted in 1995, it became an urgent issue first after the Turkish president's visit to Germany in the fall of 1997. The German government demanded explicitly from the Turkish state a cessation of the practice of allowing Turkish immigrants to retain their nationality upon naturalization—a practice of *de facto* dual citizenship. Only then did the "pink card" become an important issue on Turkish authorities' as well as Turkish immigrants' agendas.

The "pink card" allows us to explore the nature of the changes and challenges immigration and immigrants introduce to nation-states and to the given conceptions of citizenship. Two different approaches to the relationship between the models of membership and immigrant incorporation into the host polities dominate and divide the field of discussions on immigrant membership and participation in Europe. While one model focuses on formal citizenship status, the other underlines the resident non-citizens' access to substantive rights and argues that these immigrants often possess identical socio-economic and civil rights as citizens despite their non-citizen status (Soysal 1994). The former brings the differences between the polities in terms of their principles of membership to the forefront (the contrast between the principle of *ius sanguinis* and *ius soli*) in the analysis of immigrant incorporation. The latter draws attention to a disjuncture between formal status and substantive citizenship rights and underlines the importance of the frames in which these rights are anchored (e.g. human rights). According to this view, the new order of sovereignty, which decenters and constrains the nation-state by multiple actors, operates above and below the state. Thus, the dynamics of immigrant policies in Europe are better understood through these frames rather than different countries' varying principles of citizenship. The human rights discourses and the supranational institutions constraining the states are conceived as the key factors responsible for the unbundling of rights tied to formal citizenship (Soysal 1994; Sassen 1998b; Bauböck 1994).

The "pink card" can be seen as a clear case of extending substantive rights without formal citizenship status. The "pink card" holders are legally no longer Turkish citizens, but they are entitled to rights (such as residence, work, mobility, investments, inheritance, and property rights like buying, selling, and renting land) free from the restrictions the foreigners are subject to in Turkey.[10]

In the literature that emphasizes the decoupling of formal membership status and substantive rights, the examples are mostly drawn from post-war European countries and their immigration practices. According to this position, the immigration policies and practices of these countries converge independent of their principles of membership and their models of incorporation for immigrants (Bauböck 1994; Faist 1998; Joppke 1998; Sassen 1998b). There is a *de facto* homogenization of immigrant rights independent of their formal status in the host countries (Sassen 1998b). On this basis, the advocates of this position plead for the reconceptualization of citizenship in supranational and non-local terms in which rights are available through conventions anchored in human rights discourses. Not the formal status but the legal resident status is crucial for immigrant access to substantive rights. Interestingly, the "pink card" is conceptualized or defined as a document of legal domicile (*ikamet belgesi*). In the bill that introduced the "pink card", it is explicit that the "pink card" functions as an *ikamet belgesi* (residence permit) and could be used in all kinds of transactions in which *ikamet belges* is required (Genelge 1998, 3).[11]

According to Turkish citizenship law, with the loss of citizenship, a person's entry in the State Register (*nüfus kütügü*) is dropped out automatically. In this way the member becomes, from the legal point of view, an "alien". However, the "pink card" enables one to keep the entry at the Register open. On the "pink card" the place where the registration entry is made is noted as if it were the place of residence of the "pink card" holder. Thus, although the holders of the "pink card" reside in different countries other than Turkey, they are all treated (legally) to be residents of Turkey. It is noteworthy that the way of granting rights even to expatriots goes through the residence status (in this case virtual) by way of a residence permit.

If denizens (Hammar 1990) refer to permanent residents who for all practical purposes hold the full set of rights—except the voting rights—accorded to citizens, it could be argued that the "pink card" transforms or rather transfigures its holders into denizens in their "home" country. The difference here is that the non-resident ex-members are treated as residents. In a way, the "pink card" unifies two places of residence. If citizenship encompasses the individual's relation to the state, then in the case of the "pink card", this relationship is redefined in such a way that it is shared across territorial divisions.

Turkey is not unique in this practice. The Declaration of Mexican Nationality ID is very similar to the "pink card" and was in fact introduced by the Mexican government on the basis of similar concerns as those mentioned above (Chavez 1997). The aim was to eliminate the significant barrier for their nationals to acquire citizenship in their host countries (in this case mainly in the US). Like the "pink card", it allows the ex-members to keep their property and inheritance rights, to attend public schools and universities, and allows access to government jobs and services in Mexico. The "Non-Resident Indian" (NRI) status providing a series of rights, incentives, and privileges for investment to Indians abroad was also introduced by the Indian government due to similar concerns.

The transfigurations brought about by the "pink card" are important. First, it points out that immigration does not initiate a coexistence of multiple systems of rule only in the receiving countries, but also in the sending countries. The fact that membership becomes multilayered through immigration is usually dealt with within the context of host countries in the literature.[12] "Pink card" practice draws our attention to what Sassen (1999) urges us to do, namely to develop a new narrative of immigration in which the receiving and sending countries would be conceptualized to form an entangled and a unified space. The sending and receiving countries analytically become part of the same social space. The dynamics of this new status of membership, that is to say, of the "pink card" are intertwined by the dynamics of dual citizenship, so that they form, to use Chavez's designation for this phenomenon, a "double helix".

If we understand globalization predominantly to be a process of local transformation (see Friedman in this volume), then the "pink card" could be considered a good example of such transformations. The local becomes transnationalized in the sense that the content and the practice of membership in the locality is changed in such a way that the dynamics of the rule of membership could only be analyzed as part of a network that ties different localities together (in this case Turkey and other countries of immigration hosting Turkish immigrants without accepting dual citizenship). Moreover, as mentioned before, other labor-sending countries (like Mexico or India) have introduced similar kinds of membership options due to similar kinds of concerns. Thus, the changes in the status and practice of membership in Turkey have a directionality and need to be considered as a part of such constructions. By means of the "pink card", membership comes to be shared not only across territorial divisions, but a new category of members (the "pink card" holders) with a distinct legal status and who are different from the citizens, aliens, and the dual nationals is constituted.[13]

The Role of States in the Formation of Transnational Membership

The "pink card" practice draws attention to the fact that extension of substantive rights does not necessarily take place within the framework of supranational institutions and human rights discourses that challenge the sovereignty of the nation-state. The basic motive behind the introduction of the "pink card" is the desire of the government of the sending country to enhance and sustain homeland/expatriate relationships—for economic and political reasons—despite their citizens' naturalization in the country of immigration. With the introduction of the "pink card", the Turkish state initiated a structure of incorporation for its ex-members. It is difficult to interpret the "pink card" as a sign of a straight transcendence of the nation-state. Thus, the phenomenon of nation-states' declining sovereignty should not be dealt with as a zero-sum game but as a multifaceted negotiation process in which the nation-states are still powerful actors.

It is true that for a range of transnational activities, states cease to be the central point of reference for actors but become only one of a multiplicity of references. However, even in the case of establishing crosscutting economic, religious, and political ties, it is questionable to what extent these networks are developed outside of state institutions and influences. The "pink card" is a good example of the constitutive role of the states in the institutionalization of a social space and a bundle of ties that criss-cross borders. The states, as seen in the case of the "pink card", are the major actors in the proliferation of membership forms.

From the point of view of the nation-states, the inclusion of such people who have a multiplicity of involvements in more than one place (and who are consequently entangled in multiple solidarities among people who are spatially located at different places) into the national imaginary is undesirable and dangerous for the solidarity of the imagined community.[14] Ironically it is the nation-states that contribute to these formations. The multilayered attachments of immigrants are not the consequence of their alleged divided allegiance or loyalty, but the outcome of processes shaped and sustained actively by state centered projects and policies. Thus the nation-states involved should be given their due as institutionalized actors implicated in the process of forming and reconstituting transnational ties (Smith 1999, 15).

As Smith correctly underlines, the nation-states "are re-inventing their own role in the 'new world order'" (1999, 10). Thus, instead of facing an "inexorable decline", nation-states are transforming themselves. The new political constructions in labor-sending states that encompass those residing abroad as part of their body politic could be interpreted as part of such transformations. The introduction of visa and travel facilities (for the "nationals" abroad), levying taxes on incomes earned abroad, development of programs and incentives for the investment and funding of projects in the "homeland", or the collaboration with the migrants for lobbying activities in the countries of immigration are all examples of the state activism of labor-sending states (like Granada, Philippines, Haiti, El Salvador, etc.) to forge and sustain transnational ties and social fields.[15] Hence, it is not necessary to conclude that transnational networks would be subversive to state power. They could well be state-initiated and sponsored and the transnationalisms could be "nationalized" to an extent.[16] In fact the contrast between the Kurdish and Turkish transnational networks *vis-à-vis* state power show that the subversiveness of transnational networks depends on the articulation of migration, the state structures, and the immigrants' access to resources (including to the dominant discourses) both in the sending and receiving countries at particular historical conjunctures.[17]

The maintenance of German Turks' "homeland" ties are encouraged and supported institutionally by the state policies of the states involved. These policies lay the ground for the sustained ties of, for example Turkish immigrants in Germany, to Turkey and to other Turkish immigrants elsewhere.[18] German institutions also supported and cherished German-Turks' homeland ties. For a long time Germany, which officially defined itself as a non-immigration country, defined the immigrants as a temporary labor force. As a result, long-term policy measures were not formulated.[19]

The Lightness of the "Pink Card"

Despite the "pink card", the rates of naturalization still remain low in Germany among Turkish immigrants. In Berlin it is estimated that more than 110,000 Turks would be eligible for German citizenship under the new *Ausländegesetz*. Contrary to expectations, the applications for German citizenship among Turks dropped drastically (especially in Berlin) after the introduction of the new citizenship law.[20] In comparison to the first six months of 1999, the number of Turks applying for German citizenship dropped from 4,000 to 2,102 in the first six months of 2000.[21] The number of Turks who applied and received a "pink card" also remains low. By the end of June 2000, there were only 2,302 "pink card" holders in Berlin,[22] though their number increased slightly in 2000 (in the first six months) to 502 from 300 in 1999.

The "pink card" failed to achieve what it aimed to: namely, to encourage Turkish immigrant to acquire host country citizenship. Turkish immigrants still propagate and campaign for dual citizenship. What is lacking in the "pink card"? What could this failure hint to us about the nature of the ties citizenship encompass? Why is access to formal citizenship in two places so important?[23]

Turkish immigrants' reluctance to be satisfied with the "pink card" forces us to rethink the nature of relations construed around citizenship. Citizenship is not a simple cluster of rights but stands for something whose value cannot be comprehended solely by the rights granted to members and denied to aliens. Other than rights (and duties), there is an excess involved in citizenship. By excess I definitely do not refer to a necessary link between identity, citizenship, and loyalty. It is clear that today citizenship and identity are decoupled so that the link between the individual and the state is more of an instrumental link than of a relationship grounded in mutual loyalty (Soysal 1994). However, reducing citizenship to a mere instrumental relationship would be as misleading as reducing it to a relationship of a mystified loyalty. Both positions fail to comprehend the complexity of the ties citizenship entails. Citizenship is not only a (vertical) relationship between the individual and the state, but also a (horizontal) relationship between the members of a political entity. It entails substantial ties to fellow citizens (Offe 1999, 44–46; Faist 2000a, 3, 12). Thus, it is a phenomenon of social reciprocity. In that sense citizenship is a network of trust among strangers in a political entity. Most importantly, this relationship of trust—unlike the mystified and essentialized notions of loyalty—has sources in the institutions of society.

Both the "failure" of the "pink card" and the persistent charm of dual citizenship for Turkish immigrants could be read as indicators of flaws both in the horizontal and in the vertical ties into which Turkish immigrants are embedded in German *and* Turkish societies. Immigrants' insistence on dual citizenship in Germany could be considered a means to draw attention to the weaknesses of immigrants' trust relations with their fellow citizens in Germany. Along the same line, the failure of the "pink card" could be interpreted as a sign of weakness of Turkish immigrant's vertical ties to the Turkish state.

According to Offe (1999, 50), when both personal interaction and categorical trust fail to establish horizontal networks of trust among their fellow citizens then there is a need to rely on institutions to act as the mediators and generalizers of trust (*ibid.*, 65). The crucial thing here is that trust is a cognitive phenomenon and depends on knowledge and most importantly on belief that is built upon perceptions and images of the others (*ibid.*, 55). In the encounters between Turkish immigrants and Germans as members of German society (though with differentiated rights), these two basic trust-generating mechanisms seem to have failed to develop fully.

Turkish immigrants' awareness of (or belief in)[24] their negative stigmatization in German society (both as *Ausländer*[25] and as Muslims) and the increasing hostility against foreigners, as well as the public debates on the rising danger of "*Ausländerfeindlichkeit*" (hostility against foreigners) and racism all contribute to the failure of categorical trust between Turkish immigrants and Germans. The recent "survey" conducted by *Persembe*—the weekly bilingual (Turkish and German) supplement of *die Tageszeitung*—strikingly illustrates the resignation among Turkish immigrants regarding the future relations between Germans and German Turks in German society.[26]

In order to be able to build bridges between strangers, the institutions should, according to Offe (1999, 75) be (or be believed to be) "truth telling", "promise keeping", "fair", and anti-discriminatory. There are signs that from the point of "foreigners", institutions in Germany are believed to have flaws in performing these functions. Most importantly, the acquisition of German citizenship is not seen as an effective check against these built in preferences in the society—at least in the short-term. This contention that German citizenship would not change the nature of their encounters is strengthened by the immigrants' daily experience. It is believed that they would be discriminated against despite their German passport.[27] The fact that the "*Ausländerbeauftragte*" in Berlin pleads for anti-discrimination laws in Germany is itself a confirmation of their belief in the lack of fairness and discrimination despite their passport.[28] To my question of why he didn't apply for German citizenship (although he fulfills the requirements), 32 year-old Riza answered,

> In handling me they are not going to look at my passport. They are going to look at my hair (color). No matter whether you have a German passport or not, as long as your hair is black and your name is Riza, nothing will change.

Although formulated in a very crude way, this widely held belief draws attention to the weaknesses in the trust-inducing capacities of the institutions in the society. Moreover, the formative function of institutions—be it through education or citizenship—are believed to be weak at mediating trust among fellow citizens.[29]

The German state's failure and/or reluctance to provide full protection to its new members (namely, to the naturalized Turks) is usually given as a proof of the absence of color-blindness in institutions.[30] As a result of this perception or observation of the malfunctioning of institutional regimes, trust and reciprocity could not be generalized to "everyone else" in the society. In that sense, one could claim that there are problems in recognizing and trusting each other as the constituent participants of a political community (Offe 1999, 76). In that sense, there are cracks in the horizontal networks of trust and reciprocity between immigrants and the "natives" in the society.

If flaws in the horizontal ties of trust are responsible for Turkish immigrants' insistence on dual citizenship, it is the flaws in the vertical ties of trust, namely the relationship between the individual and the state (in this case between German Turks and the Turkish state) that contribute to the relative failure of the "pink card". The reasons behind its failure are twofold. First, some anomalies were observed in the operation of the "pink card." In some cases, the administrative staff or the state executives who were responsible for the task of implementation and enforcement of rules refused to take the "pink card" into account. German Turks are also aware of their negative stigmatization (as the category of *Almancis–Germanites*) in Turkey, and they have a strong deficit in social and symbolic capital there (Caglar 1995). In the context of these deficits, the thick inter-personal component that is crucial for the functioning of institutions makes the "pink card" a more doubtful practice. The fact that rules can be made, remade, and then changed and, most importantly, that their making and unmaking is in the hands of decision-makers to whom German Turks' access and influence are very limited (due to their low social and symbolic capital as well as their lack of influential networks and power) also cast doubt on the "pink card".

As a result of inconsistent practices affecting German Turks, no confidence in the continuity of (state) institutions in Turkey developed.[31] Moreover the "pink card" construes its holders as an ambivalent category. It breaks the uniformity of the law. One interview partner expressed the common sentiment against the "pink card" quite clearly—"the state which gives (rights) easily with one decision could also take it away with another decision. Then everything—all that labor, money, investment—would be in vain" (Interview March 21, 1999).[32] In a context in which the durability of institutions is in doubt, the "pink card" encompasses too many risks for the immigrants who lack resources to mobilize networks to reach the decision makers.

With the introduction of the "pink card", the Turkish state created a third category between citizens and aliens. One of the consequences of immigration (and the influx of refugees) is that membership becomes a continuum at "home" as well as in the "host" country. The category of the "pink card" could be designated as a syncretic category of membership at the "home" end of the continuum. Its holders are neither citizens nor aliens and despite its inclusionary content, the "pink card" still signifies to others the Turkish "diaspora".[33] The ambivalent character of the status acquired through the "pink card" made Turkish immigrants in Europe perceive their situation as vulnerable (especially in the context of the missing voting rights) to Turkish state politics and practices. In that sense, the "pink card" is too light *vis-à-vis* the Turkish state.

Conclusion

The "failure" of the "pink card" might encourage us to reconsider the attempts to reconceive citizenship in supranational and non-local terms. If the civic ideal is replaced with a more passive sense of entitlement to benefits which seem to derive from remote sources (like human rights) without the well developed corresponding institutions backing their implementation, would people be persuaded of the value and "durability" of their substantive citizenship rights at the cost of formal membership? Maybe in our endeavor to understand the social dynamics of different rules of membership, it is more appropriate to shift the emphasis from the disjuncture between the formal status and substantive rights of citizenship to the *performance* or *practice* of citizenship (Holsten & Appadurai 1997). As the case of the Turkish immigrants illustrates, without disentangling the practices of citizenship rights in a given context, neither the substantive rights nor the formal status of citizenship reveal much about the horizontal as well as the vertical ties mediated in the society. The largest immigrant group's low rates of naturalization in Germany, their insistence on dual citizenship, and the "failure" of the "pink card" all draw attention to Germany's as well as Turkey's weaknesses in terms of political governance regarding German Turks. They bring the importance of cultural and social resources (i.e. horizontal ties) in society, mediated through institutions, to the forefront of issues for governance. The stubborn charm of dual citizenship and the lightness of the "pink card" illustrate that, for the functioning of political communities, trust is a crucial factor. In fact, trust is the excess the citizenship ties encompass. It is what defies complete instrumentality in citizenship ties. Indeed, it was exactly this excess on which Demirel was playing in his well-calculated Berlin speech that at first sounded like a *faux pas*.

Notes

1. "Siz önce benim vatandasimsiniz sonra Alman vatandasiniz. Siz bizim vatandasimizsiniz ve sonradan nerenin vatandasi olursaniz olun Türkiye Cumhuriyeti′nin vatandasi olarak kalacaksiniz."

2. By Turks, I refer to immigrants with a Turkish passport. By no means do I use it as an ethnic category. As different groups from Turkey, like Kurds or Assyrians, all carry Turkish passports, it is not possible to obtain statistics of naturalization of immigrants from Turkey divided into different "ethnic" categories.

3. It should be noted that Berlin is the city that hosts the largest group of Turkish immigrants in Germany and until the new citizenship law it had a relatively higher naturalization rate among Turkish immigrants in comparison to other German cities.

4. However, this does not mean that there are no dual citizens in Germany. Although dual citizenship is not officially allowed, today there are around two to three million Germans who have dual citizenship. These are the "Aussiedler", "Spätaussiedler", and ethnic Germans in Poland; children of German men married to foreigners; and naturalized immigrants whose home countries do not allow expatriation, such as Iran, most of the Arab countries, China, etc.

5. In contrast to the predominant bifocality of most of the transnational networks studies, which limit the transnational social fields to arenas, spanned between the country of origin and the country of settlement, the notion of triadic relations brings the multifocality of these networks to the forefront.

6. Faist (2000a) argues that, in fact, being a labor-sending or labor-receiving country is more important than the principle of citizenship in determining state attitudes *vis-à-vis* dual citizenship.

7. For example, in 1997, the rates of naturalization among Tunisians and Moroccans in Germany were 6.6 percent and 4.8 percent respectively, while they were 1.9 percent and 1.3 percent for the Turks and the Hungarians.

8. The tenor of these criticisms was that the new law—by closing the door to dual citizenship more drastically than the former one—fell a step behind the former one. Because the new law blocked the way for Turkish immigrants to dual citizenship (contrary to the situation of other groups in Germany—like the citizens of EU countries or of Poland, who have such an option due to bilateral agreements), it was interpreted by some of the spokespersons of Turkish immigrant organizations (such as the Turkish Community Association in Germany) as a law designed to be against Turks in Germany.

9. Immigrants' refusal to naturalize at the cost of their "home" country citizenship is not unique to the immigrants from Turkey. For an elaborate discussion of the different rates of naturalization among different immigrant groups in Germany, see Faist (2000a, 9–10). As Faist (2000a, 26) points out, the changes in the rates of naturalization among Turkish immigrants in the Netherlands are quite telling on the importance of dual citizenship. At the end of a five-year period, during which the acquisition of Dutch citizenship did not depend on expatriation, 55 percent of Turkish immigrants were naturalized.

10. Foreigners are subject to a wide spectrum of restrictions in Turkey. These range from the restrictions on practicing certain professions (e.g. opticians) to buying land in the villages or in security sensitive areas. Even the funeral and burial of a foreigner in Turkey require special permission from the Interior Ministry. Thus, the rights acquired through the "pink card" are quite substantial.

11. "Baska bir deyisle bu belge ikamet tezkeresi yerine gececeginden, ikamet tezkeresi esas alinarak düzenlenen belgelerde kimlik belgesi olarak kullanilmasinda herhangi bir sakinca bulunmamaktadir" (Genelge, 1998, 3).

12. For an elaborate account of how membership became multilayered in Germany due to immigration see Bommes (1999a).

13. As an administrative category the "pink card" labels and juridically unifies a group of Turkish immigrants situated in different localities outside of Turkey.

14. For the argument of the diminished costs of dual nationality in a changed global context and how dual nationality poses little threat to the polity, see Spiro 1997; Hailbronner 1999; Kilic 1994; Faist, 2000a.

15. For an elaboration of the interplay of the emigration states' activities in the countries of immigration by means of "transmigrants", see Basch *et al.* (1992); Glick Schiller *et al.* (1995).

16. Glick Schiller *et al.* (995) argue this to be the case in Haitian transnationalism.

17. While the Turkish state supports and contributes to the transnationalization process of Turkish immigrants in Europe, the Kurdish networks developed to a large extent in opposition to state power.

18. The schemas of Turkish State Broadcasting (TRT INT) were particularly designed to reach Turkish immigrants basically in Europe (as well as to those in Australian and the US) and to help them to sustain and develop their ties to the "homeland". The lobby efforts of the Turkish state through Turkish embassies and consulates in Europe—which are largely organized through businessmen organizations—are a few examples of such state sponsored incentives to develop transnational ties. However, it should be noted that Turkish immigrants in Germany not only keep their ties to Turkey but also develop multi-local attachments that could not be limited to Germany and Turkey. Due to the adopted frameworks, which are entrapped in the linguistic and conceptual imaginary of the "receiving" and "sending" states, most often these ties escape analysis.

19. For example, in order to keep the return option open, several incentives—like schools designed for the needs of the returnees in Turkey as well as Turkish language courses in schools in Germany—were introduced and supported to sustain homeland ties. These Turkish language courses were designed not as immigrants' right to their native language, but to minimize Turkish children's alienation to their language and culture with the prospect that they will go back to Turkey.

20. Moreover, until December 2000, only three to four percent of those Turkish immigrants who would be eligible to apply for the (temporary) dual citizenship for their children (born between 1989 and 1999) in fact did so. The deadline for the applications was 31 December 2000.

21. There are no statistics available for 2000. This information is based on the information provided by the Turkish Consulate in Berlin to the author on her request.

22. The official Turkish population in Berlin is 132,000.

23. The "pink card's" "failure" is not unique. The Declaration of Mexican Nationality ID (which is very similar to the "pink card" design) was also unsuccessful in achieving the desired result. In 1998, the Mexican state introduced new provisions allowing Mexicans abroad to acquire Mexican nationality in addition to the county of residence.

24. Here I do not differentiate between belief and knowledge. In this context there is no difference between the two in terms of their consequences for the relations of trust.

25. Turks constitute the largest foreigner group in Germany and for a long time the "foreigner problem" (*Ausländerproblem*) was equated to "*Türkenproblem*" (Mandel 1988). In the recent discussions on the German "*Leitkulture*", the failure of (especially) Turkish immigrants to adopt to this "*Leitkulture*" again came to the forefront.

26. The editor of the supplement disappointedly asks how would it be possible for the both groups to live together without any hope (Erzeren 2000, 1).

27. The fact is that, no matter whether immigrants acquire German citizenship or not, they are referred to as the "*Ausländische Mitbürger*" or "*Mitbürger mit ausländischen Herkunft*", but not simply as citizens. This reveals the strength of their categorical stigmatization as "foreigners" in the society despite their German citizenship.

28. For discrimination against Turkish immigrants in the real estate market—despite their German citizenship—see Neumann (2000).

29. The public and scholarly debates on the presence of parallel societies (*Parallelgesellschaften*) in immigrant communities—especially among Turkish immigrants see Heitmeyer (1997)—and the public discussions and political mobilizations based on populist campaigns against dual citizenship which tie dual citizenship to a topo of immutable loyalty all contribute to this lack of confidence in the formative functions of institutions in German society. Here it should be noted that the popularized versions of Germany's troubled past with its foreigners and especially with the Jews (whose German citizen status was not very helpful in protecting them against the German state during World War II) also play a role in the dissemination of distrust of the functioning of institutions in the society.

30. The (correct or incorrect) reports in Turkish newspapers in Germany of the attacks against immigrants, their residences, and business places and the hostile or indifferent attitude of the police in these events contribute to the perception of the absence of color blindness in the society. Furthermore, the debates on the right wing tendencies within the police force in Germany feed this contention. An event that took place on 29 October 2000 is interesting in drawing attention to the flaws in Turkish immigrants' trust in the color-blindness of German institutions. A group of far-right youth shouting racist insults tried to storm a

Turkish family's house in a small town near Hannover. They attempted to force their way into the home of the Turkish family. The family alerted first their relatives and friends by telephone before calling the police and managed to hold some of the attackers before the police arrived (see *Frankfurter Allgemeine Zeitung*, 31 October 2000, p.2).

31. On the one hand, German Turks demand from Turkish authorities that their peculiar situation needs to be taken into account and some exceptions should be made. On the other, there is distrust of any kind of practice that single outs German Turks and sets them aside from the other Turkish citizens. Of course, cases like Merve Kavakci (a deputy from the Virtue Party in the parliament) whose dual citizenship (in this case American and Turkish) was picked up as a sign of her deficient loyalty to the Turkish state establish a very fertile ground for German Turks' suspicion of any practice that construes them as an exceptional category. M. Kavakci was stripped of her Turkish citizenship after her election to parliament and faced expulsion from the legislature. She was accused of having taken out US citizenship without permission. The same state which propagates dual citizenship for the Turks in Germany did not hesitate to expel Merve Kavakci on the basis of her dual citizenship.

32. Interestingly, a similar kind of distrust was expressed during Öcalan's (the leader of PKK) troubled residence in Italy. In relation to the pressures the Turkish state exerted on particular European countries to deliver Öcalan to Turkey—under the premise that Turkey will abolish death penalty—a similar kind of suspicion was heard among Turkish immigrants. The contention was that there was no guarantee that a state, which would abolish the death penalty so quickly, would not re-introduce it after Öcalan's delivery to Turkey.

33. I refer to Turkish immigrants as a "diaspora" not because they constitute a community whose unity is established or given on the axis of ethnicity and "homeland", but because they construe such an entity from the point of view of the Turkish state.

CHAPTER 14

Transnational Third Worlds

Boaventura de Sousa Santos

Introduction

My argument in this paper is twofold: (1) the intensification of global interactions in the last three decades cannot be reduced to transnational business transactions carried out by large and powerful world actors; and (2) transnationalization is a complex and even contradictory historical process that occurs both by deterritorializing and reterritorializing social relations. In this period, cross-border interactions in general have expanded enormously for a whole range of reasons, of which only some have directly to do with the increase in international trade. According to some estimates, on an average day more than seven million persons cross national borders by plane, train, bus, car, or on foot (Sohn & Buergenthal 1992, v). People cross borders as tourists, on business, or as migrant workers, and as scientists, students, consumers, and refugees. These cross-border movements raise a myriad of different socio-legal issues, from international contracts, binational marriages, adoptions of foreign children, legal protection of tourists, and cross-border consumer rights, to civil, political and social rights of legal and illegal foreign migrant workers, refugees, and asylum seekers. In spite of this, however, the international community has paid relatively little attention to the movement of people across national borders, especially when compared with the elaborate sets of uniform laws, international conventions, and *lex mercatoria* dealing with the movements of goods and services. Since the traditional international private law only covers a very small number of issues, the international movement of people, in many respects is a legal no-man's land. As a result, the legal protection of human beings seems to be much more territorialized than the legal protection of goods and services. International movements and interactions of people thus imply a net loss of legal protection. In a world seemingly saturated with an ideology of rights and undergoing a period of intense globalization, the challenges posed by this "black hole" heavily underscore the sociological and political need to analyze the movements of people across national borders.

This analysis is as important as it is difficult, mainly because the movements of people across national borders encompass such a wide variety of situations that they are irreducible to a single theoretical explanation or policy orientation. As a starting point, and with the objective of identifying and classifying the major forms of movements, I suggest an analytical framework based on a double criterion: the amount of autonomy and the amount of risk involved in moving across borders. Tourists, for instance, have almost total autonomy over their movements, including the autonomy to decide the amount of risk to take (they may decide to go backpacking alone into the wilderness or abide comfortably by a package organized by a travel agency). Business people may have just a little less autonomy than tourists, particularly if they are employed but have full control over the personal risks involved (safe means of transportation; travel insurance; guaranteed labor rights; and contracts). On the contrary, and though the situations may vary widely, migrants tend to move across borders with relatively little autonomy and with a great deal of personal risk. Finally, refugees are generally speaking the social group with least autonomy and highest degree of personal risk. International migrants and refugees are, therefore, the two most vulnerable groups of people moving across borders and those whose legal protection is simultaneously most needed and most difficult to sustain politically. They thus deserve special attention in this paper. Though I start by accepting as given the distinction between international migrants (economically determined migration) and refugees (politically determined migration), I will comment below on the reasons why the distinction has been blurred in the last decades.

International Migration

According to Portes and Böröcz, among the topics of interest to contemporary social science, few are more dynamic than international migration, especially as it has manifested itself in recent years (Portes & Böröcz 1989, 606; also see Portes & Walton 1981). In their view, rather than being the outcome of economic decisions governed by the law of supply and demand, international labor migration is a very complex social phenomenon, embedded in the political history of the relations between sending and receiving societies and in the networks constructed by the movement and contact of people across space, and whose basic dynamics lie in the labor needs of the world system as a whole. Such needs, as well as the means of fulfilling them, have changed over time.

International migration is hardly a new phenomenon. From the very beginning, the modern world system relied on it in the form of slavery. As Wallerstein has shown, capitalist development lies on the combination of free and coerced labor: "Free labor is the form of labor control used for skilled work in core countries, whereas coerced labor is used for less skilled work in peripheral ones. The combination thereof is the essence of capitalism" (Wallerstein 1974, 127; for a partial critique see Cohen 1987, 66). From the 16th century on, unfree labor involved coerced labor flows under the slave trade from West Africa to the New World, where the indigenous populations had drastically declined in the aftermath of the conquest (in Mexico the population fell from 11 million in 1519 to 1.5 million in about 1650). With a wholly different context from that of classical slavery, the slave trade was the first major form of international migration in the modern world system (Cohen 1987, 4). This form of labor flow involved high risk capital investment and required the active support of the colonial state (Portes & Walton 1981, ch.2; Portes & Böröcz 1989, 608). From the 19th century on and until the 1960s, a new major form of international migration emerged based on migrant recruitment through economic inducements. This was a period of dramatic emigration from Europe. Between 1846 and 1930 over 50 million of Europeans emigrated to overseas. This migration occurred in the context of active recruitment practices—by the post colonial states of the Americas, from the United States to Argentina—which were costly in terms of capital input, but required only passive support of the coercive bodies of the receiving states (Portes & Böröcz 1989, 608). From this point of view, this form of international labor flow was at mid-point between the coerced labor extraction of the slave trade and the self-initiated or spontaneous flows that came to dominate in more recent years. This third major form of international migration had its origins in the expectations raised by the cultural diffusion in the peripheral societies of the patterns of consumption typical of core societies: "The fulfillment of such expectations becomes increasingly difficult under the economies of scarcity of the periphery and growing cross-national ties make it possible for certain groups located there to seek a solution by migration abroad." (Portes & Böröcz 1989, 608; also see Portes 1979).

The succession of these three forms of international migration represents only a general tendency. Given the historical capacity of capitalism to combine different forms of labor, different forms of international migration may be resorted to at a given point in time, and the combinations among them may vary according to the regions of the world system. The existence of pockets of slave-like labor flows (e.g. sex tourism and prostitution rings) is recurrently a matter of international news, while active labor procurement systems continue to exist under different forms (Prothero 1990 for an introductory analysis of labor recruiting organizations in the developing world). One of such systems, the *bracero* program—an official agreement between the US and Mexico established in 1942—though officially brought to a halt in 1965–68, continued in reality under a different form as massive procurement of foreign workers by way of undocumented border crossers, at no risk whatsoever to the employers and under conditions that facilitated ruthless exploitation (Zolberg 1989, 407; Cohen 1987, 50). Both in its formal and informal versions, this system had some features in common with the *Gastarbeiter* model that was targeted to the labor reserves of the Mediterranean Basin and adopted by the advanced European countries (especially Germany) throughout the 1960s and early 1970s.[1]

As forms of labor and of labor recruitment change over time, so do forms of settlement. Though the world labor market has always combined temporary migration and settlement with permanent migration and settlement, the end of the period of organized capitalism, in the early-1970s, seems to coincide with the demise of permanent migration and settlement. While only four countries can be said to accept permanent migrants today (such acceptance being defined as confirming rights of citizenship upon entry)—Australia, Canada, New Zealand and US—virtually all countries are now participating in an international system of temporary migrations (Salt 1987, 241). Though temporary migration has absorbed increasingly larger numbers of people in the last two decades, its internal dynamics is now changing, due to several economic political and cultural factors that together create the context for the discussion of the two topics which, in the field of transnationalization dealt with here, I consider most important within the research agenda of this chapter: the role of the state in the regulation of international migration flows and the legal protection of international migrants.

State Regulation of Migration Flows

It is commonly agreed that one of the main features of the period of disorganized capitalism is a new international division of labor in the terms of which industrial capital from the core is moving to the periphery, where cheaper labor is located, establishing factories to produce manufactured goods for export to the worldwide market (Fröbel, Heinrichs, & Kreye 1980). This new division of labor involves a new spatial division of labor which, according to some authors, is producing some structural changes in the labor markets of the core countries to the effect that the demand for massive industrial labor of the sort usually filled by immigrants will be substantially reduced (Piore 1986; Zolberg 1989, 410). It is further claimed that, in the future, the international migration flows will grow mainly in the South, among peripheral and semiperipheral countries. Though this is disputed by other authors for whom the bulk of industrial production continues to be located at the core, it is evident that in recent years the core states have tightened the controls over entry, building imaginary fortresses or walls of China around their national boundaries.

This raises the issue of the role of the state in transnational flows of labor. A first observation is that the role of the state, no matter how drastically changed in its internal content over time, has always remained crucial in this field. Throughout the history of capitalism labor flows have gone through time-spaces of intense deterritorialization and time-spaces of intense reterritorialization, but in either case the state has always played a crucial role. The three large forms of labor displacement mentioned above required from the states—from the receiving state but also from the sending state—the performance of important tasks with the purpose either of deterritorializing labor relations (opening up national borders) or reterritorializing them (closing down the national borders) according to the circumstances. Enforcing or relaxing border controls in the interests of capital as a whole has therefore been a major function of the modern state (Petras 1980, 174; Cohen 1987, 175). But this is by no means the whole story. As the most recent migration literature has emphasized, international migration is a complex social and political process that cannot be reduced to the operation of the laws of the market. Portes has drawn our attention to the creation and consolidation of migrant networks across space: "More than individualistic calculations of gain, it is the insertion of people into such networks which helps explain differential proclivities to move and the enduring character of migrant flows" (Portes & Böröcz 1989, 612; also see Portes & Zhou 1992, 491-522; for a different view see Salt 1989). The operation of such networks is partly responsible for the often limited effectiveness of state efforts to regulate immigration. In West Germany, even though entries of migrant workers from the outside of the EC were banned in 1973, the number of foreign residents continued to grow due to family reunification. In spite of such limits, state control over national boundaries has been a crucial factor in the direction and intensity of international migration and its operational logic cannot be reduced to that of world economy (see, among others, Zolberg 1891; 1989, 405).

International migration has an irreducible political element, in that it entails not only physical relocation, but a change of jurisdiction and membership. In this respect, the policies of the receiving states are particularly important, because, after all, they determine whether the international movement, and of what kind, may or may not take place. In a world system characterized by widely varying conditions, international borders serve to maintain global inequality. State policies may aim at defending one fraction of capital to the detriment of another, or national capital to the detriment of foreign capital. They may also result from coalitions of capital and labor, particularly in core countries, as when organized labor is able to achieve some market protection by imposing limiting conditions on labor importation (for the opposition of AFL-CIO to NAFTA, for instance, see Trubek *et al.* 1993, 31–49). Furthermore, the state prerogative over national boundaries may be activated for reasons that, though related to economic factors, cannot be solely attributed to them. Racism, xenophobia, and the social construction of codes of "cultural incompatibility" between foreigners and nationals have a cultural and political leverage of their own, influencing migration policies autonomously.

The state and the national boundaries it controls have thus performed crucial roles in the creation of international migration regimes throughout the history of modern capitalism. Even when the state control is limited either by transnational economic pressures or by transnational social networks of migratory movement and settlement, the state retains the control of the legal status of migrants, a detail that has a decisive impact on migrant life and experience in the host country. This control has become more central lately in the light of the convergent impact of two recent trends. On the one hand, the trend of core states is to favor, if at all, only temporary migration and only in restrictive terms (available only to those whose skills and expertise are in demand), with the consequent tighter control over borders. On the other hand, there is the increased pressure to emigrate and the potential for large-scale population movements motivated by the struggle for survival resulting from the immiseration of significant regions of the world system and the growing disparities between the North and the South. Hence we witness the potential increase of illegal, clandestine, or undocumented migration and the consequent strengthening of the receiving states as monopoly holders of the legal status of migrants and of migrant life chances and expectations attached to it.

The Legal Rights of Migrants

In general, states do not treat aliens, including legal resident aliens, the same way they treat citizens. They regularly reserve a variety of rights for nationals and this is generally considered legitimate under international law. Thus, by definition, migrants are second or third class citizens, but their legal status varies considerably according to whether they are legal or illegal migrants. Concerning legal migrants, their legal status may still vary according to whether they are permanent immigrants (expected to settle in the host country) or temporary immigrants (seasonal migrants, "guest workers", "project-tied workers"). The legal status of illegal migrants, on the other hand, is the most precarious; accordingly, they are the most vulnerable class of immigrants, though they are also the fastest growing class of immigrants (Rogers 1992). In the early 90s, the International Labor Organization (ILO) predicted that in the next two decades there would be 25 million migrants in irregular situations throughout the world, not including refugees (ILO 1991, 3). For these reasons, and also because they represent the highest social and political tension between national and transnational perspectives, between territorial sovereignty principles and human rights principles, I will focus briefly on the status of illegal migrants.

The undocumented migrants are the hardest working and lowest paid laborers; they are especially vulnerable to arbitrary practices on the part of employers, landlords, and merchants; they are afraid to avail themselves of the few rights they may enjoy for fear of exposure to immigration authorities and, above all, for fear of deportation; they are too culturally handicapped (including limited foreign language-speaking ability) to have minimum access to the system; they are especially victimized by racial, class, ethnic, and gender discrimination (Bosniak 1991, 747). Some of their hardships are related to the specific work the undocumented migrants are engaged in. For instance, undocumented domestic workers—one fast growing group in many European countries and in the US—often lack formal contracts; their working conditions are poorly enforced, due to the dispersed, isolated, and private nature of work sites; they are often physically and sexually abused, due to close working quarters (Davis 1993, 14).

In the light of these multiple vulnerabilities, the extension of substantial human rights protection to undocumented immigrants seems particularly justified and necessary. Nonetheless, protection is as problematic as it is necessary. The problems arise from the fact that illegal immigrants question, in a very direct way, one of the state's prerogatives most closely associated with territorial sovereignty: the state's powers to decide who will enter its territory, refuse entry, and expel unwanted aliens. The very existence of illegal immigrants demonstrates that such powers are being eroded and, with them, territorial sovereignty. In theory, the improvement of the legal status of illegal immigrants seems to be obtainable only at the cost of state sovereignty. From the latter's perspective, the sole logical way of dealing with illegal immigration is to prevent its occurrence. In practice, however, state policies *vis-à-vis* illegal immigration have varied widely and in some periods they have been characterized by great tolerance toward unauthorized cross-border movements. I have already mentioned that in the US the *bracero* program continued informally after its official termination without employers necessarily being punished or workers deported. In France, undocumented immigration, which constituted up to 80 percent of all immigration until the early-1970s, was described as "spontaneous migration" and tolerated as such (Bosniak 1991, 744).

Today, in the periphery of the world system, irregular migration is a normal, often inconsequential occurrence, out of sheer incapacity on the part of the states to enforce border controls or mere lack of political will. Only in the last two decades, as a result of economic deterioration and the rise of xenophobic anti-immigration movements, have states, particularly the core states, come to view illegal immigration as a threat to national sovereignty, indeed, as a legal, social and political problem of significant proportions. Many of these countries have introduced restrictive immigration legislation with the purpose of reasserting control over the borders and eliminating illegal immigration (US, Canada, France, Australia, Japan, Germany, Argentina, Italy and, lastly, some European states in the ambit of the Schengen Agreements).

In spite of these legislative efforts, it is unlikely that illegal migration will diminish anytime soon; many factors and indicators point, rather, to its substantial increase in the coming years. If this is the tendency, the principles of territorial sovereignty will appear increasingly at odds with the dynamics of transnational migration and the tensions derived therefrom will accentuate. To a significant extent, these tensions are part of a much broader conflict between the core and the periphery of the world system, or between the North and South, and must be analyzed in this context (more on this below). As things stand now, no international consensus has been reached on the possible terms of a compromise between the principles of international human rights applicable to nationals and non-nationals and to legal and illegal aliens, on the one hand, and the principles of territorial sovereignty, on the other; in other words, no international migration regime has come into existence. The latent ideological and political conflict between these mutually inconsistent principles, both of them equally embedded in western modernity, can be easily traced in the last United Nations Convention for the Protection of the Rights of All Migrant Workers and Members of their Families, drafted in collaboration with the ILO, and adopted by the UN General Assembly of 1990.

Under the Convention, it is the obligation of states to afford to documented as well as to undocumented workers a range of civil, social and labor rights, which include, among others, rights to due process of law in criminal proceedings, free expression and religious observance, domestic privacy, equality with nationals before the courts, emergency medical care, education for children, respect for cultural identity, rights to enforce employment contracts against employers, to participate in trade unions, and to enjoy the protection of wage, hour, and health regulations in the workplace. Yet, the Convention's treatment of undocumented immigrants is deeply ambivalent. While contracting states must meet a minimum standard of treatment of irregular migrants, the rights provided to these migrants need not to be as extensive as those which must be afforded to legally admitted migrants. The states are thus entitled to discriminate against undocumented migrants in many decisive aspects, from rights to family unity and liberty of movement, to rights to social services, employment and trade union protection. The allowance for this discriminatory treatment is grounded on the Convention's overriding commitment to the principle of national sovereignty. Over and over again, the terms of the Convention state that the rights granted cannot be construed as an infringement on state power to exclude foreigners from its territory and to shape the composition of its national membership.

The tension between human rights and territorial sovereignty principles extends far beyond the migration context and in a sense is constitutive of the modern interstate system. But in the case of undocumented migrants it reaches a particularly high level, because the states here have no choice but to assert the prerogative of sovereignty against the recognition of their failure to assert it. Therefore, discrimination against undocumented migrants is a substitute for actual exclusion at the border. Under such circumstances, elimination of discrimination presupposes a radical transformation of the principle of sovereignty as we know it. Short of that, and irrespective of how many transnational migration movements, both regular and irregular, have contributed and will still contribute to world capitalist development, the situation of undocumented immigrants is bound to be structurally shaped by multiple and blatant violations of human rights. The discrimination they suffer is double: on the one hand, their legal entitlements are very low; on the other, their social vulnerability makes the struggle for the enforcement of rights almost impossible and the impunity of violations a normal occurrence. To give just an example, according to the US Immigration Reform and Control Act of 1986, regardless of their legal status, undocumented workers are entitled to the federal minimum wage. If the employer pays them less than that—which occurs very often[2]—they are unlikely to complain about it to the authorities for fear of exposure to punishment or deportation; they are less likely to quit and risk unemployment since they are not eligible for unemployment benefits; and they are also less likely to organize in defense of their rights or to join existing labor unions for the same fear of public exposure. Undocumented migrants are part of a growing transnational third world of people, a non-constituency for nationally based political processes, moving around in a legal no-man's land, living life experiences shaped by the dark side of a growing global economy whose inequities are in part guaranteed by the existence of national boundaries and the coercive powers of the states policing them. As an extreme case of subordinate transnationalization—not the most extreme case of distribution which, in many instances, is the case of those who cannot even emigrate—undocumented migrants reveal the innermost contradictions between the exclusionary powers of sovereignty and a cosmopolitan politics of rights called for to protect new transnational vulnerabilities against new transnational impunities.

Refugees and Displaced People

Though internally more diversified, another sector of the growing transnational third world of people are the refugees. As in the case of undocumented migrant workers, refugees concern me here insofar as they raise specific new issues in a broad conceptualization of the transnationalization of the legal field. Such issues have to do, in this case, with two clear-cut distinctions upon which the international refugee regime was built in post-war period: between voluntary and involuntary international migration, on the one hand, and between economically motivated and politically motivated migration, on the other. I argue here that these two distinctions have collapsed in recent years, thereby producing new inadequacies between the hegemonic principles of territorial sovereignty and the dynamics of transnational movements.

The cumulative world number of post-war refugees has been estimated at around 90 million (Hakovirta 1993, 37). Massive refugee flows have marked the period since the end of the 1970s—starting with the dramatic situation of the Vietnamese "boat people" in 1979–1981—and have increased dramatically in the last few years. Due to the political transformations in Central and Eastern Europe, applications for asylum in European countries numbered 65,400 in 1983 and 544,500 in 1991 (Rogers 1992, 35). Refugees are not evenly distributed around the world. Particularly since the early-1980s the share of the South has increased, with Asia in the range of 45–55 percent, and Africa around 30 percent of the total of refugee flows (Hakovirta 1993, 37). In the last decades massive emergencies have forced hundreds of thousands of people to cross state borders in Jordan, Somalia, Eritrea, Vietnam, Ogaden, Sudan, Liberia, Mozambique, Cambodia, Laos, Iraq, Afghanistan, Sri Lanka, Lebanon, Uganda, Nicaragua, El Salvador, Uganda, Congo-Kinshasa, Burundi, Sierra Leone, etc. The pressures on neighboring countries have been enormous. In the early-90s there were one million Mozambiquean refugees in Malawi, whose native population is only seven times larger. In the last half decade refugees have become a serious problem in Europe and they are likely to continue being seen as such in the coming years. The disintegration of the Soviet Union and Yugoslavia has already produced hundreds of thousands of displaced people. The specter of massive flows of people within Europe is already transforming the European interstate system in significant ways. I mean "Soviet-Poles" flowing into Poland, *Volksdeutsche* into Germany, Albanians into Italy, Transylvania Magyars into Hungary, ex-Yugoslavians into Croatia and elsewhere, Pontic Greeks into Greece and so on.

But who is a refugee? According to the United Nations Conventions of 1951 and 1967, refugee is any person who, "owing to a well-founded fear of being persecuted for reasons of race, religion, nationality, membership of a particular social group or political opinion, is outside the country of his nationality and is unable or, owing to such fear, is unwilling to avail himself of the protection of that country; or who, not having a nationality or being outside the country of his former habitual residence as a result of such events, is unable or, owing to such fear, is unwilling to return to it" (Sohn & Buergenthal 1992, 100). Bearing in mind the reference above to the major refugee flows of our time, the above definition excludes most of the world's displaced populations who are mainly victims of massive conflicts, human rights abuses, civil wars, external aggression and occupation, foreign domination, etc. Since they have not been personally persecuted, they are not entitled to the refugee status, even though the political nature of the causes of their flight offers no doubt. They are considered "displaced persons" and at the most may receive some humanitarian assistance. In the periphery and the semiperiphery of the world system some regional interstate agreements have taken some first steps to expand the concept of refugee in order to include the "humanitarian refugee", (for African refugees policy see Anthony 1991) but the core countries have repeatedly expressed their opposition to such an expansion. When confronted with the potential rise of applications for asylum, they have even adopted more restrictive legislation on (or rather, against) refugees and asylum seekers (Sohn & Buergenthal 1992, 102; Hathaway 1991). The most blatant examples are the Schengen countries in Europe (more on this below).

The last three decades have witnessed other "involuntary" flows of people still more at odds with international and domestic refugees legislation: hundreds of thousands of people fleeing from famine, starvation and natural disasters (droughts, earthquakes, volcano eruptions). In many cases extreme poverty and environmental crises have acted together with civil war or political repression to provoke massive displacements of people, as in Haiti or Eritrea, in Mozambique or Cambodia. These are dramatic situations, apparently ever more recurrent, in which the distinction between economic and political factors have been blurred, if not totally dissolved; situations in which the calamitous deterioration of native survival systems turns the question of the voluntary or involuntary nature of the migration into a macabre exercise. The inadequacy and the inequity of an international system that fails to provide protection for millions of people in the most vulnerable of situations are thereby fully exposed.

Notwithstanding the chauvinistic alarms in the core countries, the majority of these subordinate transnational migrations have taken place within the South and have meant an enormous burden for neighboring countries whose social conditions are often equally grim. Oughtn't burden-sharing to be conceived on a global scale? And will this be possible in an interstate system based on state self-centeredness?

Two types of "involuntary" transnational migration are most likely to grow in the coming years. The first one will be caused by environmental catastrophes, directly or indirectly caused by anthropogenic climate changes and often coupled with over-population. Refugees will be environmental refugees, seeking ecological asylum. Once again most of these flows will take place in the periphery of the world system or, at least, will start from there. More stridently even than others, environmental refugee flows portray the dark side of capitalist world development and global lifestyles. They should, therefore, become the best candidates for the application of a new and more solidary transnational conception of burden sharing. It is however very doubtful that that may ever occur. Environmental refugees occupy the outer fringes of a generally precarious system of international protection. They fall outside the competence of the United National High Commissioner for Refugees and their plight can be alleviated only to a very limited degree by the already over-committed resources of the United Nations Disaster Relief Co-ordinator. Furthermore, environmental refugees are most likely to collide with the territorial logic underlying social protection as a matter of right.

The second type of forced transnational migration likely to grow in the coming years is the most paradoxical form of migration because it consists of populations that stay put and "migrate" only because the political conditions in which they used to live "migrate" themselves so to speak. Over 25 million Russians who live outside Russia became minorities overnight when the Soviet Union ceased to exist. In some cases they became even aliens in a quasi-refugee situation. The same happened in former Yugoslavia with even more dramatic consequences. With the rise of ethnic nationalism—against the background of modern nation-state building based on ethnic supremacy and ethnic suppression—it is not far-fetched to predict new situations of standstill migration in other parts of the world, in Africa, in India, in China, and so on. Unlike other forms of refugee situations, the fate of refugees is here determined by the weakness or even by the break-up of territorial sovereignty.

The high vulnerability of refugees derives from a double adverse condition. On the one side, international human rights applicable to them are highly restricted by a highly restrictive definition of refugees that leaves out most of the current and massive situations of forced migration. On the other side, the few rights they are entitled to are grossly violated with almost total impunity. Such rights have evolved both from international human rights law and international humanitarian law, and include the obligation of the states through which refugees and displaced people transit or seek asylum or durable settlement in, to uphold their rights to life, to personal property, to shelter, to food, to basic health care, to practice religion, to non-discrimination, and so on. In reality, however, such rights are rarely respected. For alleged reasons of national security, refugees are often confined to camps and detention centers where, aside from the lack of freedom of movement and access to the outside world, they are subjected to the most degrading human conditions. The discrepancy between the refugee politics of core countries (as well illustrated by the Schengen Agreements) and that of peripheral countries (as in the Organization of African Unity's broad definition of refugees, including those fleeing natural disasters, foreign intervention and civil unrest) is creating a tension which is likely to become another dimension of the North-South conflict. This is due mainly to the stability rent that core countries continue to collect directly or indirectly at the cost of the periphery in an historical continuity that can be traced back to European colonialism. Aside from the upheavals in Central Europe in the 1990s, some of the largest, most urgent, and longest-lasting refugee situations have originated in countries where ethnic and/or religious cleavages overlap with regional inequalities and where they possibly have a significant transboundary dimension (Hakovirta 1993, 45). These situations have predominantly occurred in the South, in most instances as part of the historical process of transition from decolonization to the conflicts of postcolonialism.

Citizenship, International Migration, and Cosmopolitanism

I have focused on undocumented migrant workers and refugees because they constitute the two most vulnerable groups of subordinated transnational migration. Needless to say, many situations of often extreme vulnerability (poverty, starvation, repression) do not involve any massive movements of people or, if they do, such movements take place within the confines of national borders and for that reason have not been considered in this paper. Migration literature and international relief agencies have coined the concept of "internally displaced persons" to cover the situations in which the movement of people has kept within a given nation-state (Copeland 1992, 995). According to UN estimates, at the end of the 1980s there were in Southern Africa 10.5 million uprooted (including 3.6 million forcibly relocated within the Republic of South Africa) of whom 1.4 million had crossed transnational borders; in Afghanistan: 7–8 million uprooted of whom 5.8 million were abroad; in Palestine: 8.8 million uprooted of whom 2.2 million were abroad, under UNWRA jurisdiction; in other Middle-East countries: 2.8–3.2 million uprooted of whom 1.3 million were abroad; in Sub-Saharan Africa: 2.7–2.9 million uprooted, of whom 1.1 million abroad; in Ethiopia: 1.8–2.6 million uprooted, of whom 1.1 million abroad; in Central America: 1.9 million uprooted, of whom 850,000 abroad (Zolberg 1989, 415). The vulnerability of internally displaced people lies, among other factors, in that it remains for the most part beyond the purview of international organizations. In this situation international human rights principles collide with special intensity with the principle of sovereignty.

Subordinate transnational migration is most likely to grow in the coming years. Three main factors account for this: the increasing inequality between the North and the South; the growing instability in the interstate system (including civil wars, ethnic infra-state nationalisms, boundary disputes, and threat of nuclear holocaust) directly or indirectly related to the renewed struggle for supremacy among core states; the likelihood of a global environmental disaster due to the uncontrolled reproduction of anarchy in investment decision-making and anti-ecological consumption habits and lifestyles. In themselves and via the subordinate transnational movements of people that they will eventually generate, these factors will challenge in fundamental ways the principle of territorial sovereignty, as well as its satellite concepts of national community, citizenship, and membership. It is therefore not by coincidence that the nation-states, especially the core states, are today posed to control one of the major effects of such factors, the dramatic increase in the migration potential and the likelihood of massive irregular transnational movements.

In fact, the control over national boundaries as a major prerogative of territorial sovereignty has been growing steadily since the mid-19th century as a central dimension of the consolidation of the nation-states and of the modern interstate system. In Europe, in the second half of the 19th century, it was possible to travel from Portugal to Russia without passport or visa. Restrictions on movements of persons across borders were imposed mainly after World War I. From then on, wars and international tensions, disparities of economic development and standards of living, and differences in political and social regimes, contributed together to build up restrictions and controls of cross border movements. The general argument of this paper—that transnationalization is a complex and even contradictory historical process that occurs both by deterritorializing and reterritorializing social relations—finds here an unequivocal confirmation. While in other forms of transnationalization of the legal field (transnational factors causing changes in domestic law; *lex mercatoria*; law of regional integration) the national state seems to have lost ground and become relatively weak, in the case of subordinate transnational movements the state, particularly the core state, seems more affirmative and self-centered than ever.

The European states are in this respect specially revealing because they are now in a double process of relinquishing the control over entry and membership in the national territory within the EU (the internal boundaries) and of strengthening it as far as non-EU countries are concerned (the external boundaries). In terms of the Single European Act, the EU countries seem determined to guarantee the free movement of persons within its common borders. In spite of differences about who these persons are and the political and institutional instruments that will guarantee such freedom in practice, this is a major political development and signifies a substantial transformation of a central prerogative of modern territorial sovereignty. This transformation is even more compelling within the five EU countries that have signed the Schengen Agreements Concerning the Gradual Abolition of Controls at the Common Borders (1985, 1990). "Schengenland" is constituted by the joint territories of the following countries (ordered by the date that they signed the agreement): Belgium, France, Germany, Italy, Spain, Portugal, Greece, Luxembourg, The Netherlands, Austria, Denmark, Finland, and Sweden. One person authorized to enter at any external border of this transnational territory can move freely within it for up to three months. To guarantee this unprecedented freedom, an unprecedented system of international security cooperation is set up—police cooperation; court cooperation; the Schengen Information System, etc., etc.,—in the 142 articles that comprise the 1990

Schengen Agreement drawn upon for the purpose of "executing" the 1985 Agreement (Meijers *et al.* 1992).

The facility with which one will be allowed to move within Schengenland is only matched by the difficulty in entering it. The refugee norms of Schengen are as restrictive as the refugee legislation defined by the 1990 Dublin Convention Determining the State Responsible for Examining Applications for Asylum Lodged in One of the Member States of the European Communities. This Convention, drafted at a moment of panic before the specter of millions of refugees fleeing the disintegration of the Soviet Union,[3] not only sticks to the old, by now totally inadequate, concept of refugee, but also introduces numerous procedural and substantive controls which have led to the enactment, in the individual signing countries, of the most restrictive refugee legislation in their history. Increase in discretionary powers of the agencies in charge of asylum applications, elimination of judicial control over their decisions, granting transport carriers (almost always privately owned, like airlines), the public prerogatives (and obligations, subject to penalty if not fulfilled) of controlling entry on national borders, are some of the features of this new anti-refugee legislation. The principle of sovereignty is thus negated at the national level by the same process that confirms it with greater efficiency at the supra-state level. This enhanced confirmation and the democratic deficit that it implies is of consequence, not only for asylum seekers, but also for the nationals of this transnational space: the price of free movement will eventually be greater vulnerability *vis-à-vis* transnationalized systems of repression and information.

Though probably an extreme case, the European legal and political development epitomizes the ingenuity and resourcefulness of the principle of sovereignty, always ready to transform itself on the condition that it remains operative and, if possible, with renewed efficiency—against the truly dangerous intruders, those that remain at the external borders. And these are without exception those that come from peripheral or semiperipheral regions of the world system and dare to benefit from the social amenities accumulated in the core, often at the expense of those same regions. The exclusionary virtuosity of the principle of sovereignty is not exercised in a social or political vacuum. The state, as a set of institutions, together with the political, social, and cultural elites, is the cement with which the fortress of nationalistic chauvinism and ethnic panic is built. In an illuminating analysis of the widespread ethnic panic in the Netherlands during the first months of 1985 created by the immigration of a group of Tamil refugees from Sri Lanka—a potential minority group that up until then had been unknown to the population at large—van Dijk has found that ethnic prejudice is mainly preformulated in the prevailing discourse types of the elite—representatives of the national and local authorities, the judiciary, the police, welfare agencies, education and academic research—and that such discourse is publicly reformulated by the mass media (van Dijk 1987, 81–122).

This dialectics of deterritorialization-reterritorialization, which is observable at the macro-level of policy, legislation and opinion making, can also be observed at micro-level of sets of individual decisions by different state agencies. The European Court of Justice is one such agency. The Court has played a prominent role in deterritorializing the economic and commercial legislation of EU countries, creating in its stead a new community-wide supranational legal order of its own, grounded on a new constitutional basis derived from the interpretation of the European treaties adopted by the Court. In the light of this, it is all the more symptomatic that the Court has been extremely passive, restrictive and low profile in interpreting the limits of its human rights jurisdiction in cases concerning non-EU nationals. As Weiler aptly notes, "in relation to non-Community nationals the Court has been … particularly prudent and has eschewed the boldness which characterizes some of its jurisprudence in other areas" (Weiler 1992, 70; see also Cassese, Clapham, & Weiler 1991a, 1991b). The Court has been acting in total consonance with the political project of EU member states, deterritorializing the internal borders in order to strengthen the position of Europe as a regional trading bloc in the upcoming struggle for supremacy in the world system, on the one hand, and, on the other, reterritorializing the external borders as to prevent the strength of the position from being endangered by the disruptive presence of undesired and undeserving guests. The hard economic interest calculations that seem to fuel this dialectics are, however, in a collision course with the political and cultural principles that have been proclaimed as the essential ethos of the European project. Furthermore, the needs of electoral politics may at times require feeding on internal xenophobic sentiments or, at least, being ambiguous about them. The contradictory nature of such a course of action is well summarized by Weiler, when he speaks of "a delicate path to tread, one which is supportive of the process of European Union but acknowledges the dangers of feeding xenophobia towards non-Europeans and the even deeper danger towards one of the moral assets of

European integration—its historical down-playing of nationality as a principal referent in transnational intercourse" (Weiler 1992, 68).[4]

If the EU countries have lately become an extreme example of restrictive refugee policies, the US has been, and not only lately, an extreme example of political bias and discretionary selectivity in the application of refugee legislation formally informed by the principle of equal treatment. In 1965, Congress discarded favoritism by national origins in favor of the same immigration ceiling for every country; equal treatment was further extended in 1980 when, through the Refugee Act, the US redefined refugees as individuals fearing persecution not only from communist systems, as had been the case before, but from any regime (Little 1993, 270–271). The Refugee Act established objective criteria for determining refugee admissions which would supposedly depoliticize the refugee policy. In practice, however, the Act's provisions have been easily circumvented by an executive branch with too much discretionary authority which has been exercised to fit overarching political objectives. The Haitians' quest for political asylum illustrates best the strong bias in the implementation of US immigration laws. From June 1983 until March 1991, 74.5 percent of refugees from former Soviet Union were granted asylum compared to 1.8 percent Haitians, and the discrimination is even more blatant when Haitians are contrasted with nationals from other American countries, namely with Cubans. As Little puts it, "[i]n many ways, immigration procedures towards Cubans and Haitians that seek entry into the United States represent the extremes of United State policy. Immigration policy towards Cuba tends to be generous and humanitarian; immigration policy towards Haiti tends to be stringent and inhumane" (Little 1993, 290). Soon after Fidel Castro took power in Cuba, the United States enacted the Cuban Refugee Adjustment Act of 1966, enabling almost 800,000 Cubans to enter the US between 1966 and 1980 (Lennox 1993, 712). During the same period, the government refused to admit refugees from Haiti, though they fled from one of the bloodiest and most repressive regimes of the world, the "gangster government" of the Duvaliers. The truth of the matter lay in the fact that Haiti was anti-communist and the Duvaliers supported US's attempts to dislodge communism in Cuba. For this reason, Haitian refugees were unwelcome.

Discrimination against Haitians and in favor of Cubans has been a distinctive feature of the US refugee policy and is pursued at different levels, for instance, in detention centers. During most of the time, Haitians have been the majority of the detainees in the best well known INS detention facility, Krome North Service Processing Center located in Miami, Florida. In early January 1993, the Haitians detained here entered a nine-day hunger strike following the arrival of fifty-two Cubans who had "commandeered" a Cuban commuter flight from Havana to Varadero, Cuba, diverting it to Miami. They protested against another painful instance of the double standard: all the Cubans were released from the camp within forty-eight hours (Little 1993, 289). Plainly, the Refugee Act of 1980 has failed to eliminate ideological discrimination from immigration policy. Because the President selects the geographical locations and allotment of aliens who may enter, *de facto* discrimination based on geopolitical considerations has simply replaced *de jure* discrimination (Lennox 1993, 711).

For all their differences, recent immigration and refugee policies of the European countries and the United States illustrate the extent to which the overriding commitment of core states to national interests, defined, in this instance, as territorial prerogatives, may lead to measures against non-nationals and to distinctions among non-nationals which, when viewed from a cosmopolitan human rights perspective, are arbitrary and discriminatory. The likely intensification of subordinate transnational migrations in the coming years, together with the increasing transnationalization of its root causes, are liable to raise the contradictions between their dynamics and the logic of territorial sovereignty to such a high level that current institutional and normative structures will collapse for lack of legitimacy and feasibility, calling for a new understanding and a new political approach. In my view, such a new departure will be built upon the following normative concerns.

A New Historical Epistemology of Need and Difference

Whenever transnational migration is forced upon people, there is no ethical justification to distinguish between nationals and non-nationals. In the light of international human rights principles, whenever people cannot choose to stay within their national boundaries, except by risking their lives, they become *ipso facto* citizens of any other country. This should be the basic premise of a new political and legal cosmopolitanism. It is new to the extent that rather than based on abstract principles of individualism, universalism and generality, it is historically grounded, culturally specific, and politically discriminating. The history of the modern world system is a history of unequal exchanges which are at the roots of the war, starvation, oppression and ecological disaster that force people to migrate. Modern science has managed to separate the knowledge of this history from the history of this knowledge. For this reason, modern historical knowledge is ahistorical. Because this ahistorical knowledge benefits the countries that have benefited from the unequal exchanges, modern science is intrinsically territorial. To that extent, it is as great an obstacle to the development of a new cosmopolitan politics as the nation-state itself. Short of such a new cosmopolitanism, neither the needs nor the differences of transnational migrants can be properly addressed.

As things stand now, the needs of migrants have been codified and ranked by criteria of nationality and territoriality that are inherently biased against them, while their differences have been codified and ranked by a hegemonic form of knowledge that cannot understand them except by what they are not. Hegel conceived of modern science as a form of knowledge that progressed by distinctions, divisions and discriminations. He oversaw the fact that, in the real world, rather than calling for a philosophical *Aufhebung*, that form of knowledge became articulated with the modern state, whereupon scientific distinctions became social differences, which in turn engendered subordination. Subordinate transnational movements are movements of knowledges that have been suppressed and marginalized. Transnational third worlds of people are also transnational third worlds of knowledges, and they feed on each other. Learning from them, learning from the South, is one of the epistemological prerequisites of a cosmopolitan politics.[5] Competition among different knowledges is a prerequisite to the transformation of the history of the modern world system into a tribunal to determine culpability and liability, grant entitlements to compensation and establish the criteria for burden-sharing. It is also an epistemological prerequisite to distinguish among differences that don't generate, legitimate or occult subordination, and differences that do. Without alternative knowledges within the same hermeneutic constellation it is not possible to sustain multicultural pluralism within the same territorial time-space (Santos 1995, 479–519).

Community, Membership, Transnational Advocacy

Subordinate transnational migration represents a fundamental challenge to the concepts orbiting around the principle of territorial sovereignty, such as national community, citizenship, membership, naturalization. It is today widely recognized that national boundaries are a major political device to maintain inequality across the world system and that they do so by separating jurisdictions and defining membership. Control of entry and control over range of membership, though separate issues, are thus intimately intercon-nected. Whenever the state fails to control entry—as when illegal immigrants manage to settle inside the borders—it still can erect a wall against incorporation by virtue of the illegal status stamped on immigrant life experience. Illegal immigrants and asylum seekers thus doubly challenge the principle of territorial sovereignty, as they raise both the question of entry—to what extent the denial of entry represents a violation of international human rights?—and the question of membership—to what extent can people already present in the national territory and, eventually, with significant ties to it, be denied full membership without thereby violating international human rights? The second question deserves greater attention because the social and political impact of decisions on entry is premised upon the quality and the range of membership they give access to.

The plight of illegal immigrants and asylum seekers is one of the most dramatic consequences of the impoverishment of the principle of community once it has been reduced to the national community and the latter to the state and civil society as foils of one another. The legal and political overload of such a reduction disqualified at once both local communities and transnational communities. The concepts of citizenship, membership and, mediating between the two, the concept of naturalization, are the core of that overload and have in recent years become the most contested terrain in a politics of belonging. Walzer has argued that the national community is the most comprehensive level at which human beings have been able to develop democratic forms of political organization and mechanisms for cultural understanding and for a fairer distribution of resources, and that for that reason it is legitimate to protect it as an established and functioning community against massive immigration. According to him, "the idea of distributive justice presupposes a bounded world, a community, within which distributions take place, a group of people committed to dividing, exchanging and sharing, first of all among themselves ... At some level of political organiza-tion something like the sovereign state must take shape and claim the authority to make its own admissions policy, to control and some-times to restrain the flows of immigrants" (Walzer 1981, 10). This sophisticated defense of liberal political territoriality is a paradig-matic example of how an abstractly constructed and universally applicable principle of balanced relation between inclusion and exclusion may legitimize, under the conditions of the modern inter-state system, a politics that in fact excludes the great majority of the world population from the goods that Walzer's national community is capable of delivering. Such national community is restricted to the core countries and, with the emergence of the "interior third world", will be increasingly restricted to a partial community inside them. The relatively high level of incorporation that it achieves within the national borders, protecting 1/6 of the world population, is the other side of the extremely high level of exclusion it commands outside those borders, where five-sixths of the world population lives.

Because illegal immigrants and asylum seekers are the most vulnerable social groups contesting national boundaries, they show most clearly the radical reassessment of concepts of citizenship and membership required by a cosmopolitan politics. Conversely, they unveil the most resistant obstacles in building up a transnational coalition that would support and promote such a politics. The ideal-type of citizenship, intrinsic to the ideal-type of Walzer's national community, is a form of membership characterized by being egalitarian, sacred, national democratic, unique and socially consequential (Brubaker 1989, 3). This is not the place to analyze the "deviations" of real citizenship in relation to this ideal-type, even in core countries. For my argument here it will suffice to mention that the modern concept of citizenship has always operated in articulation with a broader concept of membership that is also territorially based and intended to cover a whole range of statuses of people that are not full citizens. Legally admitted permanent immigrants are more members than seasonal workers, while illegal immigrants or asylum seekers are not members at all or, at best, vestigial members. By means of its territorial grounding, the concept of citizenship keeps its integrity only by creating, in sociological terms, second-class, third-class, and even fourth-class citizens. Millions of subordinate transnational migrants are generally deprived from getting beyond the first steps of the citizenship ladder. The legal disenfranchising of these people, together with the sociological disenfranchising of millions of nationals confined to the interior third worlds, show the discriminatory workings of modern politics of citizenship. The collision with international human rights is evident and has been managed in different ways by different nation states. Because such differences are very relevant, the creation of a cosmopolitan coalition—transnational networks of locally, nationally, and transnationally embedded social relations of emancipation—must take them into account.

The bridge of naturalization between membership and citizenship is narrower and longer in some countries than in others. The fact that Canada entered modernity through the gate of the New Worlds (settlement) and Germany through the European gate explains, in part, the fact that the naturalization rate in Canada is more than 20 times higher than in Germany. The different traditions of nationhood in Portugal or France, on the one hand, and Germany, on the other, are, in part, explained by the fact that, while Portugal and France were colonial powers, Germany was not (Brubaker 1989, 6 ff.). In countries whose legal culture is grounded on religion, as in the Middle East, citizenship is sacred and its sacredness is reproduced by its unbridgeable reach, while in countries whose legal culture has been most pervasively secularized, as in the Nordic countries, short of nationalization, human rights can be granted more easily (e.g. the right to vote in local elections).

These differences must be analytically worked out before cosmopolitan coalitions can be built in this field. The networking of differences must be subjected to certain general orientations. A new theory of citizenship must be developed to account for the growing subordinate transnational movements and the challenges they pose to the international human rights regime (for the prolegomena of a new theory of citizenship see Santos 1995, 479–519). Citizenship must be deterritorialized (less national and more egalitarian) so that the legal diaspora of millions of displaced people may come to an end. Citizenship must be decanonized (less sacred and more democratic) so that the passport and the visa cease to be a legal fetish upon which the life changes and human dignity of so many people depend. Citizenship must be socialistically reconstructed (more socially consequential and less unique) so that dual or even triple citizenship becomes the rule rather than the exception. The objective is to disperse both citizenship and territorial sovereignty, but in such a way that citizenship is thereby re-evaluated while territorial sovereignty is devaluated: precisely the opposite of what is happening today in core countries, as I tried to show above. This general orientation must be institutionally grounded on a new transnational legal field emerging out of a new balance between international human rights and the domestic legal statuses of persons. The new theory of citizenship is just a first step toward a new cosmopolitan consciousness and politics. It must be combined with a new theory of trust globally conceived, which will replace the current paradigm of state-centered trust that is fortressed within national boundaries. The new historical epistemology of need and difference called for above will be the foundation of global trust. Since a great deal of forced transnational migration is taking place within the South, the new theory of citizenship, unaccompanied by a new theory of trust, could easily become another trap for the South. On the contrary, the cosmopolitan politics proposes that entry becomes irrelevant for membership. People may enter specific countries, but they are members of all of them and the guarantee of their human rights must be provided for by all countries according to their resources, that is to say, according to their historical responsibilities in the creation of worldwide inequalities.

Notes

1. The case of Germany is particularly striking. The federal labor office (FLO) set up labor bureaus in the Mediterranean countries, encouraging German employers wanting laborers to pay this government agency a recruitment fee. The work of FLO was supplemented by intergovernmental labor-supply contracts with Greece (1960), Turkey (1961 and 1964), Morocco (1963), Portugal (1964), Tunisia (1965) and Yugoslavia (1968). See Castles *et al.* (1984, 72); Cohen (1987, 157).

2. In the mid-1980s 24 percent of illegal workers were paid less than minimum wage (Friedman 1986, 1715).

3. Curiously enough, for more than forty years since the end of World War II millions of refugees fled from Eastern Europe because of the existence of the Soviet Union and the communist bloc. During that period Austria alone, as one of the adjacent countries, offered refuge to 2 million people. About two-thirds of them were subsequently resettled in third countries, primarily in traditional overseas immigration countries, like the United States, Canada and Australia. Nonetheless, 600,000 refugees and displaced persons chose to settle in Austria (Kussbach 1992, 646). On the asymmetric axes of European migration policy, East-West and North-South, see Manfrass (1992).

4. This topic started being intensively debated in the early-90s. As reported by Clapham (1991) at the discussion between ministers in the ACP (African, Caribbean and Pacific countries)/EEC Council of Ministers on 28–29 March 1990, ACP states said they would have liked a joint expert group to be established to deliberate on how to combat racist attacks on their citizens in the Community. The Community opposed this idea on the grounds that these questions were of the competence of the member states. As Clapham commented: "One cannot ignore the fact that community integration may exhibit nasty side effects which can rebound on 'extracommunitari' in a particularly brutal way" (1991, 84).

5. In Santos (1995), I develop the idea of learning from the south as one of the key epistemological innovations in the paradigmatic transition.

CHAPTER 15

Mediating World Order: The Human Quest for Cultural Identity versus the Discipline of Global Capital

Richard Falk

Transforming the Imagination

The imagination that dominates the collective consciousness of the world at this moment of history is generated primarily by the market-place, most vividly revealed by advertisements and franchise logos (e.g. the golden arches of McDonalds). The *International Herald Tribune* a few years ago was featuring the following slogan in large formatted ads: **"there's no such thing as the outside world. Just Outsiders."** This assertion posits a radical contention, challenging the prevailing idea of a state-centric world that rests on the organizing principle of inside/outside, which is integral to the primacy of territorial sovereignty and the whole legal tradition of unconditional control by the state over international boundaries (Walker 1993). Leaving no doubt as to the meaning, the small print text of the IHT advertisement goes on to say "[t]he global class of decision makers and opinions makers would agree" with this sense of a borderless world, and their capacity to "move easily across continents and cultures" (*International Herald Tribune* 18 October 1999).

This new freedom of the globalizing elites contrasts dramatically with those who move across borders for reasons of *necessity*, either responding to the push of circumstances and the pull of imagined opportunities. For those who are threatened economically or politi-cally in a deprived or oppressive habitat, movement continues to be dominated by the inside/outside metaphor, and the state controls both access and egress as a discretionary matter of sovereign right.[1] Indeed, the legal obstacles placed in the way of such involuntary migratory flows are spawning a series of transnational criminal enterprises that engage in smuggling persons illegally across borders, often luring their clients, mainly women, with false promises of employment or marriage, and delivering them as virtual slaves into the hands of brothel owners and sex shops (Finn 2000). Both realities are true.

There is a class of privileged nomads that travel the planet as never before, effectively operating as extensions of the global market, and then at the other extreme are streams of refugees and economic migrants desperately seeking to escape from danger and misery of their homelands (Attali 1991). The globalizing nomads take advantage of the unevenness of economic conditions in different parts of the world to gain material (and touristic) benefits. Proceeding from felt need, the refugees and economic migrants are initially victims of this unevenness, but seek to re-locate so as to gain better access to opportunity and stability, including the possibility of sending a portion of their meager earnings abroad back home where its impact rescues many families from the depths of destitution. The acute vulnerability of those in deprived circumstances is exploited by criminal entrepreneurs that make a business out of smuggling such persons across borders.

That is, the Westphalian barriers to travel, which include overcoming obstacles to entry for gainful employment, invite crime to circumvent such obstacles. But the dilemma generated by widening disparities of living standards, and the persistence of poverty, is made even more intractable due to identity politics. If, as in Europe, double-digit unemployment co-exists with high welfare benefits and living standards, the host society will oppose immigration, and mount hostility toward recent immigrants, especially those with "distant" ethnic and religious identities. Such a backlash not only tightens controls over legal and illegal immigration, it encourages chauvinism and anti-foreign modes of discrimination.

A second emblematic advertisement reveals another aspect of the spirit of the time, with this message: **"To be in the right place at the right time is to be everywhere at once"**[2] (*The Economist* 8 April 2000). Here again, with information, access to IT, the importance of a global presence is stressed. The Internet allows the advantages of "presence" to be achieved without physical movement, and the interactivity of globalization does not depend directly on the penetration of political space by persons. Again this non-physicality, which applies with particular relevance to flows of money and information, is not a response to the situation of ordinary people, especially those in need, who often find themselves both entrapped by circumstance or authority within a confined space or barred from entry into a preferred space by regulated frontiers and restrictions on access. In this sense, as well, IT paradoxically liberates business elites from several aspects of the need to move across borders, while accentuating patterns of interdependence and uneven development that widen disparities and provoke a variety of upheavals that make movement to places of sanctuary and opportunity a matter of life and death.

This chapter explores these tensions between that which flows easily in an emergent global village framework and that which flows with difficulty being subject to the constraints of statist authority in a globalizing world of polarized conditions. At the core of this exploration are the differences associated with the regulation of people and money, a governance structure that has been increasingly restructured to conceive of the world as an economic unity and a political plurality. In such a world it is imperative to facilitate the free flow of money while still predominantly dedicated to controlling the flow of people by reference to the priorities of governments representing states. An important book by Richard Rosecrance (1999, 27–42) argues that the state has itself become "a virtual state" due to the prominence of "flows" as opposed to "stocks" (in the industrial era). Such a shift has also encouraged manufacturing activity to be relocated in countries with lower labor costs and less stringent regulation. The argument is insightful, and illuminating, especially with reference to the Westphalian roles of the state as it relates to economic policy and the fundamental drive toward territorial expansion (and war) that was associated with capitalism in its industrial phase.

The overall persuasiveness of Rosecrance's position is limited by his adoption of an economistic outlook that is insufficiently attentive to the "police" functions of the state that focuses on the control and suppression of undesirable flows, and on prohibited territorial activities. For instance, in the United States, the dramatic recent expansion of prisons and prisoners, the growing reliance on capital punishment, and the harsh treatment of drug dealers, terrorists, and illegal immigrants discloses a facet of the contemporary state, that is anything but virtual. And yet Rosecrance, so blinkered in his treatment of virtuality, can write, "[a]mong major developed countries, the United States has progressed most rapidly toward virtual status" (*ibid.*, 141). Why? Because 70 percent of its GDP derives from the service sector, and another 20 percent from overseas manufacturing. It is this restructuring of the economy, away from land-based activity with tangible products that is relied upon as the exclusive test of virtuality. Although crucial in redefining the role of the state, such restructuring has yet to lapse into true virtuality!

The role of law has been derivative, mainly reflecting the influence of economics and politics, and only marginally giving expression to considerations of human values, especially those associated with upholding human rights. It is this insensitivity to the ethical aspects of migration patterns and policies that associates a state-centric system of world order with great cruelty despite the emergence of globalization and international human rights as leitmotifs of the current era. The state is normatively trapped by globalization between acknowledging the moral claims of outsiders and protecting the material position, identities, and wellbeing of insiders against precisely these claims. Particularly democratic states are responsive to such a crosscutting mixture of internal pressures. Where serious labor shortages exist in relation to skilled work, as in the United States, the state mediates between facilitating access and populist feelings that oppose further immigration, particularly by non-Caucasian ethnic populations. If labor markets are saturated, as in Europe, then states submit to chauvinistic pressures, although to varying degrees and in different ways.

But the challenge is not so neatly one-sided even if assessed exclusively from a humanistic perspective. The state-centric framework did provide protection for many types of cultural pluralism either by way of secularization (and its accompanying commitment to an ethos of toleration) or by way of nationalism. The nation-state, although as much a project of elites as an existential reality for the citizenry, did often, especially in Europe, establish its sense of community on the basis of a prevailing identity. From the French Revolution onwards, this ideology of nationalism, despite its marginalization and periodic suppression of minorities, seemed to reconcile the dual quest for community and identity under the nationalist and territorial aegis of the sovereign state. Wider cosmopolitan appeals to "humanity" failed to command serious allegiance from any significant portion of society throughout the entire modern period, including the present (Archibugi & Held 1995; Nussbaum *et al.* 1997; Walzer 1994).

Of course, throughout modernity, roughly from the formation of modern states after Westphalia, the nationalist idea also gave rise to numerous exclusions and suppressions under the authority of the state, entailing the annihilation of community. No identity suffered more from this combination of exclusion and suppression than did traditional or indigenous peoples. Diasporic peoples were also periodically victimized in the secular states of Europe where antisemitism flourished and extreme prejudice against the Roma remained pervasive. These anti-human patterns culminated in the Nazi phenomenon, which, in turn, for Jews, gave a decisive push in the Zionist direction, and the establishment of the ethnic state of Israel (that ironically imposes many prejudicial restrictions on its large minority Arab population). In effect, Jewish entrapment within European territorial states led by stages to the migration of many Jews to a Jewish territorial enclave. This enclave, itself a state, has controlled state power, although it has not yet managed to make itself secure against either internal violence or external challenge. The supposed Middle East "peace process" of the 1990s appeared to seek such a result, but whether it was ever possible to satisfy Israeli security requirements while simultaneously respecting Palestinian rights under international law is quite doubtful. The claim of Palestinian refugees to exercise "a right of return" seemed particularly vital to the Palestinians and totally unacceptable to the Israelis (Said 1994, 2000). In effect, Israel's existence resulting from a genocidal onslaught in Europe produced the tragedy of Palestinian dispossession, and cannot be legitimized and secured until these Palestinian claims are accommodated (Said 1979).

These background observations establish a contradictory field of action that has confused and complicated the role of law. Fundamentally, law upheld the spatial prerogatives of the state regardless of its treatment of persons within its territorial domain, but in so doing the legal order also insulated the commission of "human wrongs" from any form of external accountability (Booth 1995). Such insulation persists, despite the rise of international human rights as an operative dimension of international law, and its impact on the foreign policy of some states, especially the United States. The recent debate about US policy toward China was based on the appropriateness and effectiveness of using economic leverage on trade policy to encourage Chinese adherence to human rights standards. A parallel European debate, occasioned by the Austrian elections in 2000 raised the question as to whether giving right-wing extremists a partnership role in government violated European community obligations. Such a controversy is substantively relevant because support for Haider's Freedom party was primarily an expression of identity politics, a backlash against immigrants.

A more systemic exception to territoriality exists in Europe where some degree of external accountability is gradually being built into the human rights procedures of the European Union, and where strategic interests in continental stability currently support "humanitarian interventions" under certain circumstances, as in relation to Kosovo under NATO auspices (Judah 2000; Mertus 1999). Because of the absence of authorization by the United Nations Security Council, the NATO War, could not be convincingly validated by law, but it was arguably nevertheless vindicated by appeals to morality and politics, that is, saving the Albanian Kosovars from ethnic cleansing and upholding the credibility of NATO as an alliance in the post-cold war setting. As a result, considerations of legality and legitimacy appear to contradict one another in relation to the NATO War.[3]

With the emergence of globalization, the picture is further complicated in a variety of contradictory ways. The blurring of state boundaries as a result of economic and cultural interconnectivity, both changes the agenda of the state and weakens its boundary-management capacities. The logic of globalization, given the neo-liberal ideological climate that favors maximizing competitiveness would often seem to favor flexible labor markets and trading regimes, but nationalist and grassroots pressures are mounting against such tendencies.[4] For material, cultural, and security reasons an anti-immigration fervor is gaining disturbing degrees of support in the rich countries of the North. If this fervor is ignored, it could lead to a revival of chauvinistic politics, even to fascism, as the rise of fringe rightist parties in Europe, even during periods of relative prosperity, confirms. Normative pressures move in opposite directions: pointing one way, favoring giving people rights to move away from misery and oppression and to take advantage of entry into societies where opportunity and freedom exists; pointing the opposite way, endorsing the discretion of democratic societies to sustain their cultural identity, standards of living, and homeland security in the face of immigration pressures from radically different cultural backgrounds. In effect, if we live in a global village, its residents should be free to live and work in the neighborhood of choice, but if we live in nation-states, then the citizenry by way of its government should be able to decide upon conditions of entry and exclusion, including setting numerical levels to protect relative affluence and reduce vulnerability to infiltrators who are linked to global terror networks. The citizenry of a nation generally claim the right to control the size and composition of their population, at least as affected by transnational migration; at the same time, controlling internal migration, as in apartheid South Africa or the Soviet Union is looked upon as a definite expression of extreme authoritarianism, a sign of illegitimate and oppressive internal governance. In this regard, the inside/outside metaphor remains operative, although its embodiment seems paradoxical. States remain at liberty to regulate international flows as well as they can, but lose legitimacy to the extent that such controls limit movement and settlement within the state. From a strict Westphalian perspective, we would expect the reverse pattern: some mutual standards on migration and rights of asylum, with no assessment whatsoever of internal regulatory patterns restricting movement.

The contemporary challenge is most poignantly posed by the realization that we live simultaneously in both a global village and nation-states. Whether international law is capable of mediating between these seemingly contradictory poles of identity and activity is highly uncertain at this time, but the current outlook is not encouraging. The unevenness of economic and political circumstances, the increasing severity of demographic and environmental pressures in poorer countries, the rise of identity politics based on ethnic and religious criteria, and the ambiguity of the state as both arbiter of these pressures and instrument for sustaining a particular nationalist character.

Re-imagining Space, Time, and People

The state-centric world order of the Westphalian era, roughly from 1648–1990s, embodied a clear conception of world order. The guiding idea of sovereignty legitimized territorial governance as the exclusive prerogative of a central government that represented the state in its external diplomatic relations. A map of the world incorporated these spatial notions, which also made concerns about boundary-management and territorial aggression central to notions of security. Issues of identity were messier, although the growth of nationalism in the aftermath of the French Revolution, fashioned the juridical project of "the nation-state", which deliberately (con)fused formal authority to confer nationality with popular feelings about political identity and loyalty. This confusion generally succeeded in forging a sense of community to the extent that ethnic heritage, language, religion corresponded with territorial boundaries of the state, allowing some room for diversity based on the acknowledgement of "minorities". The essential normative idea was a fusion of identity and authority in political entities that qualified as states in the annals of international diplomacy, and possessing unlimited authority to restrict the inflow and outflow of persons (Krasner 1999).

In this Westphalian construct time was marginalized as a dimension of world order, with neither the past nor the future taken into fundamental account by the constitutive framework. The system was Eurocentric in conception, evolution, and administration, having little difficulty in accommodating the geopolitical realities of the colonial period. Colonies were treated as subordinate territorial units attached to a metropole that provided representation, denying a colonized people any direct form of indigenous international representation or status. There was considerable variation in relation to issues of cultural security, with sub-Saharan Africa treated in the most invasive manner, removing millions to serve as slaves in other colonized areas, a coercive migration of the most abusive character, sustained for commercial gain. As well, much of Africa was divided up among European colonial powers as spoils of the prevailing geopolitical game that accorded no deference to existing patterns of cultural and ethnic identity. These practices were accommodated by prevailing international law, although the international slave trade (as distinct from the institution of slavery itself) was finally prohibited by treaty, which is viewed as the first international human rights initiative (Congress of Berlin, 1878, 1885; on steps in international law to establish a regime of prohibition see Malanczuk 1997, 21).

The Middle East also endured such arbitrary delimitation of its territorial domains, leading to political units that later emerged post-colonially as "states". Indeed, aside from Europe the notion of nation-state was a dangerous fiction that has produced decades of violence in non-Western countries. Even in Europe, the Balkan region continues to exhibit dangerously this instability of a state structure imposed on a multi-cultural ethnic setting of rivalry and enmity. Even such established "nation-states" as Spain and France are beset by small extremist, yet troublesome, secessionist movements based on minority identity claims—being a Basque or a Bretton. As soon as the tension between state and society crosses a certain threshold of antagonism, the dimension of time enters in the form of cultural memories and national aspirations, a remembered past and an imagined future, both challenging the sacrosanct quality of the territorial status quo, and subverting the legitimacy of the existing state formation.

These tensions have gained prominence in the last decade for two fundamental reasons; the first, related to the shifting geopolitical patterns of conflict among dominant states, and the second, reflecting the transformative impact of information technology on the manner in which the world economy operates. The end of the cold war weakened the geopolitical discipline exerted by strong states over a variety of manifestations of micro-nationalism. When the ideological outcome of struggles for dominance within countries in the Third World ceased to be a geopolitical arena of struggle, as it had been throughout the cold war, then the impulse to intervene declined dramatically. At the same time, global awareness of severe abuses of human rights as linked to new concerns about regional and global stability have given rise to a new push for "humanitarian intervention" under various auspices. Kosovo 1999 raised these issues in the setting of "the new geopolitics" (Moore 1998; Murphy 1996; Wheeler 2000). Also, many dormant patterns of internal conflictual behavior in former colonial regions, especially Asia and Africa, were less easily contained by state structures. The inability of these state structures to suppress ethnic and religious rivalry within their own boundaries generated severe forms of political violence with genocidal overtones. The weakening of such state structures was further accentuated by patterns of trade and investment associated with economic globalization, as well as by trends toward democratization and the protection of human rights. These patterns were reinforced by neoliberal ideas and practices as promoted by the triad of international financial institutions, the World Trade Organization (WTO), the International Monetary Fund (IMF), and the World Bank.

Such intrusions on state/society relations engendered, in turn, a variety of resistance tendencies of transnational scope and orientation, which can be generalized as "globalization-from-below" (Falk 1999). Overall, these various convergent developments introduce several complications into any interpretation of world order. The system is no longer usefully reducible to relations among states, which provided the framework for realist assessments (Falk 1998). Under contemporary conditions, private sector actors (corporations, banks), international institutions, and civil society actors must be taken into account to achieve any real insight into the workings of the global political economy.[5] The state, while retaining its predominance, has been significantly refashioned in recent decades to serve more effectively as an agent of global capital, and in the process downgrading its traditional role as a representative of the interests and values of the human community situated within its boundaries. Of course, this changing orientation of the state, and its managers, needs to be concealed as the legitimacy of government depends on territorial elections, and more generally, on acceptance by the citizenry. As a result, the state, and its political infrastructure, including political parties and mainstream media, must "sell" its public on the benefits of globalization (and regionalization), and it is often "a hard sell" as in relation to NAFTA or the European Union.

Focusing Inquiry

The pure logic of globalization threatens traditional patterns of cultural identity, although it offers a replacement: the homogenizing singularity of a consumerist future being forged by patterns of trade and investment that applies the technological innovations of the information age to the opportunities of the global marketplace.[6] Such a future, as accompanied by architectural uniformity and corporate logos that are known everywhere, tends to offer the peoples of the world a Westernizing experience of modernity that is dominated by the United States. Resistance to these trends takes a variety of forms, including direct attacks mounted against the most visible embodiments of such a globalization, such as the WTO, the IMF, and the World Bank. Other forms of resistance generate culture wars that involve an array of struggles by particular peoples to assert a more exclusive sense of cultural identity that treats globalization as dangerous and undesirable. The Iranian Revolution of 1978–79 is paradigmatic, as well as initiating a trend toward revolutionary religious politics.[7] One notable feature of this tension between tradition and globalization is the importance of the divergent approaches adopted toward flows of people and money. The Westphalian logic has held in relation to the regulation of human flows. In contrast, a globalizing logic of freedom has dominated financial flows. The overall reality is overwritten by the pull of various forces. Labor shortages in developed countries has induced legal and illegal immigration, which in turn has induced migration from poor to rich sectors of the world economy. At the same time, the rich country is increasingly reluctant to make a full or permanent commitment, especially to those at or near the bottom of the socio-economic ladder. Economic migrants often seek to earn money abroad for limited periods of time, repatriating portions of their earnings for the sake of family members or for investment at home.

International law offers a double facilitative framework: it validates controls on the flows of people while seeking to lift controls on the flow of money. Indeed, the free flow of financial resources is a central tenet of neo-liberal globalization. Since the 1997 Asian Financial Crisis, this removal from the state of its authority over the inflow and outflow of money, with its accompanying speculative frenzy, has been challenged overtly by Malaysia, and more subtly by debates about the future "financial architecture" of the world economy. The implementation of the Maastricht Treaty with regard to the establishment of a common European currency is a massive move in the direction of limiting the international financial role of the state, and represents the early stages in an experimental embrace of a confederal regional order.

With regard to flows of people, as the European Union expands to the East, member states will insist on a compromise for Europe between the unrestricted flow of people associated with Westphalian sovereignty as operative within democratic states and the sort of unrestricted control imposed on the dynamics of immigration and emigration. In this basic respect, a confederal Europe will likely have a single currency and segmented regulation of intra-European migration patterns. Also, the EU is likely to retain, if not intensify, a statist approach to inter-regional migration patterns. Two sets of factors are involved: first of all, gaining maximum advantage from an enlarged market economy that brings peace, stability, and social wellbeing to Europeans; and secondly, not integrating to an extent that jeopardizes cultural identity based on shared traditions, language, religion, rituals, and values.

Whether the European model of extended statehood, combining diminished regional territoriality with a new set of regional boundaries, is likely to be followed in Asia, Latin America, and Africa is difficult to discern. At this point, Asia and Latin America are definitely experimenting with a variety of regional and subregional arrangements, but do not seem ready to cede sovereignty over the flow of peoples based on a norm of free regional movement.

Africa is even less able to contemplate such possibilities, being preoccupied with migratory flows of refugees generated by widespread ethnic warfare. A foreign country, especially if it shares a common ethnic (or tribal) identity, provides a sanctuary for those displaced by civil violence. The Great Lakes area of central Africa has been beset by severe struggles that have caused massive displacements of persons within countries, as well as across borders. In these circumstances, there is a virtual loss of cultural security for many

Africans. The situation is so desperate in many places that states cannot even provide security for their own citizenry, and efforts to introduce international peacekeeping forces are not succeeding (Kaplan 2000; Peterson 2000). In effect, regional unevenness makes it unlikely that the European experience will be replicated in any literal fashion. What does seem likely is that to the extent negotiable, governments will seek to enhance economic performance and development by adopting regional schemes for coordination. To the extent these schemes succeed, they will begin to address social issues of vulnerability and insecurity, but for a long time ahead, even in Asia, the responses will be shaped almost exclusively at the level of the state. The Westphalian tensions will persist in the face of economic regionalization carried out according to neo-liberal precepts.

In this global setting, the contributions of international law are likely to remain rhetorical and marginal, encouraging grants of asylum particularly to political refugees, but little else. Even in this limited setting, states are as likely to offer asylum or not based on strategic, economic, and racist considerations as they are to apply objective standards. A legal approach would imply treating equals equally, which is not likely for many years. The extension of asylum as a right to economic and environmental refugees is even less likely to be based on legal procedures and standards for the foreseeable future. As a result, with globalization generating enclaves of poverty and affluence, as well as being environmentally disruptive, the pressure to migrate will remain intense, and is likely to intensify, at the same time, the counter-pressure to shut down migration to those who come in search of basic economic needs are likely to grow even stronger. A factor in this process is the likelihood that robots can perform an increasing number of unskilled and semi-skilled jobs, reducing the economic receptivity of rich countries to the immigration of unskilled workers (Moravec 1999).

In conclusion, then, the quest for security is likely to produce controversy and contradictory priorities. The advanced economies that are moving into new phases of capitalist enterprise are increasingly likely to seek to protect the cultural security of their citizens by keeping people out. The impoverished, demographically pressured societies are likely to induce desperate efforts at escape, whether legally or not. The spectacle of boat people perishing at sea and forced repatriation is sure to be part of the unfolding future casting a shadow across claims of an ethos global humanism arising from the steady growth of the world economy.

The peoples of the world, for better and worse, will be overwhelmingly dependent for their cultural security on the orientation and practices of the territorial state. Such a fragmenting vulnerability, given the unevenness of circumstances, is not a positive prospect. At the same time, money is likely to retain its freedom of movement, although perhaps ceding some limited authority by way of capital controls over short-term transnational transactions. In one sense, the protesters at Seattle, Washington, and elsewhere are insisting that capital flows need to be regulated for the sake of human well being, and are challenging the benefits of this form of "freedom".

A Concluding Perspective

There are a few factors that may work to soften the vulnerability of persons now entrapped within Westphalian space:

- The general rise in protection for international human rights;
- The closely related moves toward humanitarian intervention, and the imposition of criminal accountability upon political and military leaders; the revival of the Nuremberg idea;
- The realignment of international financial institutions in more people-oriented directions;
- The growth of global solidarity as one expression of the transnational movement in support of global democracy;
- The further evolution of regional solidarity as a dimension of an emergent post-Westphalian world order.

Each of these favorable tendencies is subject to qualifications, including counter-tendencies, especially as a result of the security imperatives associated with the transnational challenge of mega-terrorism. The complexity of this fluid global setting provides, at the very least, political space for compassionate initiatives on behalf of vulnerable peoples.

Notes

1. International law does purport to set standards governing the treatment of those persons who qualify as "refugees", but in a loose manner that is not subject to review by third party judgment. The main international standard, such as it is, obligates governments not to repatriate refugees if they face the prospect of persecution upon their return. According to Article 1A(2) of the 1951 Convention on the Status of Refugees, a refugee status is available if there

exists in relation to a person "outside the country of his nationality ..." a "well-founded fear of being persecuted for reasons of race, religion, nationality, membership of a particular social group or political opinion", if such a person is forced to return to that country or accept its protection. This narrow legal conception of a "refugee" is reaffirmed in the 1967 Protocol on the Status of Refugees. For texts of both treaties see Weston *et al.* (1997, 391–95, 448–50). But forcible repatriation is common even in circumstances where clear and present dangers exist, and despite almost certain economic misery, as is the case in mid-2000 in relation to involuntary repatriations of Serb and other minorities to Kosovo underway from Switzerland and Germany.

2. This ad is by Instinet, a Reuters company that provides market information through an Internet service.

3. For the diversity of views on these international law issues see "Editorial Comments: NATO's Kosovo Intervention." *American Journal of International Law* 93 (1999): 824–862.

4. The Seattle protests in early December 1999 directed at ministerial meetings of the World Trade Organization were a warning signal to the exponents of neo-liberalism. For one interpretation see Falk (2000a). For a more critical account of the Seattle protests see "The Real Losers" and "After Seattle: A Global Disaster" (*The Economist* 11 December 1999, 15, 19–21).

5. In 1998 Kofi Annan proposed partnerships between the UN on one side and civil society and the private sector on the other at the World Economic Forum in Davos. In his report to the Millennial Assembly of the United Nations the Secretary General went further. He called for adherence to a "Global Compact" in which organs of the UN (ILO, UNEP, Office of UN High Commissioner of Human Rights) "engage corporations in the promotion of equitable labor standards, respect for human rights, and the protection of the environment". Elsewhere in the report the role of a people-oriented approach to all aspects of the UN are stressed, which is a challenge to state-centric and neo-liberal patterns of behavior (Annan 2000).

6. For a positive reading of this globalizing impact see Mozaffari (1998). For those who emphasize the rise of civilizationalism as more of a defining challenge than globalization, see most notably Huntington (1996).

7. For a broad study of the more extremist expressions of this trend see Juergens-meyer (2000).

References

Abel, O. 1999. "Quatorze thèses sur l'humanité universelle et le respect des différences." *Esprit* 253: 101–107.

Acuerdo de Cartagena, Junta. 1991a. *Acta Final de la 1ra. Reunion de Autoridades Migratorias del Grupo Andino. Lima: JUNAC.*

Acuerdo de Cartagena, Junta. 1991b. *Bases de Propuesta para la Integracion Fronteriza Andina. Lima: JUNAC.*

Acuerdo de Cartagena, Junta/OIM. 1991c. *La Migracion Internacional en los Procesos Regionales de Integracion en America del Sur. Lima: JUNAC.*

Aksoy, A. 1997. "Reaching the parts state television does not reach: multiculturalism in Turkish television." In: *Programming for People: From Cultural Rights to Cultural Responsibilities*, edited by Kevin Robins, 54–63. Rome: RAI.

Aksoy, A. and Robins, K. 2000. "Thinking across spaces: transnational television from Turkey." *European Journal of Cultural Studies* 3, No. 3: 543–565.

Altinay, A.G. Forthcoming. "Making citizens, making soldiers: military service, gender and National Identity in Turkey." Ph. D. Dissertation, Duke University.

Althusser, L. 1971. "Ideology and ideological state apparatuses. (notes towards an investigation)." In: *Lenin and Philosophy and Other Essays*, 121–173. London: New Left Books.

Aman, Jr. A.C. 1995. "A global perspective on current regulatory reform: rejection, relocation, or reinvention?" *Indiana Journal of Global Legal Studies* 2, No. 2: 429–464.

Anderson, B. 1983, 1991 (revised edition). *Imagined Communities: Reflections on the Origins and Spread of Nationalism.* London: Verso.

Anderson, L.E. 1994. *The Political Ecology of the Modern Peasant: Calculation and Community.* Baltimore: The Johns Hopkins University Press.

Annan, K.A. 2000. *'We the Peoples': The Role of the United Nations in the 21st Century*. New York: United Nations.

Anthias, F. 1998. "Evaluating 'diaspora': beyond ethnicity?" *Sociology* 32, No. 3: 557–580.

Anthony, C. 1991. "Africa's refugee crisis: state building in historical perspective." *International Migration Review* 25: 574–591.

Appadurai, A. 1990. "Disjuncture and difference in the global economy." *Public Culture* 2, No. 2 (Spring): 1–24.

Appadurai, A. 1993. "Patriotism and its futures." *Public Culture* 5, No. 3: 411–29.

Appadurai, A. 1996a. *Modernity at Large: Cultural Dimensions of Globalization*. Minneapolis: University of Minnesota Press.

Appadurai, A. 1996b. "Sovereignty without territoriality: notes for a postnational geography." In: *The Geography of Identity*, edited by Patricia Yaeger, 40–58. Ann Arbor: The University of Michigan Press.

Archibugi, D. and Held, D. 1995. (eds) *Cosmopolitan Democracy: An Agenda for a New World Order*. Cambridge, UK: Polity.

Armentrout-Ma, L.E. 1990. *Revolutionaries, Monarchists, and Chinatowns: Chinese Politics in the Americas and the 1911 Revolution*. Honolulu: University of Hawai'i Press.

Arrighi, G. 1997. "Globalisation, state sovereignty, and the 'endless' accumulation of capital." Revised version of a paper presented at the Conference on States and Sovereignty in the World Economy. University of California, Irvine, Feb. 21–23, 1997.

Asad, T. 1993. *Genealogies of Religion*. Baltimore: Johns Hopkins University Press.

Associated Press. 1999. "National news briefing; one U.S. resident in 10 is now foreign born." *New York Times*, September 19, p. 37.

Attali, J. 1991. *Millennium: Winners and Losers in the Coming World Order*. New York: Random House.

Ayata, A. 1997. "The emergence of identity politics in Turkey." *New Perspectives on Turkey* 17: 59–73.

Bade, K.J. 1996a. *Die Multikulturelle Herausforderung: Menschen über Grenzen—Grenzen über Menschen*. München: Beck.

Bade, K.J. 1996b. *Migration–Ethnizität–Konflikt. Systemfragen und Fallstudien*. Osnabrück: Rasch.

Bade, K.J. and Bommes, M. 1996. "Migration–Ethnizität–Konflikt. Erkenntnisprobleme und Beschreibungsnotstände: eine Einführung." In: *Migration–Ethnizität–Konflikt. Systemfragen und Fallstudien*, edited by Klaus J. Bade, 11–40. Osnabrück: Rasch.

Bairoch, P. and Kozul-Wright, R. 1996. "Globalization myths: some historical reflections on integration, industrialization and growth in the world economy." UNCTAD discussion paper 113. Geneva, Switzerland.

Bank, R. 2000. "Europeanisation of the reception of asylum seekers: the opposite of welfare state politics." In: *Immigration and Welfare: Challenging the Borders of the Welfare State*, edited by Michael Bommes and A. Geddes, 148–169. London: Routledge.

Banks, M. 1996. *Ethnicity: Anthropological Constructions*. London: Routledge.

Barber, B. 1996. *Jihad vs. McWorld: How Globalism and Tribalism are Reshaping the World*. New York: Ballantine Books.

Basch, L., Glick Schiller, N. and Szanton Blanc, C. 1994. *Nations Unbound: Transnational Projects, Postcolonial Predicaments and peterritorialized Nation-States*. Amsterdam: Gordon and Breach.

Bauböck, R. 1994. *Transnational Citizenship: Membership and Rights in International Migration*. Aldershot, England: Edward Elgar.

Baucom, I. 1999. *Out of Place. Englishness, Empire and the Locations of Identity*. Princeton, Princeton University Press.

Bauman, Z. 1990. "Modernity and ambivalence." In: *Global Culture: Nationalism, Globalization and Modernity*, edited by Mike Featherstone, 143–69. London: Sage Publications.

Bauman, Z. 1992. "A sociological theory of postmodernity." In: *Between Totalitarianism and Postmodernity: A Thesis Eleven Reader*, edited by Peter Beilharz, Gillian Robinson, and John Rundell. Cambridge, MA: MIT Press.

Bearak, B. "Trying to wreck India's romance with the bomb." *New York Times*, August 27, p. A4.

Becker, J. 1996. "Zwischen integration und dissoziation: Türkische medienkultur in Deutschland." *Aus Politik und Zeitgeschichte* 44–45: 39–47.

Becker, J. 1997. "Die ethnisierung der deutschen medienlandschaft: Türkische medienkultur zwischen assoziation und dissoziation." Paper presented to the Konferenz der Deutschen Gesellschaft für Publizistik- und Kommunikationswissenschaft, Giessen, 7–9 May.

Benjamin, W. 1980. "Das kunstwerk im zeitalter seiner technischen reprodizierbarkeit (zweite fassung)." In: *Benjamin, Walter: Gesammelte Schriften–Zweiter Band*, 470–508. Frankfurt a.M.: Suhrkamp.

Berger, P.L. 1997. "Four faces of global culture." *The National Interest*, No. 49 (Fall): 23–29.

Berking, H. 1998. "Global flows and local cultures." *Berliner Journal fuer Soziologie* 3, No. 98: 381–392.

Berman, P. 1992. (ed.) *Debating P.C.* New York: Dell Publishing.

Berry, J.W., Kim, U. and Boski, P. 1987. "Psychological acculturation of immigrants." In: *Cross-cultural Adaptation*, edited by Y.Y. Kim and W.B. Gudykunst, 62–89. Newbury Park, CA: Sage Publications.

Berry, J.W., Kim, U. and Young, S. 1989. "Acculturation attitudes in plural societies." *Applied Psychology: An International Review* 38, No. 2: 185–206.

Bey, U.S. 1996. "We are the Washitaw: Columbia via USA." The Washitaw Nation. Manuscript.

Bhabha, H. 1993. *The Location of Culture*. London: Routledge.

Biersteker, T.J., Hall, R.B. and Murphy, C.N. 2002. (eds) *Private Authority and Global Governance*. Cambridge: Cambridge University Press.

Blainey, G. 1995. "The New Racism." *The Australian*, April 8.

Bohning, W.R. and Schloeter-Paredes, M.-L. 1994. (ed.) *Aid in Place of Migration*. Geneva: International Labor Office.

Bommes, M. 1997. "Von gastarbeitern zu einwanderern: arbeitsmigration in niedersachsen." In: *Fremde im Land: Zuwanderung und Eingliederung im Raum Niedersachsen seit dem Zweiten Weltkrieg*, edited by Klaus J. Bade, 249–322. Osnabrück: Rasch.

Bommes, M. 1999. *Migration und Nationaler Wohlfahrtsstaat. Ein Systemtheoretischer Entwurf*. Wiesbaden: Westdeutscher Verlag.

Bommes, M. 1999a. "Migration, belonging and the shrinking inclusive capacity of the nation state." Paper presented at the conference "Globalization and Cultural Security: Migration and Negotiations of Identity," Berlin, 14–17 October.

Bommes, M. 2000. "National welfare state, biography and the impact of migration: Labor migrants, ethnic Germans and the re-ascription of welfare state membership." In: *Immigration and Welfare: Challenging the Borders of the Welfare State*, edited by M. Bommes and A. Geddes, 98–108. London: Routledge.

Bommes, M. and Geddes, A. 2000. (ed.) *Immigration and Welfare: Challenging the Borders of the Welfare State*. London: Routledge.

Bommes, M. and Halfmann, J. 1998. *Migration in Nationalen Wohlfahrtsstaaten. Theoretische und Vergleichende Untersuchungen*. Osnabrück: Rasch.

Bonacich, E., Cheng, L., Chinchilla, N., Hamilton, N. and Ong, P. 1994. (ed.) *Global Production: The Apparel Industry in the Pacific Rim*. Philadelphia: Temple University Press.

Booth, K. 1996. "Human wrongs in international relations." *International Affairs* 71, No. 1: 103–126.

Borjas, G. J. 1990. *Friends or Strangers: The Impact of Immigration on the US Economy.* New York: Basic Books.

Bornstein, D. 1999. "A force now in the World, citizens flex social muscle." *New York Times,* July 10, p. B7.

Bosniak, L.S. 1991. "Human rights, state sovereignty and the protection of undocumented migrants under the International Migrant Workers Convention." *International Migration Review* 25: 737–770.

Bosniak, L.S. 1992. "Human rights, state sovereignty and the protection of undocumented migrants under the International Migrant Workers Convention." *International Migration Review* 25, No. 4: 737–770.

Bourdieu, P. 1980. "L'identité et la représentation: Éléments pour une réflexion critique sur l'idée de region." *Annales de la Recherche en Sciences Sociales* 35: 63–72.

Bourdieu, P. and Wacquand, L. 1999. "On the cunning of Imperialist reason." *Theory, Culture & Society* 16, No. 1: 41–58.

Boyce, M. 1990. "Diaspora in pre-Islamic times." In: *Encyclopedia Iranica,* Vol. VI, Fascicle 4, edited by Ehsan Yarshater, 370–373. New York: Bibliotheca Persica Press.

Brah, A. 1996. *Cartographies of the Diaspora.* London: Routledge.

Briggs, A. and Snowman, D. 1996. *Fins de Siecle: How Centuries End, 1400–2000.* New Haven: Yale University Press.

Briggs, V.M., Jr. 1992. *Mass Immigration and the National Interest.* Armonk, NY: M.E. Sharpe.

Braudel, F. 1984. The perspective of the world. New York: Harper and Row.

Brubaker, W.R. 1989. *Immigration and the Politics of Citizenship in Europe and North America.* Lanhan, MD: University Press of America.

Brubaker, W.R. 1992. *Citizenship and Nationhood in France and Germany.* Cambridge, MA.: Harvard University Press.

Brubaker, W.R. 1994. "Nationhood and the national question in the Soviet Union and Post-Soviet Eurasia: An institutionalist account." *Theory and Society* 23, No. 1: 47–77.

Brumlik, M. and Leggewie, C. 1994. "Konturen der einwanderungsgesellschaft: Nationale identitaet, multikulturalismus und civil society." In: *Deutsche im Ausland—Fremde in Deutschland,* edited by Klaus Bade, 430–442. Munich: Beck.

Butterfield, F. and Kahn, J. 1999. "Chinese in the U.S. say spying case casts doubts on their loyalties." *The New York Times,* May 16.

Caglar, A. 1995. "German Turks in Berlin: Social exclusion and strategies of social mobility." *New Community* 21, No. 3: 309–323.

Cassese, A., Clapham, A. and Weiler, J. 1991a. *Human Rights and the European Community: Methods of Protection*. Baden-Baden: Nomos Verlagsgesellschaft.

Cassese, A., Clapham, A. and Weiler, J. 1991b. *Human Rights and the European Community: The Substantive Law*. Baden-Baden: Nomos Verlagsgesellschaft.

Castells, M. 1996. *The Rise of the Network Society*. Malden, MA.: Blackwell Publishers.

Castells, M. 1997. *The Power of Identity*. Malden, MA.: Blackwell Publishers.

Castells, M. 2000. *The Information Age*. Vol. I. Oxford: Blackwell.

Castles, S. 1996. "Immigration and multiculturalism in Australia." In: *Migration–Ethnizität–Konflikt. Systemfragen und Fallstudie*, edited by Klaus Bade, 249–270 Osnabrück: Rasch.

Castles, S. 1998. "Einwanderung und sozialpolitik in Australien." In: *Migration in Nationalen Wohlfahrtsstaaten. Theoretische und Vergleichende Untersuchungen*, edited by Michael Bommes and Jost Halfmann, 171–197. Osnabrück: Rasch.

Castles, S., Booth, H. and Wallace, T. 1984. *Here for Good: Western Europe's New Ethnic Minorities*. London: Pluto Press.

Castles, S. and Kosack, G. 1985. *Immigrant Workers and Class Structure in Western Europe*. Oxford: Oxford University Press.

Castles, S. and Miller, M.J. 1998. *The Age of Migration: International Population Movements in the Modern World*. New York: The Guilford Press.

Cebecioglu, T. 1995. "Änderungen im Staatsangehörigkeitsrecht der Türkei." *StAZ* 8: 234–235.

Cemal, H. 1993. "İslamcıların televizyon atağı." *Sabah*, 13 January.

CEPAL. 1994. *Desarrollo reciente delos procesos de integracion en America Latina y el Caribe*. Santiago, Chile: CEPAL.

de Certeau, M. de. 1984. *The Practice of Everyday Life*. Berkeley: University of California Press.

Cerulo, K.A. 1997. "Identity construction: New issues, new directions." *Annual Review of Sociology* 23: 385–410.

Chatterjee, P. 1997. "Beyond the nation? Or within?" *Economic and Political Weekly*, January 4–11, pp. 30–34.

Chavez, P.L. 1997. "Creating a United States-Mexico Political Double Helix: The Mexican government's proposed Dual Nationality Amendment." *Stanford Journal of International Law* 33, No. 1: 119–151.

Clapham, A. 1991. *Human Rights and the European Community: A Critical Overview*. Baden-Baden: Nomos Verlagsgesellschaft.

Clark, R.L., Passel, J., Zimmermann, W. and Fix, M. 1994. *Fiscal Impacts of Undocumented Aliens: Selected Estimates for Seven States.* Report to the Office of Management and Budget and the Department of Justice, September. Washington, D.C.: The Urban Institute.

Clastres, P. 1977. *Society Against the State.* Oxford: Blackwell.

Clifford, J. 1997. *Routes. Travel and Translation in the Late Twentieth Century.* Cambridge: Harvard University Press.

Clinton, W.J. 1999 "Remarks by President Clinton at University of Chicago Convocation Ceremonies." Office of the Press Secretary.   http://www.whitehouse.gov/WH/New/html/ 19990612.html: June 12.

Cohen, J. 1996. (ed.) *For Love of Country: Debating the Limits of Patriotism.* Boston: Beacon Press.

Cohen, R. 1987. *The New Helots: Migrants in the International Division of Labor.* Aldershot: Avebury.

Cohen, R. 1997. *Global Diasporas: An Introduction.* London: UCL Press.

Cohn-Bendit, D. and Schmid, T. 1992. *Heimat Babylon. Das Wagnis der Multikulturellen Demokratie.* Hamburg: Hoffmann and Campe.

Conzen, K.N. 1990. *Making Their Own America: Assimilation Theory and the German Peasant Pioneer.* German Historical Institute, Washington, D.C., Annual Lecture Series, No. 3. NY: Berg Publishers.

Copeland, E. 1992. "Global refugee policy: An agenda for the 1990s." *International Migration Review* 26: 992–999.

Cornelius, W.A., Martin, P.L. and Hollifield, J.F. 1994. (ed.) *Controlling Immigration. A Global Perspective.* Stanford: Standford University Press.

Cox, R. 1987. *Production, Power, and World Order: Social Forces in the Making of History.* New York: Columbia University Press.

Dahl, G. 1997. "God save our county! Radical localism in the American heartland." Manuscript.

Davis, M. 1993. "Domestic workers: Out of the shadows." *Human Rights* 20, No. 2: 14–15, 28–29.

Davis, M. 1999. "Magical urbanism: Latinos reinvent the US Big City." *New Left Review* 234: 3–43.

Derrida, J. 1978. *Writing and Difference.* Translated by A. Bass. London: Routledge.

Diriklik, A.S. 1993. *Danimarkali Gelin.* Istanbul: Ihlas Flim Produksiyon A.S.

Dirlik, A., 1995. "Global capitalism and the reinvention of Confucianism." *Boundary* 22, No. 3: 229–273.

Dirlik, A. 2001. "Place-based imagination: Globalism and the politics of place." In: *Places and Politics in an Age of Globalization*, edited by Roxann Prazniak and Arif Dirlik, 15–51. Lanham, MD: Rowman and Littlefield.

Doane, A. 1997. "Dominant group ethnic identity In The United States: The role of "hidden" ethnicity in intergroup relations." *The Sociological Quarterly* 38, No. 3: 375–397.

Dona, G. and Berry, J.W. 1994. "Acculturation attitudes and acculturative stress of Central American refugees." *International Journal of Psychology* 29, No. 1: 57–70.

Dorra. M. 1996. "La traversée des apparences." *Le Monde Diplomatique*, June, p. 32.

Drache, D. and Gertler, M. 1991. (ed.) *The New Era of Global Competition: State Policy and Market Power*. Montreal: McGill-Queen's University Press.

Dubet, F. and Lapeyronnie, D. 1994. *Im Aus der Vorstädte. Der Zerfall der Demokratischen Gesellschaft*. Stuttgart: Klett-Cotta.

Dunlap, J.C. and Morse, A. 1995. "States sue Feds to recover immigration costs." *NCSL Legisbrief*, January 3, 1. Washington D.C. National Conference of State Legislatures.

D'Souza, D. 1996. *The End of Racism: Principles for a Multiracial Society*. New York: Free Press.

D'Souza, D. 1998. "The century the Earth stood still." December 20, 1997–January 2, 1998, pp. 71–73.

Eichenhofer, E. 1996. "Arbeitsbedingungen bei entsendung von arbeitnehmern." *Zeitschrift für Ausländisches und Internationales Sozialrecht* 10, No. 1: 55–82.

Eichenhofer, E. 1997. *Social Security of Migrants in the European Union of Tomorrow*. Osnabrück: Rasch.

Entzinger, H.B. 1985. "The Netherlands." In: *European Immigration Policy: A Comparative Study*, edited by Tomas Hammer, 50–88. Cambridge: Cambridge University Press.

Entzinger, H.B. 1998 "Zu einem modell der inkorporation von einwanderern: Das beispiel der Niederlande." In: Bommes and Halfmann 1998, 105–122.

Erikson, E.H. 1980. *Identity and the Life Cycle*. NY: Norton.

Erzeren, Ö. 2000. "Hoffnung Zerstört?" *Persembe Haftalik Gazete*, September 14, p. 1.

Esperitu, Yen Le. 1992. *Asian American Pan-ethnicity: Bridging Institutions and Identities*. Philadelphia. Temple University Press.

Espenshade, T.J. and King, V.E. 1994. "State and local fiscal impacts of U.S. immigrants: Evidence from New Jersey." *Population Research and Policy Review* 13, No. 3: 225–256.

Esping-Andersen, G. 1990. *The Three Worlds of Welfare Capitalism.* Cambridge: Polity Press.

Esping-Andersen, G. 1996. *Welfare States in Transition: National Adaptations in Global Economies.* London: Sage.

Esman, M.J. 1977. *Ethnic Conflict in the Western World.* Ithaca: Cornell University Press.

Esman, M.J. 1994. *Ethnic Politics.* Ithaca. Cornell University.

Ewing, K.P. 1990. "The illusion of wholeness: 'Culture,' 'self,' and the experience of inconsistency." *Ethos* 18, No. 3: 251–278.

Ewing, K.P. 2000a. "The violence of non-recognition: Becoming a 'conscious' Muslim in Turkey." In: *Cultures Under Siege: Collective Violence and Trauma in Anthropological and Psychoanalytic Perspective,* edited by Antonius Robben and Marcelo Suarez-Orozco, 248–271. Cambridge: Cambridge University Press.

Ewing, K.P. 2000b. "Legislating religious freedom: Muslim challenges to the relationship between 'Church' and 'State' in Germany and France." *Daedalus* 129, No. 4: 31–54. Special issue on "The free exercise of culture: How free is it? How free ought it to be?" edited by Richard A. Shweder, Martha Minow, and Hazel R. Markus.

Ewing, K.P. 2001. "Images of order and authority: Shifting identities and legal consciousness in a runaway immigrant daughter." In: *Power and the Self,* edited by Jeanette Mageo and Bruce Knauft, 93–113. Cambridge: Cambridge University Press.

Fabian, J. 1983. *Time and the Other. How Anthropology Makes its Object.* New York: Columbia University Press.

Fagen, P.W. and Eldridge, J. 1991. "Salvadorean repatriation from Honduras." In: *Repatriation under Conflict: The Central American Case,* edited by Mary Ann Larkin, Frederick Cuny, and Barry Stein, 117–86. Washington D.C.: HMPCIPRA, Georgetown University.

Faist, T. 1998. "International migration and transnational social spaces." *Archives Européennes de Sociologie* 34, No. 2: 213–247.

Faist, T. 1999. "Developing transnational social spaces: The Turkish-German example." In: *Migration and Transnational Social Spaces,* edited by Ludwig Preis, 36–72. Aldershot: Ashgate.

Faist, T. 1999a. "Transnationalization and immigrant membership: Moving from assimilation and ethnic pluralism to the border-crossing expansion of social space." Paper presented at the

Conference on Redefinition of National Identity and Citizenship in the Age of Culturalist Politics in Germany, Israel, Lebanon and Turkey, Istanbul, 17–19 June.

Faist, T. 2000. *The Volume and Dynamics of International Migration and Transnational Social Spaces*. Oxford: Oxford University Press.

Faist, T. 2000a. "Überlappende mitgliedschaft in politischen gemeinschaften: Doppelte Staatsbürgerschaft." Unpublished Manuscript.

Falk, R. 1998. *Law in an Emerging Global Village: A Post-Westphalian Perspective*. Ardsley, NY: Transnational Publishers.

Falk, R. 1999. *Predatory Globalization: A Critique*. Cambridge, UK: Polity Press.

Falk, R. 2000. *Predatory Globalization*. Cambridge, UK: Polity Press.

Falk, R. 2000a. *Australian Financial Review*, 7 January 2000, p. 17

Finn, P. 2000. "Sex slavery flourishes in Kosovo." Washington Post, April 24, p. 1, 20.

Finnegan, W. 1999. "Letter from the Balkans: The next war." *The New Yorker*, September 20, pp. 66–72.

Foucault, M. 1978. *The History of Sexuality*. NY: Pantheon Books.

Foucault, M. 1984. "The subject and power." In: *Art after Modernism: Rethinking Representation*, edited by Brian Wallis, 417–432. Boston: David R. Godine.

Franck, T.M. 1992. "The emerging right to democratic governance." *American Journal of International Law* 86, No. 1: 46–91.

Freud, S. 1953. *The Interpretation of Dreams. The Standard Edition of the Complete Works of Sigmund Freud*, edited and translated by James Strachey. Vols 4–5. London: Hogarth Press.

Freud, S. 1957. "Mourning and melancholia." *The Standard Edition of the Complete Works of Sigmund Freud*, edited and translated by James Strachey, 243–260. Vol. 14. London: Hogarth Press.

Freud, S. 1958. "Remembering, repeating, and working through (further recommendations on the technique of psychoanalysis)." *The Standard Edition of the Complete Works of Sigmund Freud*, edited and translated by James Strachey, 145–156. Vol. 12. London: Hogarth Press.

Friedman, J. 1994. *Cultural Identity and Global Processes*. Sage: Newbury Park.

Friedman, J. 1997. "Global crises, the struggle for cultural identity and intellectual pork-barreling: Cosmopolitans, nationals and locals in an era of de-hegemonisation." In: *The Dialectics of Hybridity*, edited by P. Werbner, 70–89. London: Zed Press.

Friedman, J. 1998. The hybridisation of roots and the abhorrence of the bush." *Spaces of Culture: City, Nation, World*, edited by M. Featherstone and S. Lash, 230–256. London: Sage.

Friedman, J. 1999. "The Rhinoceros 2." *Current Anthropology*, 40, No. 5 1999: 679–688.

Friedman, J. 1999a. *Concept for the Conference: Globalization and Cultural Security: Migration and Negotiations of Identity.* The House of World Cultures Berlin and the Toda Institute for Global Peace and Policy Research. October 14–17, 1999. House of World Cultures Berlin.

Friedman, J. 2002. *PC Worlds: An Anthropology of Political Correctness.* Berkeley: University of California Press (in press).

Friedman, N. 1986. "A Human Rights approach to the Labor rights of undocumented workers." *California Law Review* 74: 1715–1745.

Fröbel, F., Heinrichs, J. and Kreye, O. 1980. *The New International Division of Labor.* Cambridge: Cambridge University Press.

Furnivall, S. 1948. *Colonial Policy and Practice.* Cambridge: Cambridge University Press.

Gans, H. 1979. "Symbolic ethnicity: The future of ethnic groups and cultures in America." *Ethnic and Racial Studies* 2: 1–20.

Geertz, C. 1963. *Old Societies and New States: The Quest for Modernity in Asia and Africa.* Glencoe, IL: Free Press.

Geertz, C. 1973. *The Interpretation of Cultures: Selected Essays.* NY: Basic Books.

Geertz, C. 1994: "Reason, religion and Professor Gellner." In: Proceedings of the Erasmus Ascension Symposium 1994 on the Limitis of Pluralism, 167–173. Amsterdam: Praemium Erasmianum Foundation.

Geißler, R. 1996. *Die Sozialstruktur Deutschlands.* Opladen: (2. Auflage) Westdeutscher Verlag.

Gellner, E. 1988. *Nations and Nationalism.* Oxford: Blackwell.

Genelge 1998/10. *Circular. T.C. Isisleri Bakanligi Nüfus ve Vatandaslik Isleri Genel Müdürlügü.* Ankara.

Gerber, D.A. 2000 "Theories and lives: Transnationalism and the conceptualization of international migrations to the United States." IMIS-Beiträge, No. 15: 31–53.

General Accounting Office. 1994. *Illegal Aliens: Assessing Estimates of Financial Burden on California.* November, GAO/HEHS-95-22. Washington D.C.: U.S. GAO.

General Accounting Office. 1995. *Illegal Aliens: National Net Cost Estimates Very Widely.* July, GAO/HEHS-95-133. Washington D.C.: U.S. GAO.

343

Gergen, K.J. 1991. *The Saturated Self: Dilemmas of Identity in Contemporary Life*. NY: Basic Books.

Gilroy, P. 1990/1991. "It ain't where you're from, it's where you're at: The dialectics of diasporic identification." Third Text, 13 (Winter): 3–16.

Gilroy, P. 1993. *The Black Atlantic*. London: Verso.

Gilroy, P. 1996. "'The whisper wakes, the shudder plays': Race, nation and ethnic absolutism." In: *Contemporary Postcolonial Theory: A Reader*, edited by Padmini Mongia, 248–274. London: Arnold.

Gilroy, P. 1993a. *Small Acts: Thoughts on the Politics of Black Cultures*. London: Serpent's Tail.

Glick Schiller, N., Basch, L. and Blanc-Szanton, C. 1995. "From immigrant to transmigrant: Theorizing transnational migration." *Anthropological Quarterly* 68, No. 1 : 48–65.

Glick Schiller, N., Basch, L. and Blanc-Szanton, C. 1997. "From immigrant to transmigrant: Theorising transnational migration." In: *Transnationale Migration*, edited by Ludger Pries, 121–140. Soziale Welt. Sonderband 12. Baden-Baden: Nomos.

Glick Schiller, N., Basch, L. and Blanc-Szanton, C. 1997a. "Transnationalismus: Ein neuer analytischer rahmen zum verständnis von migration." In: *Transnationale Staatsbürgerschaft*, edited by Heinz Kleger, 81–107. Frankfurt: Campus-Verlag.

Goldring, L. 1997. "Power and status in transnational social spaces." In: *Transnationale Migration*, edited by Ludger Pries, 179–195. Soziale Welt. Sonderband 12. Baden-Baden: Nomos.

Gordon, R. 1999. "Has the 'New economy' rendered the productivity slowdown obsolete?" Manuscript.

Greenblatt, S. 1980. *Renaissance Self-fashioning*. Chicago: University of Chicago Press.

Guarnizo, L. and Smith, M.P. 1998 "Transnationalism from below." In: *Transnationalism from Below* (Special issue of *Comparative Urban and Community Research* 6), edited by Michael Peter Smith and Luis Eduardo Guarnizo, 3–34. New Brunswick, NJ: Transaction Publishers.

Hailbronner, K. 1999. "Doppelte Staatsangehörigkeit." *Zar-Abhandlungen* 2: 51–58.

Halfmann, J. 1996. *Makrosoziologie der Modernen Gesellschaft*. Weinheim/München: Juventa.

Hall, S. 1990. "Cultural identity and diaspora." In *Identity: Community, Culture, Difference*, edited by John Rutherford, 222-237. London: Lawrence and Wishart.

Hall, S. 1995. "Fantasy, identity, politics." In: *Cultural Remix: Theories of Politics and the Popular,* edited by Erica Carter, James Donald and Judith Squires, 63–69. London: Lawrence and Wishart.

Hall, S. 1997. "Old and new identities, Old and new ethnicities." *Culture, Globalization and the World-System: Contemporary Conditions for the Representation of Identity,* edited by Anthony D. King, 41–68. Minneapolis: University of Minnesota Press.

Hall, S. 1997a. "Introduction: Who needs 'identity'?" In: *Questions of Cultural Identity,* edited by Stuart Hall and Paul du Gay, 1–17. London: Sage Publications.

Hakovirta, H. 1993. "The Global refugee problem: A model and its application." *International Political Science Review* 14: 35–57.

Hammar, T. 1989. "State, nation and dual citizenship." In: *Immigration and the Politics of Citizenship in Europe and North America,* edited by Rogers Brubaker, 81–95. London: University Press of America.

Hammar, T. 1990. *Democracy and the Nation State: Aliens, Denizens and Citizens in a World of International Migration.* Aldershot: Avebury.

Hannerz, U. 1974. "Ethnicity and opportunity in urban America." In: *Urban Ethnicity,* edited by Abner Cohen, 37–76. London: Tavistock Publications.

Hannerz, U. 1996. *Transnational Connections.* London: Routledge.

Hannerz, U. 1999. "Epilogue: On some reports from a free space." In: *Globalization and Identity: Dialectics of Flow and Closure,* edited by B. Meyer and P. Geschiere, 325–329. Oxford: Blackwell Publishers.

Hansen, T.B. 1999. *The Saffron Wave.* Princeton: Princeton University Press.

Hargreaves, A. 1999. "Transnational broadcasting audiences: New diasporas for old?" Paper presented to the workshop on Media in Multilingual and Multicultural Settings, Klagenfurt, 11–13 November.

Hargreaves, A. and Mahdjoub. D. 1997. "Satellite television among the ethnic minorities in France." *European Journal of Communication* 12, No. 4: 459–477.

Hartmann, H. 1964. *Essays on Ego Psychology, Selected Problems in Psychoanalytic Theory.* New York: International Universities Press.

Harvey, D. 1989 *The Condition of Postmodernity.* Oxford: Blackwell.

Harvey, D. 1997. "Contested cities." In: *Transforming Cities,* edited by Nick Jewson and Susanne MacGregor, 19–27. London: Routledge.

Hassanpour, A. 1998. "Satellite footprints as national borders: MED-TV and the extraterritoriality of state sovereignty." *Journal of Muslim Minority Affairs* 18, No. 1: 53–72.

Hathaway, J. 1991. *The Law of Refugee Status*. Toronto: Butterworths.

Held, D., McGrew, A., Golblatt, D. and Perraton, J. 1999. *Global Transformations*. Cambridge: Polity Press.

Heitmeyer, W., Schröder, H. and Müller, J. 1997. "Desintegration und islamischer fundamentalismus: Über lebenssituation, alltagserfahrungen und ihre verarbeitungsformen bei türkischen jugendlichen in Deutschland." *Aus Politik und Zeitgeschichte* 7-8: 17–31.

Heitmeyer, W., Schröder, H. and Müller, J. 1997a. *Verlockender Fundamentalismus*. Frankfurt a.M: Suhrkamp.

Hawaii Tribune-Herald. 1998. "Entrepreneur applauds U.S. money move." June 18, pp. 1, 10.

Henkin, L. 1990. *The Age of Rights*. New York: Columbia University Press.

Hertzberg, H. 1997. "Star-spangled banter," *The New Yorker*, July 21, pp. 4–5.

Hirst, P. and Thompson, G. 1996. *Globalization in Question*. Cambridge: Polity.

Hock, D.W. 1994. "Institutions in the age of mindcrafting." Paper presented at the Bionomics Annual conference, San Francisco, CA. October 22.

Hoffmann-Nowotny, H.-J. 1996. "Soziologische aspekte der multikulturalität." In: *Migration–Ethnizität–Konflikt. Systemfragen und Fallstudien*, edited by Klaus Bade, 103–126. Osnabrück: Rasch.

Hollifield, J.F. 1992. *Immigrants, Markets and States: The Political Economy of Postwar Europe*. Cambridge, MA: Harvard University Press.

Holton, J. and Appadurai, A. 1996. "Cities and citizenship." *Public Culture*, 8, No. 2: 187–204.

Hönekopp, E. 1997. "The new labor migration as an instrument of German foreign policy." In: *Migrants, Refugees, and Foreign Policy*, edited by Reiner Münz and Myron Weiner, 165–181. Providence, RI: Berghahn Books.

Hours, B. 2000. *L'idéologie Humanitaire ou le Spectacle de l'Alterité Perdue*. Paris: Broché.

Huntington, S.P. 1996. *The Clash of Civilizations and the Remaking of World Order*. NY: Simon & Schuster.

Ignatieff, M. 1999. "Human Rights: The midlife crisis." *The New York Review of Books* 46, May 20, pp. 58–60.

Ikenberry, G.J. 1996. "The myth of post-Cold War chaos." *Foreign Affairs* 75 (May/June): 79–91.

Internal Displacement Consultation on Refugee and Migratory Movements. 1995. Colombo, 25–27 September.

International Labor Organization. 1991. *Migration News Sheet.* February.

Isbister, J. 1996. *The Immigration Debate. Remaking America.* West Hartford, CN: Kumarian Books.

Isin, E.F. 2000. (ed.) *Democracy, Citizenship and the Global City.* London: Routledge.

Jameson, F. 1991. *Postmodernism, or, the Cultural Logic of Late Capitalism.* Durham, NC: Duke University Press.

Jessop, R. 1999. "Reflections on globalization and its illogics." In: *Globalisation and the Asian Pacific: Contested Territories,* edited by Kris Olds *et al.,* 19–38. London: Routledge.

Joppke, C. 1997. "Asylum and state sovereignty: A comparison of the United States, Germany, and Britain." *Comparative Political Studies* 30. No. 3: 259–298.

Joppke, C. 1998. "Introduction." In: *Challange to the Nation-State: Immigration in Western Europe and the United States,* edited by Christian Joppke, 5–48. Oxford: Oxford University Press.

Journal fur Entwicklungspolitik. Schwerpunkt: Migration. 1995. Special Issue on Migration edited by Christoff Parnreiter. XI, No. 3. Frankfurt: Brandes & Apsel Verlag.

Judah, T. 2000. *Kosovo: War and Revenge.* New Haven, CT: Yale University Press.

Jusdanis, G. 1996. "Culture, culture everywhere: The swell of globalization theory." *Diaspora* 5, No. 1: 141–161.

Juergensmeyer, M. 2000. *Terror in the Mind of God: The Global Rise of Religious Violence.* Berkeley, CA: University of California Press.

Jussawala, F. 1997. "South Asian diaspora writers in Britain: 'Home' versus 'hybridity'." In: *Ideas of Home: Literature of Asian Migration,* edited by Geoffrey Kaine, 17–37. East Lansing, MI: Michigan State University Press.

Jussim, L. 1986. "Self-fulfilling prophesies: A aheoretical and integrative review." *Psychological Review* 93, No. 4: 429–445.

Kapferer, B. 1988. *Legends of People, Myths of State.* Washington D.C.: Smithsonian Institution Press.

Kaplan, R.D. 2000. *The Coming Anarchy: Shattering the Dreams of the Post-Cold War.* NY: Random House.

Karakullukçu, E. 1999. "Çifte vatandaşlığı sırtından vuranlar." *Hürriyet*, February 11 (Avrupa Gazetesi supplement).

Karim, K.H. 1998. *From Ethnic Media to Global Media: Transnational Communication Networks Among Diasporic Communities*. Hull, Québec: International Comparative Research Group, Department of Canadian Heritage.

Kastoryano, R. 1996. *La France, l'Allemagne et Leurs Immigrés: Négocier l'Identité*. Paris: Armand Colin.

Kastoryano, R. 1999. "Les turcs d'Europe: une communauté transnationale." In: *La Turquie et l'Europe: Une Coopération Tumultueuse*, edited by Ahmet Insel, 117–137. Paris: L'Harmattan.

Kelly, J.D. 1999. "Time and the global: Against the homogeneous, empty communities in contemporary social theory." In: *Globalization and Identity: Dialectics of Flow and Closure*, edited by B. Meyer and P. Geschiere, 239–271. Oxford: Blackwell Publishers.

Kelly, R., Friedlander, J. and Colby, A. 1993. *Irangeles: Iranians in Los Angeles*.

Kilic, M. 1994. "Deutsch-türkische Doppelstaatsangehörigkeit?" *StAZ* 3:73–78.

King, A. 1997. "The politics of vision." In: *Understanding Ordinary Landscapes*, edited by Paul Groth and Todd Bressi, 134–144. New Haven: Yale University Press.

Knox, P.L. and Taylor, P.J. 1995. (ed.) *World Cities in a World-System*. Cambridge, UK: Cambridge University Press.

Konrad, G. 1984. *Antipolitics*. NY: Harcourt Brace Jovanovich.

Koselleck, R. 1992. "Volk, nation. Einleitung." In: *Geschichtliche Grundbegriffe. Historisches Lexikon zur Politisch-Sozialen Sprache in Deutschland*, edited by Otto Brunner, Werner Conze and Reinhart Koselleck, 142–149. Stuttgart: Klett-Cotta.

Kosnick, K. 2000. "Building bridges: Media for migrants and the public-service mission in Germany." *European Journal of Cultural Studies* 3, No. 3: 319–342.

Kotkin, J. 1996. "The New Yankee traders." *INC*, March 1996, p. 25.

Krasner, S.D. 1995. "Power politics, institutions and transnational relations." In: *Bringing Transnational Relations Back In: Non-State Actors, Domestic Structures and International Institutions*, edited by Thomas Risse-Kappen, 257–279. Cambridge: Cambridge University Press.

Krasner, S.D. 1999. *Sovereignty: Organized Hypocracy*. Princeton, NJ: Princeton University Press.

Kratochwil, K.H. 1995. "Movilidad transfronteriza de personas y procesos de integracion regional en America Latina." *Revista de la OIM sobre Migraciones en America Latina* 13, No. 2: 3–12.

Kussbach, E. 1992. "European challenge: East-West migration." *International Migration Review* 26: 646–667.

Kwong, P. 1997. *Forbidden Workers: Illegal Chinese Immigrants and American Labor.* NY: The New Press.

Kyle, D. 1998. "Transparent economies and invisible workers: Human smuggling under Global economic liberalism. Europäisches Hochschulinstitut" Conference Paper MIG/60, Florenz.

Kymlicka, W. 1995. *Multicultural Citizenship: A Liberal Theory of Minority Rights.* Oxford: Claredon Press.

Lasch, C. 1995. *The Revolt of the Elites and the Betrayal of Democracy.* NY: W.W. Norton & Co.

Lattas, A. 1997. "Aborigines and contemporary Australian nationalism: Primordiality and the cultural politics of otherness." In: *Race Matters*, edited by G. Cowlishaw and B. Morris. Canberra: Aboriginal Studies Press.

Lederer, H.W. 1999. "Zur typologie und statistischen erfassung von illegaler zuwanderung." In: *Migration und Illegalität*, edited by Eberhard Eichenhofer. Osnabrück: Rasch.

Lee, S. 1993. "Racial classifications in the U.S. census 1890–1990." *Racial and Ethnic Studies* 17, No. 2: 75–94.

Leggewie, C. 1990. *Multi Kulti – Spielregeln für die Vielvölkerrepublik.* Berlin: Rotbuch-Verlag.

Le Monde. 2000. "Le Débat Fischer-Chevenement." June 21, pp. 1, 15–17.

Lennox, M. 1993. "Refugees, racism, and reparations: A critique of the United States' Haitian immigration policy." *Stanford Law Review* 45: 687–724.

Leon, R. and Kratochwil, K.H. 1993. "Integracion, migraciones y desarrollo sostenido en el Grupo Andino." *Revista de la OIM sobre Migraciones en America Latina* 11, No. 1: 5–28.

Lerner, D. 1958. *The Passing of Traditional Society: Modernizing the Middle East.* NY: The Free Press.

Levitt, P. 1998a. "Forms of transnational community and their implications for immigrant incorporation: Preliminary findings." Europäisches Hochschulinstitut, Conference Paper MIG/ 35, Florenz.

Levitt, P. 1998b. "Local level global religion: The case of U.S.-Dominican Migration." *Journal for the Scientific Study of Relegion* 37, No. 1: 74–89.

Levitt, P. 2000. "They prayed in Brazil and it rained in Boston: Dominican and Brazilian transnational religious life." Paper presented to the GAFOSS Symposium 23–26 March, Atlanta.

Lindner, R. 1999. Drei Arten "Stadtkultur" zu verstehen. *IFK-news* (1/99): 27–28.

Lintner, B. 1999. "The third wave: A new generation of Chinese immigrants fans across the globe." *Far Eastern Economic Review*, June 24, pp. 28–29.

Little, C. 1993. "United States Haitian Policy: A history of discrimination." New York Law School Journal of Human Rights 10: 269–323.

Liu, E. 1999. "China-bashing, Chinese-American lynchings, and the climate of neo-McCarthyism." Internet Communication to the ISSCO Community, March 18, 4 pp.

Liu, J.H. and Rosenau, J.N. 1999. "The psychology of fragmegration: On the uses of a simultaneity of consciousness in the 'New World Order'." Paper presented at the Third Conference of the Asian Association of Social Psychology. Taipei, Taiwan: August 4–7.

Lowenthal, D. 1995. *Possessed By The Past: The Heritage Crusade and the Spoils of History*. NY: Free Press.

Los Angeles Times. 1999. "Asian American employees fear repercussions of spy inquiries." June 12.

Lucassen, J. and Lucassen, L. 1997a. *Migration, Migration History, History: Old Paradigms and New Perspectives*. Bern: Lang.

Lucassen, J. and Lucassen, L. 1997b. "Migration, migration history, history: Old paradigms and new perspectives." In: *Migration, Migration History, History. Old Paradigms and New Perspectives*, edited by Jan and Leo Lucassen, 9–38. Frankfurt a.M:Suhrkamp.

Luhmann, N. 1997. *Die Gesellschaft der Gesellschaft*. Frankfurt a.M: Suhrkamp.

Luke, T.W. and Tuathail, G.Ó. 1998. "Global flowmations, local fundamentalism, and fast geopolitics: 'America' in an accelerating World order." In: *An Unruly World? Globalization, Governance and Geography*, edited by A. Herod, G.Ó. Tuathail, and S.M. Roberts. London and New York: Routledge.

Maalouf, A. 1998. *Les Identités Meurtrières*. Paris: Grasset.

Malanczuk, P. 1997. (ed.) *Akehurst's Modern Introduction to International Law*. New York: Routledge, 7th rev. ed.

Mandel, R. 1988. "'We called for manpower, but people came instead': The foreigner problem and Turkish guestworkers in West Germany." Unpublished Ph.D dissertation, University of Chicago, Department of Anthropology.

Mandelstam, O. 1977 [1913]. "About an interlocutor." In: *Osip Mandelstam: Selected* Essays, 58–64. Austin: University of Texas Press.

Manfrass, K. 1992. "Europe: South-North or East-West migration?" *International Migration Review* 26: 388–400.

Mannitz, S. 1999. "Students' negotiations of cultural difference: Discursive assimilation and identity management." In: *Civil Enculturation. Nation-State, School and Ethnic Difference in Four European Countries*, edited by Schiffauer, Werner, Gerd Baumann, Riva Kastoryano, and Steven Vertovec, 295–359. Frankfurt/Oder Report for the Volkswagen Stiftung.

Marmora, L. 1994. "Desarrollo sostenido y politicas migratorias: su tratamiento en los espacios latinoamericanos de integracion." *Revista de la OIM sobre Migraciones en America Latina* 12, No. 1/3: 5–50.

Markoff, J. 1999. "Tiniest circuits hold prospect of explosive computer speeds." *New York Times*, July 16, p. A1.

Martin, P.L. 1993. *Trade and Migration: NAFTA and Agriculture*. Washington D.C.: Institute for International Economics.

Massey, D.S., Arango, J., Hugo, G., Kouaouci, A., Pellegrino, A. and Taylor, J.E. 1993. "Theories of international migration: A review and appraisal." *Population and Development Review* 19, No. 3: 431–466.

Matin, A. 1999/1378. *Tarikh-I-junbesh-I-daneshjuyan-I-irani dar kharej az keshvar 1332–1357*. Tehran: Nashr-e-Shirazeh.

Mauss, M. 1969. *Oeuvres*. III. Paris: Minuit

McNeil, Jr. D. 2000. "Europeans move against Austrians on Nativist Party." *New York Times*, February 1, p. A1.

Meijers, H., Bolten, J.J. and Cruz, A. 1992. *Schengen: Internationalization of Central Chapters of the Law on Aliens, Refugees, Privacy, Security and the Police*. 2nd edition. Leiden: Stichting NJCM-Boekerij.

Mertus, J.A. 1999. *Kosovo: How Myths and Truths Started a War*. Berkeley, CA: University of California Press.

Meyer, B. and Geschiere, G. 1999. "Introduction." In: *Globalization and Identity: Dialectics of Flow and Closure*, edited by B. Meyer and P. Geschiere, 2–11. Oxford: Blackwell Publishers.

Miller, D. and Turnbull, W. 1986. "Expectancies and interpersonal processes." *Annual Review of Psychology* 37: 233–256.

Miller, J.J. 1998. "Loyalty duel: Dual citizenship means one loyalty too many." *National Review* 50, No. 9: 32–33.

Mitchell, C. 1989. "International migration, international relations and foreign policy." *International Migration Review* 23, No. 3.

Mitchell, K. 1997. "Different diasporas and the hype of hybridity." *Environment and Planning D: Society and Space* 15, No. 5: 533–553.

Mittelman, J. 1999. (ed.) *Globalization: Critical Reflections. International Political Economy Yearbook* Vol. 9. Boulder, CO: Lynne Rienner Publishers.

Moore, J. 1998 (ed.) *Hard Choices: Moral Dilemmas in Humanitarian Intervention*. Lanham, MD: Rowan & Littlefield.

Moravec, H. 1999. *Robot*. Oxford: Oxford University Press.

Morawska, E. 1998. "Structuring migration in a historical perspective: The case of travelling East Europeans." Europäisches Hochschulinstitut, Working Papers EUF No. 98/3, Florenz.

Mozaffari, M. 1998. *Mega Civilization: Global Capital and New Standard of Civilization*. Aarhus, Denmark: Aarhus University Press.

Müller-Mahn, D. 2000. "Ein ägyptisches Dorf in Paris. Eine empirische Studie zur Süd-Nord-Migration am Beispiel ägyptischer 'Sans-papiers' in Frankreich." IMIS-Beiträge 2000, No. 15: 79–110.

Murphy, S.D. 1996. *Humanitarian Intervention: The United Nations in an Evolving World Order*. Philadelphia, PA: University of Pennsylvania Press.

Naficy, H. 1993. *The Making of Exile Cultures: Iranian Television in Los Angeles*. Minneapolis: University of Minnesota Press.

Naipaul, V.S. 1987. *The Enigma of Arrival*. New York: Knopf.

Nassehi, A. 1997. "Das stahlharte Gehäuse der Zugehörigkeit. Unschärfen im Diskurs um die, multikulturelle Gesellschaft." In: *Nation, Ethnie, Minderheit. Beiträge zur Aktualität ethnischer Konflikte*, edited by Arnim Nassehi, 177–208. Köln, Weimar, Wien: Böhlau.

National Geographic Society. 1999. *Millennium in Maps:* Cultures. Washington, D.C. (June).

Needham, R. 1972. *Belief, Language, and Experience*. Oxford: Basil Blackwell.

Neisser, U. 1998. *The Rising Curve: Long-Term Gains in IQ and Related Measures*. Washington, D.C. American Psychological Association.

Newland, K. 2000. "The decade in review." *World Refugee Survey 1999*. Washington, D.C.: U.S. Committee for Refugees, pp. 14–21.

Neumann, J. 2000. "Der deutsche pass hilft nicht." *Die Tageszeitung*, September 28, p. 19.

Noirel, G. 1996. *The French Melting Pot: Immigration Citizenship, and National Identity*. Minneapolis: University of Minnesota Press.

Nuckolls, C.W. 1998. *Culture: A Problem that Cannot be Solved*. Madison: The University of Wisconsin Press.

Nussbaum, M. *et al.* 1997. *For Love of Country*. Boston, MA: Beacon Press.

Offe, K. 1999. "How can we trust our fellow citizens?" In: *Democracy and Trust*, edited by Mark Warren, 42–88. Cambridge: Cambridge University Press.

Olds, K., Dicken, P. and Kelly, P.F. 1999. (ed.) *Globalisation and the Asian Pacific: Contested Territories*. London: Routledge.

Olsen, E. 1985. "Muslim identity and secularism in contemporary Turkey: 'The headscarf dispute'." *Anthropological Quarterly* 58, No. 4: 161–169.

Öncü, A. 1994. "Packaging Islam: Cultural politics on the landscape of Turkish commercial television." *New Perspectives on Turkey* 10: 13–36.

Öncü, A. 2000. "The banal and the subversive: Politics of language on Turkish television." *European Journal of Cultural Studies* 3, No. 3: 296–318.

Ong, A. 1999. *Flexible Citizenship: The Cultural Logics of Transnationality*. Durham, NC: Duke University Press.

Ong A. and Nonini, D. 1997. (ed.) *Ungrounded Empires: The Cultural Politics of Modern Chinese Nationalism*. New York: Routledge.

Ong, A. and Nonini, D. 1997a. "Toward a cultural politics of diaspora and transnationalism." In: *Ungrounded Empires: The Cultural Politics of Modern Chinese Nationalism*, edited by Ong Aihwa and Donald Nonini, 3–33. New York: Routledge.

Opitz, P.J. 1997. *Der Globale Marsch: Flucht und Migration als Weltproblem*. München: Beck.

Pahlavan, T. 1992. *On New Regional Structures* (in Persian). Tehran: Goftego.

Pahlavan, T. 1999. *Farhang Shenasi*. Tehran: Ghotneh Publishing House.

Pahlavan, T. 1999a. *Afghanistan: The End of Mugaheddin and the Rise of Taliban*. Tehran.

Pan, L. 1990. *Sons of the Yellow Emperor*. New York: Little, Brown.

Panitch, L. 1996. "Rethinking the role of the state in an era of globalization." In: *Globalization: Critical Reflections. International Political Economy Yearbook*, edited by James H. Mittelman, 83–113. Boulder, CO: Lynne Rienner Publishers.

Peterson, S. 2000. *Me Against My Brother: At War in Somalia, Sudan, and Rwanda*. New York: Routledge.

Petras, E. 1980. "The role of national boundaries in a cross-national labour market." *International Journal of Urban and Regional Research* 4: 157–195.

Pieterse, J.N. 1997. "Globalization and emancipation: From local empowerment to global reform." *New Political Economy* 2 (March): 79–92.

Piore, M.J. 1986. "The shifting grounds for immigration." *Annals of the American Academy of Political and Social Science* 485: 23–33.

Portes, A. 1979. "Illegal immigration and the international system." *Social Problems* 26: 425–438.

Portes, A. 1995. *The Economic Sociology of Immigration: Essays on Networks, Ethnicity and Entrepreneurship.* New York: Russel Sage Foundation.

Portes, A. 1996. *A New Second Generation.* Beverly Hills, CA: Russel Sage Foundation.

Portes, A. and Böröcz, J. 1989. "Contemporary immigration: Theoretical perspectives on its determinants and modes of incorporation." *International Migration Review* 23: 606–629.

Portes, A., Guernizo, L.E. and Landolt, P. 1999. "Introduction." Special Issue: Transnational Communities. *Ethnic and Racial Studies* 22, No. 2: 217–237.

Portes, A. and Rumbault, R. 1996. *Immigrant America: A Portrait.* University of California Press. 2nd ed.

Portes, A. and Walton, J. 1981. *Labor Class and the International System.* New York: Academic Press.

Portes, A. and Zhou, M. 1992. "Gaining the upper hand: Economic mobility among immigrant and domestic minorities." *Ethnic and Racial Studies* 15: 491–522.

Poulton, H. 1999. "The struggle for hegemony in Turkey: Turkish nationalism as a contemporary force." *Journal of Southern Europe and the Balkans* 1, No. 1: 15–31.

Powell, W. and DiMaggio, P. 1991. (ed.) *The New Institutionalism in Organizational Analysis.* Chicago: University of Chicago Press.

Pries, L. 1996. "Internationale migration und die emergenz transnationaler sozialer räume." In: *Differenz und Integration: Die Zukunft Moderner Gesellschaften*, edited by Karl-Siegbert Rehberg, 313–318. 28. Kongreß der Deutschen Gesellschaft für Soziologie, Kongreßband II, Opladen.

Pries, L. 1997. (ed.) *Transnationale Migration.* Soziale Welt. Sonderband 12. Baden-Baden: Nomos.

Pries, L. 1998. "Transnationale soziale räume." In: Beck 55–86.

Pries, L. 2000. "Transnationalisierung der migrationsforschung und entnationalisierung der migrationspolitik: Das entstehen transnationaler sozialräume durch arbeitswanderung am beispiel Mexiko–USA." In: *IMIS-Beiträge, Themenheft "Transnationalismus und Kulturvergleich"*, edited by Michael Bommes, 55–77. Osnabrück: Rasch.

Prothero, R.M. 1990. "Labor recruiting organizations in the developing world." *International Migration Review* 24: 221–228.

Radtke, F.-O. 1990. "Multikulti: Das gesellschaftsdesign der 90er jahre?" *Informationsdienst zur Ausländerarbeit* 4, No. 1: 27–34.

Rafael, V. 1993. *Contracting Colonialism: Translation and Christian Conversion in Tagalog Society under Early Spanish Rule*. Durham: Duke University Press.

Rancière, J. 1995. *On the Shores of Politics*. London: Verso.

Rata, E.M. 2000. "Global capitalism and the revival of ethnic traditionalism in New Zealand: The emergence of tribal-capitalism." Ph.D. thesis University of Auckland.

Reding, A. 1995. *Democracy and Human Rights in Mexico*. New York: World Policy Institute, World Policy Papers.

Reich, R. 1991. *The Work of Nations: Preparing Ourselves for 21st Century Capitalism*. New York: Alfred A. Knopf.

Remarque, E.M. 1999. *All Quiet on the Western Front* (in German). Verlag: Kiepenhever & Whitsch. G. Auflage.

Reyna, S. 2002. "Imagining monsters: A structural history of warfare in Chad." In: *Globalization, Transnationalism and Violence*, edited by Jonathan Friedman. Walnut Creek: Altamira Press (Rowman and Littlefield) (in press).

Riches, D. 1986. "The phenomenon of violence." In: *The Anthropology of Violence*, edited by David Riches, 1–27. Oxford: Basil Blackwell.

Rigoni, I. 1997. "Les migrants de Turquie: Réseaux ou diaspora?" *L'Homme et la Société* 123–4: 39–57.

Ring, H. 1998. "Einwanderungspolitik im schwedischen Wohlfahrtsstaat." In: Bommes and Halfmann 1998, 239–249.

Ringmar, E. 1998. "Nationalism: The idiocy of intimacy." *British Journal of Sociology* 49, No. 4: 534–549.

Ritzer, G. 1996. *The McDonaldization of Society*. Pine Forge Press.

Robertson, R. 1990. "Mapping the global condition: Globalization as the central concept." In: *Global Culture: Nationalism, Globalization, and Modernity*, edited by Mike Featherstone, 15–30. London: Sage Publications.

Robertson, R. 1997. "Social theory, cultural relativity and the problem of globality." In: *Culture, Globalization and the World-System: Contemporary Conditions for the Representation of Identity*, edited by Anthony D. King, 69–90. Minneapolis: University of Minnesota Press.

Robins, K. 1996. "Interrupting identities: Turkey/Europe." In: *Questions of Cultural Identity*, edited by Stuart Hall and Paul du Gay, 61–86. London: Sage.

Robins, K. 1999. "Europe." In: *Introducing Human Geographies*, edited by Paul Cloke, Philip Crang and Mark Hudson, 268–276. London: Arnold.

Robins, K. and Aksoy, A. 1997. "Peripheral vision: Cultural industries and cultural identities in Turkey." *Environment and Planning A* 29, No. 1: 1937–1952.

Rogers, R. 1992. "The politics of migration in the contemporary world." *International Migration* 30 (special issue): 33–52.

Rosecrance, R. 1999. The Rise of the Virtual State. NY: Basic Books.

Rosen, F. and McFadyen, D. 1995. (eds) *Free Trade and Economic Restructuring in Latin America.* (A NACLA Reader). New York: Monthly Review Press.

Rosenau, J.N. 1983. "'Fragmegrative' challenges to national security." In: *Understanding U.S. Strategy: A Reader*, edited by Terry Heyns. Washington, D.C.: National Defense University: 65–82.

Rosenau, J.N. 1990. Turbulence in World Politics: A Theory of Change and Continuity. Princeton: Princeton University Press, 1990.

Rosenau, J.N. 1992. "Governance, order, and change in world politics." In: *Governance without Government: Order and Change in World Politics*, edited by James N. Rosenau and Ernst-Otto Czempiel, 1–29. Cambridge: Cambridge University Press.

Rosenau, J.N. 1994a. "New dimensions of security: The interaction of globalizing and localizing dynamics." *Security Dialogue* 25 (September): 255–282.

Rosenau, J.N. 1994b. "Globalisation or glocalisation." *Journal of International Communication* 1, No. 1: 33–52.

Rosenau, J.N. 1995. "Glocalization: Time-space and homogeneity-heterogeneity." In: *Global Modernities*, edited by Mike Featherstone, Scott Lash, and Roland Robertson, 25–44. Thousand Oaks, CA: Sage Publications.

Rosenau, J.N. 1997. *Along the Domestic-Foreign Frontier: Exploring Governance in a Turbulent World*. Cambridge: Cambridge University Press.

Rosenau, J.N. 1999. "In search of institutional contexts." Paper presented at the Conference on International Institutions: Global Processes-Domestic Consequences, Duke University, Durham, North Carolina, April 9–11.

Rosenau, J.N. Forthcoming. *Distant Proximities: Dynamics Beyond Globalization*. Princeton: Princeton University Press.

Rosenau, J.N. and Fagen, W.M. 1997. "Increasingly skillful citizens: A new dynamism in world politics?" *International Studies Quarterly* 41 (December): 655–86.

Rosenthal, R. and Jacobson, L. 1968. *Pygmalion in the Classroom.* New York: Holt, Rinehart & Winston.

Rumbault, R. 1991. "Passages to America: Perspectives on the new immigration." In: *America at Century's End*, edited by Alan Wolfe, 208-244. Berkely: University of California Press.

Safran, W. 1991. "Diasporas in modern societies: Myths of homeland and return." *Diaspora* 1, No. 1: 83–99.

Şahin, H. and Aksoy, A. 1993. "Global media and cultural identity in Turkey." *Journal of Communication* 43, No. 2: 31–41.

Sahlins, M. 1999. "Two or three things that I know about culture." *Journal of the Royal Anthropological Institute* 5, No. 3: 399–422.

Said, E. 1979. *The Question of Palestine.* New York: Times Books.

Said, E. 1993. *Culture and Imperialism.* New York: Knopf.

Said, E. *The Politics of Dispossession: The Struggle for Palestinian Self-Determination 1969-1994.* New York: Pantheon.

Said, E. 2000. *The End of the Peace Process: Oslo and After.* New York: Pantheon.

Salacuse, J. 1991. *Making Global Deals: Negotiating in the International Marketplace.* Boston: Houghton Mifflin.

Salt, J. 1987. "Contemporary trends in international migration study." *International Migration* 25: 241–250.

Salt, J. 1989. "A comparative overview of international trends and types, 1950–80." *International Migration Review* 23: 431–456.

Santel, B. 1995. *Migration in und nach Europa: Erfahrungen, Strukturen, Politik.* Opladen: Leske+Budrich.

Santel, B. and Hollifield, J.F. 1998. "Erfolgreiche integrationsmodelle? Zur wirtschaftlichen situation von einwanderern in Deutschland und den USA." *Migration in Nationalen Wohlfahrtsstaaten. Theoretische und Vergleichende Untersuchungen*, edited by Michael Bommes and Jost Halfmann, 123–145. Osnabrück: Rasch.

Santel, B. and Hunger, U. 1997. "Gespaltener sozialstaat, gespaltener arbeitsmarkt. Die etablierung postwohlfahrtsstaatlicher einwanderungspolitiken in Deutschland und den Vereinigten Staaten." *Soziale Welt* 48, No. 4: 379–396.

Santos, Boaventura de Sousa. 1995. *Toward a New Common Sense: Law, Science, and Politics in the Paradigmatic Transition.* New York: Routledge.

Sassen, S. 1996. *Losing Control? Sovereignty in an Age of Globalisation.* The 1995 Columbia University Leonard Hastings Schoff Memorial Lectures. New York: Columbia University Press.

Sassen, S. 1997. Territory and territoriality in the global economy." Manuscript.

Sassen, S. 1988. *The Mobility of Labor and Capital.* Cambridge: Cambridge University Press.

Sassen, S. 1998a. *Globalization and its Discontents.* New York: New Press.

Sassen, S. 1998b. "The *de facto* transnationalization of immigration policy." In: *Challange to the Nation-State*, edited by Christian Joppke, 49–85. Oxford: Oxford University Press.

Sassen, S. 1999. *Guests and Aliens.* New York: New Press.

Sassen, S. 1999a. "Embedding the global in the national: Implications for the role of the state." In: *States and Sovereignty in the Global Economy*, edited by David A. Smith, Dorothy J. Solinger, and Steven Topik, 158–171. London: Routledge.

Sassen, S. 1999b. "Beyond sovereignty: *De-facto* transnationalism in immigration policy." *European Journal of Migration and Law* 1, No 1: 177–198.

Sassen, S. 2001. *The Global City: New York, London, Tokyo.* Princeton, NJ: Princeton University Press.

Sassen, S. 2002. "Towards post-national and denationalized citizenship." In: *Handbook of Citizenship Studies*, edited by E. Isin and B. Turner. London: Sage.

Sayad, A. 1999. "Immigration et 'pensée d'état'." *Annales de la Recherche en Sciences Sociales* 129: 5–14.

Schiffauer, W. 1997. "Zur logik von kulturellen strömungen in großstädten." In: *Fremde in der Stadt*, edited by Werner Schiffauer, 92–128. Frankfurt/Main: Suhrkamp Verlag.

Schiffauer, W. 1997a. "Das ideal der segregation. Annäherungen an die urbane kultur der türkischen großstadt." In: *Fremde in der Stadt*, edited by Werner Schiffauer, 128–144. Frankfurt/Main: Suhrkamp Verlag.

Schiffauer, W. 1999. *Islamism in the Diaspora: The Fascination of Political Islam among Second Generation German Turks.* Transnational Communities Program. Oxford.

Schiffauer, W. 2000. *Die Gottesmännerä: Türkische Islamisten in Deutschland. Eine Studie zur Herstellung Religiöser Evidenz.* Frankfurt am Main: Suhrkamp.

Schiffauer, W., Baumann, G., Kastoryano, R. and Vertovec, S. 1999. *Civil Enculturation. Nation-State, School and Ethnic Difference in Four European Countries.* Frankfurt/Oder Report for the Volkswagen Stiftung.

Schlesinger, A.M., Jr. 1992. *The Disuniting of America: Reflections on a Multicultural Society.* New York. W. W. Norton & Co.

Schlesinger, P. 1994. "Europe's contradictory communicative space." *Daedalus* 123, No. 2: 25–52.

Schmidt-Hornstein, C. 1995. *Das Dilemma der Einbürgerung: Porträts türkischer Akademiker*. Opladen: Leske+Budrich.

Schmidt-Hornstein, C. Forthcoming. *Identität und Alterität: Eine Studie zu Kulturellen Grenzgängern*. Dissertation, Frankfurt/Main.

Shevchuk, Y.I. 1996. "Dual citizenship in old and new states." *Archives Européennes de Sociologie* 37, No. 1: 47–76.

Shokat, H. 1999/1358. *Confederacion jahani mohaselin va daneshjuyan irani (ettadieh melli)*. Tehran: Entesharat-e Ataii.

Sikkink, K. 1993. "Human rights, principled issue-networks, and sovereignty in Latin America." *International Organization* 47, No. 3: 411–41.

Sinclair, J., Jacka, E. and Cunningham, S. 1996. (ed.) *New Patterns in Global Television: Peripheral Vision*. Oxford: Oxford University Press.

Sklair, L. 1995. *Sociology of the Global System*. Baltimore: Johns Hopkins University Press.

Sloterdijk, P. 1998. "Der starke grund, zusammen zu sein." *Die Zeit*, January 2, pp. 9–12.

Smith, D.A., Solinger, D.J. and Topik, S.C. 1999. (ed.) *States and Sovereignty in the Global Economy*. London: Routledge.

Smith, M.P. 1999. "New approaches to migration and transnationalism: Locating transnational practices." Keynote address to the Conference on New Approaches to Migration: Transnational Communities and the Transformation of Home. University of Sussex, September 21–2.

Smith, M.P. and Guarnizo, L.E. 1998. (ed.) *Transnationalism from Below*. New Brunswick: Transaction Publishers.

Smith, R. 1997. "Reflections on migration, the state and the construction, durability and newness of transnational life." In: *Transnationale Migration*, edited by Ludger Pries, 197–217. Soziale Welt. Sonderband 12. Baden-Baden: Nomos.

Social Justice. 1993. "Global crisis, local struggles." Special Issue, *Social Justice* 20, Nos 3–4.

Sohn, L. and Buergenthal, T. 1992. (ed.) *The Movement of Persons Across Borders*. Washington, D.C.: The American Society of International Law.

Soja, E. 1996. *Thirdspace: Journeys to Los Angeles and Other Real- and Imagined Places*. Oxford and Boston: Blackwell Publishers.

Soros, G. 1997. "The capitalist threat." *The Atlantic Monthly*, 279, No. 2: 45–58.

Soysal, Y.N. 1994. *Limits of Citizenship: Migrants and Postnational Membership in Europe*. Chicago: University of Chicago Press.

Soysal, Y.N. 1997. "Changing parameters of citizenship and claims-making: Organized Islam in European public spheres." *Theory and Society* 26: 509–527.

Spindler, A.M. 1998. "Tracing the look of alienation" *New York Times*, March 24, p. A25.

Spiro, P.J. 1997. "Dual nationality and the meaning of citizenship." *Emory Law Journal* 46, No. 4: 1412–1485.

Spivak, G.C. 1990. *The Post-Colonial Critic: Interviews, Strategies, Dialogues*. London: Routledge.

Spruyt, H. 1994. *The Sovereign State and its Competitors: An Analysis of Systems Change*. Princeton: Princeton University Press.

Stannard, D.E. 1989. *Before the Horror: The Population of Hawaii on the Eve of Western Contact*. Honolulu: Social Science Research Institute, Univ. of Hawai'i.

Stannard, D.E. 1992. *American Holocaust: The Conquest of the New World*. New York: Oxford University Press.

Stein, E. 1993. "Las dinamicas migratorias en el Istmo Centroamericano en al perspectiva de la integracion y el imperativo de la sostenibilidad." *Revista de la OIM sobre Migraciones en America Latina* 11, No. 2: 5–51.

Stevenson, N. 1998. "Globalization, national cultures and cultural citizenship." *The Sociological Quarterly* 38, No. 1: 41–66.

Stryker, S. 1992. "Identity theory." In: *Encyclopedia of Sociology*, edited by E.F. Borgatta and M.L. Borgatta, 871–876. New York: Macmillan.

Sub-Commandante Marcos. 1999. "Why we are fighting: The Fourth World War has begun" *Le Monde Diplomatique*, August–September (Internet version, 5pp).

Swaan, A. de. 1988. *In Care of the State*. Cambridge: Polity Press.

Tai, S.H.C. and Wong, Y.H. 1998. "Advertising decision making in Asia: 'Glocal' versus 'Regcal' approach," *Journal of Managerial Issues* 10 (Fall): 318–339.

Tapia, S. de. 1994. "L'émigration turque: circulation migratoire et diaspora." *L'Espace Géographique* 23, No. 1: 19–28.

Taylor, C. 1993. *Multikulturalismus und die Politik der Anerkennung*. Frankfurt: Fischer.

Tharoor, S. 1999. "The future of civil conflict." *World Policy Journal* XVI (Spring):1–11.

Taylor, C. and Gutman, A. 1994. (ed.) Multiculturalism: Examining the politics of recognition. Princeton: Princeton University Press.

Tehranian, K.K. 1998. "Global communication and pluralization of identities." *Futures* 30:2/3. March–April, 211–218.

Tehranian, K.K. 2000. "Consuming identities: Pancapitalism and postmodern formations." *PROSPECTS: An Annual of American Cultural Studies* 24: 33–47.

Tehranian, M. 1992. "Communication and theories of social change: A communitarian perspective." *Asian Journal of Communication* 2, No. 1: 1–30.

Tehranian, M. 1999a. *Global Communication and World Politics: Domination, Development, and Discourse.* Boulder, CO: Lynne Rienner Publishers.

Tehranian, M. 1999b. *Democratizing Global Governance: Problems, Prospects, Proposals.* Honolulu: Toda Institute for Global Peace and Policy Research.

Tertilt, H. 1996. *Turkish Power Boys: Ethnographie einer Jugendbande.* Frankfurt (Main): Suhrkamp.

Thranhardt, D. 1992. (ed.) *Europe: A New Immigration Continent.* Hamburg: Lit Verlag.

Tilly, C. 1975. (ed.) *The Formation of National States in Western Europe.* Princeton, NJ: Princeton University Press.

Todorov, T. 1997. "The coexistence of cultures." *Oxford Literary Review* 19, No. 1–2: 3–17.

Tölölyan, K. 1991. "The nation state and its others." *Diaspora* 1, No. 1: 3–7.

Tölölyan, K. 1996. "Rethinking diaspora(s): Stateless power in the transnational moment." *Diaspora* 5. No. 1: 3–36.

Torales, P. 1993. *Migracion e Integracion en el Cono Sur. La Experiencia del Mercosur.* Buenos Aires: OIM.

Treibel, A. 1990. *Migration in Modernen Gesellschaften.* Weinheim/München: Juventa.

Triandis, H.C. 1995. *Individualism and Collectivism.* Boulder: Westview Press.

Trubek, D., Dezalay, Y., Buchanan, R. and Davis, J. 1993. "Global restructuring and the law: The internationalization of legal fields and the creation of transnational arenas." *Case Western Reserve Law Review* 44: 407–498.

Tucker, R.W., Keely, C.B. and Wrigley, L. 1990. (ed.) *Immigration and U.S. Foreign Policy.* Boulder, CO: Westview Press.

Turner, J.C., Hogg, M.A., Oakes, P.J., Reicher, S.D. and Wetherell, M.S. 1987. *Rediscovering the Social Group: A Self-Categorization Theory.* New York: Basil Blackwell.

Turner, V. 1967. *The Forest of Symbols*. Ithaca: Cornell University Press.

Ugrešic, D. 1998. *The Culture of Lies: Antipolitical Essays*. London: Phoenix House.

Uğur, A. 1996. "Media, identity and the search for a cultural synthesis." *Private View* 1, No. 1: 56–62.

United Nations. 1996. *World Population Monitoring 1993.With a Special Report on Refugees*. New York: UN Department for Economic and Social Information and Policy Analysis. Population Division.

United Nations High Commissioner for Refugees (UNHCR). 1995. *The State of the World's Refugees*. Oxford: Oxford University Press.

UNHCR, CASAWAME. 1997. *Amman 12–13 March* Geneva: UNHCR (April).

UNIICR, CASAWAME. 1998. *Ashagabat 3–4 March*. Geneva: UNHCR (May).

UNHCR, CASAWANE. 1998a. *Sub-regional Consultation on Afghan Refugees in South West Asia, Tehran, 16–17 June*. Geneva: UNHCR.

UNHCR Regional Bureau for Europe. 1996. *The CIS Conference on Refugees and Migrants* 2, No. 1 (January).

U.S. Committee for Refugees. 1999. *World Refugee Survey 1999*. Washington, D.C., U.S. Committee for Refugees.

van Binsbergen, W. 1999. "Globalization and virtuality: Analytic problems posed by the contemporary transformation of African societies." In: *Globalization and Identity: Dialectics of Flow and Closure*, edited by B. Meyer and P. Geschiere, 273–303. Oxford: Blackwell Publishers.

van der Veer, P. 1995. (ed.) *Nation and Migration*. Philadelphia, University of Pennsylvania Press.

van der Veer, P. 1995a. *Modern Orientalism* (in Dutch). Amsterdam, Meulenhoff.

van der Veer, P. 1997. "The Enigma of arrival: Hybridity and authenticity in the global space." In: *Debating Cultural Hybridity*, edited by Pnina Werbner and Tariq Modood, 90–105. London: Zed Books.

van der Veer, P. 1999. "Political religion in the twenty-first century." In: *International Order and the Future of World Politics*, edited by T.V. Paul and John Hall, 311–328. Cambridge, Cambridge University Press.

van der Veer, P. 2001. *Imperial Encounters: Religion and Modernity in India and Britain*. Princeton: Princeton University Press.

van der Veer, P. and Lehmann, H. 1999. (ed.) *Nation and Religion: Perpectives on Europe and Asia*. Princeton: Princeton University Press.

van Dijk, T.A. 1987. "Elite discourse and racism." In: *Approaches to Discourse, Poetics and Psychiatry*, edited by Zavala, Dijk, and Diaz-Diocaretz, 81–122. Amsterdam: Benjamins Publishing Company.

Verhulst, S. 1999. "Diasporic and transnational communication: Technologies, policies and regulation." *Javnost/The Public* 6, No. 1: 29–36.

Verschave, F. 2000. *Noire Silence*. Paris: Les Arènes.

Vertovec, S. 1999. "Conceiving and researching transnationalism." *Ethnic and Racial Studies* 22, No. 2: 447–462.

Vertovec, S. 2000. "Fostering Cosmopolitanisms: A conceptual survey and a media experiment in Berlin." Oxford: ESRC Transnational Communities Programme Working Paper WPTC-2K-06 [www.transcomm.ox.ac.uk].

Viviano, F. 1993. "Separatist party on rise in Italy." *San Francisco Chronicle*, March 3, p. 1.

Viviant, A. 1999. "La Grande-Messe télévisuelle." *La Quinzaine Littéraire* 767: 21.

Walker, R.B.J. 1993. *Inside/Outside: International Relations as Political Theory*. Cambridge: Cambridge University Press.

Wallerstein, I. 1974. *The Modern World-System I: Capitalist Agriculture and the Origins of the European World-Economy in the Sixteenth Century*. New York: Academic Press.

Wallerstein, T. 1988. *The Modern World-System III*. New York: Academic Press.

Wallerstein, T. 1991. "Does India exist?" In: *Unthinking Social Science: The Limits of Nineteenth-Century* Paradigms, 130–134. Cambridge: Polity Press.

Wallman, S. 1986. "Ethnicity and boundary processes." In: *Theories of Race and Ethnic Relations*, edited by J. Rex and D. Mason. Cambridge: Cambridge University Press.

Walzer, M. 1981. "The distribution of membership." In: *Boundaries: National Autonomy and its Limits*, edited by Peter Brown and Henry Shue, 1–35. Totowa, NJ: Rowman and Littlefield.

Walzer, M. 1994. *Thick and Thin: Moral Argument at Home and Abroad*. Notre Dame, IN: Notre Dame University Press.

Wang, L. 1991. "Roots and changing identity of the Chinese in the U.S." *Daedalus* 120, No. 4: 181–206.

Wang, L. 1997. "Foreign money is no friend of ours." *AsianWeek* November 8, p. 7.

Watson, J.L. 1997. (ed.) *Golden Arches East: McDonald's in East Asia*. Palo Alto: Stanford University Press.

Weici, H. and Shaosheng, X. 1991. *Huaqiao dui zuguo kangzhande gongxian.* Guangzhou: Guangdong renmin chubanshe.

Weiler, J. 1992. "Thou shalt not oppress stranger: On the judicial protection of the Human Rights of non-EC nationals—A critique." *European Journal of International Law* 3: 65–91.

Werbner, P. 1999. "Global pathways: Working class cosmopolitans and the creation of transnational ethnic worlds." *Social Anthropology* 7, No. 1: 17–35.

Werbner, P. and Modood, T. 1997. *Debating Cultural Hybridity: Multi-Cultural Identities and the Politics of Anti-Racism.* London: Zed Books.

Weston, B.H. *et al.* 1997. (ed.) *Basic Documents in International Law and World Order.* St. Paul, MN: West Publishing Co., 3rd editon.

Wheeler, N.J. 2000. *Saving Strangers: Humanitarian Intervention in International Society.* Oxford: Oxford University Press.

Wieviorka, M. 1998. "Racism and diasporas." *Thesis Eleven* 52: 69–81.

Wolf, C. 1997. *Parting From Phantoms: Selected Writings, 1990-1994.* Chicago: University of Chicago Press.

World Bank. 2000. *World Development Report 1999/2000: Entering the 21st Century.* New York: Oxford University Press.

Yu, H. 1995. "Thinking about Orientals: Modernity, social science, and Asians in twentieth-century America." Ph.D. Dissertation, Department of History, Princeton University.

Yuval-Davis, N. 1997. "Ethnicity, gender relations and multiculturalism." In: *Debating Cultural Hybridity: Multicultural Identities and the Politics of Anti-Racism*, edited by Pnina Werbner and Tariq Modood, 193–208. London: Zed Books.

Zentrum für Türkeistudien. 1997. *Medienkonsum in der Türkischen Bevölkerung in Deutschland und Deutschlandbild im Türkischen Fernsehen.* Bonn: Presse- und Informationsamt der Bundesregierung der Bundesrepublik Deutschland.

Zizek, S. 1989. *The Sublime Object of Ideology.* London: Verso.

Zolberg, A. 1981. "Origins of the modern world system: A missing link." *World Politics* 33: 253–281.

Zolberg, A. 1989. "The next waves: Migration theory for a changing world." *International Migration Review* 23: 403–429.

Index